The Liturgy of Vatican II

The Liturgy o

A Symposiu

CONTRIBUTORS

Evaristo Paulo Arns O.F.M.
William Baraúna O.F.M.
Marcos Barbosa
Estevão Bettencourt O.S.B.
Ferdinando Dell'Oro S.D.B.
Luigi Della Torre
João de Castro Engler C.M.P.
Gebhard Fesenmayer O.F.M. Cap.
Joseph Gelineau S.J.
Louis Heuschen
Josef Andreas Jungmann S.J.
Jorge Kémérer S.V.D.
Bonaventura Kloppenburg O.F.M.
Constantine Koser O.F.M.
William J. Leonard S.J.
Salvatore Marsili O.S.B.
Joseph Masson S.J.
Oskar Mueller S.J.
Burkhard Neunheuser O.S.B.
Adrien Nocent O.S.B.
Cipriano Vagagini O.S.B.
François Vanderbroucke

Guilherme Baraúna, editor

Vatican II

In Two Volumes

VOLUME I

Edited by
William Baraúna
Peritus of the Council

ENGLISH EDITION
edited by
JOVIAN LANG O.F.M.

FRANCISCAN HERALD PRESS
CHICAGO, ILLINOIS 60609

THE LITURGY OF VATICAN II: A Symposium in Two Volumes, edited by William Barauna O.F.M.

Library of Congress Catalog Number: 65-16674

Designed by Publication Associates.

Made in the United States of America.

Imprimi Potest:
GERMAIN SCHWAB O.F.M.
Minister Provincial

Nihil Obstat:
MARION A. HABIG O.F.M.
Censor Deputatus

Imprimatur:
MOST REV. CLETUS F. O'DONNELL, D.D.
Vicer General, Archdiocese of Chicago

August 16, 1966

Introduction

With the publication of the Constitution on the Sacred Liturgy, the II Vatican Council entered upon its last phase, the phase of carrying out the decrees promulgated by the supreme teaching authority of the Church. Upon this phase depends, to a great extent, the whole outcome of the immense amount of work which has been done ever since January, 1959, when Pope John XXIII first announced his intention of convoking a general council.

That this phase of Vatican II may follow without interruption after the two which preceded it, namely those of preparation and discussion, it will be well to recall the Council's nature and purpose. Pope John XXIII desired this Council to be a second spring, an awakening, a return to the pure fonts which Christ himself left to his Church. He wanted it to be another Pentecost, a new Epiphany for the modern world. Pope Paul VI has often expressed the same hopes. Thus, in a forceful allocution to the Italian hierarchy, he said: "The Council is an hour of God, a *transitus Domini* in the life of the Church and in the history of the world" (*L'Osservatore Romano,* April 4, 1964).

The parable of the Sower comes naturally to our mind. "Behold, the sower went out to sow. . . . Some seeds fell by the wayside. . . . Other seeds fell upon stony ground. . . . Some seeds fell among thorns. . . . And still other seeds fell upon good ground" (Mt. 13, 4-8). The Constitution *Sacrosanctum Concilium* is a seed sown in the soil of the Church. This is a fertile soil, but it is productive only when it is watered by the waters of the Holy Spirit which "spring up into life everlasting" (Jn. 4, 14). These waters are a fresh stream destined to irrigate abundantly the soil upon which has fallen the redemptive Blood of our Lord Jesus Christ.

In many places, however, and not infrequently, these bounteous waters are covered still by a layer of ice which must first be broken and melted. This layer represents, not so much real opposition to the liturgy, as a lack of proper understanding and appreciation of the liturgy, which developed in the course of centuries; and it may be characterized by four marks, namely, rubricism, clericalism, passiveness, and excessive conservatism.

We are already tasting in some measure the marvelous fruits hidden in the Constitution on the Liturgy. Many things have already changed, even in the attitude of Christians and especially of the clergy. But a great deal more remains to be accomplished. By this we do not mean additional liturgical reforms, which undoubtedly will come in their own good time. What is of greater importance is a certain "conversion" on the part of Christians and especially of the clergy. It is in the lower layers, as it were, of the Conciliar Constitution, that the true riches and the great new tidings are contained; and these will be found only by those who break through the layer of ice.

Before the Constitution, therefore, can bear all the fruits it should, a true conversion will be necessary, that is, a real education or rather liturgical re-education of the Christian and especially of the clergy. And since the Council has sought to correct the mistakes and repair the ruts which have accumulated through the centuries, this re-education may be the work of years, perhaps even of centuries.

These reflections explain, at least to some extent, the nature and purpose of the work which we now present to English-speaking peoples. The editor and collaborators wished to clear the land which is destined to receive the seed. It was not their aim to offer studies on everything contained in the Constitution or to compile an exhaustive commentary. Their work is meant to be rather an introduction to the Constitution so that its spirit can be lived and experienced. It is not intended to be a substitute for personal reflection on the Constitution and assimilation of its contents. That is a part of liturgical re-education which can be done only by the individual. What we hoped to achieve was to clear the ground gradually and to awaken in the reader the desire of becoming better acquainted, through his own efforts, with the fruitful field of the liturgy, the purest fonts of a life of union with God.

This book was planned as a work of international collaboration. Different specialists in the fields of research and of pastoral liturgy, representing as far as possible the various strata of the Church and the Council, have contributed the several chapters. While this work has the advantage of presenting a diversity of ideas and observations, we have also endeavored to give to it a desirable continuity.

Originally this book was written for Brazil, at the request of a number of bishops of that country. Frankly, we did not expect it to reach a wide circle of readers; but we were mistaken. Interest in the work has become world-wide. In Brazil it was so well received as to surpass by far our fondest expectations; and this indicated that there was an urgent need for such a work at the present time also in other countries. An Italian edition was published (by Editrice Elle Di Ci, Torino), and the printing was sold out in less than three months. A Spanish edition (by Ediciones "Studium," Madrid), which appeared recently, met a similar response. A French edition will be published soon in Canada. We were glad, therefore, to accept the offer of Franciscan Herald Press of Chicago to publish also an English edition for the United States and other English-speaking countries. To Fr. Mark Hegener, Manager of Franciscan Herald Press, and his co-workers, we wish to express our heartfelt thanks; and we sincerely hope that the publication of this book will enjoy the same success it has had in other countries.

There is no need for any further introduction, especially since it has a foreword by His Eminence James Cardinal Lercaro, Archbishop of Bologna, the pioneer promoter of the liturgical movement in Italy and now the President of the Post-Conciliar Liturgical Commission, the organization which has been set up for the correct interpretation and proper implementation of the Constitution on the Liturgy. To His Eminence we are deeply grateful. For permission to include their articles, we are indebted also to C. Vagaggini and F. Dell'Oro (Editrice Elle DI CI), J. Kemerer (Semaines Missiologiques de Louvain), J. Gelineau (*Teaching All Nations,* a review published in Manila), and J. A. Jungmann (Aschendorffsche Verlagsbuchhandlung, Münster).

Timeo transeuntem Dominum. We ought to fear the Lord passing by. It will be well for us to pray that the Council's Constitution on the Sacred Liturgy may not find us sleeping the sleep of inertia or apathy and so become like the barren fig tree which was cursed by Christ or the unfaithful steward or the foolish virgins.

WILLIAM BARAUNA O.F.M.

ROME, PENTECOST, 1965

Contents

VOLUME I

Foreword

The Conciliar Constitution promulgated on December 4, 1963, aims to bring about a liturgical renewal in the world; and a collection of studies on this subject is certainly opportune and most useful.

The Constitution is strikingly clear and at the same time profound. Rich in Biblical and Patristic references, it has a studied felicity of expression and a diction that is crisp and concise. In other words, it is full of meaning, and so it requires study and reflection.

Hence everyone who reads it with the attention of a scholar and the spirit of a pastor will find it to be a treasure-trove of information, while a reader who is unprepared to digest it will be disconcerted by insurmountable problems.

A group of scholars examining this, the first, document of the Council can readily grasp its "height and width and depth" and fathom the meaning of this great masterpiece which seeks to promote spiritual progress in souls and in the Church.

For this reason the symposium presented in these volumes is a very timely work and it will prove to be very useful.

With these remarks, however, I have by no means said everything. Solicitous pastors of souls will gradually acquaint their flocks with the contents of the Constitution; and thus the long awaited reforms will be carried out, and the deep and far-reaching significance of this providential document's teaching will be recognized more and more clearly.... Who can tell the fruit it will bear, for example, its affirmation of the principle of "adaptation to the mentality of the people"? What effect will it have on the Christianizing of traditions, cultures, and ideas, which up till now have been outside the Church's influence, and so have made the Church almost a stranger in its own house? The Constitution evidently seeks to achieve a Catholicity that makes the Church universal, not only in a geographical sense, but also in a deeper and dynamic sense, inasmuch as it makes and renders Christian everything that is good; for, "all is ours, but we are of Christ, and Christ is God."

This is just a little hint that I offer; but it suffices to indicate, that while this study, which has been lovingly made by many minds, is opportune at the present time, it will be such even more tomorrow when the seed sown by the Constitution will have blossomed.

May God bless these volumes, so that his praise on earth may ever become a better imitation of that which is sung in heaven: "illi canentes jungimur, almae Sionis aemuli" - "as imitators of dear Sion, we are joined to it in song."

Giacomo Cardinal Lercaro
Archbishop of Bologna, Italy

Preface

"The Liturgy of Vatican II" was written so all Christians may better understand the mind of the Council Fathers whose first document, *The Constitution on the Sacred Liturgy,* gave direction to and was the foundation for their later work. Articles from experts throughout the world comment on the *Constitution on the Sacred Liturgy* and related documents with the hope that the reader will attain deeper understanding and knowledge of his faith and learn effectively to express it in their external manner of worshipping God. In modernizing the Church, the Council has tried to facilitate matters, in order that the faithful, participating more consciously and actively in Church affairs, may more meaningfully act as members of the Mystical Body of Christ.

The content of this book is not difficult to grasp, but when read with deep thought, the faithful will be able to note the progress made so far and anticipate further renovations for Christian living according to the guide lines of this Constitution. Following Christ as their model, good Catholics will accept the reforms in the Church, especially during the trying period of transition, and assume their roles in the Church as they live more fully the new liturgy of the Mass and the Sacraments.

Furthermore, this book will have much value as supplementary material for college courses, study-clubs, workshops, Confraternity of Christian Doctrine meetings, etc. It can be useful to instruct seminarians in the role of the laity during liturgical functions, and their own in later life. Priests will find it most interesting to bring them up-to-date on liturgical thinking. Consequently, a good deal of time was spent in compiling the general index to increase the worth of the material by analyzing the related ideas for the benefit of the user. The correlated thinking of the experts can help the laity to try to live liturgically in modern day society at the pace of our age.

Special acknowledgments must be given to Barbara Kozleuchar who spent many hours proof-reading and to Stephanie Scherr who helped organize the index. Without their aid and devotion to the project, the editor would have found it almost impossible.

JOVIAN P. LANG O.F.M.
Editor for the American edition

The Liturgy of Vatican II

1
Documents

1 The Constitution on the Sacred Liturgy

2 Instruction for the Proper Implementation of the Constitution on the Liturgy

3 *Sacram Liturgiam,* Motu Proprio of Pope Paul VI

4 Decree on Concelebration and Communion under Both Species

5 Replies of the Vatican Commission

1

CONSTITUTION ON THE SACRED LITURGY

Promulgated by Pope Paul VI at the closing of the Second Session of the II Vatican Council, December 4, 1963

INTRODUCTION

1. This sacred Council has several aims in view: it desires to impart an ever increasing vigor to the Christian life of the faithful; to adapt more suitably to the needs of our own times those institutions which are subject to change; to foster whatever can promote union among all who believe in Christ; to strengthen whatever can help to call the whole of mankind into the household of the Church. The Council therefore sees particularly cogent reasons for undertaking the reform and promotion of the liturgy.

2. For the liturgy, "through which the work of our redemption is accomplished," [1] most of all in the divine sacrifice of the Eucharist, is the outstanding means whereby the faithful may express in their lives, and manifest to others, the mystery of Christ and the real nature of the true Church. It is of the essence of the Church that she be both human and divine, visible and yet invisibly equipped, eager to act and yet intent on contemplation, present in this world and yet not at home in it; and she is all these things in such wise that in her the human is directed and subordinated to the divine, the visible likewise to the invisible, action to contemplation, and this present world to that city yet to come, which we seek. [2] While the liturgy daily builds up those who are within into a holy temple of the Lord, into a dwelling place for God in the Spirit,[3] to the mature measure of the fulness of Christ,[4] at the same time it marvelously strengthens their power to preach Christ, and thus shows forth the Church to those who are outside as a sign lifted up among the nations[5] under which the scattered children of God may be gathered together,[6] until there is one sheepfold and one shepherd.[7]

3. Wherefore the sacred Council judges that the following principles concerning the promotion and reform of the liturgy should be called to mind, and that practical norms should be established.

Among these principles and norms there are some which can and should be applied both to the Roman rite and also to all the other rites. The practical norms which follow, however, should be taken as applying only to the Roman rite, except for those which, in the very nature of things, affect other rites as well.

4. Lastly, in faithful obedience to tradition, the sacred Council declares that holy Mother Church holds all lawfully acknowledged rites to be of equal right and dignity; that she wishes to preserve them in the future and to foster them in every way. The Council also desires that, where necessary, the rites be revised carefully in the light of sound tradition, and that they be given new vigor to meet the circumstances and needs of modern times.

Chapter I

GENERAL PRINCIPLES FOR THE RESTORATION AND PROMOTION OF THE SACRED LITURGY

I. The Nature of the Sacred Liturgy and Its Importance in the Church's Life

5. God who "wills that all men be saved and come to the knowledge of the truth" (1 Tim. 2,4), "who in many and various ways spoke in times past to the fathers by the prophets" (Heb. 1,1), when the fulness of time had come sent his Son, the Word made flesh, anointed by the Holy Spirit, to preach the gospel to the poor, to heal the contrite of heart,[8] to be a "bodily and spiritual medicine,"[9] the Mediator between God and man.[10] For his humanity, united with the person of the Word, was the instrument of our salvation. Therefore in Christ "the perfect achievement of our reconciliation came forth, and the fulness of divine worship was given to us."[11]

The wonderful works of God among the people of the Old Testament were but a prelude to the work of Christ the Lord in redeeming mankind and giving perfect glory to God. He achieved his task principally by the paschal mystery of his blessed passion, resurrection from the dead, and glorious ascension, whereby "dying, he destroyed our death and, rising, he restored our life."[12] For it was from the side of Christ as he slept the sleep of death upon the cross that there came forth "the wondrous sacrament of the whole Church."[13]

6. Just as Christ was sent by the Father, so also he sent the apostles, filled with the Holy Spirit. This he did that, by preaching the gospel to every creature,[14] they might proclaim that the Son of God, by his death and resurrection, had freed us from the power of Satan[15] and from death, and brought us into the kingdom of his Father. His purpose also was that they might accomplish the work of salvation which they had proclaimed, by means of sacrifice and sacraments, around which the entire liturgical life revolves. Thus by baptism men are plunged into the paschal mystery of Christ: they die with him, are buried with him, and rise with him;[16] they receive the spirit of adoption as sons "in which we cry: Abba, Father" (Rom. 8,15), and thus become true adorers whom the Father seeks.[17] In like manner, as often as they eat the supper of the Lord they proclaim the death of the Lord until he comes.[18] For

that reason, on the very day of Pentecost, when the Church appeared before the world, "those who received the word" of Peter "were baptized." And "they continued steadfastly in the teaching of the apostles and in the communion of the breaking of bread and in prayers . . . praising God and being in favor with all the people" (Acts 2,41-47). From that time onwards the Church has never failed to come together to celebrate the paschal mystery: reading those things "which were in all the scriptures concerning him" (Lk. 24,27), celebrating the Eucharist in which "the victory and triumph of his death are again made present," [19] and at the same time giving thanks "to God for his unspeakable gift" (2 Cor. 9,15) in Christ Jesus, "in praise of his glory" (Eph. 1,12), through the power of the Holy Spirit.

7. To accomplish so great a work, Christ is always present in his Church, especially in her liturgical celebrations. He is present in the sacrifice of the Mass, not only in the person of his minister, "the same now offering, through the ministry of priest, who formerly offered himself on the cross"[20] but especially under the Eucharistic species. By his power he is present in the sacraments, so that when a man baptizes it is really Christ himself who baptizes. [21] He is present in his word, since it is he himself who speaks when the holy scriptures are read in the Church. He is present, lastly, when the Church prays and sings, for he promised: "Where two or three are gathered together in my name, there am I in the midst of them" (Mt. 18,20).

Christ indeed always associates the Church with himself in this great work wherein God is perfectly glorified and men are sanctified. The Church is his beloved Bride who calls to her Lord, and through him offers worship to the Eternal Father.

Rightly, then, the liturgy is considered as an exercise of the priestly office of Jesus Christ. In the liturgy the sanctification of man is signified by signs perceptible to the senses, and is effected in a way which corresponds with each of these signs; in the liturgy the whole public worship is performed by the Mystical Body of Jesus Christ, that is, by the Head and his members.

From this it follows that every liturgical celebration, because it is an action of Christ the priest and of his Body which is the Church, is a sacred action surpassing all others; no other action of the Church can equal its efficacy by the same title and to the same degree.

8. In the earthly liturgy we take part in a foretaste of that heavenly liturgy which is celebrated in the holy city of Jerusalem toward which we journey as pilgrims, where Christ is sitting at the right hand of God, a minister of the holies and of the true tabernacle;[22] we sing a hymn to the Lord's glory with all the warriors of the heavenly army; venerating the memory of the saints, we hope for some part and fellowship with them; we eagerly await the Savior, our Lord Jesus Christ, until he, our life, shall appear and we too will appear with him in glory.[23]

9. The sacred liturgy does not exhaust the entire activity of the Church. Before men can come to the liturgy they must be called to faith and to

conversion: "How then are they to call upon him in whom they have not yet believed? But how are they to believe him whom they have not heard? And how are they to hear if no one preaches? And how are men to preach unless they be sent?" (Rom. 10,14-15).

Therefore the Church announces the good tidings of salvation to those who do not believe, so that all men may know the true God and Jesus Christ whom he has sent, and may be converted from their ways, doing penance.[24] To believers also the Church must ever preach faith and penance; she must prepare them for the sacraments, teach them to observe all that Christ has commanded,[25] and invite them to all the works of charity, piety, and the apostolate. For all these works make it clear that Christ's faithful, though not of this world, are to be the light of the world and to glorify the Father before men.

10. Nevertheless the liturgy is the summit toward which the activity of the Church is directed; at the same time it is the fount from which all her power flows. For the aim and object of apostolic works is that all who are made sons of God by faith and baptism should come together to praise God in the midst of his Church, to take part in the sacrifice, and to eat the Lord's supper.

The liturgy in its turn moves the faithful, filled with "the paschal sacraments," to be "one in holiness;"[26] it prays that "they may hold fast in their lives to what they have grasped by their faith;"[27] the renewal in the Eucharist of the covenant between the Lord and man draws the faithful into the compelling love of Christ and sets them on fire. From the liturgy, therefore, and especially from the Eucharist, as from a fount, grace is poured forth upon us; and the sanctification of men in Christ and the glorification of God, to which all other activities of the Church are directed as toward their end, is achieved in the most efficacious possible way.

11. But in order that the liturgy may be able to produce its full effects, it is necessary that the faithful come to it with proper dispositions, that their minds should be attuned to their voices, and that they should cooperate with divine grace lest they receive it in vain.[28] Pastors of souls must therefore realize that, when the liturgy is celebrated, something more is required than the mere observation of the laws governing valid and licit celebration; it is their duty also to ensure that the faithful take part fully aware of what they are doing, actively engaged in the rite, and enriched by its effects.

12. The spiritual life, however, is not limited solely to participation in the liturgy. The Christian is indeed called to pray with his brethren, but he must also enter into his chamber to pray to the Father in secret;[29] yet more, according to the teaching of the Apostle, he should pray without ceasing.[30] We learn from the same Apostle that we must always bear about in our body the dying of Jesus, so that the life also of Jesus may be made manifest in our bodily frame.[31] This is why we ask the Lord in the sacrifice of the Mass that, "receiving the offering of the spiritual victim," he may fashion us for himself "as an eternal gift."[32]

13. Popular devotions of the Christian people are to be highly commended, provided they accord with the laws and norms of the Church, above all when they are ordered by the Apostolic See.

Devotions proper to individual Churches also have a special dignity if they are undertaken by mandate of the bishops according to customs or books lawfully approved.

But these devotions should be so drawn up that they harmonize with the liturgical seasons, accord with the sacred liturgy, are in some fashion derived from it, and lead the people to it, since, in fact, the liturgy by its very nature far surpasses any of them.

II. The Promotion of Liturgical Instruction and Active Participation

14. Mother Church earnestly desires that all the faithful should be led to that full, conscious, and active participation in liturgical celebrations which is demanded by the very nature of the liturgy. Such participation by the Christian people as "a chosen race, a royal priesthood, a holy nation, a redeemed people" (1 Pet. 2,9; cf. 2,4-5), is their right and duty by reason of their baptism.

In the restoration and promotion of the sacred liturgy, this full and active participation by all the people is the aim to be considered befor all else) for it is the primary and indispensable source from which the faithful are to derive the true Christian spirit; and therefore pastors of souls must zealously strive to achieve it, by means of the necessary instruction, in all their pastoral work.

Yet it would be futile to entertain any hopes of realizing this unless the pastors themselves, in the first place, become thoroughly imbued with the spirit and power of the liturgy, and undertake to give instruction about it. A prime need, therefore, is that attention be directed, first of all, to the liturgical instruction of the clergy. Therefore the sacred Council has decided to enact as follows:

15. Professors who are appointed to teach liturgy in seminaries, religious houses of study, and theological faculties must be properly trained for their work in institutes which specialize in this subject.

16. The study of sacred liturgy is to be ranked among the compulsory and major courses in seminaries and religious houses of studies; in theological faculties it is to rank among the principal courses. It is to be taught under its theological, historical, spiritual, pastoral, and juridical aspects. Moreover, other professors, while striving to expound the mystery of Christ and the history of salvation from the angle proper to each of their own subjects, must nevertheless do so in a way which clearly bring out the connection between their subjects and the liturgy, as also the unity which underlies all priestly training. This consideration is especially important for professors of dogmatic, spiritual, and pastoral theology and for those of holy scripture.

17. In seminaries and houses of religious, clerics shall be given a liturgical formation in their spiritual life. For this they will need proper direction, so that they may be able to understand the sacred rites and

take part in them wholeheartedly; and they will also need personally to celebrate the sacred mysteries, as well as popular devotions which are imbued with the spirit of the liturgy. In addition they must learn how to observe the liturgical laws, so that life in seminaries and houses of religion may be thoroughly influenced by the spirit of the liturgy.

18. Priests, both secular and religious, who are already working in the Lord's vineyard are to be helped by every suitable means to understand ever more fully what it is that they are doing when they perform sacred rites; they are to be aided to live the liturgical life and to share it with the faithful entrusted to their care.

19. With zeal and patience, pastors of souls must promote the liturgical instruction of the faithful, and also their active participation in the liturgy both internally and externally, taking into account their age and condition, their way of life, and standard of religious culture. By so doing, pastors will be fulfilling one of the chief duties of a faithful dispenser of the mysteries of God; and in this matter they must lead their flock not only in word but also by example.

20. Transmissions of the sacred rites by radio and television shall be done with discretion and dignity, under the leadership and direction of a suitable person appointed for this office by the bishops. This is especially important when the service to be broadcast is the Mass.

III. The Reform of the Sacred Liturgy

21. In order that the Christian people may more certainly derive an abundance of graces from the sacred liturgy, holy Mother Church desires to undertake with great care a general restoration of the liturgy itself. For the liturgy is made up of immutable elements divinely instituted, and of elements subject to change. These not only may but ought to be changed with the passage of time if they have suffered from the intrusion of anything out of harmony with the inner nature of the liturgy or have become unsuited to it.

In this restoration, both texts and rites should be drawn up so that they express more clearly the holy things which they signify; the Christian people, so far as possible, should be enabled to understand them with ease and to take part in them fully, actively, and as befits a community.

Wherefore the sacred Council establishes the following general norms:

(A) *General Norms*

22. §1. Regulation of the sacred liturgy depends solely on the authority of the Church, that is, on the Apostolic See and, as laws may determine, on the bishop.

§2. In virtue of power conceded by the law, the regulation of the liturgy within certain defined limits belongs also to various kinds of competent territorial bodies of bishops legitimately established.

§3. Therefore no other person, even if he be a priest, may add, remove, or change anything in the liturgy on his own authority.

23. That sound tradition may be retained, and yet the way remain open to legitimate progress, a careful investigation is always to be made into each part of the liturgy which is to be revised. This investigation should be theological, historical, and pastoral. Also the general laws governing the structure and meaning of the liturgy must be studied in conjunction with the experience derived from recent liturgical reforms and from the indults conceded to various places. Finally, there must be no innovations unless the good of the Church genuinely and certainly requires them; and care must be taken that any new forms adopted should in some way grow organically from forms already existing.

As far as possible, notable differences between the rites used in adjacent regions must be carefully avoided.

24. Sacred scripture is of the greatest importance in the celebration of the liturgy. For it is from scripture that lessons are read and explained in the homily, and psalms are sung; the prayers, collects, and liturgical songs are scriptural in their inspiration, and it is from the scriptures that actions and signs derive their meaning. Thus to achieve the restoration, progress, and adaptation of the sacred liturgy, it is essential to promote that warm and living love for scripture to which the venerable tradition of both eastern and western rites gives testimony.

25. The liturgical books are to be revised as soon as possible; experts are to be employed on the task, and bishops are to be consulted, from various parts of the world.

(B) *Norms Drawn from the Hierarchic and Communal Nature of the Liturgy*

26. Liturgical services are not private functions, but are celebrations of the Church, which is the "sacrament of unity," namely, the holy people united and ordered under their bishops.[33]

Therefore liturgical services pertain to the whole body of the Church; they manifest it and have effects upon it; but they concern the individual members of the Church in different ways, according to their differing rank, office, and actual participation.

27. It is to be stressed that whenever rites, according to their specific nature, make provision for communal celebration involving the presence and active participation of the faithful, this way of celebrating them is to be preferred, so far as possible, to a celebration that is individual and quasi-private.

This applies with especial force to the celebration of Mass and the administration of the sacraments, even though every Mass has of itself a public and social nature.

28. In liturgical celebrations each person, minister or layman, who has an office to perform, should do all of, but only, those parts which pertain to his office by the nature of the rite and the principles of liturgy.

29. Servers, lectors, commentators, and members of the choir also exercise a genuine liturgical function. They ought, therefore, to discharge

their office with the sincere piety and decorum demanded by so exalted a ministry and rightly expected of them by God's people.

Consequently they must all be deeply imbued with the spirit of the liturgy, each in his own measure, and they must be trained to perform their functions in a correct and orderly manner.

30. To promote active participation, the people should be encouraged to take part by means of acclamations, responses, psalmody, antiphons, and songs, as well as by actions, gestures, and bodily attitudes. And at the proper times all should observe a reverent silence.

31. The revision of the liturgical books must carefully attend to the provision of rubrics also for the people's parts.

32. The liturgy makes distinctions between persons according to their liturgical function and sacred Orders, and there are liturgical laws providing for due honors to be given to civil authorities. Apart from these instances, no special honors are to be paid in the liturgy to any private persons or classes of persons, whether in the ceremonies or by external display.

(C) *Norms Based upon the Didactic and Pastoral Nature of the Liturgy*

33. Although the sacred liturgy is above all things the worship of the divine Majesty, it likewise contains much instruction for the faithful.[34] For in the liturgy God speaks to His people and Christ is still proclaiming His gospel. And the people reply to God both by song and prayer.

Moreover, the prayers addressed to God by the priest who presides over the assembly in the person of Christ are said in the name of the entire holy people and of all present. And the visible signs used by the liturgy to signify invisible divine things have been chosen by Christ or the Church. Thus not only when things are read "which were written for our instruction" (Rom. 15,4), but also when the Church prays or sings or acts, the faith of those taking part is nourished and their minds are raised to God, so that they may offer Him their rational service and more abundantly receive his grace.

Wherefore, in the revision of the liturgy, the following general norms should be observed:

34. The rites should be distinguished by a noble simplicity; they should be short, clear, and unencumbered by useless repetitions; they should be within the people's powers of comprehension, and normally should not require much explanation.

35. That the intimate connection between words and rites may be apparent in the liturgy:

(1) In sacred celebrations there is to be more reading from holy scripture, and it is to be more varied and suitable.

(2) Because the sermon is part of the liturgical service, the best place for it is to be indicated even in the rubrics, as far as the nature of the rite will allow; the ministry of preaching is to be fulfilled with

exactitude and fidelity. The sermon, moreover, should draw its content mainly from scriptural and liturgical sources, and its character should be that of a proclamation of God's wonderful works in the history of salvation, the mystery of Christ, ever made present and active within us, especially in the celebration of the liturgy.

(3) Instruction which is more explicitly liturgical should also be given in a variety of ways; if necessary, short directives to be spoken by the priest or proper minister should be provided within the rites themselves. But they should occur only at the more suitable moments, and be in prescribed or similar words.

(4) Bible services should be encouraged, especially on the vigils of the more solemn feasts, on some weekdays in Advent and Lent, and on Sundays and feast days. They are particularly to be commended in places where no priest is available; when this is so, a deacon or some other person authorized by the bishop should preside over the celebration.

36. §1. Particular law remaining in force, the use of the Latin language is to be preserved in the Latin rites.

§2. But since the use of the mother tongue, whether in the Mass, the administration of the sacraments, or other parts of the liturgy, frequently may be of great advantage to the people, the limits of its employment may be extended. This will apply in the first place to the readings and directives, and to some of the prayers and chants, according to the regulations on this matter to be laid down separately in subsequent chapters.

§3. These norms being observed, it is for the competent territorial ecclesiastical authority mentioned in Art. 22, §2, to decide whether, and to what extent, the vernacular language is to be used; their decrees are to be approved, that is, confirmed, by the Apostolic See. And, whenever it seems to be called for, this authority is to consult with bishops of neighboring regions which have the same language.

§4. Translations from the Latin text into the mother tongue intended for use in the liturgy must be approved by the competent territorial ecclesiastical authority mentioned above.

(D) *Norms for Adapting the Liturgy to the Culture and Traditions of Peoples*

37. Even in the liturgy, the Church has no wish to impose a rigid uniformity in matters which do not implicate the faith or the good of the whole community; rather does she respect and foster the genius and talents of the various races and peoples. Anything in these peoples' way of life which is not indissolubly bound up with superstition and error she studies with sympathy and, if possible, preserves intact. Sometimes in fact she admits such things into the liturgy itself, so long as they harmonize with its true and authentic spirit.

38. Provisions shall also be made, when revising the liturgical books, for legitimate variations and adaptations to different groups, regions,

and peoples, especially in mission lands, provided that the substantial unity of the Roman rite is preserved; and this should be borne in mind when drawing up the rites and devising rubrics.

39. Within the limits set by the typical editions of the liturgical books, it shall be for the competent territorial ecclesiastical authority mentioned in Art. 22 §2, to specify adaptations, especially in the case of the administration of the sacraments, the sacramentals, processions, liturgical language, sacred music, and the arts, but according to the fundamental norms laid down in this Constitution.

40. In some places and circumstances, however, an even more radical adaptation of the liturgy is needed, and this entails greater difficulties. Wherefore:

(1) The competent territorial ecclesiastical authority mentioned in Art. 22, §2, must, in this matter, carefully and prudently consider which elements from the traditions and culture of individual peoples might appropriately be admitted into divine worship. Adaptations which are judged to be useful or necessary should then be submitted to the Apostolic See, by whose consent they may be introduced.

(2) To ensure that adaptations may be made with all the circumspection which they demand, the Apostolic See will grant power to this same territorial ecclesiastical authority to permit and to direct, as the case requires, the necessary preliminary experiments over a determined period of time among certain groups suited for the purpose.

(3) Because liturgical laws often involve special difficulties with respect to adaptation, particularly in mission lands, men who are experts in these matters must be employed to formulate them.

IV. Promotion of Liturgical Life in Diocese and Parish

41. The bishop is to be considered as the high priest of his flock, from whom the life in Christ of his faithful is in some way derived and dependent.

Therefore all should hold in great esteem the liturgical life of the diocese centered around the bishop, especially in the cathedral church; they must be convinced that the pre-eminent manifestation of the Church consists in the full active participation of all God's holy people in these liturgical celebrations, especially in the same Eucharist, in a single prayer, at one altar, at which there presides the bishop surrounded by his college of priests and by his ministers.[35]

42. But because it is impossible for the bishop always and everywhere to preside over the whole flock in his Church, he can not do other than establish lesser groupings of the faithful. Among these the parishes, set up locally under a pastor who takes the place of the bishop, are the most important: for in some manner they represent the visible Church constituted throughout the world.

And therefore the liturgical life of the parish and its relationship to the bishop must be fostered theoretically and practically among the faithful and clergy; efforts also must be made to encourage a sense of community within the parish, above all in the common celebration of the Sunday Mass.

V. The Promotion of Pastoral-Liturgical Action

43. Zeal for the promotion and restoration of the liturgy is rightly held to be a sign of the providential dispositions of God in our time, as a movement of the Holy Spirit in His Church. It is today a distinguishing mark of the Church's life, indeed of the whole tenor of contemporary religious thought and action.

So that this pastoral-liturgical action may become even more vigorous in the Church, the sacred Council decrees:

44. It is desirable that the competent territorial ecclesiastical authority mentioned in Art. 22, §2, set up a liturgical commission, to be assisted by experts in liturgical science, sacred music, art, and pastoral practice. So far as possible the commission should be aided by some kind of Institute for Pastoral Liturgy, consisting of persons who are eminent in these matters, and including laymen as circumstances suggest. Under the direction of the above-mentioned territorial ecclesiastical authority the commission is to regulate pastoral-liturgical action throughout the territory, and to promote studies and necessary experiments whenever there is question of adaptations to be proposed to the Apostolic See.

45. For the same reason every diocese is to have a commission on the sacred liturgy under the direction of the bishop, for promoting the liturgical apostolate.

Sometimes it may be expedient that several dioceses should form between them one single commission which will be able to promote the liturgy by common consultation.

46. Besides the commission on the sacred liturgy, every diocese, as far as possible, should have commissions for sacred music and sacred art.

These three commissions must work in closest collaboration; indeed it will often be best to fuse the three of them into one single commission.

Chapter II

THE MOST SACRED MYSTERY OF THE EUCHARIST

47. At the Last Supper, on the night when He was betrayed, our Savior instituted the Eucharistic sacrifice of His Body and Blood. He did this in order to perpetuate the sacrifice of the Cross throughout the centuries until He should come again, and so to entrust to His beloved spouse, the Church, a memorial of His death and resurrection: a sacrament of love, a sign of unity, a bond of charity,[36] a paschal banquet in which Christ is eaten, the mind is filled with grace, and a pledge of future glory is given to us.[37]

48. The Church, therefore, earnestly desires that Christ's faithful, when present at this mystery of faith, should not be there as strangers or silent spectators; on the contrary, through a good understanding of the rites and prayers they should take part in the sacred action conscious of what they are doing, with devotion and full collaboration. They should be instructed by God's word and be nourished at the table of the Lord's body; they should give thanks to God; by offering the Immaculate Victim, not only through the hands of the priest, but also with him, they should learn also to offer themselves; through Christ the Mediator,[38] they should be drawn day by day into ever more perfect union with God and with each other, so that finally God may be all in all.

49. For this reason the sacred Council, having in mind those Masses which are celebrated with the assistance of the faithful, especially on Sundays and feasts of obligation, has made the following decrees in order that the sacrifice of the Mass, even in the ritual forms of its celebration, may become pastorally efficacious to the fullest degree.

50. The rite of the Mass is to be revised in such a way that the intrinsic nature and purpose of its several parts, as also the connection between them, may be more clearly manifested, and that devout and active participation by the faithful may be more easily achieved.

For this purpose the rites are to be simplified, due care being taken to preserve their substance; elements which, with the passage of time, came to be duplicated, or were added with but little advantage, are now to be discarded; other elements which have suffered injury through accidents of history are now to be restored to the vigor which they had in the days of the holy Fathers, as may seem useful or necessary.

51. The treasures of the bible are to be opened up more lavishly, so that richer fare may be provided for the faithful at the table of God's word. In this way a more representative portion of the holy scriptures will be read to the people in the course of a prescribed number of years.

52. By means of the homily the mysteries of the faith and the guiding principles of the Christian life are expounded from the sacred text, during the course of the liturgical year; the homily, therefore, is to be highly esteemed as part of the liturgy itself; in fact, at those Masses which are celebrated with the assistance of the people on Sundays and feasts of obligation, it should not be omitted except for a serious reason.

53. Especially on Sundays and feasts of obligation there is to be restored, after the Gospel and the homily, "the common prayer" or "the prayer of the faithful." By this prayer, in which the people are to take part, intercession will be made for holy Church, for the civil authorities, for those oppressed by various needs, for all mankind, and for the salvation of the entire world.[39]

54. In Masses which are celebrated with the people, a suitable place may be allotted to their mother tongue. This is to apply in the first place to the readings and "the common prayer," but also, as local conditions may warrant, to those parts which pertain to the people, according to the norm laid down in Art. 36 of this Constitution.

Nevertheless steps should be taken so that the faithful may also be able to say or to sing together in Latin those parts of the Ordinary of the Mass which pertain to them.

And wherever a more extended use of the mother tongue within the Mass appears desirable, the regulation laid down in Art. 40 of this Constitution is to be observed.

55. That more perfect form of participation in the Mass whereby the faithful, after the priest's communion, receive the Lord's body from the same sacrifice, is strongly commended.

The dogmatic principles which were laid down by the Council of Trent remaining intact,[40] communion under both kinds may be granted when the bishops think fit, not only to clerics and religious, but also to the laity, in cases to be determined by the Apostolic See, as, for instance, to the newly ordained in the Mass of their sacred ordination, to the newly professed in the Mass of their religious profession, and to the newly baptized in the Mass which follows their baptism.

56. The two parts which, in a certain sense, go to make up the Mass, namely, the liturgy of the word and the Eucharistic liturgy, are so closely connected with each other that they form but one single act of worship. Accordingly this sacred Synod strongly urges pastors of souls that, when instructing the faithful, they insistently teach them to take their part in the entire Mass, especially on Sundays and feasts of obligation.

57. §1. Concelebration, whereby the unity of the priesthood is appropriately manifested, has remained in use to this day in the Church both in the east and in the west. For this reason it has seemed good to the Council to extend permission for concelebration to the following cases:

1. (a) on the Thursday of the Lord's Supper, not only at the Mass of the Chrism, but also at the evening Mass;
   (b) at Masses during councils, bishops' conferences, and synods;
   (c) at the Mass for the blessing of an abbot.
2. Also, with permission of the ordinary, to whom it belongs to decide whether concelebration is opportune:
   (a) at conventual Mass, and at the principal Mass in churches when the needs of the faithful do not require that all the priests available should celebrate individually;
   (b) at Masses celebrated at any kind of priests' meetings, whether the priests be secular clergy or religious.

§2. 1. The regulation, however, of the discipline of concelebration in the diocese pertains to the bishop.

2. Nevertheless, each priest shall always retain his right to celebrate Mass individually, though not at the same time in the same church as a concelebrated Mass, nor on Thursday of the Lord's Supper.

58. A new rite for concelebration is to be drawn up and inserted into the Pontifical and into the Roman Missal.

Chapter III

THE OTHER SACRAMENTS AND THE SACRAMENTALS

59. The purpose of the sacraments is to sanctify men, to build up the body of Christ, and, finally, to give worship to God; because they are signs they also instruct. They not only presuppose faith, but by words and objects they also nourish, strengthen, and express it; that is why they are called "sacraments of faith." They do indeed impart grace, but, in addition, the very act of celebrating them most effectively disposes the faithful to receive this grace in a fruitful manner, to worship God duly, and to practice charity.

It is therefore of the highest importance that the faithful should easily understand the sacramentals signs, and should frequent with great eagerness those sacraments which were instituted to nourish the Christian life.

60. Holy Mother Church has, moreover, instituted sacramentals. These are sacred signs which bear a resemblance to the sacraments: they signify effects, particularly of a spiritual kind, which are obtained through the Church's intercession. By them men are disposed to receive the chief effect of the sacraments, and various occasions in life are rendered holy.

61. Thus, for well-disposed members of the faithful, the liturgy of the sacraments and sacramentals sanctifies almost every event in their lives; they are given access to the stream of divine grace which flows from the paschal mystery of the passion, death, and resurrection of Christ, the fount from which all sacraments and sacramentals draw their power. There is hardly any proper use of material things which cannot thus be directed toward the sanctification of men and the praise of God.

62. With the passage of time, however, there have crept into the rites of the sacraments and sacramentals certain features which have rendered their nature and purpose far from clear to the people of today; hence some changes have become necessary to adapt them to the needs of our own times. For this reason the sacred Council decrees as follows concerning their revision.

63. Because the use of the mother tongue in the administration of the sacraments and sacramentals can often be of considerable help to the people, this use is to be extended according to the following norms:

(a) The vernacular language may be used in administering the sacraments and sacramentals, according to the norm of Art. 36.

(b) In harmony with the new edition of the Roman Ritual, particular rituals shall be prepared without delay by the competent territorial ecclesiastical authority mentioned in Art. 22, §2, of this Constitution. These rituals, which are to be adapted, also as regards the language employed, to the needs of the different regions, are to be reviewed by the Apostolic See and then introduced into the regions for which they have been prepared. But in drawing up these rituals or particular collections of rites, the instructions prefixed to the individual rites in the Roman Ritual, whether they be pastoral and rubrical or whether they have special social import, shall not be omitted.

64. The catechumenate for adults, comprising several distinct steps is to be restored and to be taken into use at the discretion of the local ordinary. By this means the time of the catechumenate, which is intended as a period of suitable instruction, may be sanctified by sacred rites to be celebrated at successive intervals of time.

65. In mission lands it is found that some of the peoples already make use of initiation rites. Elements from these, when capable of being adapted to Christian ritual, may be admitted along with those already found in Christian tradition, according to the norm laid down in Art. 37-40 of this Constitution.

66. Both of the rites for the baptism of adults are to be revised: not only the simpler rite, but also the more solemn one, which must take into account the restored catechumenate. A special Mass "for the conferring of baptism" is to be inserted into the Roman Missal.

67. The rite for the baptism of infants is to be revised, and it should be adapted to the circumstance that those to be baptized are, in fact, infants. The roles of parents and godparents, and also their duties, should be brought out more clearly in the rite itself.

68. The baptismal rite should contain variants, to be used at the discretion of the local ordinary, for occasions when a very large number are to be baptized together. Moreover, a shorter rite is to be drawn up, especially for mission lands, to be used by catechists, but also by the faithful in general when there is danger of death, and neither priest nor deacon is available.

69. In place of the rite called the "Order of supplying what was omitted in the baptism of an infant," a new rite is to be drawn up. This should manifest more fittingly and clearly that the infant, baptized by the short rite, has already been received into the Church.

And a new rite is to be drawn up for converts who have already been validly baptized; it should indicate that they are now admitted to communion with the Church.

70. Except during Eastertide, baptismal water may be blessed within the rite of baptism itself by an approved shorter formula.

71. The rite of confirmation is to be revised and the intimate connection which this sacrament has with the whole of Christian initiation is to be more clearly set forth; for this reason it is fitting for candidates to renew their baptismal promises just before they are confirmed.

Confirmation may be given within the Mass when convenient; when it is given outside the Mass, the rite that is used should be introduced by a formula to be drawn up for this purpose.

72. The rite and formulas for the sacrament of penance are to be revised so that they more clearly express both the nature and effect of the sacrament.

73. "Extreme unction," which may also and more fittingly be called

"anointing of the sick," is not a sacrament for those only who are at the point of death. Hence, as soon as any one of the faithful begins to be in danger of death from sickness or old age, the fitting time for him to receive this sacrament has certainly already arrived.

74. In addition to the separate rites for anointing of the sick and for Viaticum, a continuous rite shall be prepared according to which the sick man is anointed after he has made his confession and before he receives Viaticum.

75. The number of the anointings is to be adapted to the occasion, and the prayers which belong to the rite of anointing are to be revised so as to correspond with the varying conditions of the sick who receive the sacrament.

76. Both the ceremonies and texts of the ordination rites are to be revised. The address given by the bishop at the beginning of each ordination or consecration may be in the mother tongue.

When a bishop is consecrated, the laying of hands may be done by all the bishops present.

77. The marriage rite now found in the Roman Ritual is to be revised and enriched in such a way that the grace of the sacrament is more clearly signified and the duties of the spouses are taught.

"If any regions are wont to use other praiseworthy customs and ceremonies when celebrating the sacrament of matrimony, the sacred Synod earnestly desires that these by all means be retained."[41]

Moreover the competent territorial ecclesiastical authority mentioned in Art. 22, §2, of this Constitution is free to draw up its own rite suited to the usages of place and people, according to the provision of Art. 63. But the rite must always conform to the law that the priest assisting at the marriage must ask for and obtain the consent of the contracting parties.

78. Matrimony is normally to be celebrated within the Mass, after the reading of the gospel and the homily, and before "the prayer of the faithful." The prayer for the bride, duly amended to remind both spouses of their equal obligation to remain faithful to each other, may be said in the mother tongue.

But if the sacrament of matrimony is celebrated apart from Mass, the epistle and gospel from the nuptial Mass are to be read at the beginning of the rite, and the blessing should always be given to the spouses.

79. The sacramentals are to undergo a revision which takes into account the primary principle of enabling the faithful to participate intelligently, actively, and easily; the circumstances of our own days must also be considered. When rituals are revised, as laid down in Art. 63, new sacramentals may also be added as the need for these becomes apparent.

Reserved blessings shall be very few; reservations shall be in favor only of bishops or ordinaries.

Let provision be made that some sacramentals, at least in special circumstances and at the discretion of the ordinary, may be administered by qualified lay persons.

80. The rite for the consecration of virgins at present found in the Roman Pontifical is to be revised.

Moreover, a rite of religious profession and renewal of vows shall be drawn up in order to achieve greater unity, sobriety, and dignity. Apart from exceptions in particular law, this rite should be adopted by those who make their profession or renewal of vows within the Mass.

Religious profession should preferably be made within the Mass.

81. The rite for the burial of the dead should express more clearly the paschal character of Christian death, and should correspond more closely to the circumstances and traditions found in various regions. This holds good also for the liturgical color to be used.

82. The rite for the burial of infants is to be revised, and a special Mass for the occasion should be provided.

Chapter IV

THE DIVINE OFFICE

83. Christ Jesus, high priest of the new and eternal covenant, taking human nature, introduced into this earthly exile that hymn which is sung throughout all ages in the halls of heaven. He joins the entire community of mankind to himself, associating it with his own singing of this canticle of divine praise.

For he continues his priestly work through the agency of his Church, which is ceaselessly engaged in praising the Lord and interceding for the salvation of the whole world. She does this, not only by celebrating the Eucharist, but also in other ways, especially by praying the divine office.

84. By tradition going back to early Christian times, the divine office is devised so that the whole course of the day and night is made holy by the praises of God. Therefore, when this wonderful song of praise is rightly performed by priests and others who are deputed for this purpose by the Church's ordinance, or by the faithful praying together with the priest in the approved form, then it is truly the voice of the bride addressed to her bridegroom; it is the very prayer which Christ himself, together with his body, addresses to the Father.

85. Hence all who render this service are not only fulfilling a duty of the Church, but also are sharing in the greatest honor of Christ's spouse, for by offering these praises to God they are standing before God's throne in the name of the Church their Mother.

86. Priests who are engaged in the sacred pastoral ministry will offer the praises of the hours with greater fervor the more vividly they realize that they must heed St. Paul's exhortation: "Pray without ceasing" (1 Thess. 5,17). For the work in which they labor will effect nothing and bring forth no fruit except by the power of the Lord who said: "Without me you can do nothing" (Jn. 15,5). That is why the apostles, instituting

deacons, said: "We will devote ourselves to prayer and to the ministry of the word" (Acts 6,4).

87. In order that the divine office may be better and more perfectly prayed in existing circumstances, whether by priests or by other members of the Church, the sacred Council, carrying further the restoration already so happily begun by the Apostolic See, has seen fit to decree as follows concerning the office of the Roman rite.

88. Because the purpose of the office is to sanctify the day, the traditional sequence of the hours is to be restored so that once again they may be genuinely related to the time of the day when they are prayed, as far as this may be possible. Moreover, it will be necessary to take into account the modern conditions in which daily life has to be lived, especially by those who are called to labor in apostolic works.

89. Therefore, when the office is revised, these norms are to be observed:

(a) By the venerable tradition of the universal Church, Lauds as morning prayer and Vespers as evening prayer are the two hinges on which the daily office turns; hence they are to be considered as the chief hours and are to be celebrated as such.

(b) Compline is to be drawn up so that it will be a suitable prayer for the end of the day.

(c) The hour known as Matins, although it should retain the character of nocturnal praise when celebrated in choir, shall be adapted so that it may be recited at any hour of the day; it shall be made up of fewer psalms and longer readings.

(d) The hour of Prime is to be suppressed.

(e) In choir the minor hours of Tierce, Sext, and None are to be observed. But outside choir it will be lawful to select any one of these three, according to the respective time of the day.

90. The divine office, because it is the public prayer of the Church, is a source of piety and nourishment for personal prayer. And therefore priests and all others who take part in the divine office are earnestly exhorted in the Lord to attune their minds to their voices when praying it. The better to achieve this, let them take steps to improve their understanding of the liturgy and of the bible, especially of the psalms.

In revising the Roman office, its ancient and venerable treasures are to be so adapted that all those to whom they are handed on may more extensively and easily draw profit from them.

91. So that it may really be possible in practice to observe the course of the hours proposed in Art. 89, the psalms are no longer to be distributed throughout one week, but through some longer period of time.

The work of revising the psalter, already happily begun, is to be finished as soon as possible, and is to take into account the style of Christian Latin, the liturgical use of psalms, also when sung, and the entire tradition of the Latin Church.

92. As regards the readings, the following shall be observed:

(a) Readings from sacred scripture shall be arranged so that the riches of God's word may be easily accessible in more abundant measure.

(b) Readings excerpted from the works of the fathers, doctors, and ecclesiastical writers shall be better selected.

(c) The accounts of martyrdom or the lives of the saints are to accord with the facts of history.

93. To whatever extent may seem desirable, the hymns are to be restored to their original form, and whatever smacks of mythology or ill accords with Christian piety is to be removed or changed. Also, as occasion may arise, let other selections from the treasury of hymns be incorporated.

94. That the day may be truly sanctified, and that the hours themselves may be recited with spiritual advantage, it is best that each of them be prayed at a time which most closely corresponds with its true canonical time.

95. Communities obliged to choral office are bound to celebrate the office in choir every day in addition to the conventual Mass. In particular:

(a) Orders of canons, of monks and of nuns, and of other regulars bound by law or constitutions to choral office must celebrate the entire office.

(b) Cathedral or collegiate chapters are bound to recite those parts of the office imposed on them by general or particular law.

(c) All members of the above communities who are in major orders or who are solemnly professed, except for lay brothers, are bound to recite individually those canonical hours which they do not pray in choir.

96. Clerics not bound to office in choir, if they are in major orders, are bound to pray the entire office every day, either in common or individually, as laid down in Art. 89.

97. Appropriate instances are to be defined by the rubrics in which a liturgical service may be substituted for the divine office.

In particular cases, and for a just reason, ordinaries can dispense their subjects wholly or in part from the obligation of reciting the divine office, or may commute the obligation.

98. Members of any institute dedicated to acquiring perfection who, according to their constitutions, are to recite any parts of the divine office are thereby performing the public prayer of the Church.

They too perform the public prayer of the Church who, in virtue of their constitutions, recite any short office, provided this is drawn up after the pattern of the divine office and is duly approved.

99. Since the divine office is the voice of the Church, that is, of the whole mystical body publicly praising God, those clerics who are not obliged to office in choir, especially priests who live together or who assemble for any purpose, are urged to pray at least some part of the divine office in common.

All who pray the divine office, whether in choir or in common, should fulfil the task entrusted to them as perfectly as possible: this refers not only to the internal devotion of their minds but also to their external manner of celebration.

It is, moreover, fitting that the office, both in choir and in common, be sung when possible.

100. Pastors of souls should see to it that the chief hours, especially Vespers, are celebrated in common in church on Sundays and the more solemn feasts. And the laity, too, are encouraged to recite the divine office, either with the priests, or among themselves, or even individually.

101. §1. In accordance with the centuries-old tradition of the Latin rite, the Latin language is to be retained by clerics in the divine office. But in individual cases the ordinary has the power of granting the use of a translation to those clerics for whom the use of Latin constitutes a grave obstacle to their praying the office properly. The vernacular version, however, must be one that is drawn up according to the provision of Art. 36.

§2. The competent superior has the power to grant the use of the vernacular in the celebration of the divine office, even in choir, to nuns and to members of institutes dedicated to acquiring perfection, both men who are not clerics and women. The version, however, must be one that is approved.

§3. Any cleric bound to the divine office fulfills his obligation if he prays the office in the vernacular together with a group of the faithful or with those mentioned in §2 above, provided that the text of the translation is approved.

Chapter V

THE LITURGICAL YEAR

102. Holy Mother Church is conscious that she must celebrate the saving work of her divine Spouse by devoutly recalling it on certain days throughout the course of the year. Every week, on the day which she has called the Lord's day, she keeps the memory of the Lord's resurrection, which she also celebrates once in the year, together with His blessed passion, in the most solemn festival of Easter.

Within the cycle of a year, moreover, she unfolds the whole mystery of Christ, from the incarnation and birth until the ascension, the day of Pentecost, and the expectation of blessed hope and of the coming of the Lord.

Recalling thus the mysteries of redemption, the Church opens to the faithful the riches of her Lord's powers and merits, so that these are in some way made present for all time, and the faithful are enabled to lay hold upon them and become filled with saving grace.

103. In celebrating this annual cycle of Christ's mysteries, holy Church honors with especial love the Blessed Mary, Mother of God, who is joined by an inseparable bond to the saving work of her Son. In her the Church holds up and admires the most excellent fruit of the redemption, and joyfully contemplates, as in a faultless image, that which she herself desires and hopes wholly to be.

104. The Church has also included in the annual cycle days devoted to the memory of the martyrs and the other saints. Raised up to perfection by the manifold grace of God, and already in possession of eternal salvation, they sing God's perfect praise in heaven and offer prayers for us. By celebrating the passage of these saints from earth to heaven the Church proclaims the paschal mystery achieved in the saints who have suffered and been glorified with Christ; she proposes them to the faithful as examples drawing all to the Father through Christ, and through their merits she pleads for God's favors.

105. Finally, in the various seasons of the year and according to her traditional discipline, the Church completes the formation of the faithful by means of pious practices for soul and body, by instruction, prayer, and works of penance and of mercy.

Accordingly the sacred Council has seen fit to decree as follows.

106. By a tradition handed down from the apostles which took its origin from the very day of Christ's resurrection, the Church celebrates the paschal mystery every eighth day; with good reason this, then, bears the name of the Lord's day or Sunday. For on this day Christ's faithful should come together into one place so that, by hearing the word of God and taking part in the Eucharist, they may call to mind the passion, the resurrection, and the glorification of the Lord Jesus, and may thank God who "has begotten them again, through the resurrection of Jesus Christ from the dead, unto a living hope" (1 Pet. 1,3). Hence the Lord's day is the original feast day, and it should be proposed to the piety of the faithful and taught to them so that it may become in fact a day of joy and of freedom from work. Other celebrations, unless they be truly of greatest importance, shall not have precedence over the Sunday which is the foundation and kernel of the whole liturgical year.

107. The liturgical year is to be revised so that the traditional customs and discipline of the sacred seasons shall be preserved or restored to suit the conditions of modern times; their specific character is to be retained, so that they duly nourish the piety of the faithful who celebrate the mysteries of Christian redemption, and above all the paschal mystery. If certain adaptations are considered necessary on account of local conditions, they are to be made in accordance with the provisions of Art. 39 and 40.

108. The minds of the faithful must be directed primarily toward the feasts of the Lord whereby the mysteries of salvation are celebrated in the course of the year. Therefore, the proper of the time shall be given the preference which is its due over the feasts of the saints, so that the entire cycle of the mysteries of salvation may be suitably recalled.

109. The season of Lent has a twofold character; primarily by recalling or preparing for baptism and by penance, it disposes the faithful, who more diligently hear the word of God and devote themselves to prayer, to celebrate the paschal mystery. This twofold character is to be brought into greater prominence both in the liturgy and by liturgical catechesis. Hence:

(a) More use is made of the baptismal features proper to the Lenten liturgy; some of them, which used to flourish in bygone days, are to be restored as may seem good.

(b) The same is to apply to the penitential elements. As regards instruction it is important to impress on the minds of the faithful not only the social consequences of sin but also that essence of the virtue of penance which leads to the detestation of sin as an offense against God; the role of the Church in penitential practices is not to be passed over, and the people must be exhorted to pray for sinners.

110. During Lent penance should not be only internal and individual, but also external and social. The practice of penance should be fostered in ways that are possible in our own times and in different regions, and according to the circumstances of the faithful; it should be encouraged by the authorities mentioned in Art. 22.

Nevertheless, let the paschal fast be kept sacred. Let it be celebrated everywhere on Good Friday and, where possible, prolonged throughout Holy Saturday, so that the joys of the Sunday of the resurrection may be attained with uplifted and clear mind.

111. The saints have been traditionally honored in the Church and their authentic relics and images held in veneration. For the feasts of the saints proclaim the wonderful works of Christ in his servants, and display to the faithful fitting examples for their imitation.

Lest the feasts of the saints should take precedence over the feasts which commemorate the very mysteries of salvation, many of them should be left to be celebrated by a particular Church or nation or family of religious; only those should be extended to the universal Church which commemorate saints who are truly of universal importance.

Chapter VI

SACRED MUSIC

112. The musical tradition of the universal Church is a treasure of inestimable value, greater even than that of any other art. The main reason for this pre-eminence is that, as sacred song united to the words, it forms a necessary or integral part of the solemn liturgy.

Holy Scripture, indeed, has bestowed praise upon sacred song,[42] and the same may be said of the fathers of the Church and of the Roman pontiffs who in recent times, led by St. Pius X, have explained more precisely the ministerial function supplied by sacred music in the service of the Lord.

Therefore sacred music is to be considered the more holy in proportion as it is more closely connected with the liturgical action, whether it adds delight to prayer, fosters unity of minds, or confers greater solemnity upon the sacred rites. But the Church approves of all forms of true art having the needed qualities, and admits them into divine worship.

Accordingly, the sacred Council, keeping to the norms and precepts of ecclesiastical tradition and discipline, and having regard to the purpose of sacred music, which is the glory of God and the sanctification of the faithful, decrees as follows.

113. Liturgical worship is given a more noble form when the divine offices are celebrated solemnly in song, with the assistance of sacred ministers and the active participation of the people.

As regards the language to be used, the provisions of Art. 36 are to be observed; for the Mass, Art. 54; for the sacraments, Art. 63; for the divine office, Art. 101.

114. The treasure of sacred music is to be preserved and fostered with great care. Choirs must be diligently promoted, especially in cathedral churches; but bishops and other pastors of souls must be at pains to ensure that, whenever the sacred action is to be celebrated with song, the whole body of the faithful may be able to contribute that active participation which is rightly theirs, as laid down in Art. 28 and 30.

115. Great importance is to be attached to the teaching and practice of music in seminaries, in the novitiates and houses of study of religious of both sexes, and also in other Catholic institutions and schools. To impart this instruction, teachers are to be carefully trained and put in charge of the teaching of sacred music.

It is desirable also to found higher institutes of sacred music whenever this can be done.

Composers and singers, especially boys, must also be given a genuine liturgical training.

116. The Church acknowledges Gregorian chant as specially suited to the Roman liturgy: therefore, other things being equal, it should be given pride of place in liturgical services.

But other kinds of sacred music, especially polyphony, are by no means excluded from liturgical celebrations, so long as they accord with the spirit of the liturgical action, as laid down in Art. 30.

117. The typical edition of the books of Gregorian chant is to be completed; and a more critical edition is to be prepared of those books already published since the restoration by St. Pius X.

It is desirable also that an edition be prepared containing simpler melodies, for use in small churches.

118. Religious singing by the people is to be skillfully fostered, so that in devotions and sacred exercises, as also during liturgical services, the voices of the faithful may ring out according to the norms and requirements of the rubrics.

119. In certain parts of the world, especially mission lands, there are peoples who have their own musical traditions, and these play a great part in their religious and social life. For this reason due importance is to be attached to their music, and a suitable place is to be given to it, not only in forming their attitude toward religion, but also in adapting worship to their native genius, as indicated in Art. 39 and 40.

Therefore, when missionaries are being given training in music, every effort should be made to see that they become competent in promoting the traditional music of these peoples, both in schools and in sacred services, as far as may be practicable.

120. In the Latin Church the pipe organ is to be held in high esteem, for it is the traditional musical instrument which adds a wonderful splendor to the Church's ceremonies and powerfully lifts up man's mind to God and to higher things.

But other instruments also may be admitted for use in divine worship, with the knowledge and consent of the competent territorial authority, as laid down in Art. 22, §2, 37, and 40. This may be done, however, only on condition that the instruments are suitable, or can be made suitable, for sacred use, accord with the dignity of the temple, and truly contribute to the edification of the faithful.

121. Composers, filled with the Christian spirit, should feel that their vocation is to cultivate sacred music and increase its store of treasures.

Let them produce compositions which have the qualities proper to genuine sacred music, not confining themselves to works which can be sung only by large choirs, but providing also for the needs of small choirs and for the active participation of the entire assembly of the faithful.

The texts intended to be sung must always be in conformity with Catholic doctrine; indeed they should be drawn chiefly from holy scripture and from liturgical sources.

Chapter VII

SACRED ART AND SACRED FURNISHINGS

122. Very rightly the fine arts are considered to rank among the noblest activities of man's genius, and this applies especially to religious art and to its highest achievement, which is sacred art. These arts, by their very nature, are oriented toward the infinite beauty of God which they attempt in some way to portray by the work of human hands; they achieve their purpose of redounding to God's praise and glory in proportion as they are directed the more exclusively to the single aim of turning men's minds devoutly toward God.

Holy Mother Church has therefore always been the friend of the fine arts and has ever sought their noble help, with the special aim that all things set apart for use in divine worship should be truly worthy, becoming, and beautiful, signs and symbols of the supernatural world, and for this purpose she has trained artists. In fact, the Church has, with good reason, always reserved to herself the right to pass judgment upon the arts, deciding which of the works of artists are in accordance with faith, piety, and cherished traditional laws, and thereby fitted for sacred use.

The Church has been particularly careful to see that sacred furnishings should worthily and beautifully serve the dignity of worship, and has admitted changes in materials, style, or ornamentation prompted by the progress of the technical arts with the passage of time.

Wherefore it has pleased the Fathers to issue the following decrees on these matters.

123. The Church has not adopted any particular style of art as her very own; she has admitted styles from every period according to the natural talents and circumstances of peoples, and the needs of the various rites. Thus, in the course of the centuries, she has brought into being a treasury of art which must be very carefully preserved. The art of our own days, coming from every race and region, shall also be given free scope in the Church, provided that it adorns the sacred buildings and holy rites with due reverence and honor; thereby it is enabled to contribute its own voice to that wonderful chorus of praise in honor of the Catholic faith sung by great men in times gone by.

124. Ordinaries, by the encouragement and favor they show to art which is truly sacred, should strive after noble beauty rather than mere sumptuous display. This principle is to apply also in the matter of sacred vestments and ornaments.

Let bishops carefully remove from the house of God and from other sacred places those works of artists which are repugnant to faith, morals, and Christian piety, and which offend true religious sense either by depraved forms or by lack of artistic worth, mediocrity and pretense.

And when churches are to be built, let great care be taken that they be suitable for the celebration of liturgical services and for the active participation of the faithful.

125. The practice of placing sacred images in churches so that they may be venerated by the faithful is to be maintained. Nevertheless their number should be moderate and their relative positions should reflect right order. For otherwise they may create confusion among the Christian people and foster devotion of doubtful orthodoxy.

126. When passing judgment on works of art, local ordinaries shall give a hearing to the diocesan commission on sacred art and, if needed, also to others who are especially expert, and to the commissions referred to in Art. 44, 45, and 46.

Ordinaries must be very careful to see that sacred furnishings and works of value are not disposed of or dispersed; for they are the ornaments of the house of God.

127. Bishops should have a special concern for artists, so as to imbue them with the spirit of sacred art and of the sacred liturgy. This they may do in person or through suitable priests who are gifted with a knowledge and love of art.

It is also desirable that schools or academies of sacred art should be founded in those parts of the world where they would be useful, so that artists may be trained.

All artists who, prompted by their talents, desire to serve God's glory in holy Church, should ever bear in mind that they are engaged in a kind of sacred imitation of God the Creator, and are concerned with works destined to be used in Catholic worship, to edify the faithful, and to foster their piety and their religious formation.

128. Along with the revision of the liturgical books, as laid down in Art. 25, there is to be an early revision of the canons and ecclesiastical statutes which govern the provision of material things involved in sacred worship. These laws refer especially to the worthy and well planned construction of sacred buildings, the shape and construction of altars, the nobility, placing, and safety of the Eucharistic tabernacle, the dignity and suitability of the baptistery, the proper ordering of sacred images, embellishments, and vestments. Laws which seem less suited to the reformed liturgy are to be brought into harmony with it, or else abolished; and any which are helpful are to be retained if already in use, or introduced where they are lacking.

According to the norm of Art. 22 of this Constitution, the territorial bodies of bishops are empowered to adapt such things to the needs and customs of their different regions; this applies especially to the materials and form of sacred furnishings and vestments.

129. During their philosophical and theological studies, clerics are to be taught about the history and development of sacred art, and about the sound principles governing the production of its works. In consequence they will be able to appreciate and preserve the Church's venerable monuments, and be in a position to aid, by good advice, artists who are engaged in producing works of art.

130. It is fitting that the use of pontificals be reserved to those ecclesiastical persons who have episcopal rank or some particular jurisdiction.

Appendix

A DECLARATION OF THE SECOND ECUMENICAL COUNCIL OF THE VATICAN ON REVISION OF THE CALENDAR

The Second Ecumenical Council of the Vatican, recognizing the importance of the wishes expressed by many concerning the assignment of the feast of Easter to a fixed Sunday and concerning an unchanging calendar, having carefully considered the effects which could result from the introduction of a new calendar, declares as follows:

1. The sacred Council would not object if the feast of Easter were assigned to a particular Sunday of the Gregorian Calendar, provided that those whom it may concern, especially the brethren who are not in communion with the Apostolic See, give their assent.

2. The sacred Council likewise declares that it does not oppose efforts designed to introduce a perpetual calendar into civil society.

But, among the various systems which are being suggested to stabilize a perpetual calendar and to introduce it into civil life, the Church has no objection only in the case of those systems which retain and safeguard a seven-day week with Sunday, without the introduction of any days outside the week, so that the succession of weeks may be left intact, unless there is question of the most serious reasons. Concerning these the Apostolic See shall judge.

* * * * *

In the name of the most holy and undivided Trinity, the Father, and the Son and the Holy Spirit. The Decrees, which have now been read in this Sacred and Universal Second Vatican Synod lawfully assembled, have pleased the Fathers.

And We, by the Apostolic power given to Us by Christ, together with the venerable Fathers approve, enact, and establish these Decrees in the Holy Spirit and command that what has been thus established in the Synod be promulgated unto the glory of God.

Paul Pp. VI

NOTES TO CONSTITUTION

1 Secret of the ninth Sunday after Pentecost.

2 Cf. Heb. 13,14.

3 Cf. Eph. 2,21-22.

4 Cf. Eph. 4,13.

5 Cf. Is. 11,12.

6 Cf. Jn. 11,52.

7 Cf. Jn. 10,16.

8 Cf. Is. 61,1; 4,18.

9 St. Ignatius of Antioch, *To the Ephesians,* 7, 2.

10 Cf. 1 Tim. 2,5.

11 *Sacramentarium Veronese* (ed. Mohlberg), n. 1265; cf. also n. 1241, 1248.

12 Easter Preface of the Roman Missal.

13 Prayer before the second lesson for Holy Saturday, as it was in the Roman Missal before the restoration of Holy Week.

14 Cf. Mk. 16,15.

15 Cf. Acts 26,18.

16 Cf. Rom. 6,4; Eph. 2,6; Col. 3,1; 2 Tim. 2,11.

17 Cf. Jn. 4,23.

18 Cf. 1 Cor. 11,26.

19 Council of Trent, Session XIII, Decree on the Holy Eucharist, c. 5.

20 Council of Trent, Session XXII, Doctrine on the Holy Sacrifice of the Mass, c. 2.

21 Cf. St. Augustine, *Tractatus in Joannem,* VI, n. 7.

22 Cf. Apoc. 21,2; Col. 3,1; Heb. 8,2.

23 Cf. Phil. 3,20; Col. 3,4.

24 Cf. Jn. 17,3; 24,27; Acts 2,38.

25 Cf. Mt. 28,20.

26 Postcommunion for both Masses of Easter Sunday.

27 Collect of the Mass for Tuesday of Easter Week.

28 Cf. 2 Cor. 6,1.

29 Cf. Mt. 6,6.

30 Cf. 1 Thess. 5,17.

31 Cf. 2 Cor. 4,10-11.

32 Secret for Monday of Pentecost Week.

33 St. Cyprian, *On the Unity of the Catholic Church,* 7; cf. Letter 66, n. 8, 3.

34 Cf. Council of Trent, Session XXII, Doctrine on the Holy Sacrifice of the Mass, c. 8.

35 Cf. St. Ignatius of Antioch, *To the Smyrnians,* 8; *To the Magnesians,* 7; *To the Philadelphians,* 4.

36 Cf. St. Augustine, *Tractatus in Ioannem,* VI, n. 13.

37 Roman Breviary, feast of Corpus Christi, Second Vespers, antiphon to the Magnificat.

38 Cf. St. Cyril of Alexandria, *Commentary on the Gospel of John,* book XI, chap. XI-XII: Migne, *Patrologia Graeca,* 74, 557-564.

39 Cf. 1 Tim. 2,1-2.

40 Session XXI, July 16, 1562. Doctrine on Communion under Both Species, chap. 1-3: *Concilium Tridentinum. Diariorum, Actorum, Epistolarum, Tractatuum nova collectio,* ed. Soc. Goerresiana, tome VIII (Freiburg in Br., 1919), 698-699.

41 Council of Trent, Session XXIV, November 11, 1563, On Reform, chap. I. Cf. Roman Ritual, title VIII, chap. II, n. 6.

42 Cf. Eph. 5,19; Col. 3,16.

2

INSTRUCTION FOR THE PROPER IMPLEMENTATION OF THE CONSTITUTION ON THE SACRED LITURGY

INTRODUCTION

I. Nature of this Instruction

1. The Constitution on the Sacred Liturgy is deservedly counted among the first fruits of the Second Ecumenical Vatican Council, since it governs the most excellent part of the Church's activity. It will bear more abundant fruit the more profoundly the pastors and the faithful of Christ perceive its genuine spirit and put it into practice with good will.

2. The Commission for the Implementation of the Constitution on the Sacred Liturgy, established by the Supreme Pontiff, Paul VI, in the apostolic letter *Sacram Liturgiam* has already speedily undertaken the task entrusted to it, to bring the directives of the Constitution and of the apostolic letter to a proper fulfillment and to provide for the interpretation and execution of these documents.

3. It is of the greatest importance that the documents, from the very beginning, should be properly applied everywhere, with doubts, if there are any, concerning their interpretation being removed. Therefore, the commission, by mandate of the Supreme Pontiff, has prepared this Instruction, in which the functions of the bodies of bishops in liturgical matters are more clearly defined, some principles given in general words in the above-mentioned documents are explained more precisely, and finally some matters, which can be put into practice now, before the restoration of the liturgical books, are allowed or required.

II. Some principles to be noted

4. What is now defined as to be put into practice has the purpose of making the liturgy correspond always more perfectly to the mind of the Council concerning the promotion of active participation of the faithful.

The general reform of the sacred liturgy, moreover, will be accepted more readily by the faithful if it proceeds gradually and by stages and if the reform is proposed to the faithful and explained to them by the pastors by means of the required catechesis.

5. Nevertheless, it is necessary first that all be persuaded of the intention of the Constitution on the Sacred Liturgy of the II Vatican Council: not only to change liturgical forms and texts, but rather to stir up that formation of the faithful and pastoral activity which has the sacred lit-

urgy as summit and fount (cf. Constitution, Art. 10). The changes thus far introduced and to be introduced into the sacred liturgy in the future are directed toward this end.

6. The power of pastoral-liturgical activity rests in this, that the Christian life may express the paschal mystery in which the Son of God, incarnate and made obedient even to the death of the cross, is so exalted in His resurrection and ascension that He may share His divine life with the world. By this life men, dead to sin and conformed to Christ, "may live no longer for themselves but for Him who died for them and rose again" (2 Cor. 5, 15).

This is done through faith and through the sacraments of faith, that is, chiefly through baptism (cf. Constitution, Art. 6) and the most sacred mystery of the Eucharist (cf. Constitution, Art. 47). Around the Eucharist are ranged the other sacraments and the sacramentals (cf. Constitution, Art. 61) and the cycle of celebrations by which the paschal mystery of Christ is unfolded in the Church during the course of the year (cf. Constitution, Arts. 102-107).

7. Therefore, even if the liturgy does not exhaust the entire action of the Church (cf. Constitution, Art. 9), nevertheless the greatest attention must be paid to the liturgy, so that pastoral-liturgical action is not exercised as if separate and abstract, but as intimately joined to other pastoral activities.

It is especially necessary that there be a close union between the liturgy and catechesis, religious formation, and preaching.

III. Fruits to be hoped for

8. Thus, the bishops and their assistants in the priesthood should relate their entire pastoral ministry ever more closely to the liturgy. In this way the faithful may derive the divine life in abundance from the perfect participation in the sacred celebration. Having been made the ferment of Christ and the salt of the earth, the faithful will proclaim the divine life and communicate it to others.

Chapter I

SOME GENERAL NORMS

I. Application of these norms

9. The practical norms, found in the Constitution or in this Instruction, and whatever is permitted or determined now by this Instruction before the restoration of the liturgical books, even if they pertain to the Roman rite alone, may nevertheless be applied to the other Latin rites, the provisions of law being observed.

10. Those matters which are entrusted to the competent territorial ecclesiastical authority in this Instruction may and should be put into effect by that authority alone through legitimate decrees.

In individual cases, the time and the circumstances in which these decrees will take effect shall be defined, always with a reasonable interval of time for the faithful to be instructed and prepared for their observance.

II. Liturgical formation of clerics (Constitution, Arts. 15-16 and 18)

11. With regard to the liturgical formation of clerics:

a) In theological faculties there shall be a chair of liturgy, so that all the students may receive the necessary liturgical instruction; in seminaries and in the houses of studies of religious, local ordinaries and major superiors shall see to it that as soon as possible there be a special and properly prepared teacher of liturgy.

b) Professors who are appointed to teach sacred liturgy shall be prepared as soon as possible, in accordance with the norm of Art. 15 of the Constitution.

c) For the further liturgical instruction of clerics, particularly of those who are already working in the Lord's vineyard, pastoral-liturgical institutes shall be established where possible.

12. The liturgy shall be taught for a suitable period of time, to be indicated in the curriculum of studies by the competent authority, and according to an appropriate method in accordance with the norm of Art. 16 of the Constitution.

13. Liturgical services shall be celebrated as perfectly as possible. Therefore:

a) The directions shall be carefully observed and the ceremonies performed with dignity, under the diligent vigilance of the seminary directors, with the necessary preparations beforehand.

b) Clerics shall frequently fulfill the liturgical functions of their order, that is, of deacon, subdeacon, acolyte, lector, and, in addition, of commentator and cantor.

c) The churches and oratories, the sacred furnishings in general, and sacred vestments shall afford an example of genuine Christian art, including contemporary art.

III. Liturgical formation of the spiritual life of clerics (Constitution, Art. 17)

14. In order that clerics may be formed for the full participation in liturgical celebrations and for the spiritual life to be derived from these celebrations, while being prepared to share this participation and life with others, the Constitution on the Sacred Liturgy shall be put into full effect in seminaries and houses of studies of religious, in accordance with the norm of documents from the Apostolic See, with the unanimous and harmonious co-operation of all the directors and teachers to this end. A suitable formation in the sacred liturgy shall be provided for the clerics together with the recommendation of books dealing with the liturgy, especially under its theological and spiritual aspect, which should

be available in the library in sufficient numbers; as well as by meditations and conferences which shall be drawn above all from the fount of sacred Scripture and the liturgy (cf. Constitution, Art. 35, 2); and by common exercises, in accord with Christian custom and usage, but suited to the various seasons of the liturgical year.

15. The Eucharist, the center of the entire spiritual life, shall be celebrated daily with the use of different and appropriate forms which best correspond to the condition of the participants (cf. Constitution, Art. 19).

On Sunday, however, and on other major feast days, a sung Mass shall be celebrated with the participation of all who are in the seminary or house of studies, with a homily and, as far as possible, with the sacramental communion of those who are not priests. The priests may concelebrate, especially on the more solemn feast days, if the needs of the faithful do not require that they celebrate individually, and after the new rite of concelebration has been published.

It is desirable that, at least on major feast days, the students should participate in the celebration of the Eucharist assembled around the bishop in the cathedral church (cf. Constitution, Art. 41).

16. It is most fitting that the clerics, even if they are not yet bound by the obligation of the divine office, should each day recite or chant in common Lauds, in the morning as morning prayer, and Vespers, in the evening as evening prayer, or compline, at the end of the day. The directors themselves shall take part in this common recitation, as far as possible. In addition, sufficient time shall be provided in the order of the day for clerics in sacred orders to pray the divine office.

It is desirable that, at least on major feast days, the students should chant vespers in the cathedral church, where possible.

17. Exercises of piety, arranged according to the laws or customs of each place or institute, shall be held in due esteem. Nevertheless, care should be taken, especially if these exercises are celebrated in common, that they be in harmony with the sacred liturgy, according to the purpose of Art. 13, of the Constitution, and that they be related to the seasons of the liturgical year.

IV. Liturgical formation of members of institutes dedicated to acquiring perfection

18. What has been said in the preceding articles concerning the liturgical formation of the spiritual life of clerics must be applied also to the members, both men and women, of institutes dedicated to acquiring perfection, with the necessary adaptations.

V. Liturgical formation of the faithful (Constitution, Art. 19)

19. Pastors of souls shall strive diligently and patiently to carry out the command of the Constitution concerning the liturgical formation of the faithful and their active participation, both internal and external,

"according to their age and condition, their way of life, and standard of religious culture" (Constitution, Art. 19). They should be especially concerned about the liturgical formation and the active participation of those who are engaged in religious associations of the laity, since it is the latter's duty to share more intimately in the life of the Church and also to assist the pastors of souls in properly promoting the liturgical life of the parish (cf. Constitution, Art. 42).

VI. Competent authority in liturgical matters (Constitution, Art. 22)

20. Regulation of the sacred liturgy pertains to the authority of the Church: therefore, no other person shall proceed in this matter on his own authority to the detriment, as may often happen, of the liturgy itself and of its restoration by the competent authority.

21. It pertains to the Apostolic See to reform and to approve the general liturgical books; to order the sacred liturgy in those matters which affect the universal Church; to approve, that is, confirm the acts and deliberations of the territorial authority; and to receive the proposals and petitions of the same territorial authority.

22. It pertains to the bishop to regulate the liturgy within the limits of his diocese, in accordance with the norms and spirit of the Constitution on the Sacred Liturgy as well as the decrees of the Apostolic See and of the competent territorial authority.

23. The various kinds of territorial bodies of bishops, to which the regulation of the liturgy pertains in virtue of Art. 22, 2 of the Constitution, must be understood to be, for the interim:

a) either the body of all the bishops of a nation, in accordance with the norm of the apostolic letter *Sacram Liturgiam,* n. X;

b) or a body already lawfully constituted which consists of the bishops, or of the bishops and other local ordinaries, of several nations;

c) or a body to be established, with the permission of the Apostolic See, consisting of the bishops or of the bishops and the local ordinaries of several nations, especially if in the individual nations the bishops are so few that they may convene more profitably from various nations of the same language or of the same culture.

If the particular local conditions suggest another solution, the matter should be proposed to the Apostolic See.

24. The following must be invited to the above-mentioned bodies:

a) residential bishops;
b) abbots and prelates *nullius;*
c) vicars and prefects apostolic;
d) apostolic administrators of dioceses who have been appointed permanently;
e) all other local ordinaries except vicars general.

Coadjutor and auxilliary bishops may be invited by the president, with the consent of the majority of those who take part in the body with deliberative vote.

25. Unless the law provides otherwise for certain places in view of

particular circumstances, the convocation of the body must be made:

a) by the respective president, in the case of bodies already lawfully established;

b) in other cases, by the archbishop or bishop who has the right of precedence in accordance with the norm of law.

26. The president, with the consent of the Fathers, determines the order to be followed in the examination of questions, and opens, transfers, prorogues, and closes the conference.

27. A deliberative vote belongs to all who are named in n. 24, including coadjutor and auxilliary bishops, unless a different provision is expressly made in the document of convocation.

28. For the lawful enactment of decrees, two-thirds of the votes, taken by secret ballot, are required.

29. The acts of the competent territorial authority which are to be transmitted to the Apostolic See for approval, that is, confirmation, should contain the following:

a) the names of those who took part in the session;

b) a report of matters taken up;

c) the result of voting for the individual decrees.

Two copies of these acts, signed by the president and the secretary of the body, and with the proper seal, shall be sent to the Commission for the Implementation of the Constitution on the Sacred Liturgy.

30. When, however, it is a question of acts in which there are decrees concerning the use and extent of the vernacular language to be admitted in the liturgy, besides what is enumerated in n. 29, in accordance with Art. 36, 3, of the Constitution and the apostolic letter *Sacram Liturgiam*, n. IX, the acts should also contain:

a) an indication of the individual parts of the liturgy which are to be said in the vernacular;

b) two copies of the liturgical texts prepared in the vernacular, one copy of which will be returned to the body of bishops;

c) a brief report concerning the criteria upon which the work of translation was based.

31. The decrees of the territorial authority which need the approval, that is, the confirmation of the Apostolic See, shall be promulgated and put into practice only when they have been approved, that is, confirmed by the Apostolic See.

VII. The office of individuals in the liturgy (Constitution, Art. 28)

32. The parts which pertain to the schola or to the people, if they are sung or recited by them, are not said privately by the celebrant.

33. Likewise the celebrant does not say privately the lessons which are recited or chanted by a competent minister or by a server.

VIII. Avoiding distinctions of person (Constitution, Art. 32)

34. The individual bishops or, if it seems opportune, the regional or

national conferences of bishops shall see to it that the prescription of the holy Council which forbids any favor to private persons or any favor on the basis of social distinctions, either in ceremonies or in external pomp, shall be put into effect in their territories.

35. In addition, pastors of souls shall work with prudence and charity so that, in the liturgical services and, more especially, in the celebration of sacraments and sacramentals, the equality of the faithful shall be evident even outwardly and that, further, all appearance of money-seeking be avoided.

IX. *Simplification of certain rites* (Constitution, Art. 34)

36. In order that the liturgical services may exhibit a noble simplicity in harmony with the mentality of our times:

a) The salutations to the choir on the part of the celebrant and the ministers shall be made only at the beginning and at the end of the sacred rite;

b) The incensation of the clergy, apart from those who are bishops, shall be done once for each part of the choir, with three swings of the thurible;

c) The incensation of the altar shall be done only at that altar where the liturgical service is being celebrated;

d) The kisses of the hand and of objects which are being presented or received shall be omitted.

X. *Sacred celebrations of the word of God* (Constitution, Art. 35, 4)

37. In places which lack a priest, if no priest is available for the celebration of Mass on Sundays and feast days of precept, the sacred celebration of the word of God shall be fostered, according to the judgment of the local ordinary, with a deacon or even a layman, authorized for this purpose, presiding over the service.

The pattern of this celebration shall be almost the same as the liturgy of the word in Mass; ordinarily the epistle and gospel of the Mass of the day shall be read in the vernacular, with chants, especially from the psalms, before the lessons and between them; the one who presides shall give a homily, if he is a deacon; if not a deacon, he shall read a homily indicated by the bishop or the pastor; and the whole celebration shall be closed with the "common prayer" or "prayer of the faithful" and with the *Lord's Prayer.*

38. It is also fitting that sacred celebrations of the word of God, which are to be encouraged on the vigils of the more solemn feasts, on some weekdays in Advent and Lent, and on Sundays and feast days, should take into account the pattern of the liturgy of the word in Mass, although there may be only a single reading.

In the arrangement of several readings, however, in order that the history of salvation may be clearly discerned, the reading from the Old Testament shall generally precede the reading from the New Testament, and the reading of the holy gospel shall appear as the climax.

39. In order that these celebrations may be held with dignity and piety, it shall be the task of the liturgical commissions in the individual dioceses to indicate and provide appropriate aids.

XI. Vernacular translations of liturgical texts (Constitution, Art. 36, 3)

40. In vernacular translations of liturgical texts prepared in accordance with the norm of Art. 36, 3, it is fitting that the following be observed:

a) The vernacular translations of liturgical texts shall be made from the Latin liturgical text. The version of the biblical pericopes, however, should conform to the Latin liturgical text, but with the possibility of revising this translation, if deemed advisable in accordance with the original text or some other clearer translation.

b) The preparation of the translation of liturgical texts should be entrusted, as a special concern, to the liturgical commission mentioned in Art. 44 of the Constitution and in n. 44 of this Instruction. So far as possible, the institute of pastoral liturgy should assist the commission. But if there is no such commission, the supervision of the translation should be entrusted to two or three bishops, who will choose persons, including lay persons, expert in scripture, liturgy, biblical languages, Latin, the vernacular language, and music. For the perfect translation of the liturgical text into the language of the people must necessarily and properly fulfill many conditions at the same time.

c) Whenever it is called for, there should be consultation concerning translations with the bishops of neighboring regions which have the same language.

d) In nations which have several languages, different vernacular translations should be prepared for these languages and submitted to the special examination of the bishops concerned.

e) Consideration should be given to the dignity of the books from which the liturgical text is read to the people in the vernacular language, so that the dignity of the book itself may move the faithful to a greater reverence for the word of God and for sacred things.

41. In liturgical services which are celebrated in some places with people of another language, it is lawful with the consent of the local ordinary to use the vernacular language known to these faithful, especially in the case of groups of immigrants, or of members of a personal parish, or similar instances. This shall be done in accordance with the extent of the use of the vernacular and its translation as legitimately approved by a competent territorial ecclesiastical authority of the respective language.

42. New melodies for parts to be sung in the vernacular language by the celebrant and the ministers must be approved by the competent territorial ecclesiastical authority.

43. Particular liturgical books which were lawfully approved before the promulgation of the Constitution on the Sacred Liturgy and in-

dults conceded up to that day retain their force, unless they are opposed to the Constitution, until other provision is made in the liturgical restoration, as it will be completed in whole or in part.

XII. The liturgical commission of the body of bishops (Constitution, Art. 44)

44. The liturgical commission, which it is desirable that the territorial authority establish, shall be chosen from among the bishops themselves, as far as possible. At least it shall consist of one or other bishop, with the addition of some priests expert in liturgical and pastoral matters, who are designated by name for this office.

It is desirable that the members of this commission be convened several times a year with the consultors of the commission that they may deal with questions together.

45. The territorial authority may, as circumstances suggest, entrust the following to this commission:

a) studies and experiments to be promoted in accordance with the norm of Art. 40, 1 and 2 of the Constitution;

b) practical initiatives to be undertaken for the entire territory, by which the liturgy and the application of the Constitution on the Liturgy may be encouraged;

c) studies and the preparation of aids which become necessary in virtue of the decrees of the plenary body of bishops;

d) the office of regulating the pastoral-liturgical action in the entire nation, supervising the application of the decrees of the plenary body, and reporting concerning all these matters to the body;

e) consultations to be undertaken frequently and common initiatives to be promoted with associations in the same region which are concerned with scripture, catechetics, pastoral care, music, and sacred art, and with every kind of religious association of the laity.

46. The members of the institute of pastoral liturgy as well as individual experts who are called to assist the liturgical commission shall also freely offer their assistance to individual bishops for the more effective promotion of pastoral-liturgical action in their territory.

XIII. The diocesan liturgical commission (Constitution, Art. 45)

47. The following duties pertain to the diocesan liturgical commission, under the direction of the bishop:

a) to be informed about the state of pastoral-liturgical action in the diocese;

b) to implement carefully what is proposed in liturgical matters by the competent authority, and to obtain information concerning studies and programs which are taking place elsewhere in this field;

c) to suggest and promote practical undertakings of every kind which may help to promote the liturgy, especially those which will assist priests already working in the Lord's vineyard;

d) in individual cases, or also for the entire diocese, to suggest opportune and progressive steps in the work of pastoral liturgy; to indicate and also to call upon suitable persons who on occasion may help priests in this matter; and to propose suitable materials and aids;

e) to see to it that programs in the diocese to promote the liturgy progress with a harmonious spirit and with the assistance of other associations, in a way similar to that indicated for the commission established within the body of bishops (n. 45e).

Chapter II

THE MOST HOLY MYSTERY OF THE EUCHARIST

I. The rite of the Mass (Constitution, Art. 50)

48. Until the entire rite of the Mass is restored, the following shall be observed.

a) The parts of the Proper which are sung or recited by the schola or by the people are not said privately by the celebrant.

b) The celebrant may sing or recite the parts of the Ordinary together with the people or the schola.

c) In the prayers to be said at the foot of the altar at the beginning of Mass, psalm 42 is omitted. All the prayers at the foot of the altar are omitted whenever another liturgical service immediately precedes the Mass.

d) In solemn Masses the paten is not held by the subdeacon, but is left upon the altar.

e) The secret prayer or prayer over the offerings shall be chanted in sung Masses, and recited in a loud voice in other Masses.

f) The doxology at the end of the Canon, from the words *Per ipsum* up to *Per omnia saecula saeculorum. R. Amen,* inclusively, shall be chanted or recited in a loud voice. Throughout the entire doxology the celebrant lifts up the chalice and the host for the little elevation, omitting the signs of the cross, and at the end genuflects only after the response *Amen* is given by the people.

g) In low Masses the *Lord's Prayer* may be recited by the people together with the celebrant in the vernacular language; in sung Masses it may be chanted by the people together with the celebrant in the Latin language and, if the territorial ecclesiastical authority shall so decree, also in the vernacular language, to melodies approved by the same authority.

h) The embolism after the *Lord's Prayer* shall be chanted or recited in a loud voice.

i) In distributing holy communion the formula, *Corpus Christi,* shall be used. The celebrant, as he says these words, lifts up the host a little above the ciborium to show it to the communicant, who responds: *Amen,* and afterward is communicated by the celebrant. The sign of the cross with the host is omitted.

j) The last gospel is omitted; the Leonine prayers are suppressed.

k) It is lawful to celebrate a sung Mass with a deacon only.

l) It is lawful for bishops, if necessary, to celebrate a sung Mass according to the form used by priests.

II. Lessons and chants between the lessons (Constitution, Art. 51)

49. In Masses celebrated with the people, the lessons, epistle, and gospel shall be read or chanted facing the people:

a) in solemn Mass, at the ambo or at the edge of the sanctuary area;

b) in high Mass or in low Mass, if they are read or chanted by the celebrant, either at the altar or at the ambo or at the edge of the sanctuary area, as may be more convenient; if they are read or chanted by another, at the ambo or at the edge of the santuary area.

50. In Masses celebrated with the people which are not solemn Masses, the lessons and epistle, together with the intervenient chants, may be read by a qualified lector or server, while the celebrant sits and listens. The gospel, however, may be read by a deacon or by a second priest, who says *Munda cor meum,* seeks the blessing, and at the end presents the book of gospels for the celebrant to kiss.

51. In sung Masses, the lessons, epistle, and gospel, if they are proclaimed in the vernacular, may be recited without chant.

52. In reciting or chanting the lessons, epistle, the chants which occur after them, and the gospel, the order is as follows:

a) In solemn Mass, the celebrants sits and listens to the lessons and epistle as well as to the intervenient chants. After the epistle has been chanted or recited, the subdeacon goes to the celebrant and is blessed by him. Then the celebrant, seated, places incense in the thurible and blesses it. While the *Alleluia* and its verse are being chanted or toward the end of other chants following the epistle, the celebrant rises to bless the deacon. At his seat he listens to the gospel, kisses the book of gospels, and, after the homily, intones the creed, if the latter is to be said. At the end of the creed he returns to the altar with the ministers, unless he is to direct the prayer of the faithful.

b) In high or low Masses in which the lessons, epistle, the chants following them, and the gospel are sung or recited by the minister mentioned in n. 50, the celebrant acts in the manner described above.

c) In high or low Masses in which the gospel is chanted or read by the celebrant, while the *Alleluia* and its verse are being chanted or recited or toward the end of other chants following the epistle, he goes to the lowest step of the altar and there bows deeply while saying *Munda cor meum*. Then he goes to the ambo or to the edge of the sanctuary area to chant or recite the gospel.

d) But if, in a high Mass or low Mass, all the lessons are chanted or recited by the celebrant at the ambo or at the edge of the sanctuary area, then, standing in the same place, he also recites the chants occurring after the lessons and the epistle, if this is necessary; he says *Munda cor meum* turned toward the altar.

III. The homily (Constitution, Art. 52)

53. There shall be a homily on Sundays and feast days of precept in all Masses which are celebrated with the people present. No exception may be made for conventual, sung, or pontifical Masses.

On other days, a homily is recommended, especially on some of the weekdays of Advent and Lent, as well as in other circumstances when the people come to church in larger numbers.

54. By a homily from the sacred text is understood an explanation either of some aspect of the readings from holy Scripture or of another text from the Ordinary or Proper of the Mass of the day, taking into account the mystery which is being celebrated and the particular needs of the hearers.

55. If plans of preaching within Mass are proposed for certain periods, the intimate connection with at least the principal seasons and feasts of the liturgical year (cf. Constitution, Arts. 102-104), that is, with the mystery of the Redemption, is to be harmoniously preserved: for the homily is part of the liturgy of the day.

IV. The common prayer or prayer of the faithful (Constitution, Art. 53)

56. In places where the custom is already in force of having the common prayer or prayer of the faithful, for the interim it shall take place before the offertory, after the word *Oremus,* according to the formulas now in use in the individual regions. The celebrant shall direct the prayer either from his seat, from the altar, from the ambo, or from the edge of the sanctuary area.

The intentions or invocations may be chanted by a deacon or a cantor or other qualified server, reserving to the celebrant the words of introduction and the concluding prayer. This latter will ordinarily be: *Deus, refugium nostrum et virtus* (cf. *Missale Romanum, Orationes diversae,* n. 20) or another prayer which corresponds better to a particular need.

In places where the common prayer or prayer of the faithful is not in use, the competent territorial authority may decree that it be done in the manner indicated above, with formulas approved for the interim by that authority.

V. The place which may be granted to the vernacular language in the Mass (Constitution, Art. 54)

57. In Masses, whether sung or low, which are celebrated with the people, the competent territorial ecclesiastical authority may admit the vernacular language, the decrees having been approved, that is, confirmed, by the Apostolic See:

a) especially in proclaiming the lessons, epistle, and gospel, as well as in the common prayer or prayer of the faithful;

b) according to the circumstances of the place, also in the chants of the Ordinary of the Mass, namely, Kyrie, Gloria, Creed, Sanctus-Benedictus, and Agnus Dei, and in the antiphons at the Introit, offertory, and communion, as well as in the chants that occur between the lessons.

c) moreover, in the acclamations, salutations, and dialogue formulas, together with the formulas at the communion of the faithful: *Ecce Agnus Dei, Domine, non sum dignus,* and *Corpus Christi,* and in the *Lord's Prayer* with its introduction and embolism.

Missals for liturgical use, however, should contain the Latin text in addition to the vernacular translation.

58. It pertains solely to the Apostolic See to concede the vernacular language in other parts of the Mass which are chanted or recited by the celebrant alone.

59. Pastors of souls shall carefully see to it that the faithful, more particularly the members of lay religious associations, also know how to say or to sing together in the Latin language those parts of the Ordinary of the Mass which pertains to them, especially with the use of simpler melodies.

VI. The faculty of repeating communion on the same day (Constitution, Art. 55)

60. The faithful who communicate in the Mass of the Easter Vigil or in the midnight Mass of Christmas may also receive communion again in the second Mass of Easter and in one of the Masses which is celebrated on Christmas in the daytime.

Chapter III

THE OTHER SACRAMENTS AND THE SACRAMENTALS

I. The place which may be granted to the vernacular language (Constitution, Art. 63)

61. The competent territorial authority may admit the vernacular language, the decrees having been approved, that is, confirmed, by the Apostolic See;

a) in the rites of baptism, confirmation, penance, anointing of the sick, and matrimony, including the essential forms, as well as in the distribution of Holy Communion;

b) in the conferral of orders; in the allocutions at the beginning of each ordination or consecration, as well as in the examination of the bishop-elect in episcopal consecration, and in the instructions;

c) in the sacramentals;

d) in funeral rites.

Wherever a more extended use of the vernacular language appears desirable, the regulation of Art. 40 of the Constitution is to be observed.

II. Things to be suppressed in the rite for supplying omissions in baptism (Constitution, Art. 69)

62. In the rite for supplying omissions in the case of a baptized infant, which is given in the Roman Ritual, tit. II, cap. 5, those exorcisms shall be omitted which are found under n. 6 (*Exi ab eo*), 10 (*Exorcizo te, immunde spiritus–Ergo maledicte diabole*), and 15 (*Exorcizo te, omnis spiritus*).

63. In the rite for supplying omissions in the case of a baptized adult, which is given in the Roman Ritual, tit. II, cap. 6, those exorcisms shall be omitted which are found under n. 5 (*Exi ab eo*), 15 (*Ergo, maledicte diabole*), 17 (*Audi maledicte satana*), 19 (*Exorcizo te, Ergo, maledicte diabole*), 21 (*Ergo, maledicte diabole*), 23 (*Ergo, maledicte diabole*), 25 (*Exorcizo te–Ergo maledicte diabole*), 31 (*Nec te lateat*), *and* 35 (*Exi, immunde spiritus*).

III. Confirmation (Constitution, Art. 71)

64. If confirmation is conferred within Mass, it is fitting that the Mass be celebrated by the bishop himself. In this case he confers confirmation while vested in the Mass vestments.

The Mass within which confirmation is conferred may be celebrated as a votive Mass of Class II, of the Holy Spirit.

65. After the gospel and homily, before the reception of confirmation, it is praiseworthy that those to be confirmed should renew the promises of baptism, according to the rite legitimately in use in the individual regions, unless this has already taken place before Mass.

66. If the Mass is celebrated by another, it is fitting that the bishop assist at the Mass wearing the vestments prescribed for the conferral of confirmation, which may be either the color of the Mass or white. The bishop himself shall give the homily, and the celebrant shall resume the Mass only after confirmation.

67. Confirmation is conferred according to the rite prescribed in the Roman Pontifical, but at the words *In nomine Patris, et Filii, et Spiritus Sancti* which follow the formula *Signo Te,* a single sign of the cross shall be made.

IV. Continuous rite for anointing of the sick and Viaticum (Constitution, Art. 74)

68. When anointing of the sick and Viaticum are administered at the same time, unless a continuous rite is already found in a particular ritual, the rite shall be arranged as follows: after the sprinkling with holy water and the prayers of entrance which are given in the rite of anointing, the priest shall hear the confession of the sick person, if necessary, then administer anointing, and finally give Viaticum, omitting the sprinkling with its formulas and the Confiteor and absolution.

If, however, the apostolic blessing with a plenary indulgence at the hour of death is to be imparted on the same occasion, this shall be given immediately before anointing, omitting the sprinkling with its formulas and the Confiteor and absolution.

V. Imposition of hands in episcopal consecration (Constitution, Art. 76)

69. All the bishops present at an episcopal consecration may impose hands; they vest in choir dress. The words *Accipe Spiritum Sanctum,* however, shall be said only by the bishop consecrator and by the two co-consecrating bishops.

VI. Rite of matrimony (Constitution, Art. 78)

70. Matrimony, unless a just cause excuses from the celebration of Mass, shall be celebrated within Mass after the gospel and the homily. The latter is never omitted.

71. Whenever matrimony is celebrated within Mass, the votive Mass for the spouses shall always be celebrated or a commemoration made of it, according to the rubrics, even during the prohibited season.

72. As far as possible, the pastor or his delegate who assists at the marriage shall celebrate the Mass; but if another priest assists the celebrant shall not continue the Mass until the rite of matrimony has been completed.

The priest who assists at the marriage but does not celebrate the Mass shall be vested in surplice and white stole and, according to the local custom, also in cope, and shall give the homily. The blessing after the *Lord's Prayer* before the *Placeat,* however, is always to be imparted by the priest who celebrates the Mass.

73. The nuptial blessing shall always be imparted within the Mass, even in the prohibited season and even if one or both of the spouses is entering a second marriage.

74. In the celebration of matrimony without Mass:

a) at the beginning of the rite, according to the apostolic letter *Sacram Liturgiam,* n. V, a brief admonition shall be given. This is not a homily, but only a simple instruction for the celebration of marriage (cf. Constitution, Art. 35, 3). There shall be, however, a sermon or homily drawn from the sacred text (cf. Constitution, Art. 52), after the reading of the epistle and gospel from the Mass for the spouses, so that the order of the whole rite shall be: brief admonition, reading of the epistle and gospel in the vernacular language, homily, celebration of marriage, nuptial blessing.

b) For the reading of the epistle and gospel from the Mass for the spouses, in the absence of a vernacular text approved by the competent territorial ecclesiastical authority, it is lawful for the interim to use a text approved by the local ordinary.

c) A chant may be sung between the epistle and the gospel. Likewise the prayer of the faithful is highly recommended after the completion of the rite of matrimony, according to a formula approved by the local ordinary, in which petitions for the spouses are also to be included.

d) At the end of the rite the blessing shall always be imparted to the spouses, even in the prohibited season and even if one or both of the spouses is entering a second marriage, according to the formula which is found in the Roman Ritual, tit. VIII, cap. III, unless another blessing is given in particular rituals.

75. If marriage is celebrated during the prohibited season, the pastor shall advise the spouses to take into account the special character of this liturgical season.

VII. Sacramentals (Constitution, Art. 79)

76. In the blessing of candles on February 2 and in the blessing of ashes at the beginning of Lent, a single prayer from among the prayers which are found in the Roman Missal for these blessings may be said.

77. Blessings which have been reserved up to the present time and which are contained in the Roman Ritual, tit. IX, cap. 9, 10, 11, may be given by any priest, with the exception of the blessing of a bell for the use of a blessed church or oratory (cap. 9, n. 11), the blessing of the first stone for the building of a church (cap. 9, n. 16), the blessing of a new church or public oratory (cap. 9, n. 17), the blessing of an antimension (cap. 9, n. 21), the blessing of a new cemetery (cap. 9, n. 22), the papal blessings (cap. 10, n. 1-3), and the blessing and erection of the stations of the Way of the Cross (cap. 11, n. 1) inasmuch as this is reserved to the Bishop.

Chapter IV

THE DIVINE OFFICE

I. The celebration of the divine office by those bound to the obligation of choir (Constitution, Art. 95)

78. Until the restoration of the divine office is completed:

a) Communities of canons, monks, nuns, and other regulars or religious bound to choir by law or constitutions must celebrate the entire divine office daily in choir, in addition to the conventual Mass.

Individual members of these communities who are in major orders or are solemnly professed, except for the *conversi,* even if they are lawfully dispensed from choir, must recite individually each day the canonical hours which they do not celebrate in choir.

b) Cathedral and collegiate chapters must celebrate those parts of the office in choir which are imposed upon them by the common law or by particular law, in addition to the conventual Mass.

Individual members of these chapters, in addition to the canonical hours which all clerics in major orders are bound to celebrate (cf. Constitution, Art. 96 and 89), must recite individually those hours which are celebrated by their chapter.

c) In mission lands, however, while preserving the religious or capitular choral discipline established by law, religious or members of chapters who are lawfully absent from choir by reason of the pastoral ministry may enjoy the concession made in the apostolic letter *Sacram Liturgiam,* n. VI, with the permission of the local ordinary, but not of the vicar general or delegate.

II. Faculty of dispensing from or commuting the divine office (Constitution, Art. 97)

79. The faculty conceded to all ordinaries of dispensing their subjects, in individual cases and for a just cause, from the obligation of the divine office in whole or in part or of commuting it, is also extended to major superiors of non-exempt clerical religious institutes and of societies of clerics who live the common life without vows.

III. Short offices (Constitution, Art. 98)

80. No short office is considered as drawn up after the pattern of the divine office which does not consist of psalms, lessons, hymns, and prayers and which does not take into some account the hours of the day and the respective liturgical seasons.

81. In order to celebrate the public prayer of the Church, for the interim those short offices may be used which have been lawfully approved up to the present time, provided that they have been drawn up according to the requirements enumerated in No. 80.

New short offices, however, must be approved by the Apostolic See in order to be used for the public prayer of the Church.

82. The translation of the text of a short office into the vernacular language for use as the public prayer of the Church must be approved by the competent territorial ecclesiastical authority, the decrees having been approved, that is, confirmed by the Apostolic See.

83. The competent authority for conceding the vernacular in the recitation of a short office to those who are bound to this office by the constitutions, or for dispensing from or commuting the obligation of recitation, is the ordinary or the major superior of the respective subject.

IV. Divine office or short offices celebrated in common by members of institutes dedicated to acquiring perfection (Constitution, Art. 99)

84. The obligation of celebrating in common the divine office or a short office or parts of either imposed by their constitutions on members of institutes dedicated to acquiring perfection does not take away the faculty of omitting the hour of prime and of selecting from among the other minor hours one that best suits the time of day (cf. Apostolic Letter *Sacram Liturgiam,* n. VI).

V. The language to be used in the recitation of the divine office (Constitution, Art. 101)

85. In the celebration of the divine office in choir, clerics are bound to retain the Latin language.

86. The faculty granted to the ordinary of conceding the use of the vernacular language, in individual cases, to those clerics for whom the use of Latin constitutes a grave impediment to their praying the office properly, is extended also to the major superiors of nonexempt clerical religious institutes and of societies of clerics who live the common life without vows.

87. The grave obstacle which is required for the grant of the preceding concession must be weighed by taking into consideration the physical, moral, intellectual and spiritual condition of the petitioner.

Nevertheless, this faculty, which is granted solely to make the recitation of the divine office easier and more devout, is in no way intended to detract from the obligation incumbent upon priests of the Latin rite to learn the Latin language.

88. The vernacular translation of the divine office according to a rite other than the Roman rite shall be prepared and approved by the respective ordinaries of that language, employing for elements common to both rites those translations approved by the territorial authority, and then proposed for the confirmation of the Apostolic See.

89. Breviaries to be used by clerics to whom the use of the vernacular language in the celebration of the divine office is conceded in accordance with Art. 101, No. 1, of the Constitution, should contain the Latin text in addition to the vernacular translation.

Chapter V

THE PROPER CONSTRUCTION OF CHURCHES AND ALTARS IN ORDER TO FACILITATE THE ACTIVE PARTICIPATION OF THE FAITHFUL

I. The arrangement of churches

90. In the new construction, repair, or adaptation of churches great care shall be taken that they are suitable for the celebration of divine services according to the true nature of the services and for the active participation of the faithful (cf. Constitution, Art. 124).

II. The main altar

91. It is proper that the main altar be constructed separately from the wall, so that one may go around it with ease and so that celebration may take place facing the people; it shall occupy a place in the sacred building which is truly central, so that the attention of the whole congregation of the faithful is spontaneously turned to it.

In choosing the material for the construction or ornamentation of the altar, the prescriptions of law shall be observed.

Moreover, the presbyterium or sanctuary area around the altar shall be of sufficient size that the sacred rites may be conveniently celebrated.

III. The seat of the celebrant and ministers

92. The seat for the celebrant and ministers, according to the structure of individual churches, shall be so placed that it may be easily seen by the faithful and that the celebrant may truly appear to preside over the entire community of the faithful.

Nevertheless, if the seat is placed behind the altar, the form of a throne is to be avoided, as this belongs to the bishop alone.

IV. Minor altars

93. The minor altars shall be few in number. In fact, to the extent permitted by the structure of the building, it is highly suitable that they be placed in chapels in some way separated from the principal part of the church.

V. Ornamentation of altars

94. The cross and candlesticks, which are required on the altar for the individual liturgical services, may also, in accordance with the judgment of the local ordinary, be placed next to it.

VI. The reservation of the most holy Eucharist

95. The most holy Eucharist shall be reserved in a solid and inviolable tabernacle placed in the middle of the main altar or of a minor, but truly outstanding, altar, or, according to lawful customs and in particular cases to be approved by the local ordinary, also in some other noble and properly adorned part of the church.

It is lawful to celebrate Mass facing the people even if there is a tabernacle, small but suitable, on the altar.

VII. The ambo

96. It is fitting that there be an ambo or ambos for the proclamation of the sacred readings, so arranged that the ministers can be easily seen and heard by the faithful.

VIII. The place of the schola and organ

97. The places for the schola and the organ shall be so arranged that it will be clearly evident that the singers and the organist form a part of the united community of the faithful and so that they may fulfill their liturgical function more suitably.

IX. The places of the faithful

98. The places for the faithful shall be arranged with particular care, so that they may participate in the sacred celebrations visually and with proper spirit. It is desirable that ordinarily benches or seats

be provided for their use. Nevertheless, the custom of reserving seats for certain private persons is to be reprobated, in accordance with Art. 32 of the Constitution.

Care shall also be taken that the faithful may not only see the celebrant and the other ministers but may also hear them easily, with the use of present-day technical means.

X. *Baptistry*

99. In the construction and ornamentation of the baptistry, care shall be taken that the dignity of the sacrament of baptism is clearly apparent and that the place is suitable for the community celebration of the sacrament (cf. Constitution, Art. 27).

* * * *

The present Instruction, prepared at the command of Pope Paul VI, by the Commission for the Implementation of the Constitution on the Sacred Liturgy, was presented to His Holiness by James Cardinal Lercaro, president of the Commission.

The Holy Father, after having given due consideration to this Instruction, with the help of the above-mentioned Commission and of this Sacred Congregation of Rites, in an audience granted to Arcadio Maria Cardinal Larraona, prefect of the Congregation, on September 26, 1964, approved it in a special way as a whole and in its parts, confirmed it by his authority, and ordered it to be published, and to be diligently observed by all concerned, beginning the First Sunday of Lent, March 7, 1965.

All things to the contrary notwithstanding.

Rome, September 26, 1964.

James Cardinal Lercaro
Archbishop of Bologna
President of the Commission
for the Implementation of
the Constitution on the
Sacred Liturgy.

Arcadio M. Cardinal Larraona
Prefect of the Congregation of
Sacred Rites
✠ Henry Dante
Titular Archbishop of Carpasia
Secretary of the Congregation
of Sacred Rites

3

SACRAM LITURGIAM

Motu Proprio of Pope Paul VI on implementing the Ecumenical Council's Constitution on the Liturgy

The many documents on liturgical questions that have been published and are well known to all demonstrate how it was the ceaseless concern of our predecessors in the supreme pontificate, of ourselves, and of the holy shepherds to preserve diligently, to cultivate and to renew the sacred liturgy according to need. Another proof of this solicitude is given by the Liturgical Constitution which the Second Ecumenical Vatican Council has approved by general consent and which we in the solemn public session of December 4, 1963, ordered to be promulgated.

This lively interest stems from the fact that "in the earthly liturgy we take part in a foretaste of that heavenly liturgy which is celebrated in the holy city of Jerusalem toward which we journey as pilgrims, where Christ is sitting at the right hand of God, a minister of the holy rites and of the true tabernacle. We sing a hymn to the Lord's glory with all the warriors of the heavenly army. Venerating the memory of the saints, we hope for some part and fellowship with them. We eagerly await the Savior, our Lord Jesus Christ, until he, our life, shall appear and we too will appear with him in glory" (Art. 8, Liturgy Constitution).

For this reason the souls of the faithful worship God, the principle and model of all holiness, in such a way as to be, in this earthly pilgrimage, "imitators of the heavenly Zion" (from hymn of Lauds of the Feast of the Dedication of a Church).

For these reasons it is apparent to all that it is our uppermost concern that all Christians, and especially all priests, should consecrate themselves first of all to the study of the already mentioned constitution and from now on, resolve to implement its individual prescription in good faith as soon as they enter into force. And since it is necessary by the very nature of things that the prescriptions concerning the knowledge and spread of the liturgical laws should take place immediately, we earnestly exhort shepherds of dioceses that with the help of the sacred ministers, "dispensers of God's mysteries" (Constitution, Art. 19), they should hasten to act in order that the faithful entrusted to their care may understand, to the degree permitted by age, by the conditions of their own life and by their mental formation, the strength and inner value of the liturgy and at the same time participate very devoutly, internally and externally, in the rites of the Church (Constitution, Art. 19).

Meanwhile, it seems evident that many prescriptions of the constitution cannot be applied in a short period of time, especially since some rites must first be revised and new liturgical books prepared. In order that this work may be carried out with the necessary wisdom and prudence, we are establishing a special commission whose principal task will be to implement in the best possible way the prescriptions of the Constitution on the Sacred Liturgy itself.

However, since among the norms of the constitution there are some which can be made effective now, we desire that they enter immediately into force, so that the souls of the faithful may not be further deprived of the fruits of the grace which are hoped for from them.

Therefore, with our apostolic authority and on our own initiative, we order and decree from the coming first Sunday of Lent, that is, from February 16, 1964, the statutory interval for a law to go into force being waived, the following norms enter into force:

I. We desire that the norms contained in Arts. 15, 16 and 17 concerning teaching of the liturgy in seminaries, in schools of religious communities and in theological faculties immediately should be worked into the programs in such a way that beginning in the next school year students may devote themselves to such study in an orderly and diligent way.

II. We also decree that, according to the norms of Arts. 45 and 46, there be established as soon as possible in the various dioceses a commission whose task is, under direction of the bishop, to foster knowledge of the liturgy and advance the liturgical apostolate.

It will also be opportune that in certain cases, several dioceses should have a single commission.

Furthermore, in all dioceses let two other commissions be established: one for sacred music and the other for sacred art.

These three diocesan commissions may also be merged into one if necessary.

III. From the date established above, we desire that the norms of Art. 52 should enter into force, prescribing the homily during holy Mass on Sunday and holy days.

IV. In the same way, we also put into immediate effect the norms contained in Art. 71, which permits, when convenient, administration of the sacrament of confirmation during holy Mass after the reading of the gospel and the preaching of the homily.

V. Concerning Art. 78, we admonish all concerned that the sacrament of matrimony must normally be celebrated during holy Mass, after the reading of the gospel and the sermon.

If matrimony is administered outside the Mass, we order that the following rules be observed until a new ritual is established: At the beginning of this sacred rite (Constitution, Art. 35, paragraph 3), after a brief exhortation, the gospel and epistle of the Nuptial Mass must be read; and then let spouses receive the blessing which is contained in the Roman Ritual in Section 8, Chapter III.

VI. Although the divine office has not yet been revised and renewed according to the norms of article 89, we nevertheless grant immediately the following permission to all who are obliged to recite the divine office. From February 16, in recitation of the office outside of choir, they may omit the hour of Prime and choose from among the three other little hours one that best suits the time of day, always without prejudice to the dispositions of Arts. 95 and 96 of the Constitution.

We make this concession with strong confidence this will not detract in any way from the piety of the clergy, but rather that in diligently carrying out the duties of their priestly office for the love of God, they may feel more closely united to God throughout the day.

VII. Still regarding the divine office, we ordain that ordinaries may for just and well-considered reasons dispense their own subjects wholly or in part from the obligation of reciting it, or commute it to something else (Constitution, Art. 97).

VIII. Still regarding the divine office, we desire that those members of institutes of perfection who, according to their constitutions, recite some part of the divine office, or some "little office," provided this is drawn up on the pattern of the divine office and regularly approved, are to be considered as taking part in the public prayer of the Church (Constitution, Art. 98).

IX. Since according to Art. 101 of the Constitution those who are obliged to recite the divine office may in various ways be permitted to use the vernacular instead of Latin, we deem it proper to specify that the various versions proposed by the competent territorial bishops' conference, according to Art. 36, paragraphs 3 and 4, must always be reviewed and approved by the Holy See, according to the norm of the same article, paragraph 3. We order that this practice always be observed whenever a liturgical Latin text is translated into the vernacular on behalf of the territorial authority.

X. Since in accord with Art. 22, paragraph 2, the direction of the liturgy within geographical limits comes within the competence of the legitimately constituted territorial episcopal conference of various kinds, we establish that the term "territorial" be understood as meaning national.

In addition to residential bishops, all who are mentioned in Canon 292 of the Code of Canon Law may participate in these national conferences, with the right to vote.

In addition, coadjutor and auxilliary bishops may also be called to these conferences. In these conferences, legitimate approval of decrees requires a two-third majority, with the voting secret.

XI. Finally we wish to emphasize that—beyond what we in this apostolic letter on liturgical matters have either changed or have ordered carried out at the established time—regulation of the liturgy comes solely within the authority of the Church: that is, of this Apostolic See and, in accordance with the law, of the bishop. Consequently, absolutely no one else, not even a priest, can on his own initiative add or subtract or change anything in liturgical matters (Constitution, Art. 22, paragraphs 1 and 3).

We ordain that all we have established with this *motu proprio* should remain valid, and in force, everything to the contrary notwithstanding.

Given in Rome, at St. Peter's, January 25, 1964, the feast of the Conversion of St. Paul the Apostle, in the first year of our pontificate.

PAUL PP. VI

4

DECREE ON CONCELEBRATION AND COMMUNION UNDER BOTH SPECIES

The Church has always been concerned about the order and renewal of the celebration of her sacred mysteries. For she wishes that the very rites achieve two things: to communicate the inexhaustible riches of Christ which they contain and to make the rites more meaningful in the best possible way, to the faithful who receive them with proper dispositions so that they may more easily penetrate the very souls and life of the faithful who take part in them.

The Church shows a special zeal and concern for the celebration of the Eucharist. For she compares and arranges its various forms that they express and inculcate the various aspects of the Eucharistic Sacrifice in the minds and hearts of the faithful.

In each form, no matter how simple, in which Mass is celebrated, all the gifts (dotes) and properties of the Mass are actively present. These by their very nature are necessarily proper to the most holy sacrifice of the Mass. Among these gifts and properties the following are to be noted for their own peculiar reason:

Above all the oneness of the Sacrifice of the Cross, in as far as the many Masses represent only the one sacrifice of Christ[1] and from this fact take on the character of a sacrifice, because they are a memorial of the bloody immolation once offered on the cross, whose fruits are perceived by this present unbloody immolation.

Then the unity of the priesthood, in as far as there are many priests who celebrate the Mass, while the individuals are ministers of Christ who exercises his priesthood through them and who for this purpose in a very special way has the individuals share his own priesthood. Furthermore on this account when the individual priests offer the sacrifice, all do this by virtue of the same priesthood and act in the person of the High Priest, who is at liberty to have one priest or many priests together consecrate the sacrament of his body and blood.[2]

Finally the action of the whole people of God appears more clearly; for every Mass, as the celebration of that sacrament by which the Church continuously lives and grows[3] and in which the genuine nature of the same Church is especially manifested,[4] is even more than all the other liturgical actions[5] the action of the whole people of God as it is acting in hierarchical fashion (*hierarchice ordinati*).

Then, too, this triple prerogative, which is proper to every Mass, is shown before our very eyes in the rite when several priests concelebrate the same Mass.

For in this way of celebrating Mass, several priests by virtue of the same Priesthood and in person of the High Priest act at the same time with one will and one voice and at the same time by one act confect and offer one and the same sacrifice and at the same time participate of the same.

Wherefore in the celebration of such a sacrifice, which the faithful together, consciously and actively participate in the manner proper to a community, especially if the bishop is present, we have in truth the principal manifestation of the Church[6] in its unity of priesthood and sacrifice, in one act of thanks, around one altar with ministers and holy people.

In this way by the rite of concelebration, truths of great moment, which pertain to the spiritual and pastoral life of the priest and to the education of the faithful are clearly proposed and inculcated in a life-like manner.

For these reasons, more than for other reasons of a practical nature, concelebration of the Eucharistic Mystery in various ways and forms has been recognized and evolved in various ways, both in the East and in the West and has been in use up to the present time.

For these same reasons liturgical experts have carried on investigations and have requested that the faculty of concelebration be extended and that a more adapted renewal of this rite be drawn up.

Then the II Vatican Council duly considered the matter and extended the faculty of concelebration for several occasions and decreed that a new rite of concelebration be drawn up and be inserted in the Roman Pontifical and Missal. Therefore His Holiness, Pope Paul VI, after the solemn approval and promulgation of the Constitution on the Sacred Liturgy, entrusted to the Commission for the proper implementation of the said Constitution, to draw up, as soon as possible, a rite to be observed in the concelebration of Mass. Several times the Commission closely examined this rite and after perfecting it unanimously approved it on June 19, 1964, and decided that, if it so pleased our Holy Father before it be definitely approved, it be released for practical experiment in various parts of the world and under different conditions.

Likewise according to the will of the Sacred Council the same Commission for the implementation of the liturgy also drew up a rite of Communion under both species defining clearly the occasions and the forms, in which clerics, religious and laity are allowed to receive the Eucharist under both species.

For several months many experiments have been made with regard to the rite of concelebration and of Communion under both species. They were conducted everywhere with the best results and reports with accompanying observations and suggestions were sent in to the Secretariate of the Commission. After due consideration each rite was finally perfected and brought to the Holy See by His Eminence Cardinal Lercaro, the President of this Commission.

After diligently examining both rites with the help of the above Commission and this Sacred Congregation, Our most Holy Father, in an audience on the 4th of March with the Prefect of the Congregation of Sacred Rites, His Eminence Arcadius Cardinal Larraona, approved them completely in a special way and decreed them to be made public and to be observed from Holy Thursday, April 5th 1965, and to be inserted in the Pontifical and the Missal.

All to the contrary notwithstanding.

March 7, 1965.

James Card. Lercaro
Archbishop of Bologna
President of the Commission for the
Implementation of the Constitution
of the Sacred Liturgy

Arcadius M. Card. Larraona
Pref. of the Congregation
of Sacred Rites

Ferdinandus Antonelli O.F.M.
Secretary of the Congregation
of Sacred Rites

NOTES TO DECREE

1 Cf. Concilium Trid., Sess. XXII, Cap. I.

2 Cf. S. Thomas Aq., S. Th. III, 82, a. 3, ad 2 et ad 3.

3 Cf. Conv. Vat. II, Const. de Ecclesia, Art. 26.

4 Cf. Conc. Vat. II, Const. de Sacra Lit., Art. 2 et 41.

5 Cf. ibid., Art. 26.

6 Cf. Conc. Vat. II, Const. de Sacra Lit., Art. 41.

5

REPLIES OF THE VATICAN COMMISSION

VATICAN CITY—(NC)—The Church body charged with co-ordinating the Ecumenical Council's liturgical reforms has warned against experimentation by persons claiming a general permission.

The Consilium (commission) for the Implementation of the Liturgy Constitution, in the June, 1965 issue of its publications, *Notitiae,* which was published early in July, declared that aside from one case it has "never given any general indult to begin experimentation."

The one exception, it said, was a temporary indult for experimentation in concelebration and Communion under both species, granted from July 3, 1964, until Apr. 15, 1965, after which the general decree on these practices went into effect.

The consilium said the liturgy constitution provides that authority for such general experimentations will be granted to territorial bodies of bishops by the Holy See. They are to be performed only by determined groups suited for such experiments and for a determined length of time.

"If the consilium permits experiments," *Notitiae* said, "it will always communicate the faculty to perform them to territorial ecclesiastical authority, and this in writing, with the addition of conditions and limits within which the experiments may be performed.

"Likewise when rites or ceremonies or innovations of any kind seem out of harmony with today's laws in liturgical matters, all of them are to be considered 'personal' innovations, arising from 'private agitation' . . . and by that very fact disapproved by the constitution and the consilium."

The consilium said it was publishing its declaration because "sometimes rumors are spread here and there of certain innovations which go beyond either the rubrics in force or the constitution or the instruction concerning the sacred liturgy. Authors of these innovations, as is very often the case, claim they have obtained a faculty or indult from the consilium to conduct experiments."

Clarifying doubts arising in the interpretation of the liturgy constitution, *Notitiae* said it is permissible to celebrate Mass in the vernacular even if those assisting do not actually participate by making responses.

Answering another difficulty concerning the use of the laity to read the Epistles and lessons or perform the function of commentator, *Notitiae* noted that even in houses of religious women or girls' schools, the Epistles and lessons must be read by a man. Women, however, can perform the function of commentator in a restricted sense: they can "as it were, lead singing or prayers."

Notitiae set down the general guidelines the consilium will follow in proposing liturgical changes. "Only those elements are to be set forth which already manifest some sort of certainty on the part of the consilium. Others, although they may have been discussed and examined frequently, will simply be omitted if they seem not yet sufficiently mature."

Expressions used by the consilium, such as "it has pleased the Fathers" or "the Fathers have given their vote" or "they have approved," are to be accepted in a broad sense. That is, *Notitiae* said, "they show the mind of the consilium, not the definitive solution to questions. In the pursuit of their work a matter can be established otherwise if new elements arise . . . .

"It is especially superfluous to note that the judgment of the consilium constitutes no binding rule for ultimate and definitive approbation by supreme authority."

Two proposals, reported out of the committees of experts at work within the consilium, were published in *Notitiae*. One concerned the general principles or criteria for the reform of the liturgical calendar. The other concerned the redistribution of psalms in the priests' breviary.

In the former, it was proposed that the calendar of saints' feasts be revised to represent more equally saints from various regions "so that it is demonstrated that sanctity is diffused throughout the universal Church, avoiding making the Roman calendar a Mediterranean calendar." The committee specifically proposed by way of example the inclusion of the Japanese, Canadian and Uganda martyrs.

It was suggested that several saints' feasts be assigned to the same day, leaving an option on which is to be celebrated.

As guidelines for the selection of saints for the universal calendar, the committee proposed the retention of all the Apostles and Evangelists, of all the more ancient martyrs who are universally celebrated or have a special universal import for the life of the Church, and of a selection from all areas of Church life—clerical and lay.

The "major" doctors of the Church are to be retained, while the "minor" ones are to be selected individually. Saints should be kept in the universal calendar whose lives have a universal bearing on Church piety, either because of the particular form of their spirituality or their apostolate.

In general, the proposals for breviary changes suggested the spacing of 150 psalms over a two-week period in a priest's recitation instead of one week as in the present breviary. The committee recommends this "not for brevity or relaxation (of the breviary obligation; per se, but for spiritual advantage. The length of the hours (parts) of the breviary . . . can be preserved by the addition of readings if it is desired."

One suggestion is for a reduction in the first and longest part of the breviary—Matins—from nine to three psalms except on more solemn feasts.

On June 2, 1965, the Apostolic See granted to Major Religious superiors, according to their prudent judgment, the power to retain or declare non-obligatory the recitation of Prime by their subjects.

The permission of the ordinary is not required for concelebration on Holy Thursday's evening mass, for the Constitution itself gives this right.

The Sacred Ministers, who perform their duties in a concelebrated mass twice in one day, can receive twice under both species.

The reason why Communion can be received twice on Christmas and Easter is because there are two distinct liturgical offices involved.

'ITE, MISSA EST' FINDS DIFFERENT TRANSLATIONS

VATICAN CITY—(NC)—The varied approach in translating parts of the Mass into the vernacular was put in bold relief by the bulletin of the postconciliar liturgy commission here.

The just-released June issue of *Notitiae* published a list of approved translations of the familiar "Ite missa est" at the conclusion of the Mass.

Aside from "Go, the Mass is ended," which is used in the United States, Canada, Australia and New Guinea, *Notitiae* lists the following in English:

"Go, this is the dismissal"—England and Wales.

"You may go. The Mass is ended"—Scotland.

"Go in peace and the Lord be with you"—New Zealand.

"Go, you are sent forth"—elsewhere where English is spoken.

In Ireland, the Latin has been retained for the dismissal. In France, the usage is equivalent to "Go, in the peace of Christ." In Italy, it is "The Mass is finished: Go in peace."

As of March 27, 1966, the approved translation in the United States is "The Mass is ended. Go in peace."

FURTHER REPLIES OF THE VATICAN COMMISSION
(From *Notitiae,* no. 11)

The International Advisory Committee on English in the Liturgy received as authorization and guide the following Mandate from the International Episcopal Committee:

1. To work out a plan for the translation of liturgical texts and the provision of original texts where required in language which would be correct, dignified, intelligible, and suitable for public recitation and singing.

to propose the engagement of experts in various fields as translators, composers, and critics and to provide for the exchange of information with the sponsoring Hierarchies and with other interested Hierarchies; and

to give special attention, within the scope of this plan, to the question of a single English version of the Bible for liturgical use or at least of common translations of biblical texts used in the liturgy.

2. To submit this plan to the interested Hierarchies with a view to obtaining their consent.

3. To implement the approved plan.

4. To submit final recommendations to the interested Hierarchies for their approval.

5. To use such funds as shall be made available for these purposes by the Hierarchies under the general control of the Episcopal Secretary representing them for the time being, the Most Reverend Paul J. Hallinan, Archbishop of Atlanta.

To fulfill this mandate, the first stages of this work is envisioned as:

1. Setting up general norms for translation.

2. Determining a program or project of translation of texts (or selection of existing translations).

3. Obtaining samples and proposals from prospective translators, whether individuals or teams.

4. Proposing to the Hierarchies a definitive project of translation, including refined norms of translation, method of procedure, names of translators, estimated costs, etc.

First Principles of Liturgical Translation agreed by the Advisory Committee:

1. The task of the Advisory Committee and of its associates is limited to the provision of acceptable English translations from the Liturgical books of the Latin rite. It does not extend to the composition of new (and in places possibly better) texts.

2. Translators will therefore work from the latest typical editions of the Roman Missal, Ritual, and Pontifical.

3. To be acceptable in substance, a translation must faithfully express the meaning of the original texts. If the meaning of a passage is not certainly known, the translator may take some liberty of reasonable conjecture.

4. To be acceptable in style, translation must take account of (a) the sacral character of the original texts; (b) the tradition of devotional writing in the English language; (c) contemporary linguistic usage; (d) euphony; and (e) the practice of other Christian bodies.

5. Respect for the sacral character of the original texts and the demands of corporate public worship will prescribe a vocabulary and style not necessarily identical with those admissible in private and personal prayer.

6. Respect for contemporary linguistic usage will dictate the avoidance of words and phrases not in living use today.

7. Respect for euphony will involve the testing of all draft versions by reciting them aloud.

8. The word "acceptable" in the foregoing paragraphs is to be understood as requiring translators to work mainly with an eye to the middle range of church-goers rather than to the least or the most intelligent and literate.

9. Translators are entitled to assume that such words, as e.g. grace, absolution, and salvation will not be altogether foreign to their hearers.

10. Any question not covered by these norms is to be treated as an open question.

Other pertinent matters discussed informally by the Episcopal Committee should be noted.

1. It was thought that the collaboration with other Christians interested in the liturgical use of English should be developed after the first meeting of the Advisory Committee. At least the principal churches should be consulted. Mention was made of the Anglicans (Episcopalians), Lutherans, and Presbyterians.

2. With regard to the version of the Scriptures to be proposed ultimately, it was agreed that all versions should be considered. This would not necessarily preclude a proposal from the Advisory Committee of a new translation, either of the Scriptures or of some part, for example, the Book of Psalms.

3. Although the entire project is planned with a view to the complete revision of the Roman liturgical books, expected within a period of from four to eight years, it was considered desirable that an early agreement be reached, if possible, on the ordinary chants of Mass, responses, and acclamations, etc. This would be of help to composers.

4. Some discussion by the Episcopal Committee during the second period of the Council (1963) was directed to the broad division of material to be translated. It was evident that at least three categories must be considered:

a. the scriptural readings, presumably to be taken from a single translation of the Bible and thus available no matter what changes take place in the lectionary;

b. the hymns, psalms, and other poetic materials which are to be sung; and

c. non-scriptural prose texts, including collects, prefaces, blessings, the eucharistic Canon, etc.

2
A great gift of God to the Church

Josef Andreas Jungmann S.J.

1 The liturgy is not unchangeable
2 Decentralization
3 Participation
4 Pastoral character of the reform
5 Limits and compromises

Father Jungmann is professor of liturgy at the University of Innsbruck in Austria, and was consultor of the Preconciliar Liturgical Commission, and *peritus* of the II Vatican Council. His article was translated into English by Salvatore Attanasio.

A grandiose work, which nobody would have dared imagine a few years ago, has been happily completed. A springtime, which began to bud a half century ago, and which has come to full bloom everywhere, has found its fulfillment in a rich harvest. A great gift of God has been placed into our hands. It is a gift of God, but at the same time it is also a work shaped and created by human hands, an undertaking which has emerged from the hands of man but is nevertheless animated by those vital powers which God has given to his Church.

Only the fundamental lines of the new form which the divine service of the Church is to assume in the future are laid down in the Constitution of the sacred liturgy; the new liturgical books and the full actualization are to come later. Most of the important decisions, however, have been made. We shall briefly point out some of them.

1 THE LITURGY IS NOT UNCHANGEABLE

The Constitution has broken the spell which for four hundred years has kept our liturgy in a state of immutability and hence in a state of paralysis. We all have grown up with the idea that liturgical matters are not only holy and inviolable but also exempt from change for all time. In this sense the liturgy was viewed as being not much different in status from holy scripture, not a letter of which can be changed down the course of the centuries. According to the Council of Trent this absolute immutability was a necessity and a blessing. Toward the end of the Middle Ages, the liturgical forms had in many instances fallen into a chaotic state. Further confusion was created by the often immoderate attacks of the reformers who denied the hierarchic structure of the priesthood and the sacrificial character of the Mass, and who abolished all distinctions between the priests and the people. It became necessary to formulate precise and hard rules, to draw a clear line of demarcation between the priests and people. Further, there was an obvious need to prescribe a universal unconditional adherence to the Latin language.

Conditions have substantially changed since then. What above all is urgently necessary at the beginning of this new epoch is to facilitate access to the riches of the mystery of Christ to the faithful and to strengthen their bond of union with the altar. Therefore the Constitution speaks boldly of a fundamental reform (*instauratio*) of the liturgy, a word in the drafts which at first some Council Fathers read not without some trepidation. Indeed, this renovation even includes the entire order of the Mass (Art. 50).

The proposal shows how determined the Council is to make adjustments to the needs of the times and to what extent the Church proves itself to be a living organism.

2 DECENTRALIZATION

A further basic feature of the reform lies in the fact that it renounces the idea of a liturgy that is strictly uniform for all countries. To be sure, the rites and forms of the liturgy used in the Orient have always been recognized, their continuance down the centuries was viewed as a privilege, or a relic from the past to be lovingly and reverentially preserved. Certain variants of the Roman rite have also been continued in the Latin Church up to this day: the Ambrosian rite, the Dominican rite, etc. But these are negligible exceptions doomed to disappear. For the rest, from Japan to South Africa, from Alaska to Ceylon, the only norm that remained was the letter of the missal. Understandably enough, it was precisely in the young and the flourishing Churches in countries rich in ancient cultures that voices were raised demanding a relaxation of the uniformity. These voices made their weight felt at the Missionary Liturgical Congress which was held in Nimwegen in 1959. Actually, the principle of strict uniformity was unknown before the Council of Trent. At that time the Roman liturgy was adhered to, but the individual church provinces claimed the right to prescribe the details. This principle has now been revived. Whereas up to now the Apostolic See, in accordance with Canon 1256, was the exclusive competent body with respect to the ordering of the liturgy, now a larger radius of initiative on the part of the bishops is recognized and very broad powers are granted to the bishops' conferences (Arts. 36; 40).

3 PARTICIPATION

Another factor is linked to all this, namely that today within the Universal Church, not only in the local churches but also in the individual dioceses, the community of the faithful, here and now, has been given a new valuation. Essentially, the Church is a gathering of the faithful. Hence the worship of the Church in its true meaning is essentially that which the community of the faithful performs under the guidance of the priest appointed and commissioned to this office from above. What was emphasized in the Council discussions with reference to the schema *De Ecclesia* on the nature of the Church, namely, that the Church is primarily to be viewed as the people of God whom the hierarchy must serve, was already anticipated in different passages of the Constitution on the Sacred Liturgy.

Certain important conclusions were to be drawn therefrom and these conclusions have been drawn. Full justice is not done to the significance of a liturgical act merely by the presence of the faithful, or when they "reverently hear" Mass. What is expected of them is a *plena et actuosa participatio* (Art. 14) an *actuosa participatio interna et externa* (Art. 19). They are to participate in the holy act *conscie, pie et actuose* (Art. 48). At bottom this does not call for anything new. All it does is to reach back to the concrete meaning of the forms that have been handed down by tradition, to the fact that since time immemorial, all the official prayers of the priest were spoken in the plural, that in the *Oremus* the faithful are invited to pray, and that they are expected to pronounce the *Amen* by way of confirmation.

If now the faithful are expected to participate in the liturgy in a conscious and intelligent way, it follows that a further conclusion must be drawn, namely that the veil of the language enveloping the sacred texts must be made transparent. Although it is an easy matter to draw this conclusion, it had to be actualized in harmony with the different situations of a multi-faceted reality. For example, it would be necessary to make this total transition possible even in the mother languages of the old high cultures, such as those of the Far East, which are as far removed from the Graeco-Roman cultural foundations as we are from the Chinese. This is provided for in Art. 40. Some of the neo-Latin peoples have no desire at all to depart from the traditional Latin to which they are dearly and fondly attached. It would be necessary to leave them the freedom to persevere in the old tradition just as it would be necessary to grant the possibility of at least a partial use of their national language. This was effected by granting greater powers to the bishops' conferences as stipulated in Art. 36, and/or 54.

As regards the situation in Germany, where since ancient times many dioceses celebrated the so-called "German office" (since the Roman indult of December 24, 1943 it constitutes a privilege extended to the entire area of the ancient Reich), the Constitution essentially marks a further step forward because in addition to the hymns, the readings of the Mass may also be made in German. These are to be generously enriched through the reform of the liturgical books (Art. 51). If proper use is made then of this privilege in the hymns—and here excellent experiments are already in progress—and if in the Prayer of the Faithful the voice of the people achieves the recognition that is due to it in a new way (Art. 53), we shall truly be able to say that the gates of the sanctuary are no longer barred to the faithful.

The re-ordering of the entire rite of the Mass, through which its structure is to become conspicuous and the meaning and logical connection of the individual parts stand out with greater clarity (Art. 15), will further facilitate the internal and external participation of the faithful. The stipulation of the details will be the task of a special commission in the near future. The regulation with which the Holy Father, in the light of the coming reform, has already put into effect several innovations which do not require further elaboration, should be understood as a guarantee that the eucharistic celebration on Sundays particularly will be a culmination point of Christian life and, at the same time, a source of new power to the community of the faithful present (cf. Art. 10).

4 PASTORAL CHARACTER OF THE REFORM

Regarding the reform, which is merely outlined in the Constitution, it can be stated that it is truly a pastoral reform and that in the field of the divine service it is in keeping with the pastoral aims set forth by Pope John XXIII and by Pope Paul VI, who has followed in his footsteps.

The pastoral character of the reform is not at all a product of spontaneity and sudden inspiration. The last great reform of the liturgy, which was undertaken four hundred years ago, was not primarily of a pastoral character. It was apologetically and historically oriented. Through the elimination of numerous excrescences and deformations it sought to restore to the liturgy of the Church the form that it had had up to a few centuries before then. Its aim was not to go toward the Christian people, but only to guard it from error. The liturgical reform of the II Vatican Council also reaches back to old, indeed even older traditions—those in which the liturgy was still to be a living expression of the whole community. In this sense it even repeats the watchword with which Pius V at the time officially introduced the new missal: the reform is to be carried out according to the "norm of the old Fathers" (Art. 50). Now, however, the orientation of the reform is wholly pastoral. This return to the past is to be carried out as "advantage or necessity may require." The reform takes a giant step toward the Christian people, in short, it is a pastoral reform.

Whereas the regulations regarding the reform of the Mass effect the entire Christian people, those concerning the divine office particularly apply to the clergy. The great complaint in this area was that the office as arranged in the breviary with its eight hours spread over the day no longer meets the changed situation of the priest charged with the care of souls. Indeed many a priest, in trying mechanically to fulfill his duty to read the breviary, actually forgets what authentic prayer is. Here, too, the regulations regarding the reform indicate a readiness to cope with the real requirements of the pastoral ministry. The breviary must not be viewed merely as a duty to be discharged and done with—it must be a prayer. The priest is no longer expected to fulfill a *pensum,* which at one time was designed to fill the day of a monk. It will no longer be necessary to string together a series of hours in the morning, violating their nature, or to catch up with them late in the evening. Moreover, the Constitution by its emphasis on the two principal hours, Lauds and Vespers, which in their original form invited the participation of the faithful, reveals an effort to restore to the office some of its original significance (Art. 100). In this context we also refer to the new evaluation of the religious celebrations and devotions, under the responsibility of the bishops, which were practiced in certain dioceses, and contained in the respective devotional books (Art. 13, 2) and particularly to "celebrations of the Word of God" (Art. 35) which point out new ways leading to a rebirth of genuine Christian piety.

5 LIMITS AND COMPROMISES

Certain principal points stand out prominently in what has been said, which show the great gains that the Constitution will assure to the liturgy of the Church. On the other hand, those who have worked hard in the preparation of the reform know better than anybody else that not all wishes have been fulfilled. This does not only apply to those wishes which, since the announcement of the Council, were formulated by more or less competent advisers in writing and verbally, in soaring visions of the future, but also to those which were espoused by authorative persons in the Council hall. Apart from the fact that many important questions had to be left open because their solution can be entrusted only to special commissions which must now set to work, the pastoral commitment to reform was also obliged to seek a compromise arrangement with the weight of tradition—and not only the venerable tradition of the early centuries, but also the more recent tradition in which we ourselves have grown up. The line of such a compromise had to be regulated according to the forces which are operative in the Church at this time. This explains why more than one article shows the marks of a compromise. We shall cite one example: in the discussions of the second session of the meeting, the Fathers gave different answers to the question as to whether in the concept of the Church primacy should be given to the hierarchy or to the people of God. Likewise, in the preparation of the liturgical scheme there were different answers to the question as to whether the liturgical prayer acquires its full validity only if it is actualized on the authorization of the highest hierarchical authority which legitimates such prayer "in the name of the Church," or whether for this purpose it suffices that the community is gathered *hic et nunc* under the delegated authority of the official minister, since such a community is already the Church. This is a theoretical question from which however, conclusions of vast importance derive (cf. Art. 13; 84; 99). Another example of a compromise decision was the answer given to the question as to whether the breviary, born of the tradition of choral prayer of the monks and of the canonical communities, should be replaced by a new breviary for the secular priest. A clear-cut "yes" to this question would not have been over-daring, but a middle course was chosen. Finally, many of us would have expected a more radical solution regarding the problem concerning the language of the liturgy.

In all these and similar questions it should be remembered that the reform work of the Constitution represents all that was possible to achieve in 1963, on the part of an assembly of two thousand bishops coming from all the nations of the world, at a time when far-reaching developments are in progress not only in the world, but also in the Church. Many doors have been opened and new perspectives of liturgical possibility have been authorized. We must thank God for the gift that he has given us.

3
Chronicle of amendments of the Constitution

Bonaventura Kloppenburg O.F.M.

1 The Introduction of the Constitution
2 Chapter I of the Constitution: General principles for the restoration and promotion of the sacred liturgy
3 Chapter II: The most sacred mystery of the Eucharist
4 Chapter III: The other sacraments and the sacramentals
5 Chapter IV: The divine office
6 Chapter V: The liturgical year
7 The last two chapters
8 The votes "Placet juxta modum"

Father Kloppenburg is professor of dogmatic theology in the clericate of the Franciscans at Petrópolis, Brazil, consultor of the II Vatican Council. His article was translated into English by Father Rufino Rexing O.F.M.

Discussion of the liturgy schema came to a close in November 13, 1962. With it came to a close also the eighteenth General Assembly of Vatican II.[1] At the opening of the nineteenth General Assembly, a communique was read in Latin, Spanish, English, French, German, and Arabic.[2] The chapters of the schema were then submitted to a vote. The results, out of 2,215 votes cast: 2,162 yes; 46 no; 7 invalid.

For the work of revision, the liturgy commission was divided into thirteen groups, thus forming thirteen sub-commissions:

1. Theological – to discuss theological and dogmatic questions
2. Juridical – to weigh the juridical problems
3. For general observations
4. For the Preface and Section One of Chapter I
5. For Section Two of Chapter I
6. For Section Three of Chapter I
7. For Chapter II
8. For Chapter III
9. For Chapter IV
10. For Chapter V
11. For Chapter VI
12. For Chapter VII
13. For Chapter VIII[3]

These sub-commissions were charged with the task of examining the various opinions and suggestions made by the Fathers in the council hall (a total of 328 speeches) and the written proposals (350 in all) handed into the Secretary General. The sub-commissions would have to coordinate and study them. All the speeches, both written and oral, were therefore mimeographed and passed out among the commission members and experts. From October 21 to December 6 the commission met twenty-one times in general sessions. They thus terminated the work charged to the first six sub-commissions. Here is how they went about their work: As soon as the Fathers were finished discussing a certain chapter, the sub-commission president would present a summary of the various proposed amendments. These were then thoroughly and freely discussed in the general session of the sub-commission. Even the experts could speak freely. The pastoral experience of the Fathers and the knowledge of the experts made up a wonderfully well-balanced whole.[4]

1 THE INTRODUCTION OF THE CONSTITUTION

Twenty-First General Assembly
November 17, 1962

The commission presented four amendments to the Introduction. Each was voted on individually:

Art. 1: Where before we read: "separated brothers in the Church"; now we read: "all who believe in Christ."
2,206 votes: 2,181 yes; 14 no; 11 invalid.

Art. 2: This was a most notable correction. Now we read: "manifest to others, the mystery of Christ and the real nature of the true Church. It is of the essence of the Church that she be both human and divine, visible and yet invisibly equipped, eager to act and yet intent on contemplation. . . ." Before we read: "manifest to others, the mystery of Christ and the real nature of the Church: whose essence is at the same time human and divine, visible and invisible – a Church of action and contemplation. . . ."
2,202 votes: 2,175 yes; 26 no; 1 invalid.

Art. 3: The present text omits the following: "The present Constitution wishes to make no dogmatic definitions"
2,203 votes: 2,175 yes; 21 no; 7 invalid.

On November 28, 1962, *L'Osservatore Romano* commented that this elimination was made "perhaps because the Fathers wished greater freedom to reform the liturgy.

Instead of merely making a few rubrical changes they wished to touch even some liturgical elements which are not of divine institution."

Art. 4: Nothing really notable.
2,204 votes: 2,191 yes; 10 no; 3 invalid.

2 CHAPTER I: GENERAL PRINCIPLES FOR THE RESTORATION AND PROMOTION OF THE SACRED LITURGY

Thirtieth General Assembly
November 30, 1962

For details of the discussion, see our book.[5]

Art. 5: After the words "the Word made flesh," add: "anointed by the Holy Spirit."
2,145 votes: 2,096 yes; 41 no; 8 invalid.

Art. 5: Before we read: "cause of our salvation"; now we read: "instruments of our salvation."
2,143 votes: 2,103 yes; 34 no; 6 invalid.

Art. 6: Before we read: "accomplished by means of the sacraments"; now we read: "accomplished by means of sacrifice and sacraments."
2,139 votes: 1,984 yes; 150 no; 5 invalid.

Art. 6: Add onto the end: "through the power of the Holy Spirit."
2,135 votes: 2,113 yes; 13 no; 9 invalid.

Art. 7: Add that whole beautiful section on the four ways Christ is present in the Church and especially in the liturgical action. The

section begins with the words: "He is present" and goes on to the end of this paragraph.
2,125 votes: 2,049 yes; 66 no; 10 invalid.

Thirty-First General Assembly
December 1, 1962

Art. 7: After the words: "and men are sanctified," add: "the Church is his beloved Bride who calls to her Lord, and through him offers worship to the eternal Father."
2,122 votes: 2,101 yes; 15 no; 6 invalid.

Art. 10: At the beginning, add: "Nevertheless the liturgy is the summit toward which the activity of the Church is directed; at the same time it is the font from which all her power flows."
2,120 votes: 2,004 yes; 101 no; 5 invalid.

Art. 10: After the words: "to praise God in the midst of his Church," add: "to take part in the sacrifice."
2,116 votes: 2,079 yes; 19 no; 5 invalid.

Art. 12: Instead of: "Although the Christian is sometimes called to prayer in common, he is also sometimes called to enter into his chamber to pray to the Father in secret," read: "The Christian is indeed called to pray with his brethren, but he must also enter into his chamber to pray to the Father in secret."
2,117 votes: 2,097 yes; 13 no; 7 invalid.

Thirty-Second General Assembly
December 3, 1962

His Excellency Francis Grimshaw, Archbishop of Birmingham, England, presented various amendments on Articles 14-20. As official spokesman he called for only two votes:

Art. 14: After the words: "redeemed people," add: "by reason of their Baptism" to show, as the spokesman explained, the fundamental priestly character of the faithful who actively participate in the liturgical acts.
2,113 votes: 2096 yes; 10 no; 7 invalid.

Art. 16: Add: "in theological faculties it is to rank among the principal courses," to put due emphasis on the liturgy in seminaries and houses of religious formation.
2,109 votes: 2,051 yes; 52 no; 6 invalid.

Thirty-Fourth General Assembly
December 5, 1962

As official spokesman, His Excellency Charles Calewaert, Bishop of Ghent, Belgium, presented the amendments on Articles 21-40 of the First Chapter, along with the general norms for the restoration of the sacred liturgy, "which are the basis for almost this whole chapter." The spokesman adjoined that these amendments almost always met with unanimous approval in the commission's ballots. There were eleven votes cast on these 20 articles.[6]

Art. 25: After: "on the task," add "and bishops are to be consulted."
2,110 votes: 2,087 yes; 14 no; 11 invalid.

Art. 37: Add onto the end: "Sometimes in fact she admits such things into the liturgy itself, so long as they harmonize with its true and authentic spirit." This amendment is very important because of its principle to adapt the liturgy to the various customs and peoples.
2,114 votes: 2,083 yes; 21 no; 10 invalid.

Art. 39: Speaks of the bishops' competence to make some adaptations in the liturgical books. The text presents the following new words: "Within the limits set by the typical editions of the liturgical books, it shall be for the competent territorial ecclesiastical authority mentioned in Art. 22, 2 to specify adaptations."
2,109 votes: 2,044 yes; 50 no; 15 invalid.

Art. 36, 1: Maintains the use of Latin, "particular law remaining in force."
2,073 votes: 2,033 yes; 36 no; 4 invalid.

Art. 36, 2: Adds the words: "whether in the Mass, the administration of the sacraments, or other parts of the liturgy . . . according to the regulations on this matter to be laid down separately in subsequent chapters."
2,072 votes: 2,011 yes; 54 no; 5 invalid.

Art. 36, 3: The main change in this paragraph: instead of "proposed by the Holy See," read "to decide whether, and to what extent, the vernacular language is to be used; their decrees are to be approved, that is, confirmed, by the Apostolic See." The spokesman explained that the commission had chosen the words "approved, that is confirmed," so that the desire of those Fathers who spoke on this subject might be granted. The word "approved" is a general term specified by the word "confirmed." This word shows the right which is legitimately instituted by inferior authority and at the same time is acknowledged and completed by superior authority. This brings us a harmony, since inferior authority condones the right and superior authority adds a new juridical power.
2,082 votes: 2,016 yes; 56 no; 10 invalid.

Art. 36, 4: A whole new paragraph.
2,079 votes: 2,041 yes; 30 no; 8 invalid.

Art. 35, 4: A whole new paragraph. The large number of invalid votes was explained by the Secretary General. The General Assembly was about to terminate at the time of voting and some did not have time to finish. Since the yes votes already made a majority (the admendment had already been given a solid majority of 1,384), the Board of Presidents decided it useless to repeat the vote.
2,086 votes: 1,903 yes; 38 no; 145 invalid.

Thirty-Fifth General Assembly
December 6, 1962

Voting continued on the amendments presented by Bishop Calewaert.

Art. 27: Add the sentence beginning with: "This applies . . ." This is a completely new text.
2,082 votes: 2,054 yes; 22 no; 6 invalid.

Art. 22, 2: This is a new text which consecrated the fundamental principle of decentralization. The spokesman explained that this decision only ripened after discussion in the council hall. "It was a very difficult thing to do," he explained, "but yet very important." For this whole constitution has as its principal axis, around which the whole liturgical reform revolves, that this reform, according to the various regional conditions, be in great part given to the bishops and not any more to the Holy See. Since the so-called episcopal conferences are still in an experimental stage without juridical statutes, the commission met many difficulties in their search for a juridically acceptable formulation "so the constitution might not remain ineffective and suspended in the meanwhile." Finally they came to an agreement on the following: "In virtue of power conceded by the law, the regulation of the liturgy within certain defined limits belongs also to various kinds of competent territorial bodies of bishops legitimately established." It is evident that the subject of this power has been carefully determined: "competent territorial bodies of bishops legitimately established." The spokesman explained the basic motive for this scrupulous formulation: "That way not only the conferences strictly so called are included, but also provincial and plenary councils, or even, if the case may be, a gathering of bishops from many regions." In order to make this point very clear, the spokesman directed the Fathers to add onto the end of article 22, 1: "on the bishop" instead of "on the bishops" — "so that the powers of the bishops together as a college will be more clearly distinguished from those of each individual bishop in his own diocese, either already possessed by him or granted by this constitution."
2,058 votes: 2,023 yes; 31 no; 4 invalid.

On January 25, 1964, Pope Paul VI determined that for the time being this territorial ecclesiastical authority be always national; and also that coadjutor and auxiliary bishops may be called to participate; and that in order for the decree to pass legitimately it must obtain at least two-thirds of the secret votes in these national bishops' conferences.

Art. 32: The previous text read: "except by customs approved by the ordinary." The commission decided to suppress these words.
2,078 votes: 1,981 yes; 37 no; 4 invalid.

During this same General Assembly, His Excellency, Francis Grimshaw, Archbishop of Birmingham, England, presented, as official spokesman, amendments on the last six articles of Chapter I. He said that the commission did not accept many of the suggestions proposed on the competence of bishops because frequently it was a juridical matter and could not be included in the present council document. He only asked for two votes:

Art. 42: Previously the text included the phrase: "Therefore, unless for a reasonable cause, Baptism, Confirmation, first Communion, Matrimony and funerals may be allowed to take place outside the parish." The commission now proposes that the words be omitted because of their content. These topics should be treated in a disciplinary document.
2,037 votes: 1,916 yes; 115 no; 6 invalid.

Art. 44: This text was modified to agree with the new article 22, 2.
2,014 votes; 1,981 yes; 22 no; 11 invalid.

Thirty-Sixth General Assembly
December 7, 1962

A global vote was asked for on Chapter I. The Fathers were allowed to cast three types of votes: *yes; yes, if modified; no.* This is the first time the *yes, if modified* vote can legally be cast. The Secretary General explained that such a vote is actually positive, approving the text, but asking for a modification. Whoever should decide to vote in this way must hand in their modification before December 31 of this year or their vote will be counted as *yes.*

2,118 votes [1,412 votes necessary for a majority]: 1,922 yes; 180 yes, if modified; 11 no; 5 invalid.

Since the *yes* votes reached a majority, the Secretary General told the Fathers that they no longer need explain their *yes, if modified* votes.

3 CHAPTER II: THE MOST SACRED MYSTERY OF THE EUCHARIST

Forty-First General Assembly
October 4, 1963

On October 4, 1963, during the forty-first General Assembly, amendments on Chapter II were handed out to the Council Fathers. This chapter treats of the most sacred mystery of the Eucharist. The 32 pages contain first of all 19 amendments, those considered most important, which will be given in individual vote. Then follows the official summary by the spokesman, His Excellency Jesus Enciso Viana, Bishop of Mallorca, Spain, which presented the official mind of the commission with regard to the amendments; then the text of Chapter II in two columns, one the discussed text and in the other the corrected text. It was said that ballots on the 19 amendments would be cast during the forty-third General Assembly on October 8, 1963.

Forty-Third General Assembly
October 8, 1963

Cardinal Giacomo Lercaro, Archbishop of Bologna, member of the liturgical commission and one of the four council moderators, presented a summary of the commission's studies. He said that although the first session of the Council had ended in December of 1962, the subcommissions of the liturgical commission continued to meet during the interim. From April 24 to May 10, 1963, the sub-commissions held nine plenary sessions in which all the members were present except two experts. The commission always cast secret ballots and almost always reached a unanimous decision. After the text had been corrected by the subcommission it was handed over to Latinists and stylists. From their hands it returned to the commission, who re-examined it in a plenary session during the month of July, 1963. Finally on September 27, 28 and 30 the commission gathered once more to give the final touches. This is the text which has now been submitted to the Fathers for voting.

Art. 47: Describes the sacrificial character of the Eucharist in clearer words, stating that it was instituted as a sacrifice to perpetuate until the end of time the sacrifice of the cross.
2,298 votes: 2,278 yes; 12 no; 1 yes, if modified [this was not a legal vote since only a yes-no ballot could be cast and it was therefore counted as invalid]; *7 invalid.*

Art. 49: Affirms that the reason for the innovations is pastoral; favors Sunday and festive Masses.
2,290 votes: 2,264 yes; 14 no; 2 yes, if modified; 10 invalid.

Art. 50: Affirms the necessity to simplify the rites, to omit everything added during the passing of time which is not truly useful, to restore according to the norms laid down by the Holy Fathers what has fallen into disuse but seems good or necessary in our own day.
2,285 votes: 2,249 yes; 31 no; 4 invalid. [I would like to call attention to the supreme importance of this amendment.]

Art. 52: Defines the homily to be given at Sunday Mass as a sermon by means of which the sacred text, the mysteries and norms of Christian life are presented to the faithful during the liturgical year.
2,285 votes: 2,263 yes; 15 no; 7 invalid.

Art. 52: Prescribes a sermon on Sundays and holy days of obligation.
2,284 votes: 2,261 yes; 18 no; 5 invalid.

Forty-Fourth General Assembly
October 9, 1963

Art. 54: Refers to the use of the vernacular at Mass, affirming that

such languages might be given a worthy place (*tribui possit*) instead of the (*tribuatur*) which seemed to prescribe the vernacular usage.
2,275 votes: 2,215 yes; 52 no; 1 yes, if modified; 7 invalid.

Art. 54: Gives the episcopal conferences the faculties to introduce the vernacular in certain parts of the Mass.
2,278 votes: 2,212 yes; 47 no; 2 yes, if modified; 17 invalid.

Art. 54: Recommends that even though the vernacular may be used at Mass, the faithful should still learn to pray and sing the ordinary parts in Latin (so that travelers and various nationalities can pray and sing songs).
2,251 votes: 2,193 yes; 44 no; 3 yes, if modified; 11 invalid.

His Excellency Jesus Enciso Viana presented a summary of these amendments to the Fathers. In the name of the liturgical commission he clearly stated that the only reason for this amendment was international encounters where all members would have a common language in prayer and song. It might be good here to give his exact words: "*Unum tantum in hoc articulo praecipitur: 'Provideatur tamen ut christifideles etiam lingua latina partes Ordinarii Missae, quae ad ipsos spectant, possint simul dicere vel cantare.' His vero nihil aliud facimus nisi respondere, et quidem libenti animo, desiderio sollemniter expresso a relatore Excmo. Calewaert in insigni sua ad Patres conciliares relatione de Art. 36, cum declaravit: 'Nos autem, re perpensa, omnia particularia remittenda censuimus ad respectivos articulos subsequentium capitum. Attamen expresse optavimus UT IN CAPITE DE MISSA ALIQUA COMMONITIO INSERATUR, ad praecavendum ne fideles ex diversis linguis et nationibus peregrini convenientes incapaces evadant simul communiter orandi.' Idem desiderium manifestaverant alii Patres in disceptatione ad aulam.*" This observation expresses very forcefully the mind of the Council with relation to this amendment: it is exclusively in favor of international travelers. It would seem that where international travelers are few, there would be no reason to insist on Latin.

Art. 54: It foresees, under the guidance of the Holy See, the possibility of a more ample use of the vernacular in all parts of the Mass including the Canon; as His Excellency Enciso explained.
2,219 votes: 2,149 yes; 67 no; 13 invalid.

Art. 55: Recommends a more perfect participation in the holy Sacrifice by receiving a host consecrated at that particular Mass.
2,218 votes: 2,159 yes; 46 no; 2 yes, if modified, 11 invalid.

Art. 55: That communion under two species be allowed, though recalling the doctrinal principles of the Council of Trent.
2,236 votes: 2,131 yes; 96 no; 9 invalid.

Art. 56: Asks the faithful to assist at the entire Mass on Sundays and holy days of obligation, including the instructive part before the Offertory.
2,254 votes: 2,232 yes; 14 no; 8 invalid.

While voting, the Secretary General explained in the name of the presidential board a doubt which had arisen: someone, for example, did not agree with Communion under two species. How should he vote if he wished to correct a particular point to which he was opposed? The board of presidents answered that last year the schema had been voted upon and approved in general. Hence now we must consider the principle innovations as approved. (This refers to the vote on November 14, 1962, during the nineteenth General Assembly.) Nevertheless, one could if he wished simply vote *no*. Or, he might vote *yes, if modified* when the whole chapter is put to a vote.

Forty-Fifth General Assembly
October 10, 1963

Art. 57: Declares that the reason for concelebration is to express the unity of the priesthood (and not the difficulty or impossibility of individual celebrations).
2,263 votes: 2,166 yes; 92 no; 1 yes, if modified; 4 invalid.

Art. 57: Allows concelebration for both Holy Thursday Masses – the pontifical and the evening Mass.
2,265 votes: 2,088 yes; 168 no; 9 invalid.

Art. 57: Allows concelebrated Masses at the Council, episcopal reunions, and synods.
2,261 votes: 2,111 yes; 142 no; 2 yes, if modified; 6 invalid.

Art. 57: Allows concelebration at the blessing of an abbot.
2,166 votes: 2,006 yes; 142 no; 18 invalid.

Art. 57: Allows concelebration, with the ordinary's permission, for conventual Masses, for the principal Mass in churches (or semipublic oratories, the spokesman explained) always when the necessity of the faithful does not demand individual Masses of those priests present.
2,163 votes: 1,839 yes; 315 no; 2 yes, if modified; 7 invalid.

When the official spokesman presented this amendment, he clarified: It requires the ordinary's consent. It was discussed whether we should say bishop or ordinary in order to avoid conflicts among major religious superiors. The expression "ordinary" prevailed. Perhaps this observation caused the rise in *no* votes. Even so, however, the amendment was approved by more than 80 per cent of the Council Fathers. [An observer will have noted the curious oscillation in the number of votes cast. For this particular amendment it hit a minimum. The explanation is simple: on both sides of the council hall there were excellent bars, "Bar Jona" and "Bar Abbas," with coffee furnished from ten to noon by the Brazilian government.]

Art. 57: Allows concelebration with the ordinary's permission to reunions of secular or religious priests.
2,224 votes: 1,975 yes; 245 no; 4 invalid.

Art. 57: Declares that every priest remains free to celebrate Mass individually if he so desires, but not at the same time and in the same church as the concelebrated Masses – nor on Holy Thursday.
2,231 votes: 2,159 yes; 66 no; 1 yes, if modified; 5 invalid.

The text reads "though not at the same time in the same church." These words could mean a prohibition of several simultaneous Masses at any time in the same church (one on the high altar and others on side altars). Some Brazilian Franciscan bishops suggested this doubt to the Secretariat and received the following answer from Bishop Kempf: "only when there is a question of a concelebrated Mass."

Forty-Seventh General Assembly
October 14, 1963

The Secretary General announced that the second chapter of the liturgy schema, the amendments of which were voted on and approved the preceding week, would be put to a global votation.

2,242 votes: 1,417 yes; 781 yes, if modified; 36 no; 8 invalid.

The chapter did not receive a sufficient majority (1,495) because of the large number of *yes, if modified* votes. Thus the commission received 781 proposals of amendments which would have to be studied and evaluated during the following days. The large number of *yes, if modified* votes was not expected. It will be recalled that only 180 *yes, if modified* votes were cast on Chapter I.

4 CHAPTER III: THE OTHER SACRAMENTS AND SACRAMENTALS

Forty-Eighth General Assembly
October 15, 1963

His Excellency, Paul J. Hallinan, Archbishop of Atlanta, Georgia, gave the official presentation of Chapter III. Only ten amendments would be submitted to a vote:

Art. 60: Gives a definition of sacramentals.
2,239 votes: 2,224 yes; 12 no; 1 yes, if modified; 2 invalid.

Art. 63: Grants the use of the vernacular in the administration of the sacramentals and sacraments except in the form of some of them.
2,159 votes: 2,103 yes; 49 no; 3 yes, if modified; 4 invalid.

Art. 68: Grants bishops the right to accommodate the Baptism rite, when the number to be baptized is quite large.
2,100 votes: 2,058 yes; 42 no.

Art. 73: Gives preference to the expression "Anointing of the Sick" instead of "Extreme Unction." This amendment declares that this is not merely a sacrament of the dying.
2,178 votes: 2,143 yes; 35 no.

Forty-Ninth General Assembly
October 16, 1963

While the voting continued, the Fathers in the council hall discussed the collegiality of the bishops and the restoration of the permanent deaconate.

Art. 73: Declares that the opportune time to receive the sacrament of the Anointing of the Sick is the moment when a person begins to run the danger of death through sickness or old age.
2,259 votes: 2,219 yes; 37 no; 3 invalid.

Art. 75: Proposes to omit the following phrase which was in number 60 of the schema: "Anointing of the Sick may be administered three times during a long sickness" (to avoid a disputed question, the official spokesman said).
2,216 votes: 1,964 yes; 247 no; 1 yes, if modified; 4 invalid.

Art. 76: Grants the right to all bishops present at an episcopal consecration the right to impose their hands on the newly consecrated.
2,175 votes: 2,124 yes; 50 no; 1 invalid.

Art. 78: In the administration of the sacrament of matrimony the blessing must always be given to the spouses.
2,220 votes: 2,194 yes; 24 no; 1 yes, if modified; 1 invalid.

Fiftieth General Assembly
October 17, 1963

Art. 79: In certain circumstances some sacramentals may be adminitered by the laity if the local ordinary so desires.
2,250 votes: 1,637 yes; 607 no; 1 yes, if modified; 5 invalid.

Art. 80: Asks for a special rite for religious profession and the renewal of vows, to be observed by those who make profession or renew their profession during Mass, except in case of special law.
2,248 votes: 2,207 yes; 39 no; 2 invalid.

Fifty-First General Assembly
October 18, 1963

A global votation of Chapter III of the liturgy schema.
2,217 votes: 1,130 yes; 30 no; 1,054 yes, if modified; 3 invalid.

Hence, the chapter must return to the liturgical commission. The large number of *yes, if modified* votes can be traced back to the tremendous propaganda put forward by the liturgist Martimort. His point of attack was Article 63 (amendment number 2, passed by a vote of 2,103 to 52 during the Forty-Eighth General Assembly). This particular amendment grants the use of the vernacular in the administration of the sacraments, "but in the form of the sacrament Latin must be generally used." The 1,054 *yes, if modified* votes wanted to eliminate this phrase. This would be a tremendous victory for Martimort. As we shall see later on, it was achieved.

5 CHAPTER IV: THE DIVINE OFFICE

Fifty-Second General Assembly
October 21, 1963

The Secretary General announced that today the first three ammendments to Chapter IV of the liturgy schema (on the breviary) would be put to a vote. The official spokesman for Chapter IV was His Excellency, Joseph Albertus Martin, Bishop of Nicolet, Canada. Because of the exceptional importance of the breviary reform, the official speech will be summarized here. That talk fills a total of 30 pages.

The discussion last year on the breviary reform began during the 14th General Assembly (November 7, 1962) and lasted until the 17th (November 11, 1962) with a sum of 39 speeches.[5] In fact, Pius XII had already set up a special commission for breviary reform. That commission had made a general research on the priests' desires and composed a *Memoria* in 1957. All this material (the written and spoken speeches of last year's discussion and the *Memoria* of Pope Pius' commission) were studied by the liturgical commission in choosing the amendments for Chapter IV. The summary of that study consists of five parts:

1. Doctrinal and general questions on the breviary (not too practical nor interesting; so I will not enumerate them).
2. The general norms for the breviary reform:
   a. General principles: The following served as a starting point: The breviary is the public prayer of the Church. It cannot be confused with particular exercises of piety. The office said in the name of the Church has objective value in itself. But it must also be subjective prayer, of the priest, sincere and fruitful prayer. As such it must be understandable by all, so that all might love it and recite it with devotion.
   b. The question of "the truth of the hours." There was a lot of discussion last year, and in the commission, on this point. Evidently the breviary reform depends fundamentally on the way this problem is solved. While acknowledging the modern way of life, the commission decided to maintain the principle of dividing the divine office into "hours." The commission set up by Pius XII had come to the same conclusion in 1957.
   c. Should the breviary be abbreviated? There were many reasons presented for not shortening the breviary. Others asked that the prayers be changed into liturgical prayers, for example when a priest is already fully occupied during the day by many prayers (saying three Masses). Others begged that only some parts be obligatory while others could be left up to one's choosing. Still others proposed two types of breviaries: for those who work in the apostolate, and for the contemplatives. Some simply asked for a shorter breviary. Faced by so many diverse suggestions the commission decided to resolve the question.

d. What to do in the concrete? Abstracting from the contemplative way of life, the commission decided to consider the office as said by the diocesan or regular priests in the care of souls. The following was decided: Lauds and Vespers, the morning and evening prayers, would be considered the principal hours. Prime would be suppressed; there is no need for two morning prayers. Compline would be retained but could be reduced to, perhaps, Psalm 90. After much discussion in the council hall as well as in the commission, it was decided that Tierce, Sext, and None would be obligatory in choral recitation. In private recitation the more appropriate hour could be chosen and it would suffice for the other hours. The commission recognized that the word Matins was not too fitting, but gave permission to recite it at any hour of the day. It would therefore be transformed into "Divine Reading," however, maintaining the quality of prayer and not simply that of spiritual reading as many suggested. The post-Council liturgical commission will have to reconstruct this part of the breviary, reducing the number of psalms and increasing the lessons.

3. The reform of the various elements in the breviary:

The Psalter: The revision of the text should be completed as soon as possible (Weber, O.S.B. was given special credit for his attempt). The Latin should be Christian and not classical. Some Fathers asked that certain psalms be omitted, but the commission did not accept this proposal. The principle that the whole Psalter must be recited every week is to be abolished. The rest will be handed over to the post-Council commission.

The Readings: Many asked that there be more readings from the Bible and that the texts to be read be better chosen—especially that readings from the New Testament be chosen. The traditional hour for the reading of the New Testament is during the Mass and the Old Testament during the divine office. Others asked greater freedom in choosing texts for the readings: each should be allowed to choose the texts he desires to read. The liturgical commission decided that all these particular questions should be left up to the post-Council commission. The aim of the Council is actually to set down general lines.

4. The obligation of reciting the breviary: The main discussion concerned those who are bound to choral recitation. Some thought this question should be included in the schema on the discipline of the clergy. Others maintained that the obligation should be explicitly grave. One opinion had it that only the more important hours should bind under grave obligation. The commission decided to retain the obligation in general: "the whole office is obligatory" while some parts are left to the will of each as has already been described. The principle of substitution was admitted: "the suitable substitution of the divine office by other liturgical acts should be defined by the rubrics." The ordinaries were given the power to dispense in particular cases.

5. The use of the vernacular in the recitation of the breviary: This

caused much discussion in both the hall and in the commission. In the primitive schema we read simply: "clerics must use the Latin language in reciting the divine office." However, this was sharply criticized by many council Fathers. The commission decided to retain the general law, granting the ordinaries, however, the power to allow "in certain cases" the recitation of the breviary in the vernacular, "for those clerics who must recite the office and to whom the Latin language presents serious difficulties." At this point the spokesman became very explicit in showing the mind of the commission: "Our ordinaries should humanly consider and weigh each case out of charity for our priests when deciding upon the seriousness of the difficulty." That is to say: not too rigorously, but generously and out of the sentiment of charity. The spokesman declared on behalf of the commission that Article 101, 1 contains a completely new text: "This text seems to us to be honest, reasonable, and quite desirable by many of you." Hence, it is quite evident that the commission does not wish to insist on Latin recitation. It goes so far as to recommend that the post-Council commission organize a bilingual breviary, "whatever might please the Council concerning Article 101."

Art. 83: Declares that the recitation of the divine office is, next to the Eucharist celebration, a continuation of Christ's priestly function.
2,163 votes: 2,151 yes; 8 no; 2 yes, if modified; 2 invalid.

Art. 84: Declares that the divine office is the voice of the Bride speaking with her Groom; it is Christ's prayer with his Body to the Father.
2,022 votes: 2,009 yes; 12 no; 1 invalid.

Art. 86: Recommends praying the breviary particularly to the priests who work in the ministry.
2,141 votes: 2,130 yes; 9 no; 2 invalid.

Fifty-Third General Assembly
October 22, 1963

While the following votation was taken by the Fathers, there took place in the council hall a lively discussion concerning the chapter on "The Laity."

Art. 89, c: Matins should be so modified that it may be recited at any hour of the day. It should have less psalms and longer lessons.
2,234 votes: 2,113 yes; 118 no; 2 yes, if modified; 1 invalid.

Art. 89, d: suppresses Prime.
2,231 votes: 1,722 yes; 509 no (nevertheless the amendment is approved).

Art. 89, e: makes the following observation with regards to the so-called hours, Tierce, Sext, and None: They must be retained in choral recitation; in private recitation one of them can be chosen which is the more appropriate for the hour at which it is being recited. This will then suffice for the whole.
2,216 votes: 1,840 yes; 371 no; 4 yes, if modified; 1 invalid.

Art. 90: A new article. "The divine office, because it is the public prayer of the Church, is a source of piety and nourishment for personal prayer. And therefore priests and all others who take part in the divine office are earnestly exhorted in the Lord to attune their minds to their voices when praying it. The better to achieve this, let them take steps to improve their understanding of the liturgy and the Bible, especially of the psalms. In revising the Roman office, its ancient and venerable treasures are to be so adapted that all those to whom they are handed on may more extensively and easily draw profit from them."

2,123 votes: 2,111 yes; 12 (!) *no.*

Art. 91: Revision work on the psalms should be concluded as soon as possible. This work is to take into account the style of Christian Latin, the liturgical use of psalms, also when sung, and the entire tradition of the Latin Church.

2,110 votes: 2,088 yes; 20 no; 1 yes, if modified; 1 invalid.

Fifty-Fourth General Assembly
October 23, 1963

The ninth amendment of Chapter IV of the liturgy schema suppresses Article 72 which entered into particular questions more properly treated by the post-Council commission.

2,230 votes: 2,111 yes; 118 no; 1 invalid.

Art. 97: A new article. "Appropriate instances are to be defined by the rubrics in which a liturgical service may be substituted for the divine office."

2,225 votes: 2,200 yes; 24 no; 1 invalid.

Art. 97: "In particular cases, and for a just reason, ordinaries can dispense their subjects wholly or in part from the obligation of reciting the divine office, or may commute the obligation."

2,160 votes: 2,125 yes; 34 no; 1 invalid.

Art. 101, 1: By a general law stipulates that Latin must be used in the recitation of the breviary by clerics, but grants at the same time the ordinary faculties to allow the vernacular in individual cases to those who cannot say the office in Latin without undue difficulties.

2,040 votes: (there were, therefore, 190 council Fathers tranquilly taking their morning break or conversing or . . . .) *1,904 yes; 131 no; 4 yes, if modified; 1 invalid.*

Art. 99: Recommends common recitation, of at least a part of the holy office, to those who are not obliged by choral recitation.

2,181 votes: 1,960 yes; 219 no; 2 invalid.

Fifty-Fifth General Assembly
October 24, 1963

Global vote on Chapter IV of the liturgy schema:

2,236 votes; 1,491 needed for a majority; 1,638 yes; 43 no; 552 yes, if modified; 3 invalids.

6 Chapter V: The Liturgical Year

Franz Zauner, Bishop of Linz, Austria, presented the report of the liturgical commission on Chapter V of the schema. He said that the liturgy reform could not be considered perfect if the liturgical year were not put more in harmony with the Church's tendency toward tradition and pastoral usefulness. During the first session, 85 speeches were presented on Chapter V.[6] The points which received greatest attention: The proper of the time, penitential practices during Lent, Saints' feasts, a permanent date for Easter, and a perpetual calendar. Many suggestions were more disciplinary than liturgical and were therefore handed over to the respective commissions. Many others, however, suggested particular points which will be studied later on by post-Council commissions. A rather important amendment, however, which would have granted the possibility of fulfilling one's Sunday Mass obligation on Saturday evening, was not included in the present text. The official spokesman said: "such faculties are to be given to the local ordinaries when they receive their habitual faculties." The suggestion to transfer weekly feasts to Sundays was not accepted by the commission for it is contrary to the liturgical spirit. The commission suggests that such feasts be transferred to national or local holidays or to a Saturday in those places where the so-called English Week has been introduced. The question of the perpetual calendar was taken out of the liturgy schema completely and included as an appendix since the Council alone cannot resolve the question. This same day the following amendments were voted upon and approved:

Art. 103: Speaks of the thought behind the feasts of Our Lady which are inserted into the liturgical year. This amendment contains an interesting new declaration which has definitive theological value: "In celebrating this annual cycle of Christ's mysteries, the holy Church honors with especial love the Blessed Mary, Mother of God, who is joined by an inseparable bond to the saving work of her Son. In her the Church holds up and admires the most excellent fruit of the redemption, and joyfully contemplates, as in a faultless image, that which she herself desires and hopes wholly to be."
2,232 votes: 2,217 yes; 15 no.

Art. 105: Declares that the Church, during the various periods of the year, completes the instruction of the faithful by means of various pious exercises of soul and body, "with instruction, prayers, works of penance and mercy."
2,158 votes: 2,148 yes; 9 no; 1 invalid.

Art. 107: Accepts the possibility of adaptations according to the conditions of place, as long as it agrees with Articles 39 and 40.
2,085 votes: 2,071 yes; 11 no; 3 invalid.

Art. 106: A completely new text which defines the Church's thought with regards to Sundays: "The Church celebrates the paschal mystery every eighth day; with good reason this, then, bears the name of the Lord's day or Sunday. For on this day Christ's faithful should come together into one place so that, by hearing the word of God and taking part in the Eucharist, they may call to mind the passion, the resurrection, and the glorification of the Lord Jesus, and may thank God who 'has begotten them again, through the resurrection of Jesus Christ from the dead, unto a living hope' (1 Pet. 1,3). Hence the Lord's day is the original feast day, and it should be proposed to the piety of the faithful and taught to them so that it may become in fact a day of joy and of freedom from work. Other celebrations, unless they be truly of greatest importance, shall not have precedence over Sunday which is the foundation and kernel of the whole liturgical year."

2,060 votes: 2,049 yes; 10 no; 1 yes, if modified.

Art. 109: Asks that the twofold character of Lent be made evident: principally by recalling or preparing for Baptism and by doing penance do the faithful prepare themselves for the celebration of the paschal mystery through more frequent listening to the word of God and more insistent prayer.

2,151 votes: 2,146 yes; 4 no; 1 yes, if modified.

Fifty-Sixth General Assembly
October 25, 1963

Art. 109, b: Recommends that when catechizing the faithful they be impressed with the social consequences of sin and the very nature of penance to detest sin as an offense against God.

2,192 votes: 2,181 yes; 10 no; 1 yes, if modified.

Art. 110: Besides internal and individual penance, this amendment recommends external and social penance according to the possibility of our times and the various regions and in accord with the possibilities of the faithful. These penitential practices must be recommended by the authority mentioned in Article 22 (episcopal conferences).

2,180 votes: 2,171 yes; 8 no; 1 invalid.

Art. 111: Reaffirms the cult of the saints and the veneration of relics and images.

2,071 votes: 2,057 yes; 13 no; 1 invalid.

The ninth amendment proposes to put the Council's considerations on a perpetual calendar in an appendix and take it out of the body of the text.

2,062 votes: 2,057 yes; 4 no; 1 invalid.

The tenth amendment proposes the following introduction to the appendix which will treat of a fixed date for Easter and of the perpetual calendar: "The Second Ecumenical Sacred Council of the Vatican, recognizing the importance of the wishes expressed by many concerning the assignment of the feast of Easter to a fixed Sunday and concerning an unchanging calendar, having carefully considered the effects which could result from the introduction of a new calendar, declares as follows: [then follow two declarations].

2,068 votes: 2,058 yes; 9 no; 1 invalid.

Fifty-Seventh General Assembly
October 29, 1963

A global votation was taken on Chapter V of the constitution, which treats of the liturgical year. It was almost unanimously approved.

2,193 votes: 2,154 yes; 21 no; 16 yes; if modified; 2 invalid.

It will not be necessary to return this chapter to the liturgical commission. The only thing lacking now is promulgation. It will then become a solemn council document.

7 THE LAST TWO CHAPTERS

The amended text of the sixth chapter was distributed to the Fathers during the 56th General Assembly. During the next general assembly, Abbot Cesario D'Amato, O.S.B., Titular Bishop of Sebaste in Cilicia and Abbot of St. Paul Outside the Walls made the presentation of this text. It is a rather short chapter and was subjected to only six amendments. The same day the first three amendments were submitted to a vote.

Art. 112: Declares that sacred chant is a necessary or integral part of the liturgy.
2,093 votes: 2,087 yes; 5 no; 1 invalid.

Art. 113: Declares that liturgical action takes on a more noble form when celebrated with chant.
2,120 votes: 2,106 yes; 13 no; 1 invalid.

Art. 115: Recommends the setting up of higher institutes of sacred music.
2,157 votes: 2,147 yes; 9 no; 1 invalid.

Fifty-Eighth General Assembly
October 30, 1963

This was one of the most interesting days of the whole Council (the bishops voted on the five key-point questions concerning the collegiality of the bishops and the restoration of the permanent deaconate). The Fathers also concluded the votation concerning the remaining amendments of Chapter VI, as well as the chapter as a whole.

Art. 119: Replace the expression "Christian music" with "traditional music of these peoples."
1,922 votes: 1,882 yes; 39 no; 1 invalid.

Art. 120: Speaks of the pipe organ.
1,941 votes: 1,897 yes; 41 no; 3 invalid.

Art. 121: A new article. "Composers, filled with the Christian spirit, should feel that their vocation is to cultivate sacred music and increase its store of treasures. Let them produce compositions which have the qualities proper to genuine sacred music, not confining themselves to works which can be sung only by large choirs, but providing also for the needs of small choirs and for the active participation of the entire assembly of the faithful. The text intended to be sung must always be in conformity with Catholic doctrine; indeed they should be drawn chiefly from holy scripture and from liturgical sources."

1,999 votes: 1,990 yes; 7 no; 2 invalid.

Then a global vote on the whole Chapter VI:

2,096 votes: 2,080 yes; 9 yes, if modified; 6 no; 1 invalid.

Fifty-Ninth General Assembly
October 31, 1963

His Excellency Carlo Rossi, Bishop of Biella, Italy, presented a summary on behalf of the liturgical commission of the final chapter of the liturgical constitution: On Sacred Art and Sacred Furnishings. The summary was brief. There were seven amendments. The moderators decided, however, that since not one of the amendments represents a controversial point, it would be sufficient to put the whole chapter to a vote without calling for votes on each amendment. In fact, the more important amendments are numbers 2, 3, and 4. Number two gives beauty emphasis over sumptuousness in sacred art. Number three calls attention to functional architecture in churches. Number four counsels moderation in the cult of images with regard to number and order, so that true devotion be fostered and false devotion condemned.

1,941 votes: 1,838 yes; 94 yes, if modified: 9 no.

Thus the last chapter of the liturgy schema was approved.

8 THE VOTES "PLACET JUXTA MODUM"

Sixty-Ninth General Assembly
November 16, 1963

On the occasion of the general votes taken on each chapter, the Fathers had a chance to vote *yes, if modified.* There were 180 such votes on Chapter I, 781 on Chapter II, 1,054 on Chapter III, 552 on Chapter IV, 16 on Chapter V, 9 on Chapter VI, and 94 on Chapter VII. There was a total of 2,686 *yes, if modified* votes. On November 15 the liturgy commission handed out a pamphlet containing the modifications corresponding to the 180 *yes, if modified* votes (there were actually only 52 since many were repetitions) cast by the Council Fathers on the liturgy schema. The commission patiently gave a reply to each amendment suggested by these votes, which were not all reasonable or considerate. For example, the very first reactionary modification said: *"Schema funditus renovetur et clara principia ponantur ad ritus unitatem servandam."* The Commission had the patience to answer: *"Cum caput primum quasi unanimi consensu Concilio placuerit, ut patet ex suffragatione commissio non potest illud funditus immutare."*

Sixty-Ninth General Assembly
November 18, 1963

Cardinal Lercaro presented to the Fathers the modification made by the liturgical commission and expressed the hope of the approval of the Constitution by November 22, the 60th anniversary of St. Pius X's *Motu Proprio, Tra le sollectitudine.* Then Joseph Albert Martin, Bishop of Nicolet, Canada, presented the first chapter of this same modification. Since Chapter I had no notable corrections (only two insignificant changes) it was subjected to vote by means of the following question: "Does the examination made by the Council liturgy commission on the Preface and Chapter I please the Fathers?" The Fathers voted by means of individual ballots.

2,084 votes: 2,060 yes; 20 no; 4 invalid.

Seventy-First General Assembly
November 20, 1963

His Excellency, Jesus Enciso Viana, Bishop of Mallorca, presented the modifications of the second chapter.

First vote: Add to Article 57, 2: "The regulation, however, of the discipline of concelebration in the diocese pertains to the bishop."

2,182 votes: 2,057 yes; 123 no; 2 invalid.

In order to understand better this amendment it would be good to go back to the original text. Before, the sentence read: "Moreover, with permission of the ordinary, to whom the discipline of concelebration pertains." But when the votes were counted on this paragraph, some 781 *yes, if modified* had been cast. The modification requested was the addition of the word "of the place" after the word "ordinary." These 781 Fathers had the following in mind: Only bishops and not major religious superiors (who are also ordinaries) can judge when concelebration is fitting and when not. The commission answered: "The commission unanimously declares that there is no desire whatsoever to detract from the right which the bishop has in his diocese to modify worship." Therefore, in order to clarify the point, the commission proposed this new paragraph for votation and approval. It is worthy of note that the point in question is to clarify that the bishops' competence remains intact. The commission did not, however, give the bishop faculties to decide if and when concelebration is fitting in the churches of exempt religious. The essence of the preceding text remains in Article 57: "Also, with permission of the *ordinary,* to whom it belongs to decide whether concelebration is opportune."

Second vote: The answer of the liturgical commission to the suggestion that explicit use of the vernacular be provided for in the prayers of the priest to which the faithful respond: The Fathers were asked if they approved the response of the commission that such explicit mention is not necessary since it is already contained in a more general provision.

2,182 votes: 2,047 yes; 131 no; 4 invalid.

Third vote: The suggestion had been made that permission for holy Communion under both species be extended to the Nuptial Mass. The commission's answer was that this extension could not be proposed in a brief article with all the necessary precautions, and that since the instances mentioned in the text are only examples, this extension could be provided for in individual local circumstances under the authority of national conferences according to general principles already approved.

2,143 votes: 2,014 yes; 128 no; 1 invalid.

Fourth vote: The commission asks for approval of the answers given to many other modifications suggested by the Fathers.

2,091 votes: 2,056 yes; 31 no; 4 invalid.

Fifth vote: Approval of the second chapter as it now stands.

2,152 votes: 2,112 yes; 40 no.

Seventy-Second General Assembly
November 21, 1963

Five votes were cast on Chapter III of the liturgy schema:

First vote: Some 640 Fathers had asked that Article 63 be modified in the following manner (This article conceded the use of the venacular in the administration of sacraments and sacramentals *in all parts except the form of the sacraments*): "The vernacular language may be used in administering the sacraments and sacramentals, according to the norm of Art. 36.

2,185 votes: 1,848 yes; 335 no; 2 invalid.

Therefore a grand majority has approved this new and most important amendment that from now on we can administer the sacraments, all of them including Holy Eucharist, penance, holy orders, form and all, in the vernacular.

Second vote: Determine in what sense certain blessings referred to in Article 79 are to be "reserved" to ordinaries.

2,182 votes: 2,084 yes; 96 no; 2 invalid. Article 79, 2 will remain as it was.

Third vote: Deals with the authorization for selected laymen to administer certain sacramentals with the permission of the local ordinary.

2,106 votes: 1,972 yes; 132 no; 2 invalid. This article, 79, 3, likewise will remain as it was.

Fourth vote: Asks approval for the other modifications made on Chapter III.

2,031 votes: 1,999 yes; 29 no; 3 invalid.

Fifth vote: A pure and simple approval of Chapter III as it will be with the modifications included.

2,143 votes: 2,107 yes; 35 no; 1 invalid.

Seventy-Third General Assembly
November 22, 1963

Today was a day of special importance for the Constitution on the liturgy, which received final and formal approval.

First vote: Chapter IV on the breviary received 552 *yes, if modified,* votes last October 24, 1963. In spite of them, however, the text had been approved. They actually were all resuméd into three modifications of minor importance and were presented to the Council Fathers now by the liturgical commission under one vote: Does what the commission did with the modifications please the Fathers?

2,183 votes: 2,131 yes; 50 no; 1 yes, if modified (this was not an acceptable mode of voting so was counted as invalid); *1 invalid.*

Second vote: Chapters V, VI, and VII had received only a few or no modifications. The Commission, however, answered each call for modification and asked the Fathers if the answers were acceptable.

2,156 votes: 2,149 yes; 5 no; 2 invalid.

Third vote: The commission then asked for a global vote on the whole sacred liturgy schema. This formal, all-decisive vote began at 11:30. At 12:05 the Secretary General, Archbishop Felici, read the results:

2,178 votes: 2,158 yes; 19 no; 1 yes, if modified.

The results were greeted by a jubilant, animated applause. Cardinal Tisserant, dean of the Council's board of presidents immediately arose to thank the liturgical commission, calling to mind the first president of the liturgical commission, Cardinal Caetano Cicogniani, who died February 5, 1962. Cardinal Cicogniani directed the precounciliar studies.

Now all that was lacking in order to make the liturgy schema a formal constitution was the formality of a vote in the presence of the Holy Father. This took place on December 4, 1963:

2,151 votes: 2,147 yes; 4 no.

Pope Paul VI then approved the text in the name of the Father and of the Son and of the Holy Spirit and ordered it promulgated for the glory of God.

NOTES TO CHAPTER 3

1 We made a very detailed chronicle concerning the debates; cf. B. Kloppenburg, *Second Vatican Council,* Vol. II (Editora Vozes, 1963), 87-160.

2 *Op. cit.,* 161.

3 Note that the liturgy schema had eight chapters when presented to the Council. Later, Chapter VI (sacred furnishings) and Chapter VIII (sacred art) were joined and formed Chapter VII.

4 This information was given by Cardinal Lercaro during the Forty-Third General Assembly (October 8, 1963); cf. Kloppenburg, *op. cit.,* III, 79.

5 *Op. cit.,* 228.

6 The apparent disorder in this series of amendments is due to the change made in the structure of this part of the Constitution.

7 *Op. cit.*, II, 137-147.

8 *Op. cit.*, II, 147 ff.

4
Fundamental ideas of the Constitution

Cipriano Vagagini O.S.B.

1 Pastoral bearing
2 Liturgy and ecclesiology
3 Sacrament
4 Summit and font
5 History of salvation
6 Paschal mystery
7 Sacrifice of the Church
8 Don't create useless difficulties for the people
9 Leave the door open
10 Relaxation of rigid uniformity and centralization
11 Ecumenical spirit
12 Without defects
13 Conclusion

Dom Vagagini of Italy was consultor of the Preconciliar Liturgical Commission and *peritus* of the II Vatican Council. His article was translated into English by Salvatore Attanasio.

The Constitution on the Liturgy of the II Vatican Council should be the object of a detailed commentary on every single point. But the need of the moment is to see the general spirit that animates it. Not only is this task important for understanding the exact nature of the Constitution in its entirety, but also for grasping the far-reaching trends of the Council, as well as the vital movements and thinking which under the inspiration of the Holy Spirit, makes the Church a living reality today.

In view of the task assigned to me, I shall take up a number of important points which serve to characterize quite well, if I am not mistaken, the general spirit of the Constitution, without however, writing a real commentary on every single point nor without treating exhaustively the questions touched upon.

1 PASTORAL BEARING

The precise aim of the Constitution is clearly pointed out in the Introduction: "Wherefore the sacred Council judges that the following principles concerning the promotion and reform of the liturgy should be called to mind, and that practical norms should be established" (Art. 3).

In other words, its purpose is to draw up principles and establish practical norms which are to serve as guides for increasing liturgical life and reforming the liturgy. In the first chapter "General Principles for the Restoration and Promotion of the Sacred Liturgy" the general principles are explained. These are to guide the action decided upon to increase in the faithful liturgical life in general and are to guide the general reform of the liturgy. In the six chapters which follow, the same twofold purpose is pursued. Principles and special norms are given which refer in particular to the various parts of the liturgy, namely, the Mass, the sacraments and the sacramentals, the liturgical year, sacred music, sacred art and furnishings.

Throughout the entire Constitution, the articles which contain the general and special principles drawn up for increasing an appreciation for and participation in the liturgy on the part of both clergy and faithful, are intermingled as one finds in the gradual unraveling of an idea. In the first chapter, for example, there are some entire sections which treat more of promoting liturgical life (e.g. Articles 9-20, 41-46), and this also holds for the other chapters (e.g. Articles 102-111, 113-120, 123-129); other sections more directly pertain to liturgical reform, as Articles 22-40 in the first chapter and a large number of the others in the following chapters.

If then we pay close attention to the manner in which the Constitution conceives the relationship between these two aforementioned aims, we see at once that the reform is a result of an increased appreciation for and participation in the liturgy of the Church. This principle is repeated in Articles 14 and 21 of the first chapter in a very general way, and then again explicitly or implicitly affirmed at the beginning of each succeeding chapter. "In order that the Christian people may more certainly derive an abundance of graces from celebrating the liturgy, holy Mother Church desires to undertake with great care a general restoration of the liturgy itself. For the liturgy is made up of immutable elements divinely instituted, and of elements subject to change. These not only may but ought to be changed with the passage of time if they have suffered from the intrusion of anything out of harmony with the inner nature of the liturgy or have become unsuited to it.

"In this restoration, both texts and rites should be drawn up so that they express more clearly the holy things which they signify; the Christian people, so far as possible, should be able to understand them with ease and take part in them fully, actively and as befits a community.

"Wherefore, the sacred Council establishes the following general principles" (Art. 21).

The general norms of liturgical reform viewed in their entirety follow. Hence, the reform of the liturgy has the special purpose of bringing about the full participation of the people in the liturgy.

What part does the theology of the liturgy play in all this? It plays a most important part and one that undoubtedly throws light on everything else. It is destined to remain always a beacon that will guide the life of the Church, even after the reform is completed and the people generally have learned to participate fully in the liturgy.

The introduction and the first part of the first chapter, in particular, often summarizes the better elements found in recent ecclesiastical literature. One never fails to find framed within a theological liturgical background the more important norms of a practical nature which are brought in now and then throughout the document. I purposely use the term "framed," because the norms for the reform of the liturgy and for the increase of liturgical life among the faithful are to be so framed within their natural ideological background that the basic harmony of the theologico-liturgical outlook of the Constitution is preserved.

The Constitution, without wishing to set forth at all, either in fact or merely in resume, a complete theology of the liturgy, does in any case recall the basic principles which refer to the pastoral aim and the goal of reform. The reasoning always takes this form, namely: the nature of the liturgy and its importance for the life of the Church are basic theology (Art. 5-13). Accordingly, the Church wishes that the faithful be led to participate more easily and as fully as possible in such great sources of grace (Art. 14). Wherefore, the Church wishes not only that the faithful are thoroughly educated along these lines by a clergy that are the first to know and live well that which they must communicate to others (Art. 14-19), but also that the liturgy itself be so reformed that it does not place unnecessary obstacles to the much desired full and active participation (Art. 21-40). This same reasoning is substantially repeated in the following chapters for the various parts of the liturgy, Mass, sacraments and so forth.

Conclusion: The chief concern of the Constitution is to lead the people to live the liturgy to the fullest extent. It has pastoral perspective. The ideal of "full participation" (Art. 14; 21; 41) is the catalyzing concept, while the rest only serves as its ideological background and the necessary practical means.

Now the ideological background or that theology of the liturgy which the Council reinstates does not thereby become less important. If the aim is practical, it is the ideology that characterizes and justifies it. To get the spirit of the Constitution one must get an insight into that theology on which it is founded.

2 LITURGY AND ECCLESIOLOGY

The Constitution opens with an introduction in which the Council first of all recalls the aims that led to its convocation: to impart an ever-increasing vigor to Christian life; to adapt more suitably to the needs of our age those parts subject to change; to prepare for union among all Christians; and to call all mankind into the fold of the Church (Art. 1). With these ends in mind, the Council must necessarily be concerned with the reform and promotion of liturgical life.

And why? Simply because through and in the liturgy Christian people more fully are in contact with the mystery of Christ and the Church, and at the same time more clearly manifest him to the world.

"For the liturgy, 'through which the work of our Redemption is accomplished,' most of all in the divine sacrifice of the Eucharist, is the outstanding means whereby the faithful may express in their lives, and manifest to others, the mystery of Christ and the real nature of the true Church. It is of the essence of the Church that she be both human and divine, visible and yet invisibly equipped, eager to act and yet intent on contemplation, present in this world and yet not at home in it; and she is all these things in such wise that in her the human is directed and subordinated to the divine, the visible likewise to the invisible, action to contemplation, and this present world to that city yet to come, which we seek. While the liturgy daily builds up those who are within into a holy temple of the Lord, into a dwelling place for God in the Spirit, to the mature measure of the fullness of Christ, at the same it marvelously strengthens their power to preach Christ, and thus shows forth the Church, to those who are outside, as a sign lifted up among the nations under which the scattered children of God may be gathered together until there is one sheepfold and one shepherd" (Art. 2).

When the introduction was discussed in the first session, there were those who thought this article was completely irrelevant. Under what pretext, they demanded, do liturgists presume to enter the field of dogma, reserved to the Theological Commission, and put forth their opinions on the nature of the Church? What has this to do with the liturgy? Besides, was not this manner of speaking about the nature of the Church a lot of fuzzy poetry, and for that matter, they said, that of the whole present Constitution? Where is that rigor of concept and expression that alone is worthy of a conciliar declaration?

Now after the famous discussions on the theological schemas, especially those "On the Church" and "On the Bishops" and "On Ecumenism," we see the import of their criticism. They start with a concept of the Church which not only asserts the intrinsic necessity of its visible and juridical-organizational aspect—something of course, that no Catholic has ever dreamed of denying—but besides they press the analogy of the Church with the *polis* or earthly political society beyond all imagination. They go so far as to make this aspect, at least practically, their primary concern, following slavishly in the wake of an anti-Protestant, apologetic ecclesiology of a post-Tridentine and especially Bellarminian type.

It was natural that framing the liturgy on the background of a theology of the Church, particularly one in which its various elements were put together in an entirely different system than that to which they were accustomed, would appear strange to those who never seriously asked if the post-Tridentine theological position on ecclesiology might be in need of revision. How could they be anything but completely disorientated at first contact with an image of the Church so decisively centered on a concept of the *sacrament-mystery,* that is to say, on a complex reality, both visible and even sensible, organized and present in the world, about which, however, the emphatic assertion is made that the visible aspect is subordinate, ministerial, and basically transitory? Such an assertion is made because in the Church the visible looks to the invisible, action and organization to contemplation, the exterior to the interior, the present to the future. Wouldn't they be disorientated by a concept of the Church which in the last analysis is a determining factor for the organizational and juridical, something like saying that in man the soul is the determining form of the body? Lest one habituated to looking at the Church in a predominately juridical way should think this is nothing more than a bit of fanciful poetry, we will quote what is said in Article 41:

"The bishop is to be considered as the High Priest of his flock, from whom the life in Christ of his faithful is in some way derived and dependent.

"Therefore all should hold in great esteem the liturgical life of the diocese centered around the bishop, especially in his cathedral church; they must be convinced that the pre-eminent manifestation of the Church consists in the full, active participation of all God's holy people in the same liturgical celebrations, especially in the same Eucharist, in a single prayer at one altar, at which there presides the bishop surrounded by his college of priests and ministers." In a note to this article reference is fittingly made to St. Ignatius of Antioch, *Ad Magn.* 7; *Ad Phil.* 4; *Ad Smyrn.* 8.

This text gives us a precise sacral image of the Church, one urgently in need of wide diffusion. But to win such acceptance, we must admit, demands realigning many preconceived notions.

Already from the first remarks on the liturgy made in the Council, this concept of the Church was the precise point that, as succeeding events would prove, was at the root of the differences between the two principal currents manifested in the Council. That this dispute first came up in the matter of the liturgy is not at all surprising to one who knows that even historically speaking, from 1918 on, the liturgical movement itself began revising the post-Tridentine ecclesiology. This movement culminated in the successive elaboration of the schema "On the Church" in the Council. Furthermore, in the more authoritative and recent documents, such as the two encyclicals of Pius XII, *Mystici Corporis* and *Mediator Dei,* as well as contemporary liturgico-theological thought, liturgy and ecclesiology are inseparable. And they remain inseparably linked in the present Constitution.

This union between liturgy and ecclesiology is the direct result of that very sacral, sacramental image of the Church, an image outside of the prevailing juridical tradition, an image which has helped so much to discover a more profound understanding of the liturgy.

This image, in its turn, is found in the liturgy as the very center of the Church. For in the liturgy glory is given to God in Christ Jesus in the highest degree, and divine life is transmitted to men through the instrumentality of men and visible sensible things. And this is the very reason for the existence and structure of the Church. "For the liturgy . . . is the outstanding means whereby the faithful may express in their lives, and manifest to others, the mystery of Christ and the real nature of the true Church" (Art. 2). This quotation puts the ecclesiological value of the liturgy in its true perspective, both as to the internal life of the Church as well as to its mission of showing forth Christ.

Among all the aspects of the nature of the Church which the faithful concretely live and mirror so appropriately in the liturgy, the Council places in the first place that of the human-divine Spouse of Christ. This image expresses the fact that she, in the likeness of her Spouse and Founder of whom she is the Mystical Body and the continuation of his presence on earth, is at the same time both human and divine, visible and invisible, active and contemplative, engaged in the world and a pilgrim, but in such a manner that in her the human is ordered and subordinated to the divine, the visible to the invisible, action to contemplation, the present to the future which we seek.

Certainly, not without reason, the Council takes up these precise points. In fact, on the one hand, they are hardly expressed better than in the liturgy itself, and on the other hand, they actually provide the answer to the search for a right balance between the juridico-organizational element and the sacral-mystical one. Basically this balance is the key problem in contemporary ecclesiology.

These points have besides a particular ecumenical value. It is in fact well known that in the present state of the separation of Christians among themselves, the central problem is that of ecclesiology. More exactly, it is really the problem of a right balance between the juridico-organizational aspect and the sacral-mystical element in the Church. Non-Catholics defend the invisible mystical aspect to such an extent that they devaluate the visible juridical aspect, and at the same time accuse the

Catholic Church of holding a completely inadequate view of the invisible mystical aspect.

Because of the ecumenical situation, the Council reaffirms the true position of Catholic doctrine on this point, the characteristically divine-human concept of the Church. Only this concept is capable of satisfying that which is at the heart of the matter for the Orthodox and the Protestants, without diminishing in any way the function of the Church as a visible organization established by Christ. On the other hand, they themselves, even if confusedly, feel a pressing need for such a visible Church. With such a concept of the Church, especially as manifested in the divine-human symbol of the liturgy as a most perfect expression of it, the Council feels that the Church will appear "as a sign lifted up among the nations under which the scattered children of God may be gathered together until there is one sheepfold and one shepherd" (Art. 2).

The second Article of the Introduction is formulated like a thesis. In the sections that follow, the doctrine is spelled out in detail. They treat of the nature of the liturgy from the viewpoint of the nature and work of Christ, as well as his presence and action in the sacred rites (Art. 5-7), the eschatological expectations of the liturgy (Art. 8), its place as a summit and font of the Church's activity (Art. 9-13), and as the supreme norm which is to guide liturgical reform (Art. 21; 22; 26; 23; 37), the bishop as the High Priest of the diocese (Art. 41), the meaning of the liturgical movement in general (Art. 43). This thesis is also evident in the introductions to the various chapters that follow, in which a brief reference is made to the importance of the various parts of the liturgy in the life of the Church (Art. 47; 57-61; 102-105; 112; 122).

3 SACRAMENT

The word *mystery* applied to the Church often recurs in the Constitution "On the Church." The Constitution on the liturgy explicitly cites the phrase used in the Roman Missal: "the wondrous sacrament of the whole Church" (Art. 5).

In the discussion on these texts, some protests were voiced. "Our people will think there are eight sacraments," one said. Another observed that this way of always talking about the Church as a *mystery* gives rise to the suspicion that we are accepting the errors of the Protestants about a mysterious, incomprehensible Church, one that is purely invisible. Such talk reveals a forgetfulness of the patristic and liturgical concept of *sacrament* and *mystery*.

But why resurrect a terminology, today ordinarily not understood—and we should remember that—by those who received their entire theological formation from post-Tridentine manuals? Not out of love for the archaic, but because patristic and liturgical thought has used such terminology to affirm a profound truth, unfortunately forgotten along with the terminology.

This truth must be brought to light, namely, the intimate, indissoluble bond between Christ, the Church and the liturgy in the present order of salvation. And this bond is not a mere causal connection in the sense that Christ now acts in the Church and through the Church, and the Church acts principally in the liturgy and through the liturgy, especially that of the sacraments. But there is also a close structural connection which has its prototype in Christ himself, in whose image the Church is fashioned, and the Church in turn reflects its manner of being principally in the liturgy.

And this structure is exactly that of the *sacrament* or the *mystery,* namely a sensible and visible thing which somehow contains and communicates to the well-disposed an invisible, holy and divine reality in the order of salvation, a reality which at the same time shows itself to those who have faith and hides itself from those who have not.

Thus is Christ built up, thus is the Church built up, and so too is the liturgy. Christ is the first and original *sacrament,* from whom comes that general *sacrament,* which is the Church in its wholeness, "the wondrous sacrament of the whole Church." And the Church in turn expresses itself to the greatest extent in the *sacrament* taken in a more restricted sense, namely, that of the entire liturgy, and particularly in its seven major rites, which, in today's terminology, we are accustomed to call the seven sacraments.

The perspective of the Incarnation. Within this context the Council introduces the notion of the liturgy (Art. 5-8). In Article 5, which begins an explanation of the concept of the liturgy, there is, first of all, an explanation of the structure of the person of Christ and his work, then the structure and the work of the Church, which somehow continues that of Christ (Art. 6). Finally, the section concludes with the structure and efficacy of the liturgy. In the liturgy more than in other things, the mode of being and efficacy of the Church focuses itself (Art. 7-8).

Without using the word *sacrament,* the concept that Christ is the original *sacrament* is expressed in Article 5 with the equivalent biblical and patristic expressions: "God. . .sent his Son, the Word made flesh, anointed by the Holy Spirit, to preach the Gospel to the poor, to heal the contrite of heart, to be a 'bodily and spiritual medicine,'[1] the Mediator between God and man. For his humanity, united with the Person of the Word, was the instrument of our salvation. Therefore, in Christ 'the perfect achievement of our reconciliation came forth, and the fullness of divine worship was given to us.' "[2]

Characteristic of this concept of *sacrament* in this passage is not only the expression of St. John, "the Word was made flesh," but also that of St. Ignatius of Antioch, "*bodily and spiritual medicine.*" An expression difficult to translate in the fullness of its meaning, it means that Christ is indeed a physician, just as much by means of his spirit (*pneuma*), that is through his divinity, as by means of his body (*sarx*), that is through his humanity including his flesh. And as he heals our soul to which he communicates the Holy Spirit of whom he himself is the Anointed One, so also he heals our body to which he promises a glorious resurrection in the image of his own glorious body.

Characteristic of the *sacrament* is also the patristic expression retained by the Scholastics, that in the unity of the Person of the Word the humanity of Christ was and still is the instrument of our salvation.

The conclusion of Article 5 and Article 6 develops the notion of the Church as a *sacrament* derived from the original *sacrament* which is Christ himself: "For it was from the side of Christ as he slept the sleep of death upon the cross that there came forth 'the wondrous sacrament of the whole Church' " (Art. 5).

"Just as Christ was sent by the Father, so also he sent the apostles, filled with the Holy Spirit. This he did that, by preaching the gospel to every creature, they might proclaim that the Son of God, by his death and resurrection, had freed us from the power of Satan and from death, and brought us into the kingdom of his Father. His purpose also was that they might accomplish the work of salvation they had proclaimed by means of the sacrifice and sacraments, around which the entire liturgical life revolves" (Art. 6).

The general sense of this article is that Christ on the point of leaving the world instituted the Church, in which and through which due to his invisible presence and the operation of the Holy Spirit, the works of salvation accomplished by him were applied to individual men. The plan was that mankind, after being reconciled with God and in a certain manner divinized in his very own likeness, could, through this participation in his nature and together with him, glorify God in perfect worship. (See the rest of Art. 6.)

Thus Christ instituted this Church in his own likeness—that is, with the very same make-up, in the image of the Incarnation—in such a way that it was human and divine and that in it the salvation of well-disposed believers is accomplished through the invisible operation of the Holy Spirit, by using human, even sensible means, such as the hierarchy, sacred scripture, preaching and especially the sacraments.

The sacraments must not be separated from the total context of the liturgy, for they are its nucleus and center. The rest of the liturgy, in fact, has no other meaning than to prepare and dispose us in a natural and worthy manner, with the special aid of the intercessory power of the Church, for the celebration of the sacraments and above all the eucharistic mystery.

Finally, on this background the text goes on to describe in detail the nature of the liturgy (Art. 7). The idea is set forth as follows. If the Church is so powerful and efficacious in carrying out the work of redeeming individual men through the redemption fulfilled in Christ, the reason is that Christ himself is not absent from his Church, but is intimately even if invisibly present in it, working in and through it. And this presence of his is by its very nature something unique to the liturgy.

In the eucharistic mystery he is indeed personally and substantially present, and in the other sacraments he is present by his power. For in them he himself works by means of the rites and sacred ministers whom he uses as simple instruments. And this power of his is also present in the sacramentals by a special claim, even if inferior to that of the sacraments. Hence the effect of the sacramentals is attained by means of the prayer of the Church "which is holy and works in close union with its Spouse" (*Mediator Dei*).

Besides, in this great work in which Christ gives perfect glory to the Father and men are sanctified, he always closely unites himself with his beloved Spouse.

"Rightly, then, the liturgy is considered as an exercise of the priestly office of Jesus Christ. In the liturgy the sanctification of man is signified by signs perceptible to the senses, and is effected in a way which corresponds with each of these signs; in the liturgy the whole public worship is performed by the Mystical Body of Jesus Christ, that is, by the Head and his members" (Art. 7).

The Council did not wish to give a strict definition of the liturgy in a scholastic manner by way of genus and specific difference. The problem of defining the liturgy is still disputed among theologians and it was not the intention of the Council to solve the question. Nevertheless, there are three points worthy of note in this section. In these three points the Constitution certainly marks further progress in the notion of the liturgy over that stated in *Mediator Dei.*

(1) The notion is clearly derived from the concept of *sacrament,* seen in Christ himself, in the Church in general and here applied to the liturgy. *Sacrament,* as explained above, is a sensible thing which somehow contains, manifests, and communicates to the well-disposed an invisible divine reality, but hides it from those not disposed. This notion evidently serves as a general outline of its entire development which culminates in the notion of the liturgy. Thus the "sacramentality" of the whole liturgy is sharply emphasized.

(2) Therefore the greatest prominence is given to the reality of the sensible sign. The liturgy is summed up in this concept. For the liturgy is a complex of sensible signs through which Christ the Lord in a certain way exercises his priesthood by sanctifying men and associating them with himself in the worship which he renders to God.

(3) This complex of signs does not merely refer to worship, but comprises both sanctification and worship. The twofold movement of the liturgy, the one descending from God to man, and the other rising from man to God, is much more sharply delineated in the Constitution than the one found in *Mediator Dei.*

4 SUMMIT AND FONT

Article 9 states: "The sacred liturgy does not exhaust the entire activity of the Church." For over and above the liturgy, there are certainly many other things for the Church to do, such as preaching and every kind of apostolic work, not to mention prayer and personal asceticism.

Then the Constitution continues in Article 10: "Nevertheless, the liturgy is the summit towards which the activity of the Church is directed; at the same time it is the font from which all her power flows."

This statement is explained as follows: "For the aim and object of apostolic works is that all who are made sons of God by faith and baptism should come together to praise God in the midst of his Church, to take part in the sacrifice and to eat the Lord's Supper.

"The liturgy in its turn moves the faithful, filled with 'the paschal sacraments,' to be 'one in holiness'; it prays that 'they may hold fast in their lives to what they have grasped by their faith'; the renewal in the Eucharist of the covenant between the Lord and man draws the faithful into the compelling love of Christ and sets them on fire. From the liturgy, therefore, and especially from the Eucharist, as from a font, grace is poured forth upon us; and the sanctification of men in Christ and the glorification of God, to which all other activities of the Church are directed as towards their end, are achieved in the most efficacious possible way."

On this doctrine hinges the entire problem of the relation between the liturgy and other aspects of the life of the Church. This notion is further explained in Articles 11, 12 and 13, which, in particular, treat of the relations between the liturgy and personal dispositions from which the liturgy draws its full efficacy, between the liturgy and extra-liturgical piety, and between the liturgy and devotions.

On the basis of first impressions it was said that the programmatic declaration of the Council, namely, the liturgy is the summit and font of the whole life of the Church, smacks more of "sensationalism" than of strict theological truth. Behind this impression there is without doubt the usual fear of one who has neither comprehended the nature of the liturgy, nor the true place that it has in the Church, and hence thinks that a statement of this kind wants to propagate a naive pan-liturgism for the purpose of engulfing everything within the liturgy.

The Constitution however is perfectly clear. It devotes the entire Article 9 to the statement that the sacred liturgy "does not exhaust the entire activity of the Church." Article 11 explains that proper dispositions are required if the liturgy is to have its full effect. Article 12 inculcates the necessity of piety in the whole of one's life over and above liturgical services. Article 13 recognizes within certain limits the usefulness of popular devotions. Hence there is to be no absorbing of all activity of the Church within the liturgy alone. Yet to say that the liturgy does not absorb the entire activity of the Church does not indeed prevent one from affirming at the same time that the liturgy is the summit toward which this very life in its entirety tends and from another viewpoint the font from which all else comes.

And why? In brief, the reason is that the eucharistic mystery, sacrament and sacrifice—or still better, the sacramental sacrifice—is the summit to which all the activity of the Church, both liturgical and extra-liturgical, tends and is essentially ordered, and at the same time it is the font from which all grace comes.

Now the eucharistic mystery is the very quintessence of the liturgy, without which the liturgy, as desired by Christ, is theologically inconceivable and with which it safely preserves its true nature. Hence the liturgy, in its more essential eucharistic aspect, is the summit to which all activity of the Church tends and the font from which all her supernatural power flows.

But is the eucharistic mystery really the summit to which all liturgical action is essentially ordered? "All the other sacraments are ordered to the Eucharist as to their proper end," St. Thomas says and explains in detail.[3] And with even more reason, this relation to the Eucharist is to be affirmed of the sacramentals and all the rest of the liturgy, which is one immense sacramental. And if this principle holds for the liturgical activity of the Church, all the more so for extra-liturgical actions.

Is the eucharistic mystery actually the font from which all grace flows? Yes. St. Thomas explicitly asserts that no one has grace except through some relation to the Eucharist, at least implicitly by way of desire. "This sacrament has of itself the power of conferring grace. *No one has grace before receiving this sacrament, at least through a certain desire of receiving it,* which he makes himself if he is an adult, or which infants have through the intention of the Church" (S. Th. III, 79, a. 1 ad 1).

The Catechism of the Council of Trent takes up the same notion. In explaining the nature and efficacy of the sacraments, it says that it is necessary to compare the "Eucharist to a spring and the other sacraments to brooks. It is indeed necessary to say that the Eucharist is really the *font of all graces,* since it contains in a wondrous manner the author of all the sacraments."[4]

Leo XIII merely confirmed this teaching when he said that from the Eucharist "the Church draws and possesses all its power and glory, all the divine charisms that adorn it, and every other good thing."[5] Not without reason had St. Thomas said: "Within this sacrament is contained the whole mystery of our salvation."[6]

If one were to say that all this may be true of the Eucharist but not of the liturgy, since the liturgy does not totally exhaust itself in eucharistic worship, we could give the following answer: Man in his actual being is truly the king of creation, even though he may not excel in every perfection, but only formally by reason of his intellect. That is true since the intellect pertains to man, not merely accidentally but essentially and substantially, as a substantial determinant in relation to the body and all the other faculties.

Similarly, it is perfectly valid to say that the liturgy in its actual being is the summit and font of the activity of the Church, even though it may not equally be so in every part but only formally by reason of the Eucharist. For the Eucharist pertains to the liturgy not merely accidentally but substantially as the heart, the center or determining part in relation to its other components.

Moreover, the other parts of the liturgy are primarily the other sacraments. It is clear enough that by means of them the liturgy is the summit and font of all supernatural life in the Church, since the sacraments produce their effects from the act itself (*ex opere operato*). This means that in them, every time the rite is objectively placed in a proper manner and with a right intention, Christ himself, using the sacred ministers and rites as simple instruments, infallibly works that sanctification of men and renders that worship to God which is the end to which all other works of the Church are in the last analysis ordered here below. Therefore in the actual order of salvation, every grace is sacramental.

The sacramentals, not having the same purpose nor efficacy nor importance as the sacraments, and much less than the Eucharist, still reach this end from the action of the Church (*ex opere operantis Ecclesiae*).

Therefore, if among all the activities of the Church divine services are the most sublime and in the last resort those that determine its end, Pius XI[7] could say that the liturgy is "the most excellent act of worship." And Pius XII in *Mediator Dei* in speaking of the end to be attained in all the operations of the Church, namely the sanctification of souls and the giving of glory to God, states: "It should be clear to all . . . that the worship rendered to God by the Church in union with her divine Head is the most efficacious means of achieving sancity. This efficacy, where there is question of the eucharistic sacrifice and the sacraments, derives first of all and principally from the act itself (*ex-opere operato*). But if one considers . . . the other rites instituted by the hierarchy of the Church, then the effectiveness is due rather to the action of the Church (*ex opere operantis Ecclesiae*), inasmuch as she is holy and acts always in closest union with her Head."[8]

The Constitution confirms the same teaching in the conclusion to Article 10: "From the liturgy, therefore, and especially from the Eucharist, as from a font, grace is poured forth upon us; and the sanctification of men in Christ and the glorification of God, to which all other activities of the Church are directed as towards their end, are achieved in the most efficacious possible way."

Therefore, the liturgy is the summit and font of the life of the Church.

Why is all this today so little known to many? There could be a long explanation, but the root of the matter is twofold. In general, there is a lack of theological vision in treating of the liturgy; in particular, a forgetting of a fundamental teaching of St. Paul, St. John, St. Ignatius of Antioch, St. Irenaeus, Tertullian, St. Gregory of Nyssa, St. Cyril of Jerusalem, and especially of St. Cyril of Alexandria, St. John Damascene, and St. Thomas, without which the liturgy is unintelligible, namely, the doctrine of the principal and *ever-actual* role of the humanity of Christ in the history of salvation, and especially that of his most sacred and now glorious Body and Precious Blood. And on this the whole matter hinges.

Whoever forgets this teaching cannot understand the irreplaceable function of the sacraments in the actual order willed by God, and especially that of the Eucharist and hence of the liturgy. Nor can he see why theologians rightly say that no one today can have grace without some real relation to the sacraments and especially the Eucharist. This relation must be present at least in an implicit desire, and if a desire is sincere, it must be carried out as soon as possible and permissible. Nor can he perceive the full force of the theological saying, that what saves is not only faith nor hope alone or not even charity by itself or any other act whatsoever (purely psychological), but faith *and* the *sacraments.*

Now the reason for all this is the fact that in the present order no grace comes to us except through the glorious humanity of Christ the Lord, *including his glorious Body* as the living instrument of his divinity. And therefore, to have any grace whatsoever, we must be in contact with his sacred humanity including his Body. And this contact, by the will of God—which takes into consideration human nature which both in Christ and in us is made up of spirit and body—must be not only spiritual through faith, charity, etc. (at least, implicitly desired), but also physical, even if physical in a unique sense, namely, sacramental.

In the preceding statements I have done nothing more than repeat the thought of St. Thomas, who on his part faithfully echoes the teaching of St. John Damascene and the entire Greek tradition.

"The sacraments cause grace as an instrument, which is explained as follows: Damascene[9] says that the human nature of Christ was the instrument of his divinity. . . . So in fact, the very touch of Christ instrumentally caused the cure of the leper. As the human nature of Christ was the instrument for realizing the effects of his divine power in bodily things, *so also in spiritual things.* Hence the Blood of Christ shed for us had the power of washing away our sins. . .and so the *humanity of Christ is the instrumental cause of our justification. This cause is spiritually applied to us by means of faith, corporally by means of the sacraments, for the humanity of Christ is spirit and body*. . .Therefore, the most perfect of the sacraments is that in which the Body of Christ is really contained, i.e., the Eucharist, which as Dionysius says,[10] 'brings to perfection the act of all the other sacraments.' The other sacraments participate in some of that power through which the humanity of Christ instrumentally works our justification."[11]

And on the background of this ever-actual function of the glorious Body of Christ in the work of our salvation, all the other above-mentioned texts of St. Thomas are to be considered, in which he states that all the other sacraments are ordered to the Eucharist, that no one has grace before receiving it or at least wishing to receive it, and that in it is contained the whole mystery of our salvation.

And only on this background does one clearly understand the declaration of the Council that the liturgy is the summit and font of the entire supernatural life of the Church. If we seriously apply this principle, its practical consequences for the spiritual life and the pastoral and missionary work of the Church are tremendous. In these two fields of work, then, the Council points out that the liturgy as one element does not absorb and destroy all the others, but orders and informs them.

5 HISTORY OF SALVATION

From the general theological truths on the nature of the liturgy and its function in the life of the Church (Art. 5-13), the Constitution deduces the first general norm for any pastoral liturgical service and reform of the liturgy, namely to teach the people to live so great a treasure in a "full, conscious and active participation." This is the goal that we must never lose sight of. But still there is no hope of arriving at such results, "unless the pastors themselves, in the first place, become thoroughly imbued with the spirit and power of the liturgy, and undertake to give instruction about it" (Art. 14). Herein lies the prime need for the liturgical formation of the clergy (Art. 15-19). It is time then that professors of liturgy are prepared for their task in specialized schools (Art. 15).

There is also the crucial question of the manner of teaching the liturgy (Art. 16). It is not so much a question of knowing if the liturgy is to be treated as a principal or secondary subject in the curriculum, as the Constitution decrees, but rather of the spirit in which it is to be studied and taught.

To let the teaching of the liturgy consist almost entirely in an explanation of the rubrics, or at any rate of the juridical aspects implied, is an anachronism that hopefully no professor will ever again be guilty of. But neither is a historical study enough. An integral concept of the liturgy is needed, and as such it is to be taught within a proper theological, spiritual and pastoral context, as the Constitution states so well.

Even this does not exhaust the subject. The Constitution rightly thinks that for the purpose of leading students of theology to that penetration of the liturgy which is demanded by its objective role in the life of the Church, no less important than the direct teaching of the liturgy itself, is the introduction of a new manner of conceiving all theology, and in the first place, dogma, exegesis, spiritual and pastoral theology.

"Moreover other professors, while striving to expound the mystery of Christ and the history of salvation from the angle proper to each of their own subjects, must nevertheless do so in a way which will clearly bring out the connection between their subjects and the liturgy, as also the unity which underlies all priestly training. This consideration is specially important for professors of dogmatic, ascetical and pastoral theology and for those of holy scripture" (Art. 16).

How important is this step? Here we are touching the very serious theoretical and practical problem of the function of the liturgy in seeking unity in priestly formation, a very necessary task at present, and of the role of the other theological disciplines in molding a liturgical spirit.

The question of the unity of priestly formation in relation to the manner of conceiving and teaching the various branches of theology is a serious one. Who is not aware of the fact that students hardly ever come to perceive this unity, and how as a result their intellectual, spiritual and pastoral formation suffers a grave loss? In dogma, students are not taught to uncover the great biblical, liturgical, spiritual and pastoral themes. In Sacred Scripture courses, dogmatic, liturgical, spiritual and pastoral perspectives are not sufficiently called to their attention. And the same is true of the other courses.

Instead, the Constitution affirms two things. In the first place, there really exists a basic unity among the various branches of theology, especially among dogma, Scripture, liturgy, spiritual and pastoral theology. This unity is not something extrinsic to the individual subjects and must not be artificially imposed—no matter how noble the spiritual and pastoral goals may be—but something intrinsic and natural, demanded by the very exigencies of the proper object of each discipline. How so? Every discipline of a unified theology must actually in its own way explain "the mystery of Christ and the history of salvation."

Note well that here we are not treating two different things, but only one, namely the history of salvation rooted in the mystery of Christ or the mystery of Christ as the history of salvation. This identification between the mystery of Christ and the history of salvation is, for that matter, explicitly made by the Constitution in Article 35, 2 in reference to preaching. It is stated that the sermon be a "proclamation of God's wonderful works in the history of salvation or in the mystery of Christ ever made present and active within us, especially in the celebration of the liturgy." Therefore according to the Constitution, it suffices that the individual theological disciplines, each according to the intrinsic demands of its special object and proper method, pay sufficient attention to the history of salvation, because all of them are intimately coupled together with it. The explanation of each branch contributes to the understanding of all the others, so much so that it would seem necessary to reach such a full understanding each time.

Secondly, for forming a liturgical spirit in the students, it suffices according to the Constitution, that the history of salvation be given proper emphasis in all of theology, for then dogma, Scripture, spiritual and pastoral theology, and of course liturgy itself will contribute greatly to the formation of such a spirit. Moreover, the liturgy, embracing the time from the Ascension of the Lord to his glorious return, will then appear connaturally as the centermost fact here below, for whose understanding all other disciplines are in some manner ordained. In doing this, of course, the indispensable autonomy and proper method of each is to be preserved and all confusion resulting from any overlapping of one into the field of the other is to be avoided.

All this logically supposes that nature of the liturgy and that specific function in the Church's life which the Constitution itself outlines in Articles 5-13. In fact, how else is the liturgy to be understood in these articles if not as a concrete actualization through sacred signs of the history of salvation centered on the mystery of Christ, present and active in us? For that is the mystery which the Bible announces, dogma systematically and synthetically presents in its depth, spiritual theology teaches to be lived and pastoral theology transmits to men. If this is true, the liturgy is nothing else than dogma experienced in its most sacred moments, the Bible prayed, the spirituality of the Church in its most characteristic act, the summit and font of pastoral activity.

Naturally, then, without really invading the field of any other branch of ecclesiastical learning, liturgical science plays an important role in the formation of the priest as the science which today most concretely crystallizes the profound reality of the history of salvation, a subject to be treated by all the branches of theology, each in its own way.

Even more so, that profound reality must constitute the primary object of preaching. Thus we see the sacred history of salvation as the mystery ever present and active in us, that effectively unites not only all ecclesiastical learning, but also all ecclesiastical activities. Thus the Council itself points out the way to find this much-desired deeper unity of dogmatic, biblical, spiritual and pastoral science with the practical life of the Church. And in all this we see the unmistakable mark of the liturgy.

These are not inferences, but explicit affirmations of the Council. In fact, the Council says in the text already cited from Article 35, 2 in reference to preaching: "The sermon, moreover, should draw its content mainly from scriptural and liturgical sources, and its character should be that of a proclamation of God's wonderful works in the history of salvation or in the mystery of Christ ever made present and active within us, especially in the celebration of the liturgy."

Pan-liturgism in theology too, over and above that already in the Church's life? No, though all theological learning is to be clearly ordered to a profound insight into a primary fact of the existential order, namely, the mystery of Christ present and operative first of all in the sacred rites and as the dynamic center of the history of salvation.

Perhaps some one will say: but is not the object of theology God himself? Certainly, but God himself as he shows himself to us, principally and first of all, not in a purely abstract non-temporal light, but as concretely involved in the historical existential fact of the salvation of mankind *in Christ Jesus,* which as often repeated, today crystallizes itself above all in the sacred rites.

In this way, God manifests himself to us in the revelation-history of salvation. Christ-Church-liturgy are, in the realm of history, inseparable realities. And it is always necessary to return to this concept. For these are realities of historical, existential order. And to perceive them fully and see them in their unity, theology must not only analyze them in their ontological, abstract, non-temporal aspects, but must, moreover, *expound the history of salvation,* as the Constitution states.

To understand this need is of capital importance for renewing theology and refinding that deep unity among dogmatic theology, Sacred Scripture, the theology of the Fathers, spiritual life, liturgy and pastorals. Perhaps this is the basic concern of all the theological labor we witness today. And primary too for that ecumenical dialogue so characteristic of our times. Exaggerations of liturgists? Yes, at first contact many were inclined to think so, those who heard these things for the first time in the discussions of the first session of the Council, and only then began to take serious note (and God knows with what great fears and suspicions) of the liturgical movement, as well as of the ecumenical, pastoral, theological and particularly of the ecclesiological movement. The ecumenical value of this question is evident from the fact that the Constitution on the liturgy had its effect at that moment when the *history of salvation* was given first place in the concept of theology. Doesn't this point out at the same time the central position that liturgical reality must occupy in the theological perspective?

In the memorable audience that the observers of non-Catholic confessions at the Council had with Paul VI, Professor Skydsgaard, speaking in the name of all, said to the Pope among other things that this hoped-for union calls for many conditions, certainly not yet wholly mature. And he continued, "Permit me in this regard to point out a fact that seems to me of extreme importance. I am thinking of the function of a biblical theology, which concentrates on a study of the history of salvation both in the Old and in the New Testament. The more we progress in understanding the secret and paradoxical history of the People of God, the more we begin to understand the Church of Christ both in its mystery and in its historical existence and unity. Permit me also, Your Holiness, to express our living hope that the light of such a concrete and historical theology nourished by the Bible and the teaching of the Fathers, may shine more clearly in the work of this Council."

In his answer the Pope stressed that "to this development of a concrete and historical theology which you look forward to, we willingly subscribe as to our own, and the suggestion appears to us entirely worthy of being studied and thoroughly penetrated. The Catholic Church already possesses such institutes and nothing prevents them from specializing further in this kind of research, or also creating a new institute with this purpose if the circumstances warrant it."

Naturally this is not a question of creating a new discipline along with so many others already existing, but rather of permeating all those already existing with an outlook that from the time of the Scholastics, they have neglected too much, and of instructing each of them to consider its proper object on the background of this perspective, namely, precisely that of the history of salvation.

To view this perspective in its natural setting, the liturgy is indispensable. For today the history of salvation is really focused in the prism of the liturgy, even if its rays come from the Old Testament and especially from Christ, and reach out toward the heavenly Jerusalem. The Constitution itself gives us more than one excellent example, expecially in the introduction and in the first part of the first chapter, of this manner of seeing the togetherness of revelation on the background of the history of salvation. In this regard it is worthwhile noting the prominence the Constitution gives to the trinitarian view of the plan of the divine Persons *ad extra* within the general background of Christ *sacrament* and of the Church *sacrament*. In this view everything comes from the Father —who initiated the plan and prepared its execution in the Old Testament—through the mission of the Incarnate Son and the indwelling of the Holy Spirit in us. Christ, in whom is the fullness of the Holy Spirit, sends him to us, thereby taking us to himself and leading us back to the Father, that we may finally reach the heavenly Jerusalem. This viewpoint is everywhere present in Articles 5; 6; 8.

In this perspective the liturgy plays a key role in carrying out the plan of salvation, wished by the Father and prepared in the Old Testament. For the liturgy is a complex of sensible signs through which Christ, in sending the Holy Spirit to us, sanctifies men, unites them to himself and together with them renders perfect worship to God by bringing back everything to the Father. The notion is sufficiently delineated in the Constitution, even if it does not have that perfect clarity that could be desired due to the unfortunate elimination from the text of some happy expressions contained in preceding drafts that nicely pointed it out.

Let us look at an example of what it means to view everything on the background of salvation history, and what concrete emphasis is given to the things we are discussing and how on this basis it is not difficult to find a deep unity within Scripture, dogmatic theology, patristics, spirituality, pastorals and liturgy.

Here is a typical fact. This very manner of looking at the nature of the liturgy in its trinitarian, historical and concrete setting disturbed more than one Father, as was seen when the first chapter was discussed. More than one requested that this "nebulous" manner of speaking be abandoned and that the first chapter begin instead with a clear formal definition of the liturgy—as is done in every good manual—and then from such a definition everything necessary for the liturgical reform could be systematically deduced.

Two different viewpoints? Basically, yes. Of course, no one denies the need for clear ideas of things. We simply hold that the presentation of a thing in its abstract notion without taking account of its concrete historical aspect, is to put it in a light that does not permit one to see all the aspects and all the riches the fact possesses. Anyway it is evident that the Council already in the Constitution on the liturgy opted for a view of things revealed, and of the liturgy itself, within the setting of the *history of salvation*.

6 PASCHAL MYSTERY

Setting the liturgy within the reality of the *sacrament* and the *history of salvation* has among other happy consequences that of giving great prominence to the paschal mystery in the Constitution. In it the paschal mystery always appears as the pivotal concept of salvation history. This assures it of a prominent place in the liturgy.

The paschal mystery in its liturgical concept, which is that of St. Paul and the Fathers, indicates a complex reality, historical and actual, which concerns Christ and concerns us and in some way the whole world.

In Christ the paschal mystery means the fact that he by accepting the death on the cross in obedience to the Father, not only obtained pardon from God for us, but also merited that his own human nature including his body overcame the state of the *form of a slave* and of death—consequences of sin to which he subjected himself in becoming man—and was enthroned in the glory of the risen Lord, *Kyrios,* to whom all created things are subject as to the one giver of life. This life he now communicates to us primarily through the sacraments.

For us, the paschal mystery means that primarily through the sacraments we actually receive from the sacred humanity of the glorious Christ, the instrument of his divinity, that influx of divine life, whose fullness is had in the sacred humanity of Christ. This divine life makes us pass over or more completely pass over spiritually and physically from death to divine life, by conforming us to the dead and resurrected Christ unto that perfect assimilation which will come to be in the glorious resurrection of our bodies also.

All these things taken together in their inseparable unity make up the paschal mystery. The paschal mystery as operative in the liturgy and the sacraments is continually present in the Constitution, at times in its totality, then again in some aspect or other. For instance, the first chapter speaks of the redemptive work of Christ (Art. 5), of the essential object of the apostolic message as well as the sacred functions of baptism and the Eucharist (Art. 6); the second chapter looks at Communion under the concept of the paschal meal (Art. 47); the third chapter says "from the paschal mystery of the passion, death and resurrection of Christ the font from which all sacraments and sacramentals draw their power" (Art. 61), and it hopes that "the rite for the burial of the dead should express more clearly the paschal character of Christian death" (Art. 81). Finally, the fourth chapter insistently and repeatedly inculcates that the efficacious celebration of the paschal mystery is the central object of all Christian feasts and must therefore have first place in our attention and in catechetical instruction (Art. 102-111).

This insistence on the paschal mystery also took more than one Council Father by surprise. Was not one of them, and not the least of them, heard to express his surprise that the paschal mystery would be so exalted, as if, he said, there were no other mysteries of the Lord's life, and first among them his birth and death? And did not another, a noted theologian, declare that he could not hold that the sacraments draw their power from 'the paschal mystery of the passion, death and resurrection of Christ,' since, he said, the passion and death alone are meritorious? These are eloquent testimonies of how much has been forgotten of the Pauline, liturgical and patristic concept of the paschal mystery, and we may add, of the teaching of St. Thomas on the efficient and exemplary, even if not meritorious, causality of Christ's resurrection in our justification. A deplorable consequence of such forgetfulness is the lack of understanding of the thoroughly paschal significance of the sacraments, especially of baptism and the Eucharist, and also of all life and Christian spirituality.

Who today will help us rediscover that concrete and unitary sense of all history and of the entire life of the Church and individual souls *in the dead and risen Christ,* which was the meaning that St. Paul and the Fathers had of it? We will find it only if we follow the spirit of the liturgy according to the wish of the Council.

7 SACRIFICE OF THE CHURCH

It is evident that the Constitution when speaking of the Eucharist—and it speaks a little of it everywhere—gives first preference to the sacrifice of Christ and the Church in its relation to the paschal mystery taken in its full meaning as explained above. This picture of the Eucharist appears in detail in Articles 6 and 7, where the nature of the liturgy in general is treated, and in Articles 47 and 48, which serve as a theoretical introduction to the general norms for the reform of the Mass rite.

The Eucharist is the sacrifice not only of Christ but also of the Church, of the whole Church and not only of the hierarchy but also of the *People of God,* of that Church which is the "sacrament of unity—namely the holy people united and ordered under their bishops" (Art. 26). And this is the reason why the Constitution insists so much that the people participate in the eucharistic sacrifice with that active and full participation which is the goal of pastoral liturgy.

"The Church, therefore, earnestly desires that those who have faith in Christ, when present at this mystery of faith, should not be there as strangers or silent spectators; on the contrary, through an adequate understanding of the rites and prayers they should take part in the sacred action, conscious of what they are doing, with devotion and full collaboration. They should be instructed by God's word and be nourished at the table of the Lord's Body; they should give thanks to God; by offering the immaculate victim not only through the hands of the priest, but also with him, they should learn to offer themselves; through Christ their Mediator, they should be drawn day by day into ever more perfect union with God and with each other, so that finally God may be all in all" (Art. 48).

First of all, it is a sacrificial banquet, for it ends with consuming the Victim. In a rite of this kind, those who have participated in the sacrifice, bring their participation to an ideally perfect degree, supposing of course complete conformity of mind and life. "The eucharistic sacrifice of the body and blood of the Lord" (Art. 47), then, is a paschal meal, "the table of the Lord's body" (Art. 48), the "Lord's supper" and "the breaking of bread." For this reason the Constitution insistently recommends that Holy Communion be, in the first place, a participation in the sacrifice through partaking of the Divine Victim.

In this respect, the recommendation of Article 55 is characteristic.

That the ritual significance of Holy Communion as a participation in the sacrifice at which one assists, be realized in a psychologically more perfect manner, the faithful are exhorted to communicate not only during the Mass at which they participate, but also to do so at the proper ritual moment, that is, after the communion of the priest. Furthermore they should communicate at the same sacrifice at which they participate, that is, with hosts consecrated each time at the same Mass at which they assist. This manner of participating at the Mass is called "more perfect." "That more perfect form of participation in the Mass whereby the faithful, after the priest's communion, receive the Lord's body from the same sacrifice, is strongly commended."

This text did not please all the Fathers. Some of them would have liked to remove the words "strongly commended"; others would strike out the expression "perfect form of participation"; and finally others wished to remove the clause "from the same sacrifice." The compilers of the document, however, could easily answer that they were doing nothing but taking over the teaching of Benedict XIV,[12] of Pius XII[13] and the Instruction of the Congregation of Rites of September 3, 1958.[14]

8 DON'T CREATE USELESS DIFFICULTIES FOR THE PEOPLE

So much has already been said for the purpose of illustrating the pastoral and theological spirit which animates the Constitution on the Liturgy. Now what is the spirit that pervades its wonderful directives for a practical reform of the same?

We can say in a word that the fundamental wish of the Council in this matter is to make the liturgy again genuine and authentic throughout. That means doing not only within a pastoral framework that is psychologically, didactically and socially efficacious what best corresponds to the complex integral purposes to which by its very nature it must correspond. But also the liturgy as a complex of signs—word signs, thing signs, and gesture signs—must express a sacred reality in such a way that the people by means of them perceive and take full part in it. So to have an authentic liturgy practically means to have a liturgy in which texts and rites and such signs express the sacred reality which they signify so clearly that the people can without undue difficulty fully identify themselves with them. "Without undue difficulty" means those not demanded by the very transcendence of divine things. In fact, only the difficulties necessarily connected with such transcendence cannot be avoided, for the very purpose of the liturgy is to elevate the people to such heights.

This fundamental principle of the reform is explicitly expressed in Article 21: "In this restoration, both texts and rites should be drawn up so that they express more clearly the holy things which they signify; the Christian people, so far as is possible, should be enabled to understand them with ease and take part in them fully, actively and as befits a community."

This fundamental principle implies a rethinking of those aspects of the nature of the liturgy from which one can more exactly grasp what must be its structure, for the liturgy must truly serve the people. There are principally three such aspects, namely a hierarchically structured community character, a didactic pastoral character, and adaptability to the talents and traditions of various peoples. Hence the Constitution strongly confirms these three characteristics of the liturgy. From each of them it deduces a series of practical norms which must serve as a guide to the reform of the texts and rites. The deep spirit of this section is clearly expressed in the following basic texts that constitute the very heart of the *Magna Carta* of liturgical reform.

"Liturgical services are not private functions, but are celebrations of the Church, which is 'the sacrament of unity'—namely 'the holy people united and ordered under their bishops.'

"Therefore liturgical services pertain to the whole body of the Church; they manifest it and have effects upon it; but they concern the individual members of the Church in different ways, according to their differing rank, office and activity" (Art. 26).

"Although the sacred liturgy is above all things the worship of the divine majesty, it nevertheless contains much instruction for the faithful. For in the liturgy God speaks to his people and Christ is still proclaiming his gospel. And the people reply to God by both song and prayer.

"Moreover the prayers addressed to God by the priest who presides over the assembly in the person of Christ, are said in the name of the entire holy people and of all present. And the visible signs used by the liturgy to signify invisible divine things have been chosen by Christ or his Church. Thus not only when things are read 'which were written for our instruction' (Rom. 15, 4), but also when the Church prays or sings or acts, the faith of those taking part is nourished and their minds are raised to God, so that they may offer him their rational service and more abundantly receive his grace" (Art. 33).

"Even in the liturgy, the Church has no wish to impose a rigid uniformity in matters which do not implicate the faith or the good of the whole community; rather does she respect and foster the genius and talents of the various races and nations. Anything in these peoples' way of life which is not indissolubly bound up with superstition and error she studies with sympathy, and, if possible, preserves intact. Sometimes she even admits such things into the liturgy itself, so long as they harmonize with its true and authentic spirit" (Art. 37).

All are statements of great clarity, great courage and intrepid dynamism. It could be called the declaration of the pastoral rights and duties of the liturgy. The fact that an Ecumenical Council has solemnly proclaimed these principles together with those basic ones of liturgical theology mentioned above constitutes the perfect triumph of the liturgical movement—a triumph for which so many pioneers, whom we justly remember here with gratitude, have worked and even suffered.

What are the specific consequences of these principles? They are vast and numerous. Here are a number of more typical examples.

From the community nature of the liturgy is inferred the norm that, for the most part, where the rites permit, a community celebration with an active participation of the people should be preferred to a more or less private one (Art. 27). In these celebrations each should do everything and only that which pertains to him without renunciations and without usurpations (Art. 28). The active participation of the whole congregation of the people needs to be promoted in word, song, community actions and attitudes (Art. 30). The "prayer of the faithful" in particular should be restored in the Mass (Art. 53). Polyphony should not be permitted to the detriment of active community participation (Art. 113) and popular religious songs should be seriously promoted (Art. 118).

From the didactic pastoral character of the liturgy is inferred a series of norms prescribing simplicity and perspicacity in the rites (Art. 34); prescribing a more abundant, more varied and more appropriate choice of biblical readings, both for the liturgy as a whole (Art. 35, 1) and for the Mass in particular (Art. 51) and for the divine office (Art. 92; prescribing the necessity of the homily (Art. 35, 2; 52), catechetical instructions including strictly liturgical instructions (Art. 35, 3), the importance of Bible services in the liturgy (Art. 35, 4), and especially the necessity of introducing a broader use of the vernacular in the liturgy both in general (Art. 36) and for the Mass in particular (Art. 54) for the sacraments and sacramentals (Art. 63), for the divine office (Art. 100) and for singing (Art. 113).

From the obligation of adapting the liturgy to the talents and traditions of the people are inferred practical norms concerning the necessity of providing a wider margin of liberty for local adaptations in the "typical" editions of Roman liturgical books (Art. 38; 39). In particular, the possibility is foreseen of even more radical adaptations of the Roman rite itself, where that would be deemed necessary, principally in mission countries, presupposing the initiative of the local bishops and the permission of the Holy See (Art. 40). This ultimately implies the possibility of setting out on new paths in certain cases, slowly and prudently but firmly toward the formation of new rites.

From the same adaptability of the liturgy, the practical norm is set up, of no small importance for sacred music and sacred art, especially in mission countries, that the Church "approves of all forms of true art having the needed qualities, and admits them into divine worship" (Art. 112; see also Art. 119 and 120).

In the course of the discussions, more than one, who, to speak the truth, was not much imbued with the spirit of the liturgy, believed that in this there was, now a daring revolutionary spirit of change, then again a desire to restore the ancient for love of the antique. The accusation of "the itch for novelties" and archaism often came to the surface.

As a matter of fact, the Council does not do the one nor the other, but simply takes seriously the maxim; *the salvation of souls is the highest law* and the practical norm "that sound tradition may be retained, and yet the way remain open to legitimate progress" (Art. 23).

9 LEAVE THE DOOR OPEN

There is no doubt that the Constitution gives the final blow to the prevalent excessively juridical and rubrical, even inflexible concept of the liturgy, which has been prevalent since the Council of Trent and the creation of the Congregation of Rites (1588).

The liturgy is a living and vital thing for real human beings. Such is the great proclamation of the Council, a happy consequence of its pastoral aim. Hence the Council has wished to affirm a spirit, open a road, and so it was on its guard against an attitude that could have consisted in making a few concessions and then again hermetically sealing all doors.

Once resolutely embarked on the theological and pastoral way of considering the liturgy, many and distant prospects, not all yet attainable nor perhaps now appropriate, opened up to the Council. Its watchword has been to proceed prudently, without deciding anything in haste where experience and the evolution of ideas and things is undoubtedly required, but also without closing as a matter of principle (*a priori*) any doors to future development.

Typical in this regard is its attitude, mentioned above, in the question of those possible, more radical adaptations of the Roman liturgy to the talents and traditions of the people in mission lands; adaptations which perhaps could bring to some regions not merely a marginal alteration of the Roman rite, but also the creation of new rites more or less drawn from it. In these matters the Council does not allow anyone at all, not even bishops or Episcopal Conferences, to set out right away on their own, but neither is it afraid of this possibility for it simply states:

"In some places and circumstances, however, an even more radical adaptation of the liturgy is needed, and this entails greater difficulties. Wherefore:

"(1) The competent local ecclesiastical authority mentioned in Article 22, 2, must, in this matter, carefully and prudently consider which elements from the traditions and culture of each of these peoples might appropriately be admitted into the liturgy. Adaptations which seem useful or necessary should then be submitted to the Holy See, by whose consent they may be introduced" (Art. 40, 1).

"To ensure that adaptations may be made with all the circumspection which they demand, the Holy See will grant power to this same authority to permit and direct, over a determined period of time and among certain groups specially suited for the purpose, whatever preliminary experiments may be deemed necessary" (Art. 40, 2).

The possibility of recognizing new rites within the Church beyond those existing today is included according to an authentic declaration of the relator on the meaning of the phrase of Article 4, "that Holy Mother Church holds all lawfully acknowledged rites to be of equal right and dignity." She has not wished to preclude the eventual recognition, for example of an Anglican Catholic rite within the Church.

Not less characteristic is the attitude of the Constitution toward the use of the vernacular in the liturgy. It did not wish to oblige anyone to adopt it by making a general law. But thereby, it does not exclude every possibility for those who feel it is necessary and want it. The formulation of Article 36, 2 is very elastic: "But since the use of the mother tongue is frequently of great advantage to the people in the Mass . . . the limits of its employment may be extended. This will apply in the first place to the readings and directives, and to some of the prayers and chants." No less so is that of Article 54 which specifically speaks of the vernacular in the Mass: "In those Masses which are celebrated with the people, a suitable place may be allotted to their mother tongue. This is to apply in the first place to the readings and 'Prayer of the Faithful,' but also, as local conditions may warrant, to those items of the liturgy which pertain to the people."

Also in the recitation of the divine office the use of the vernacular offers wide possibilities for those who want it: first of all for cloistered nuns and members of the institutes of perfection (Art. 101, 2), also for the clergy, first of all, when they recite it in choir with nuns or members of the institutes of perfection or with "a group of the faithful." I believe a few of the faithful can already be considered a *group,* and I think three is enough, since "three make a group." Secondly, in private recitation there are not a few possibilities of obtaining a dispensation in individual cases from the ordinary (Art. 101, 1).

Likewise, for liturgical chant in the vernacular and more so for popular religious songs, the possibilities are vast (Art. 113, 115). The Council in no way paid attention to the insistence of those who would have wished to sanction by law a solemn and perpetual prohibition of an adaptation of Gregorian chant to any vernacular whatsoever.

And if polyphony is allowed by the Constitution, it is under the express condition that it is in accord "with the spirit of the liturgical action as laid down in Article 30" (Art. 116). Now Article 30 reads: "To promote active participation, the people should be encouraged to take part by means of acclamations, responses, psalmody, antiphons and hymns, as well as by actions, gestures and bodily attitude. And at the proper times all should observe a reverent silence." This declaration clearly reechoes the real spirit of active, full and communal participation of the people in the sacred rites, so dear to the Constitution. It is no less evident that the doors are anything but closed to a serious reexamination of the theory and practice of polyphony in some of our surroundings.

In a special way, magnificent is the prospect opened to sacred and liturgical art by the solemn declaration of independence in Article 123 (cf. also Art. 113):

"The Church has not adopted any particular style of art as her very own. She has admitted styles from every period according to the natural dispositions and circumstances of her peoples, and the needs of the various rites. Thus, in the course of the centuries, she has amassed a treasury of art which must be very carefully preserved. The art of our own days coming from every race and region, is also to be given free scope provided that it adorns the sacred buildings and holy rites with due reverence and honor; thereby it is enabled to contribute its own voice to that wonderful chorus of praise in honor of the Catholic faith sung by great men in times gone by."

There are other examples of this spirit of the Council of not closing the doors to further developments in fields of no little importance. The three cases expressly cited in Article 55, in which Communion under both forms may be granted, at ordinations, religious professions and the Baptism of adults, do not comprise an exhaustive enumeration, but are only examples which do not entirely exclude other instances. In particular, the granting of this privilege by the Holy See for the spouses at the nuptial Mass is not excluded. So many good reasons suggest this and were not at the time taken into consideration due to an unfortunate accumulation of circumstances during the revision of the text.

And for the rest, once the ice of the actually rigid practices of the Latin rite is broken, and once we have some experience in the distribution of Communion under both forms, even for the laity, under the form of dipping a part of the host in the precious Blood, probably the rite will not appear quite so strange and dangerous as it seemed to so many Latin bishops for the sole reason that they had no practice.[14a]

The same could happen for concelebration. Anyway it is already permitted and in broad terms. One sees this especially in Article 57, 2 b: "at Mass celebrated at any kind of priests' meetings whether the priests be secular or religious." To deny that those words naturally lend themselves to a very broad interpretation is not easy.

The spirit of the Constitution is not at all static but, for the most part, open in areas of greater importance, to further developments which the mind of the liturgy suggests and which perhaps the good of the Church will specify ever more clearly in the near future. Of course, here more than anywhere else, the interpretation of the Constitution will depend very much on the post-conciliar Commission, charged with the reform, and the Roman Congregation which must put this spirit in effect after the reform is completed.

10 RELAXATION OF RIGID UNIFORMITY AND CENTRALIZATION

Another not insignificant point of the spirit of the Constitution is that of leaving to the jurisdiction of the bishops within the boundaries of their territorial competence some notable powers in liturgical matters.

Thus some pontifical reservations put into effect principally after the Council of Trent for the common good of the Church in specific historical situations are being done away with. Actually in various western regions, the end of the Middle Ages presented a scene of veritable anarchy in liturgical matters, due to the uncontrolled proliferation of so many local variations, often not in good taste. Moreover, the Protestant revolt often used the arm of liturgical reform—certainly necessary at the time—for inciting local authorities to carry on without Rome, as a means of introducing dogmatic innovations which corrupted the faith itself in its very foundation. In such circumstances it is understandable that the See to which by divine mandate was entrusted the supreme task of safeguarding the unity of the Church and the purity of Faith, then took steps in the liturgical field to ensure uniformity, which of course led to centralization in the liturgical field.

But today the danger of Protestantism has been overcome. And if in recent years the Latin Church has sinned in the liturgical field, it has not been through excessive and undesirable regional variations, but rather through excessive uniformity, which did not take sufficient note of various local needs. The matter is clear, if we look at the liturgical situation of the new Churches in mission lands, the good fruit of post-tridentine missionary expansion. This is why the Constitution, even if under pressure from the young Churches in mission lands, has undeniably taken a step toward the relaxation of rigid liturgical uniformity and consequently of post-Tridentine centralization.

On the other hand, in the drafting of the texts there has always been a lively desire to be on guard against reopening thereby the road to the liturgical anarchy of the late Middle Ages. Such precautions are all the more necessary, since there is already in some countries more than one symptom of impatience, which urges ordinary priests to introduce on their own authority those changes in the liturgy that they deem opportune. Movements of this kind every true liturgist desires to be blocked both for theoretical and practical reasons. Among other inconveniences, these abuses serve as flimsy pretexts for some who have not yet opened their eyes to the true nature of the liturgical movement, to continue in their indifference. Therefore, the problem consisted in finding a well-balanced formula.

The position of the Council can be summed up in three points. The first is the proclamation of the general principle that the liturgy, far from seeking a rigid uniformity in things that do not touch the faith or the common good of the whole Church, must leave a proper margin of liberty for local needs (Art. 37). And this principle holds not only in extreme cases such as can be verified in certain countries, especially in the missions, in which the problem of adaptation is so critical as to give rise to the question of profoundly changing the Roman rite (Art. 40), but also in more ordinary cases, in which the substantial retention of the rite is not in question. In view of these cases:

"Provision is to be made, when revising the liturgical books, for the legitimate variations and adaptations to different groups, regions and peoples, especially in the missions, provided always that the substantial unity of the Roman rite is preserved; and this should be borne in mind when drawing up the rites and devising rubrics for them" (Art. 38).

In other words, this means that in some points of the rites and texts, the official books of the Roman rite itself must foresee the possibility of providing various choices that are more adaptable to a given situation as may seem more opportune. This possibility is already foreseen by the Constitution itself in not a few cases of no little importance, for example, in the question of the use of the vernacular in the rites of baptism (Art. 68) and of matrimony (Art. 77).

But to whom does the choice of possible alternates pertain? To the celebrant? To individual bishops? The question can be reformulated in the following way. When the Holy See has renounced its right of imposing the same solution on all, to whom is the authority of deciding entrusted?

Without doubt, the original authority of regulating the liturgy for the universal Church resides in the Holy See alone, and in individual bishops for their own territory, excepting those cases that the same Apostolic See may reserve to herself for the common good. So it is explicitly stated in Article 22, 1: "Regulation of the sacred liturgy depends solely on the authority of the Church—which means on the Apostolic See, and, as laws may determine, on the bishops."

Now could it be left to the individual bishops, even if limited to the cases foreseen, to decide henceforth as might appear better to them? At once, there would reappear symptoms of anarchy. In as far as liturgy and pastorals are intimately united and given the ever-growing ease of communication and the mobility and intermingling of the population, so many questions on the care of souls can now no longer be solved on a purely diocesan level but require that decisions be made on at least a regional if not on a national level.

That is why the Council when speaking above of liturgical decentralization has often decided not in favor of individual bishops, but in favor of territorial groups of bishops legitimately organized in episcopal conferences. This principle is formulated in Article 22, 2: "In virtue of authority conceded by law, the regulation of the liturgy within certain defined limits belongs also to various kinds of local bishops' conferences, legitimately established." So from time to time, provincial synods and regional episcopal conferences can be convened.

Why is not the Constitution more precise? The simplest solution here would have been to indicate national episcopal conferences. If the Constitution did not do so, but has purposely chosen a more elastic formula, the simple reason is that national episcopal conferences everywhere today are not only very different structurally and operatively from country to country, but that they do not even have a determined juridical form, permitting them to make their decisions strictly obligatory on all their members. This is a question that must be decided by the schema "On Bishops and Government of Dioceses." The Constitution did not wish to anticipate matters.

If then in the single cases in which it speaks of "local bishops' conferences," the national episcopal conference or another territorial group of bishops is to be understood, there will have to be a precise determination of the matter by the schema "On Bishops" or more probably by the Holy See.

In any case, the power granted by the Constitution in matters liturgical to these territorial episcopal bodies for the sake of decentraliation and the local adaptations spoken of, is something very worthwhile. Ultimately, the decision pertains to them to use or not in their territories the permissions conceded by the Council concerning the use and extent of the vernacular in the liturgy together with the right of approving the corresponding translations (in Art. 36, 3-4 for the general principle; in Art. 54 for the Mass; in Art. 63 for the sacraments and sacramentals).

Likewise, they are to determine for their territories the adaptations of the liturgy within the limits established by the typical editions of liturgical books (Art. 39; 12;); to prepare bilingual rituals for the administration of the sacraments and sacramentals in their territories (Art. 63, b; 77); to examine, propose to the Holy See, and introduce with its consent other adaptations going beyond the permitted limits (Art. 40). In all these cases, the decisions made by the Conferences must be previously submitted to the Holy See and approved by it.[15]

Furthermore, the relaxation of liturgical centralization in favor of local adaptations is sufficiently evident from the fact that the Constitution grants to individual bishops or ordinaries the free exercise of certain faculties. The granting of such faculties conforms to the known tendencies of the Council to give greater prominence to the person of the bishop in the Church. In very many cases, individual bishops are to be the judges of the manner and extent to which the faculties granted by the Council must or can be used in their dioceses. These faculties include Communion under both forms (Art. 55), concelebration (Art. 57), organizing a catechumenate (Art. 64), the use of some rites in baptism (Art. 68), the administration of confirmation during Mass (Art. 71), the use of the vernacular in the admonitions at ordinations (Art. 76), permitting qualified members of the laity the right to administer some of the sacramentals (Art. 79), commutation of the obligation of reciting the divine office (Art. 97), permitting individual priests to recite the office in the vernacular (Art. 101, 2), granting to nuns and members of other Institutes of Perfection the choral recitation of the office in the vernacular (Art. 101, 2), promoting and watching over all forms of sacred art in their dioceses (Art. 124-130).

A third point that the Council could not fail to make is a severe admonition forbidding all private persons, even priests, to make any changes whatsoever on their own in liturgical rites and texts: "Therefore no other person, even if he be a priest, may add, remove or change anything in the liturgy on his own authority" (Art 22, 3).

11 ECUMENICAL SPIRIT

Above, in treating of the texts that speak of the Church within the background of the history of salvation, we saw that the spirit of these texts of the Constitution harmonize well with the ecumenical requirements for a dialogue with separated Christians. This important agreement was not at all directly premeditated with an ecumenical goal in mind, but simply one of the happy consequences of the fact that the theological ideology of the Constitution is abundantly nourished at the sources of the Bible, the Fathers, and the liturgy itself.

In other more specific points, however, the influence of ecumenism and the ecumenical goal has brought explicitly calculated results, or at least has been one of the determining motives of the decisions taken. That must be emphasized in order to better understand how much the liturgical Constitution reflects the more profound tendencies which were then manifested in the Council.

During the writing of the Constitution, a mixed group that represented the Secretariate for the Union of Christians and another that represented the liturgical Commission held several joint meetings. The Secretariate for Union, charged with closely watching that the Council keep in mind the ecumenical viewpoint, thus had the convenience of expressing its desires in the liturgical field, desires for the most part foreseen by the liturgists. Furthermore, during the discussion of the text on the Council floor and the subsequent making of amendments to the text, the ecumenical motive manifested itself anew in numerous questions.

For example, the solemn declaration of the Introduction—the first of its kind in an Ecumenical Council—on the equality of rights and dignity which all lawfully recognized rites have in the Church (Art. 4), has a direct ecumenical purpose. It is a statement directly opposed to the thesis of the superiority of the Latin rite, so dear to some since the time of Benedict XIV, for the sole reason that it is the rite of the Roman Church, and so more noble and more surely Catholic. This theory has so often served as a false basis for an unjustified latinization.

Secondly, the ecumenical aim—fully shared by the huge majority of the Council—was equally one of the major arguments in the drafting and in the discussions to which those appealed who wished to introduce a wider use of the vernacular in the Roman liturgy and restore to it Communion under both forms as well as concelebration.

Thirdly, notable is the importance given in the Constitution to readings, to solemn proclamations and to preaching the word of God contained in the scriptures together with the celebration of the sacrifice and the sacraments (Art. 35; 6; 9; 24; 48; 52; 56). "Bible services" were recommended without reservations as distinct liturgical rites (Art. 35, 4). In connection with the eucharistic table of the Lord they are referred to as the 'table of God's word.' In the Mass, too, a richer fare at the table of God's word should be provided for the faithful from the treasures of the Bible.

In all these points, the ecumenical aim made no small contribution. Especially in giving more liturgical importance to the Bible, the Council thereby wished to remove every pretext for the accusation that would like to see in Catholic worship a lack of perfect proportion between the celebration of the sacramental rites and the proclamation of the Word of God, between the objective aspects of the sacramental rite based on the act itself (*opus operatum*) and the action of the Church (*opus operantis Ecclesiae*) and the subjective aspect of man's correspondence to be roused through preaching, and between sacrament and faith.

One should also note the delicate ecumenical aim of the Council in its declaration on the reform of the calendar, put in the Appendix of the Constitution. The Council affirms that it "would not object if the feast of Easter were assigned to a particular Sunday of the Gregorian Calendar, provided that others whom it may concern, especially the brethren who are not in communion with the Holy See, are agreed on this matter" (n. 1).

12 WITHOUT DEFECTS

Finally, it is also for a good ecumenical reason that in the Constitution on the liturgy, on more than one occasion the use of scholastic formulas was avoided.

I say for a good ecumenical reason and on more than one occasion. For at times there was a similar influence much less praiseworthy. For in drawing up the text, some collaborators under the influence of a not too conscious nominalism and anticonceptualism which is today rather widespread in some countries, were seized with a holy horror of every formula that seemed to be scholastic. Such formulas because of their very clarity were labeled "conceptual theology" and "cartesianism." And they were inclined to eliminate them even when the "scholastic" formula alone clearly and briefly expressed what had to be said.

This affair gave rise to a curious difficulty in drafting the first chapter. In Article 5, where biblical and patristic expressions are used to explain the concept that Christ is the original *sacrament* of our salvation, there was a real struggle to know if it must be said that the humanity of Christ, in the unity of the person of the Word, was "the instrument or instrumental cause of our salvation," as the "scholastics" wished, or only the "cause of our salvation" as the "anti-conceptualists" wanted (for ecumenical motives, as they said).

At first the latter prevailed. Had the expression not been vigorously assaulted by the Fathers on the council floor, it would not have returned to that of "instrument." Only then was it accepted when the so-called scholastic formula was proven to be nothing more than the repetition of an expression in common use by the Fathers.

In another case, on the contrary, the result was less fortunate for the "scholastics," and I think not without some loss of clearness and depth in the doctrine of the Constitution. In the theological field of the liturgy, *Mediator Dei* had made some progress. Among other points, the question of the proper efficacy of the liturgy was officially clarified by introducing the distinction between the act itself and the action of the Church (*opus operatum, opus operantis Ecclesiae*) and the efficacy coming primarily from the personal disposition of the minister or those who received the sacraments or the sacramentals.

The concept of the action of the Church (*opus operantis Ecclesiae*) is indispensable for understanding the proper efficacy of the liturgy instituted by the Church, and therefore for correctly evaluating the place of the liturgy in its entirety in the Church's life. But the expression has a scholastic flavor! And that is true. That, too, was enough for stirring up the insistent opposition of the anti-conceptualists in the name of "ecumenism." And the expression was eliminated from the Constitution.

The result—the concept itself of the particular efficacy of the liturgy in virtue of the *opus operatum* and the *opus operantis Ecclesiae* remains without prominence and obscure in the Constitution. They tried to render it with the following words: "every liturgical celebration. . .is a sacred action surpassing all others; no other action of the Church can equal its efficacy by the same title and to the same degree" (Art. 7).

To understand this text it is necessary to refer to the official explanation of the relator in his answer to the *modi,* in which he had to speak of the *opus operatum* and the *opus operantis Ecclesiae*.

"The efficacy of the sacrifice and the sacraments is *ex opere operato;* the efficacy of the public prayer and the sacramentals *ex opere operantis Ecclesiae*. This efficacy is said to be of the highest degree, a statement frequently adduced in the documents of the Magisterium, and it is distinguished from other actions whether of the Church itself or its members under this very aspect of the efficacy of the actions, prescinding, of course, for the merit and communion of saints, which is an entirely different matter." On this precise point we must then hold that the Constitution in comparison with *Mediator Dei* is rather a regression than a progression.

I have used this concrete example—and there are others even if not so important—to make it understood that in sincerely thinking that the Constitution is a great gift of God to his Church, liturgists do not wish to say that it is such a perfect document that a more perfect one could not exist.

The fact that the texts of the II Vatican Council are the fruit of most extensive, truly worldwide cooperation is an enormous advantage. But at times, such representation entails a certain disadvantage, namely the texts pass often through too many hands; they lack at times a unified structure in their redaction, and not seldom are the fruit of so many compromises. Perhaps, notwithstanding everything, the Constitution on the liturgy suffers less than others through these deficiencies.

13 CONCLUSION

The Constitution on the liturgy of the II Vatican Council is first of all the fruit of 55 years of the liturgical movement. This movement, at last, thanks particularly to its deep theological research and to its ultimate connection with pastorals, has everywhere taken not only numerous but deep roots.

For one of the forces of the liturgical movement has been that of being a movement from the grass roots and from the outside. When under the influence of private individuals it was accepted, evaluated and directed by those in authority, its momentum was already formidable. This is well seen from the acceptance the Constitution found in the Council. This is well seen, for example, from the support which the missionary bishops in their great majority have given it.

And due to this fact it is not pure chance that the Constitution on the liturgy was the first to be promulgated by the Council. The first draft basically corresponded to the deep aspirations and hopes of the majority of the Fathers, while, on the contrary, the first draft of the theological schemas, which should have been the first to pass, were instead sent back to the Commission for a complete redoing.

Therefore we can say that in the history of the liturgy the emancipation from the Tridentine epoch began with the beginning of the liturgical movement in 1909. From 1909 to 1963 there was an epoch of transition, of labor, of struggle, and of successive conquests, the most memorable of them were the liturgical reforms of Pius XII.

On December 4, 1963 the profound spirit of the liturgical movement was definitively approved and solemnly sanctioned by an Ecumenical Council. All this then leads one to believe that with December 4, 1963 a new liturgical era has definitely dawned.

What will be the spirit of this new era? If the Constitution of Vatican II is not to remain a dead letter—God forbid—this spirit must be that of a profound compenetration of liturgical theology, liturgical spirituality, liturgical pastorals, in the mind, in the heart, and in the feelings of clergy and Christian peoples—a ferment capable of stirring up the entire mass, until it is wholly leavened. A great step forward in the painful reconquest of Christian essentialism over the externals and accidentals introduced in the course of time. The rediscovery of those mental and spiritual forms, Christian, simple, genuine, because primitive, because Christlike, because biblical, sacral and ecclesial without other additions.

Much will depend on the postconciliar commission which will be charged with carrying out the reform to its completion in obedience to the Council. Much and perhaps more will depend on the success of permeating priest and people with this spirit.

Never will it be too strongly stated that the more pressing are the problems of action and organization in the Church, the greater is the necessity first of all of a Christo-sacral vision of the Church itself and of all Christian life. Nothing less is in question than a proper evaluation of a scale of values and duties. Now this vision is first of all attained through a deep penetration of the liturgy and of liturgical life. Not by chance, the Holy Father, in his discourse at the closing of the second session of the Council, wished to see precisely in this fact the importance of the Constitution on the liturgy and the factual lesson that has been the first fruit of the Council.

In the following words he gives us a magnificent summary of the spirit of the liturgical movement and of the Constitution itself. "We here pay homage to a scale of values and duties. God in the first place, prayer our prime obligation, *the liturgy the primary source of that divine exchange in which the life itself of God is communicated to us; the first gift we can make to Christian people,* believing and praying with us, and *the first invitation to the world* to loose its mute tongue in blessed and truthful prayer and to feel the ineffable regenerative power of singing with us the divine praises and human hopes through Christ our Lord in the Holy Spirit. . . . It will be well for us to treasure this fruit of the Council, as *that which must animate and characterize the Church's life; in fact, the Church is a religious society, it is a praying community, it is a fervent people of interiority and spirituality moved by faith and grace. . . . We wish to make the liturgy more pure, more genuine, closer to the fonts of truth and grace, more suitable to be the spiritual patrimony of the people.*"

NOTES TO CHAPTER 4

1 St. Ignatius of Antioch, *Ad Eph.,* 7, 2.

2 *Sacr. Veronense,* Ed. Mohlberg, 1265.

3 St. Thomas Aquinas, *Summa Theologica,* III, 65 a. 3, c; cf. 72 a. 12 ad 13.

4 *Cat. ex decreto Conc. Trid.* (Roma, 1920), 228.

5 Leo XIII, *Mira caritas,* A.A.S. 34 (1901-1902), 642.

6 Aquinas, *op. cit.,* III, 83 a. 4, c.

7 Pius XI, *Divini cultus,* A.A.S. 21 (1929), 33.

8 Pius XII, *Mediator Dei,* A.A.S. 39 (1947), 532, n. 26-27.

9 St. John Damascene, *De fide orthodoxa,* III, 13.

10 Dionysius, *Eccl. Hier.,* III.

11 Aquinas, *De veritate,* 27, a. 4, c.

12 Benedict XIV, *Certiores effecti.*

13 *Mediator Dei, loc. cit.,* 565.

14 *De musica sacra et sacra liturgia,* n. 22 c.

14a See how the matter was decreed by the Sacred Congregation of Rites, March 7, 1965: *Rite to be observed in the concelebration of Mass and the Rite for Communion under both kinds.*

15 "These decrees have to be approved or confirmed by the Apostolic See" (Art. 36, 3). "These rituals are to be approved by the Holy See" (Art. 63b).

5
Active participation, the inspiring and directive principle of the Constitution

William Barauna O.F.M.

1 The meaning of active participation in the liturgy
2 The theological basis for participation
3 Origin and diagnosis of the present situation
4 Remedial means suggested
  A Liturgical formation of clergy and laity
  B The reform of the liturgy
    1 Demands of the hierarchical and group community character of the liturgy
    2 Demands of didactic and pastoral character of the liturgy
      a General indications
      b Decentralization and adaptation
      c Use of the vernacular
5 Conclusion

Father Barauna of Brazil, is a member of the Pontifical International Marian Academy and a *peritus* of the II Vatican Council. His article was translated into English by Father Tarcisio Beal O.F.M., of Washington, D.C.

It is well known that Pius X was the first pope to inaugurate the liturgical movement in this century when, on November 22, 1903, a few months after he had ascended the Chair of Peter, he issued the *Motu Proprio, Tra le sollecitudini.*

In that document we find the following words:

> Since it is our ardent desire that the true Christian spirit may flourish again in all its forms and among all the faithful, it is necessary first of all to be solicitous for the sanctity and dignity of the church, for it is there that the faithful come together to acquire that spirit from its *primary and indispensible source, which is active participation in the most sacred mysteries and in the public and solemn prayer of the Church.*[1]

We have deliberately italicized certain words in the above, and especially the words "active participation," for these words aroused the astonishment of not a few authors at the time, for they seemed to them to be too daring, and perhaps not a little less than orthodox. A faithful Latin translation would render the realistic Italian expression by the word *participatio,* but the "authentic" Latin version that was issued used the expression *actuosa communicatio.* In fact, if one were to translate in that fashion he would be overlooking certain nuances which, in the mind of the Pope, have a measure of importance, for they supply a proper theological foundation for the participation of the faithful in the liturgical life of the Church, which he desired.

Today, sixty years after the publication of the *Motu Proprio* of Pius X, we are face to face with a much more important document, the Constitution *Sacrosanctum Concilium* issued by the Council. It displays no hesitancy in speaking of "active, conscious, and full participation." It even proclaims it as the inspiring and directive principle in all the work of liturgical renewal and reform aimed at by the II Vatican Council. A simple comparison of the Latin version of the *Motu Proprio* of Pius X and the text of the liturgical Constitution of the II Vatican Council shows clearly the progress made by the liturgical movement during the brief span of sixty years.

That the entire constitution on the liturgy is focused and centered on the "people of God," and their active participation in the richness of the liturgy, appears very evident, even from a superficial reading of the Constitution. In the very first article of the Introduction, this preoccupation is unmistakable.

> The sacred Council has several aims in view: it desires to impart an ever-increasing vigor to the Christian life of the faithful; to adapt more suitably to the needs of our times those institutions which are subject to change; to foster whatever can promote union among all who believe in Christ; to strengthen whatever can help to call the whole of mankind into the household of the Church. The Council therefore sees particularly cogent reasons for undertaking the reform and promotion of the liturgy.

Fr. H. Schmidt is correct when he reminds us that "the necessity for participation in the liturgy on the part of the faithful is mentioned so many times in the Constitution that it resembles a chorus. It is like the "Pray for us" or the "spare us, O Lord" that we repeat in the litanies."[2]

In this respect there is a noticeable difference between the reform of the Council of Trent and the one published by the II Vatican Council, four centuries later. The purpose of the first was defensive and apologetic. By getting rid of certain excrescences that had grown up during the Middle Ages, it sought to protect the sacred liturgy from the attacks of the Reformers. In this it resembled some noble lady who is so eager to protect her precious jewels that she goes to the extent of displaying them no longer. She prefers to lock them up in a safe rather than run the risk of loss or theft. The liturgical reforms of the II Vatican, which officially marks the end of the Counter-reformation, have a more pastoral orientation. The Church is no longer on the defensive; it is leading a peaceful offensive, a reconquest of the enormous mass of faithful who have turned their backs on the Church, a constructive dialogue with the separated brethren, and, by having recourse to new methods, the evangelization of the multitudes who have not felt the breath of the Christian spirit. By devoting itself to this apostolic and pastoral task of offensive and conquest, the Constitution is merely attempting to channel the combined results of all the efforts of the different sectors of the ecclesiastical sciences so as to discover, or rediscover, facets of the mystery of the Church, especially of the people of God, the "chosen generation, a kingly priesthood, a holy nation, a purchased people" (1 Pet. 2, 9).

The Constitution on the liturgy is directed solely to God's people; it has no clerical overtones. Every effort is made to "de-clericalize" the liturgy so as to bring it down to the level of the people. We are reminded of the lady of nobility. Now she has decided to remove the jewels from the safe where they have reposed so long to let the people see the splendor with which she is adorned. It is the fulfillment of an ardent wish of Pope John XXIII who said, one day after he had finished a liturgical celebration in a Church in Rome: "How sad I feel when I think of those beautiful prayers which I have just said, and which you do not understand. . . . Some day these treasures must become accessible to all."[3] In short, to break down the bars that separate the sanctuary from the nave is the great preoccupation of the Council.

In the following pages, therefore, we shall try to illustrate, in a concrete way, how the participation of the faithful in the sacred liturgy constitutes the goal, the inspiring, directive, and impelling principle of all the work directed towards the promotion and restoration of the liturgy, as sought by the Constitution *Sacrosanctum Concilium*. We shall follow this procedure. First, we shall say something about the concept itself of active participation, pointing out rapidly the theological basis which it has, and which it needs. We shall then proceed to practical applications, giving a brief summary of what is wrong in the present situation, and then pointing out, and analyzing in detail, definite methods for overcoming it.

1 THE MEANING OF ACTIVE PARTICIPATION IN THE LITURGY

It is necessary to emphasize two things if we are to understand rightly the mind of the Council regarding active participation and its theological nature.

First, we must observe that in the Constitution on the liturgy there is no reference to "assistance" at Mass or at other liturgical functions as an ideal to be pursued in the care of souls. As everyone knows, "assistance" constituted the goal with which we had to be satisfied in pastoral work, at least up to the present. Most of our faithful were satisfied that they had fulfilled their Sunday obligations when they could say that they "went" to Mass, or "assisted" at it. And this, it might be added, was what could be expected, because most of our catechisms, when speaking about the Commandments of the Church, merely recommended or prescribed that each person should "assist at Mass with devotion." The catechists, in their turn, did not offer further explanation. As a rule they were satisfied, and felt completely rewarded, for their efforts, when they found that a majority of the faithful did "go" to Mass. And then they added that, in the long run, all that was needed in order to satisfy the Church's precept was, not to "come" after the Offertory, and not to "leave" before the Communion.

It is quite natural that the Council did not—and could not—condemn this form of liturgical participation which consisted in mere assistance, passive or active. But it is also quite evident that, aiming as it was at an ideal of liturgical pastoral work, it could not, and should not, be expected to recommend it. It showed a state of affairs that would have to come to an end on the part of those who are convinced that the liturgy is "the summit towards which the activity of the Church is directed . . .the font from which all its power flows" (Art. 10).

The Constitution, in fact, always speaks of "active participation," adding, here and there, words like "full" and "conscious." These qualifications make it clear that there is to be a definite type of participation in the mysteries, one which, without excluding other forms, surpasses them by its excellence and must, therefore, be considered the ideal to be attained in the pastoral ministry.

In what does active participation consist? The Constitution prefers not to give a formal definition. Instead, it gives a description which is opposed to mere assistance. This is clear from a passage such as this:

> The Church, therefore, earnestly desires that Christ's faithful, when present at this mystery of the Faith, should not be there as strangers or silent spectators; on the contrary, through a good understanding of the rites and prayers, they should take part in the sacred action conscious of what they are doing, with devotion and full collaboration. They should be instructed by God's word and be nourished at the table of the Lord's body; they should give thanks to God; by offering the Immaculate Victim, not only through the hands

> of the priest, but also with him, they should learn also to offer themselves; through Christ, the Mediator, they should be drawn day by day into ever more perfect union with God and with each other, so that finally God may be all in all (Art. 48).

From this text it follows that by speaking of "active participation," the Council imposes on the pastors of souls the grave obligation of fostering, by every means, a participation in the sacred mysteries that goes beyond mere presence, like that of spectators, no matter how recollected they may be. For active participation, it is not enough for the faithful to be physically present and to pray with recollection. It is necessary that "their minds should be attuned to their voices" (Art. 11), that they have an "active participation in liturgy both internally and externally" (Art. 19), that they participate "by actions, gestures, and bodily attitudes" (Art. 30). It is natural that active participation may and should assume many different forms, "taking into account the age [of the participants], and their condition, their way of life and standard of religious culture" (Art. 19). None the less, active participation on the part of all should be "one of the chief duties of a faithful dispenser of the mysteries of God" (Art. 19); and therefore, "pastors of souls must zealously strive to achieve it, by means of necessary instruction, in all their pastoral work" (Art. 14). The reason for this is not to be found in any simple and positive law of the Council, nor is it simply the "latest vogue"; rather, it is due to the fact that "liturgy is the summit towards which the activity of the Church is directed, and at the same time the font from which all her powers flow" (Art. 10). The same article reminds priests and bishops that the chief aim of their apostolic works is not some anthropocentric or vague "saving of souls," still less the task of "organizing" a parish well. The Constitution expressly states that "the aim and object of apostolic works is that all who are made sons of God by faith and Baptism should come together to praise God in the midst of the church, to take part in the sacrifice, and to eat the Lord's supper" (Art. 10).

Incidentally, the nature itself of the liturgy demands such an active participation, as we shall soon see. Liturgy is not a simple commemoration of a spectacle to be looked at; rather, it is an act that makes real and actual, again and again, the same saving event which is the core of the entire "history of salvation," which is simply this: the Father descends to human lowliness, through the Son, in order that the whole of mankind may return, through the Spirit and the Son, to the bosom of the Father. To repeat, liturgy is not a mere celebration of a past event. It is not a devout witnessing of a sacred drama. It is essentially an "action," one in which there is direct participation on the part of all who "join with the priest in the unity of the Father, Son, and Holy Spirit"[4] in the capacity of actors playing their roles. If this is not the purpose, there is no reason why the Church should not be satisfied with the simple "hearing" of Mass through the medium of radio or television, for in such circumstances it is certainly possible to "pray with devotion."

From what has been said, we can conclude that a truly active and fully conscious participation is possible only when body and soul, when the corporal and spiritual faculties, are perfectly attuned to the sacred action in which God and his minister take part, and with all the liturgical assembly vitally participating in it. Only a participation such as this, full and conscious, completely satisfies the nature of liturgy and the body-spirit character of man. This is participation as sought by the Council. This is the goal that inspired all its thinking, and all the measures it adopted to bring it within the reach of all.

The spirit of active participation aimed at by the Council is the one described by St. Paul in his First Epistle to the Corinthians (14, 9-23), when he spoke of charisms:

> So likewise you, except you utter by the tongue plain speech, how shall it be known what is said? For you shall be speaking into the air. There are, for example, so many kinds of tongues in this world; and none is without voice. If then I know not the power of the voice, I shall be to him to whom I speak a barbarian; and he that speaketh, a barbarian to me. So you also, forasmuch as you are zealous of spirits, seek to abound unto the edifying of the Church. And therefore he that speaketh by a tongue, let him pray that he may interpret.
>
> For if I pray in a tongue, my spirit prayeth, but my understanding is without fruit. What is it then? I will pray with the spirit. I will pray also with the understanding; I will sing with the spirit; I will sing also with the understanding. Else if thou shalt bless with the spirit, how shall he that holdeth the place of the understanding say, Amen, to the blessing? because he knoweth not what thou sayest.
>
> For thou indeed givest thanks well, but the other is not edified. I thank my God that I speak with all your tongues. But in the church I had rather speak five words with my understanding, that I may instruct others also; than ten thousand words in a tongue.
>
> Brethren, do not become children in sense: but in malice be children, and in sense be perfect.
>
> In the law it is written: In other tongues and other lips I will speak to this people; and neither so will they hear me, saith the Lord.
>
> Wherefore tongues are for a sign, not to believers, but to unbelievers; but prophesies, not to unbelievers but to believers. If therefore the whole church come together into one place, and all speak with tongues, and there come in unlearned persons or infidels, will they not say that you are mad?

Despite all this—and here we reach the second point to which there is reference in the beginning—the fact that the liturgical celebration is an action of the entire community of the baptized, does not permit us to think that there is no diversity of functions in it. As Pius XII insisted in the *Mediator Dei,* the changing of the bread and wine into the

Body and Blood of Christ, the apex of the Mass, in virtue of which Christ is placed on the altar in the state of victim, is the work of the celebrant alone in his capacity as minister of Christ, and not as a delegate representing the assembly. On the other hand, however, the offering of the sacrifice is truly made by all the faithful, since it is the whole Church which offers the sacrifice. As is emphasized in Article 48 of the Constitution, the faithful offer the immaculate host "not only through the hands of the priest, but also with him." In brief, let there be active and full participation, by all means; but let there be no "leveling down," for that is out of harmony with the character of the Church, which is essentially hierarchical; and so, too, is every liturgical celebration. Active participation means precisely that each one fulfils, in the sacred action, those parts, and only those parts, which pertain to him within the Church (Art. 28).

Furthermore, we should keep the following point in mind. Active participation, as understood in the light of the declarations of the same Council, really constitutes "a normal demand intrinsic to the liturgy, in the same way that the perfection of something, although accidental in relation to its essence, is a normal demand intrinsic to the same."[5] However, the fact that such an active participation stems from the nature itself of the liturgical celebration does not justify the conclusion that such a celebration is performed in its essentials only when there is an active and full participation of the community. A Mass celebrated without a congregation, and even without an acolyte, is essentially the same community action as a Mass offered in the presence of a congregation of monks, where everyone is perfectly attuned to the sacred action. Any study of pastoral liturgy that would ignore this dogmatic fact would, as a result, be vitiated from the beginning.

It is important to keep in mind, however, the essentially social and community character of every liturgical celebration. This leads us to conclude that no pastor of souls would be free from grave fault if he were to fail to enlist the active participation of the faithful. Such participation, especially since the days of Pius X, is not a mere recommendation; it is a command. The note of obligation in this regard has been present in the teaching of all the Popes since Pius X. Pius XI, for instance, says ". . . it is all important [*pernecesse est*] that the faithful take part in the sacred ceremonies . . . not like strangers and silent spectators, but so as to alternate their voices with those of the priest or the choir, according to the rules prescribed. If this takes place, and it is our wish, it will never again happen that the people either do not respond to the common prayers in the liturgical or vernacular language, or reply in a weak and unintelligible mumble."[6]

2 THE THEOLOGICAL BASIS FOR PARTICIPATION

His Eminence Cardinal Lercaro said recently:

> It is a matter worthy of note that despite the efforts of the pioneers in the liturgical movement who tried to bring matters home to us,

> despite the words and works of Pius X, and the encouraging efforts of his successors, despite the luminous teaching and the magnificent efforts of Pius XII in favor of the restoration of the liturgy, within the ranks of the clergy there are still not very many who devote themselves to the study, and the pastoral application, of the liturgy. There are far too many priests who, although free from the prejudices which hindered the liturgical movement in the beginning of this century, consider participation in the liturgy, and consequently the study of it, as just one among many such projects, not exactly fundamental, but things that could be useful in the apostolate, especially in certain spheres where there are particular needs. Finally, there are those who regard it as something beautiful, but unnecessary, something that, in this day, by reason of the pressing need of spreading the faith and rebuilding the Christian order, has to give way to pursuits that are more urgent and more important.[7]

It is easy to understand that the Council would miss its goal if it had not begun by summarily proscribing a mentality such as this, which does not see in the liturgical life anything beyond an added adornment to spiritual and pastoral life, an item of luxury reserved for people possessed of artistic appreciation and training, and with aristocratic tastes. These are the reasons why the entire first part of the opening chapter (Art. 5-13) is devoted to the *theological* nature of liturgy, and its place in the life of the Church.

The Council takes as its starting point the person and the labors of Christ who, in his human-divine nature, is in a sense the basic and primordial sacrament of all worship of God and of the work of sanctification of men throughout the centuries. From this primordial sacrament stems another one, the Church, a reality which is expressed in these wonderful words: "For it was from the side of Christ as he slept the sleep of death upon the Cross that there came forth 'the wondrous sacrament of the whole Church'" (Art. 5). Through this sacrament, the Church, the glorified Christ continues among men his work as Mediator, while offering to the Father the sacrifice of mankind, all united together and redeemed, for to them has been applied the fruits of sanctification acquired by him during his life on earth. This is what Christ does; and with him and in him and by him the Church, in eucharistic sacrifice, in the sacraments, in the divine office, in all the official celebrations of the Mystical Body of Christ does the same. Sacred liturgy, therefore, is the privileged place of meeting between God and man, through the mediation of Christ as Head, and by means of sensible signs (the sacraments), so appropriate to the status of man as a sojourner on earth; and they signify and produce, each in its own way, the supernatural realities of the history of salvation. The nature, greatness, and importance of the liturgy consists in its being considered as "an exercise of the priestly office of Jesus Christ. In the liturgy the sanctification of man is signified by signs perceptible to the senses, and is effected in a way which corresponds with each of these signs; in the liturgy the whole public worship is performed by the Mystical Body of Christ, that is, by the Head and his members" (Art. 7).

From this we can deduce that there is not, and there cannot be, objectively speaking, any other action that is worthier, more efficacious, and of deeper significance for Christian life than the liturgical form of worship. The Constitution expresses it in these words, and they are directed primarily, not to theologians but to pastors of souls; Nevertheless the liturgy is the summit towards which the activity of the Church is directed; at the same time it is the font from which all her power flows (Art. 10).

If the Liturgy is Christ's action *par excellence,* and the primary and indispensible font of the spirit and life of Christ, it follows that every child of the Church has a right to an active participation in it, if we wish the exercise of active participation to be something more than a practice that has been merely recommended. Article 14 speaks of active participation as a right and duty of every Christian by right of his Baptism. This being the case, liturgical life cannot be considered as a distinction awarded to chosen souls, or to a clerical aristocracy, or as a privilege reserved for souls prepared by grace and worthy of it. Such a way of thinking owes its origin to a tendency to regard the Church as something stratified, or "hierarchical," beginning with deacons and ascending to the pope, with the rank and file of the laity forming just the basis of the pyramid. The Council reminds us that, by virtue of baptism, every member of the faithful becomes a true and responsible member of the Mystical Body, acquiring thereby rights and duties which are the heritage of all, becoming a participant in the gifts of the Holy Spirit, and of the same grace which constitutes the vivifying principle for all—a grace which comes from the liturgy as its primary font.

In matters of liturgical practice, very little can be achieved if we fail to understand, and fail to enable others to understand, what the Constitution expresses in words such as these:

> Mother Church earnestly desires that all the faithful should be led to that full, conscious, and active participation in the liturgical celebrations which is demanded by the very nature of the liturgy. Such participation by the Christian people as "a chosen race, a royal priesthood, a holy nation, a redeemed people" (1 Pet. 2, 9; cf. 2, 4-5), is their right and duty by reason of their baptism (Art. 14).

Here are synthesized the great dogmatic truths which are the basis of a pastoral work, established on a solid foundation and well built, namely, the Church's liturgical life, the supreme realization of the mystery of Christ among men. This, therefore, is the center of Christian life, the alpha and the omega of all pastoral ministry, the Church as a people "living in unison by reason of the unity of the Father and the Son and the Holy Spirit," with baptism as the rite that incorporates the catechumen into the militia of Christ's Mystical Body, with the "holy people of God" as companions, and an entire "entourage" of rights and duties, including participation in the liturgy. Without a serious and calm reflection, and a genuine living according to these theological principles and a thorough instruction in them, there will be no understanding of the liturgy. There will be no liturgical life for the clergy or the faithful. Canon Martimort did not need any prophetic spirit to write these words long before the Council met:

> Have we done enough when we have given expression to our wishes and formulated projects, in the hope that the Council will carry out the rest? There is an ever-increasing number of liturgists, biblical scholars, pastors of souls, and assistants in parishes who ask the same question, in the full awareness that the Council presupposes certain other conditions which are necessary for success. A wholehearted appeal to the Holy Spirit is certainly necessary. But it is also essential that there be a change in the mentality of the clergy and the faithful, even more than a change in methods, institutions, and rites. . . . We have to renew our way of acting, our ideas, our behavior. It is through the work of the Holy Spirit that the Church is renewed.[8]

3 ORIGIN AND DIAGNOSIS OF THE PRESENT SITUATION

No pastor of souls who exercises his ministry with eyes open to daily realities will deny that among a large portion of our people there is a very superficial exercise of religion. In addition to an incalculable number of Christians who are satisfied with the mere externals of religion, there are numerous Catholics of good will who are woefully lacking in a full understanding of it. In both cases it is necessary to recognize, objectively, that one of the main reasons is that they have become estranged from the Church, from her authentic spirit, and especially from her liturgical life.

Not long ago, a bishop in Italy made the following declaration about the situation in Italy, and we believe that it has application elsewhere:

> The statistics concerning the frequency with which people attend Mass on Sundays and holydays show that there has been an amazing amount of desertion. For many who are baptized, Mass is no longer attended habitually. There are some who attend but rarely, and others who continue to go to Mass, but only by reason of custom, or simply to satisfy a precept of the Church. The majority of those who are present are present only physically. Silence and boredom surround the celebrant. The more pious among those who attend follow their own caprice. They pray as they please; they follow their own ideas; they read their own prayer books; they express their thoughts in their own ejaculatory prayers. . . .[9]

In the editorial in which Fr. Roguet indicates the purposes of the Center for Liturgical Pastoral Work in Paris, we read:

> The good shepherd is not only the one who peacefully pastures his selected and well-nourished flock in his fenced-in fold, but he

> who feels himself consumed by an immense pity for the hungry, the tired, the discouraged multitude which is like a flock without a shepherd (Mt. 9, 36; 14, 14; 15, 32). We are obsessed with concern about the vast multitudes who live without ideals, who are slaves of purely human liturgies—and sometimes liturgies that are less human; the thronging multitudes who pack the stadiums, or assemble in the somber shades of the theater, who know nothing of the inexhaustible fonts of happiness, strength and saving graces that flow from the Christian mysteries. We suffer when we see our churches so often deserted, or filled with passive multitudes who come because of custom, multitudes oppressed with the boredom of a worship which they tolerate only because it is a form of slavery which they cannot escape, or which they have reduced to an individualistic and sentimental practice.[10]

In regard to Catholicism in Latin America, an observer wrote just recently:

> Processions, medals, statues, devotion to the Blessed Virgin and the saints occupy an infinitely more important place among Latin Americans than faith in the redeeming work that flows from the death and Resurrection of Christ.[11]

A situation like this is more or less general. To what can it be attributed? There are many causes; but no one can deny that among these causes is estrangement from the liturgy.

When one asks why the great mass of Christians have abandoned the liturgy, it has to be pointed out that this is due in great part to the fossilized condition of the present liturgy: it is like something that grew out of a civilization that then changed its nature. The language of the liturgy, its idiom and symbolism—everything essentially goes back to the Bible, which came into being thousands of years ago. The most recent addition to the liturgy date practically from the Middle Ages, and they knew nothing of Cartesianism, the Enlightenment, the upward trend among the masses, the laicization of society, individualism, industrialization and all its consequences, the rise of technology, of the radio, television, and the movies, satellite and interplanetary adventures that tomorrow may lead to comfortable flights through the empyrean. Liturgy as we knew it was full of words and symbols that were meaningful for the primitive Christian and for the medieval mind, but conveyed no meaning to the modern mind which had lost familiar contact with nature.

J. Gelineau comments that:

> The worship of the Christians of the fourth and fifth centuries appears to us as an admirable synthesis. The biblical revelation in its crystal clearness, instilled into the souls of the faithful by the ardent teachings of the Fathers of the Church, is incorporated into the Mediterranean culture of the day. In their forms of worship, which blend with this culture, the classical and philosophical thought of

> the time plays a role; the spoken languages, the social customs of the era, and the symbolic expressions of religious art, manifesting itself in the common chant or in the ceremonial of prayer—all are there.[12]

The barbarian invasion put an end to this period in which there was a synthesis of the various levels of human activity. The barbarians were baptized in vast numbers, and accepted the rites and fundamentals of Christianity without fully assimilating them. The liturgy became more and more estranged from the feeling and thinking of the new ethnic groups that entered the Church. Charlemagne imported and implanted among the Franks a Roman liturgy that was not in tune with the new spirit. The same took place in regard to the Visigoths, the Germanic tribes, the Slavs, to say nothing of the developments in the sixteenth century when Christianity set out to evangelize the new world of America, and the old world of Africa and Asia.

It is an undeniable fact, then, that the estrangement of the people from the liturgy had its beginnings after the first millennium of the Christian Era. Partly because worship did not adapt itself to new forms and conditions of life, and partly because of other factors, the language and thought of Christians has been progressively departing from the language and thought of the Bible and the liturgy.

It would be instructive to take a look, for instance, at the development of the rite of the Mass in the Roman liturgy as described by J. Jungmann and G. Dix in their classic works.[13] Fr. Vagaggini, relying on these two authors, gives a summary of the most important developments in this long history,[14] and we shall now outline it.

The Mass of the primitive Christian community had the appearance of a community action, particularly a community present here and now. Without confusing the role of hierarchy and laymen, the rite was an action in which each played his part, not in commemoration of some historical event of the past, but to perform a saving event which is always new, to bring about once more the "converging" of God and man in worship and sanctification, with Christ as Mediator in the center. Nobody would have received the impression that the faithful, or groups of the faithful, were present at the liturgical celebration as mere spectators or auditors—with the exception of the "public penitents," and these regarded their exclusion from the eucharistic part of the liturgy as a severe punishment. And neither could anyone conclude that any particular part of the assemblage could hold aloof from the action and occupy itself with its own particular devotions.

The structure of the rites reflected this profoundly "common to all" aspect. That is the reason why, until the fourth century, all prayers were said in a loud voice, and there were no "secret" parts for the priest and for the faithful. There was no overlapping of hymns, chants, or ritual acts, so that the celebrant might say or do something while the choir or the faithful were saying or doing something else.[15] Parts which were intended for all were performed by all, including the celebrant. The latter never said privately those parts which were sung by the assemblage, or read by the deacon or reader. The prayers of the priest were never offered in his own name; they were offered in the name of all, and for the benefit of all, the participants and the Church in general.[16]

The language used in the primitive Roman liturgy was Greek, the cultivated language of the time, one understood by all. When Greek ceased to be commonly spoken, around the third or fourth century, Latin automatically took its place. If in Christian antiquity, in certain regions and during certain periods, the liturgy continued to be celebrated in a language unknown to the people, it was due to the fact that the language of the people was not yet a literary one, or that the Sacred Books had not yet been translated into that language.

The community and vital character of the liturgy was evident, too, in the dialogue. The bishop, or the person who represented him, at the beginning of the prayer was accustomed to address the assembly with a greeting such as: "The Lord be with you," "Let us give thanks to God," "Let us pray," "Peace be with you." This is clearly evident in the great eucharistic prayer, the Anaphora or Canon, said by the bishop or presbyter alone. The celebrant alone consecrates the offerings, but at the end, all in unison join in saying "Amen."

The same was apparent in the position of the assemblage in relation to the altar. The latter was in the center, while the faithful were grouped around it, united together around the table of the Lord. Incidentally, the altar was a real table. How different is the situation today, where the altar is at the end of the church, sometimes invisible to the people, and the priest calmly performs the functions and goes through the ceremonies, mostly with his back to the "people of God!"

In the primitive community the liturgical celebration reached its climax, in outward appearance, at the moment of Communion, the rite of participation in the sacrificial banquet. For the primitive Christian, it was inconceivable that he would assist at Mass and fail to receive Communion. It would seem an absurdity to him to take part in a sacrificial supper by merely looking on, while others partook of the nourishment. Communion was taken to those who could not attend, precisely in order that they might have a part in the sacrifice that pertained to the entire local community. Today the faithful receive Holy Communion only under the species of bread; but who is the person who would spontaneously think of "bread" when he sees the tiny white Host? Until recently he did not even say *Amen*. How different was the usage of the primitive Church! Here is how St. Cyril of Jerusalem described it:

> You will receive the Body of Christ on the palm of your hand, and you will answer *Amen*. Then, after all have received the Body of the Lord, you yourself will also approach for the chalice of his Blood. You are not to extend your hands, but you are to bow down and as an expression of respectful adoration you are to say *Amen*.

In the course of the third century, or later, the rite of the Offertory was introduced. The faithful brought their offerings to the church, and in certain regions they carried them in procession to the celebrant, and later they received Communion from the sacrificial offerings they had brought. This rite, maintained in the West until the eleventh century and later in some places, was a striking expression of the community character of the Mass. We should notice that during all this time there was no ecclesiastical commandment that placed an obligation on the faithful to attend Mass. The only thing that did exist was an express *prohibition*—a precept that denied the right to public sinners to take part in the eucharistic liturgy. It was the so-called "excommunication," the loss of the faculty of participating with the faithful in religious activities as a result of some grave fault. It was a penalty that was keenly felt by the victim, and by the local community.

There was no danger that there would be a lack of active participation on the part of the faithful. The danger was that the faithful would try to usurp functions that pertained exclusively to the hierarchy. It is against this abuse that St. Clement of Rome protested in his first Epistle to the Corinthians (Ch. 40, 41).

The ideal of worship as a community action appears in the ancient custom of celebrating only one Mass on Sundays, and that Mass was celebrated by the bishop, surrounded by the presbyters and deacons, and by the people of God. Naturally, such a custom could not last indefinitely, because of the numerical growth of communities and their members.

Unfortunately, since the fourth century, and especially in the West since the Middle Ages, the unifying and community character of the liturgy became increasingly overshadowed in the sacred rites, and, in consequence, in the psychology of the faithful. Little by little particularist elements were introduced, and their progressive accumulation, together with other factors, brought about an increasing and obvious "clericalization" of the liturgy. The latter now became something that took place between God and the priest, while the faithful were reduced to a purely passive role in relation to what took place at a distance, at the altar. In the East, as early as the fourth century, a series of prayers to be recited by the priest alone was introduced, that is, in addition to the Canon, which was always reserved to the celebrant, although he recited it in a loud voice, as is still the custom in the East. In time, the Offertory procession of the people disappeared. The iconostasis was introduced. Finally it hid the altar completely from the faithful, and during the most important parts of the Mass the veils were also closed, thus cutting off the limited view which the faithful had enjoyed. Then the celebrant began to celebrate in a low voice, and the people in general sang litanies and other prayers. Gradually all the Canon came to be recited in a low voice by the celebrant.

Such is the East; but it has the advantage that normally the language of the liturgy is understood by the people. In the West, too, the process of "clericalization" took place, and the people became separated from the altar in a still more radical way. Around the eighth and ninth centuries, Latin became a dead language; it was no longer understood except by the educated classes, and these were a small minority. Private Masses, and Masses of devotion were constantly being substituted for the community Mass, and this became common practice especially in the Middle Ages. In such private Masses, the acolyte had the exclusive privilege of making the responses to the celebrant, not only in the absence of the faithful, but even when they were present. In this way, liturgical legislation deprived the faithful of the exercise of an inalienable right of every baptized person. The liturgy was gradually becoming crowded with prayers that were entirely private, and concerned only the priest. Now he began to pray in his own name, and for himself. The entire Canon was now recited in a low voice. In sung Masses it was not merely permitted, it was prescribed that the priest was to say in a low voice what was read or sung by the sacred ministers, by the *schola cantorum,* or even by the faithful. Reception of Holy Communion, on the part of the faithful, became rarer and rarer. Long before the rise of Jansenism, the Eucharist, instead of being a sacrificial banquet, to a greater and greater extent was becoming the "awesome mystery." Instead of seeking nourishment from the Eucharistic Christ, people preferred to adore him. At this time there was introduced, in face of great opposition from Rome, the practice of elevating the Host and chalice, so that the faithful could at least "see" the Lord. The relatively few who did receive holy Communion did not see anything wrong in doing so outside of Mass, or even during its celebration.

On its part, the *schola cantorum* began to invade the small redoubt still left to the people, taking on itself the performance of the parts to be sung. To a greater and greater extent, Gregorian chant and polyphony, both beyond the capacity of the ordinary people, gained the ascendancy. The few who still came to Mass devoted their time to their own private prayers. There was nothing else to do, for even a translation of the missal was forbidden.

Thus the liturgy was transformed into something resembling a theatrical show, with lights, flowers, songs, and boring ceremonies, inspired by Byzantine and medieval pomp, when it should have been a privileged meeting with God.

Today the forest of rites, gestures, and ceremonies (on the part of the priest, ministers, and acolytes—but not of the people) is so thick that an average Christian is practically unable to distinguish the essential from the accidental. Someone has said that if St. Paul were to see a Solemn or a Pontifical Mass he would need someone to explain to him that it was the same Lord's Supper of the Gospel and of his Epistle. It is a far cry from the days of St. Augustine, who liked to emphasize the simplicity of the Christian liturgy in contrast with the Hebraic ritual. He writes:

> Now that the very apparent sign of our freedom has shone forth, thanks to the Resurrection of the Lord, we no longer bear the

> burden of all these rites.... Instead of the multitude [the Jews] had, we have but few rites. They are easy to celebrate; they have a spiritual significance; they are easy to grasp; and they are the rites that the Lord himself and the teaching of the Church have transmitted to us. The sacrament of baptism and the sacrament of the Body and Blood of the Lord are of this kind. Once he has been instructed, every Christian knows when receiving them to what they refer, and therefore feels compelled to respect them, not by a wordly form of servitude, but, on the contrary, with spiritual liberty.[17]

What we have said in regard to the Mass can be said too, and sometimes with greater truth, in regard to receiving the sacraments. As a result of all of this, the people became estranged, to a greater and greater extent, from the liturgical life of the Church. As a compensation, private devotions began to appear and develop rapidly. The cult of the saints, and especially of Our Lady, acquired an ever-increasing importance. The cult of relics and statues prevailed over liturgical piety. The denunciations of Luther and the other reformers in regard to this certainly were not arbitrary fancies of rebellious and eccentric minds. Forms of piety that made Christ the sum and center of everything were gradually declining in influence. Christ came to be considered almost exclusively in his divine nature, and therefore became an object of prayer rather than of vital communion. Or, at the other extreme, popular preachers fostered devotion to the human nature of Christ, with emphasis on the Crib and Cross.

Scholastic thinkers, especially in the decadent period since the fourteenth century, widened still further the gap between liturgical piety and popular devotions, and this inevitably had its influence on the theological level. The theology of the Fathers is pervaded with the biblical language and spirit. The emphasis is on the story of redemption, and consequently on the "mystery" of Christ and the Church. On the other hand, Scholastic theology excels in metaphysical speculation and has little regard for the historical approach. God, Christ and the Church are no longer mysteries to be lived with all the faculties of soul and body. Instead, they are an array of truth about which one may speculate, a subject for metaphysical analysis. Scholastic theology, in the days of the great masters of the thirteenth century, still kept alive a sense of mystery, and the sacred sciences were before everything else a subject of vital experience and of contemplation. But this theology of the heart, in time, was transformed into a theology of the intellect.

This was the time, too, where there appeared and developed such forces as nationalism, individualism, and anthropocentrism, of which humanism and the Renaissance are a characteristic example. The Reformation lowered theology to the level of apologetics, and forced it to live in a kind of ivory tower. Its primary function was no longer to teach the children of the Church the inexhaustible riches of the mystery of Christ and the Church. Its province now was to demonstrate to those outside the Church the truth of certain theses, especially those pertaining to the external and hierarchical aspects of the Church. Thus there was being lost, with ever-increasing tempo, a sensitivity for the inspirational aspects of Christianity, so evident in the Bible and in patristic theology. The people and the theologians began to be divorced more and more from the Bible—and for centuries its reading was practically forbidden to the faithful. An individualistic spirit, the product of historical circumstances, began to take over the piety of the faithful and the field of theology.

Such a condition continued until the end of last century and the beginning of this. Then came the epoch in which great attempts began to be made to return once more to the primitive sources of Christianity, the Bible and patristic tradition. It was this great movement of returning to early sources that gave rise to the theological, biblical, eucharistic, liturgical, missionary, and ecumenical renewal. This movement towards renewal, felt throughout the world, burst forth in an admirable way at the II Vatican Council, and it may be said that the Constitution on the liturgy is the fruit of this development—a development that matured slowly in the domains where the elite in the field of theology and Catholic pastoral work held sway. The great mission of the Council will be to ensure that the movement towards renewal will spread from the elite to the universal conscience of the Church. And this brings us to the fourth item in our exposition.

4 REMEDIAL MEANS SUGGESTED

As we stressed from the beginning, Pius X in his *Motu Proprio, Tra le sollecitudini*, gave a great impetus to the movement towards liturgical reform, which aims at bringing back the people to the altar and the altar to the people. Great efforts have been made both in the domain of specialized historical investigation and in the domain of liturgical pastoral work in order to achieve the goal of active participation of the faithful in the sacred mysteries of the liturgy. A series of measures on the part of the Holy See aimed at promoting this mainly by means of translations of the missal and by permitting the so-called bilingual ritual.

There was more pressing need, however, for a radical reform in the changeable parts of the liturgy. Pius XII took a big step forward, at the request of pastors of souls. He sanctioned new rules concerning the eucharistic fast, the issuing of a new translation of the Psalter, evening Masses, the reform of the Holy Week service, and the revision of the rubrics of the breviary and missal. In 1948, in the Congregation of Rites itself there was established a specialized commission for a general reform of the liturgy. The Council convened, therefore, at a very opportune time. The fact that the scheme of the Constitution on the liturgy was the only one accepted in substance, proves that the work which the Commission did before the Council convened was well done.

An attentive reading of the Constitution on the liturgy shows that the Council foresees two means for making possible and for fostering the active participation of the faithful in the liturgy, namely, a liturgical education of the clergy and the faithful, and a reform of the liturgy itself. Although more space is devoted to the second point, there can be no doubt that attention must be centered mainly on the first. Fr. Gelineau writes:

> The seven chapters of the Constitution do not contain anything resembling arid juridical regulations. Most of the one hundred and twenty articles exhibit a theological profoundity and an elevation of style worthy of an Ecumenical Council. Each page reveals the breath of the Spirit. It is this Spirit that we have to absorb, for before inviting us to change our habits or modify our religious attitudes, the Second Vatican Council invites us to change our mentality. If the *aggiornamento* of the liturgy is to be nothing more than a change of façade, there will be nothing but frustration. The real *aggiornamento* is spiritual. It must be given our first attention.[18]

A Liturgical Formation of Clergy and Laity

It seems opportune, at the very beginning, to call attention to the following points. Before announcing the principles that should lead to a reform of the liturgy, and the ways and means by which that reform should be effected, the Constitution on the liturgy speaks about the theological nature of the same, as we have already seen, and in particular, in six consecutive articles (14-19) speaks of the primary necessity of a solid liturgical formation of the clergy and the laity. It is evident, therefore, that in the mind of the Fathers, guided by the assistance of the Holy Spirit and by their own pastoral experience, the reform will be of little or no value unless we give first place to the effort to enable the laity to grasp the authentic liturgical spirit—for this spirit is a stranger to the people of our day, because they have little appreciation for anything that savors of symbolism, the community life, living in the spirit of the mystery of the liturgy. Even if all the liturgy of the future were in the vernacular, it would avail nothing unless people were first prepared by a deep and persevering indoctrination into the *spirit* of the liturgy. This is what Fr. Vagaggini writes in his magnificent work, *Il senso teologico della Liturgia:*

> Even if the liturgy were to be conducted in full in the vernacular, and by some incredible process the changeable parts were to be adapted to the style of expression of our own generation, the liturgy will always be composed of a large and substantial part which will remain beyond the grasp of the people, unless they are lifted up, to a notable extent, above the common level. To bring about such a transformation will always be one of the essential and urgent tasks of liturgical pastoral work. . . . The people will always be in need of instruction and of catechizing in the theological, vital meaning of the liturgical assembly and of the particular rites.[19]

This, incidentally, is the experience of all who took part in the intensive liturgical movement in the countries of Central Europe from the beginning of the century to the opening of the Council. We cannot deny that the liturgical life of the Christian communities in these countries was more dynamic than the spiritual life in countries that did not have the grace of seeing in their midst some spark of the liturgical movement. Even so, with the passing of time, a stage of paralysis and stagnation set in. When the novelty of the new forms of participation had passed, its attraction disappeared little by little. Some might feel inclined to say that the liturgy gave what it had to give! But the truth is the contrary. The liturgical movement reached this crisis of paralysis because sufficient attention had not been paid to the prime essential, which is liturgical *formation*. Without this, any form of liturgy is destined to be sterile. This is indicated by W. Duerig, professor of Liturgy and Pastoral Theology at the University of Munich. He writes:

> In the countries where the movement started, that is, where pastoral work for the past fifty years has been fostering an active participation in the worship of the Church, we observe today a stagnation, and even a crisis in the work of liturgical renovation. Will the causes of this phenomenon be found in the liturgy itself or outside it? Should we remove the cause of the stagnation by a reform of the liturgy in accordance with the needs of the present generation, or should our primary aim be a reform of the present generation in accordance with the unchangeable nature of the liturgy?[20]

The book itself gives the answer. There is need of a reform, the most profound possible. But the main factor in the renovation will be the persistent effort to enable the faithful to enter the spirit of the liturgy. This is the reason why the Constitution on the liturgy speaks repeatedly of the need for liturgical education, within and apart from the functions themselves.

The requirements for the success of the reform enjoined by the Council are enormous, and the responsibilities for the pastors of souls are heavier, for they have to make up for past negligence. D. H. Jenny, auxiliary bishop of Cambrai, and member of the Council commission thus writes:

> The Constitution will demand new efforts in all fields of Christian life. Catholics will have to read the Bible and mold their lives according to it. Priests will have to meditate on it and preach it. Teachers of youth, beginning with the humble catechism (whose importance is considerable) will have to take their inspiration from the Bible and from the liturgy. And they will have to search these, not for occasional illustrations, but deliberately study them for a better understanding of a living and evangelical faith, of a life spent as the Church would have them live it, open to God and to the world, and of a method of participating in the liturgy that will spontaneously irradiate the apostolic spirit.[21]

The reader may well meditate on the efforts demanded by these words. A person will soon be disillusioned if he thinks that the Council made easy the work of the pastors of souls, and furnished prescriptions easy to apply and infallible in efficacy. True, it opened wide vistas of possibilities; but in the region of these vistas returns and gains are possible only at the cost of intensive work directed towards the proper formation and reformation of the mentality and spirit of the faithful. It would be relatively easy to rehearse the parts of a dialog Mass; but the enchantment will soon vanish unless the priest puts forth his best efforts to elevate the people to the level and spirit of the liturgy. And this is not achieved by preaching a sermon, or even by two or three "liturgical weeks." It is a work for a lifetime, and it must pervade all sectors of the apostolic ministry, from the instruction of children up to that of adults.

Article 14, in fact, warns us that "it would be futile to entertain any hopes" of fostering and building up any enthusiasm for the liturgy "unless the pastors themselves, in the first place, become thoroughly imbued with the spirit and power of the liturgy." We should notice that the Council speaks of "spirit and power," for it is convinced that, in regard to mastery of the rubrics, there is little to be concerned about.

In the above lines, therefore, there is an implied conviction that the clergy of the present day does not have the liturgical formation that is necessary in order to fulfil what the Church demands for the benefit of the faithful. In countries such as France and Germany, statistics give ample proof of this.[22] What is the situation here at home? A French humorist once said that it is easy to determine the year in which a pastor was ordained. One had merely to watch how he celebrated Mass. This would indicate whether he left the seminary in 1930, 1945, or 1960. The fact is, that almost all priests, especially those who completed their courses in theology before the year 1950 (and the cynical would add, 1964) acquired some knowledge of rubrics, and possibly some knowledge of the historical evolution of a few rites; but few of them were ever introduced to the theological spirit of the liturgy. Few ever understood the magnificent rules that are at the basis of the whole structure and life of the liturgy.[22a]

Still more recently, Romano Guardini wrote in an open letter:

> I am not speaking for the sake of criticism when I say that the formation of the clergy is inadequate. For a long time, and in part it is still true today, the Liturgy has been considered a sort of stepmother, for it is part of that group of ill-defined studies that go under the name of Pastoral Studies. It still happens today, in the case of many young priests on whose shoulders tomorrow the burden of liturgical innovation will be placed, that they leave the seminary without a liturgical and pastoral preparation for an activity on which all the internal history of the Church and mankind, for this and the following centuries, may depend.[23]

Furthermore, the theology which many priests acquired in the seminary was little more than food for the intellect, and at the same time purely speculative. Such priests left the seminary well equipped to defend the dogma of papal primacy and the hierarchical structure of the Church, so as to be prepared to meet Christians who would deny such truths—Christians with whom they would rarely if ever have any fruitful contact. Most priests never knew what to do with the mass of data and distinctions with which their notebooks were filled, and neither did they know how to nourish the members of the faithful whom they daily met with the richness of liturgy and theology with which the seminary should have equipped them.

W. Duerig, to whom reference has already been made, further observes:

> If the clergy does not love the deeply theological and vital values of the Bible; if during its long years of formation it did not learn to meditate on, and feel at home in, a world rich in biblical imagery and symbolism; if it did not learn to build its own spirituality and theology on this basis—is it not useless and unfair to expect such a clergy to lead the people into the riches of the liturgy, for this would be impossible without an introduction into the ways of thinking and speaking peculiar to the Bible. It is useless to expect from a clergy that lacks sufficient pastoral, liturgical, ascetical, and theological formation a sudden adjustment to the demands of the liturgical movement in the Church.
>
> If, as a result of the liturgical reforms already attempted before the Council met, there was created a notable imbalance between the demands of the central headquarters and the results obtained in the field of pastoral activity, it is to be feared that an increase in these reforms will merely aggravate the present imbalance.[23a]

A liturgical renovation of the faithful, if it to be profound and effective, can begin only from the diocesan seminary, which should be transformed into a liturgical center for the diocese. Such is the opinion of another author, and Duerig subscribes to it.[24]

This is a thought that should be present in the minds of those who, up to now, have shown indifference for the liturgical movement and for other great movements of the Church in this century. But it should be present, too, in the minds of those who are constantly demanding reforms. We can be certain, Fr. Vanderbrouke, O.S.B., observes, that those who today pray their breviary with haste and without devotion, with no thought of obtaining from it the vital strength that should support their spiritual life and ministry, would take the same attitude tomorrow, even if the Church were to reform the breviary, authorize the use of the vernacular in it, and reduce to half an hour the time required to recite it.[25]

Since we have been quoting the opinions of persons who are well acquainted with today's pastoral needs and present circumstances, we now add a lengthy quotation from Fr. Botte, for it describes with finesse and realism the conditions as they are. He writes:

> Going back to my years of childhood and boyhood, I recall that at that time rubrics and liturgy were synonymous. Thus, in 1922 I

heard a professor from the university criticize the liturgical movement, saying that people would never become interested in rubrics or the missal. Besides, this is the only item I have retained from all his lectures.

In such conditions, it was quite natural that a course on liturgy could be no more than a course on rubrics. If one were to consult the manuals of the day, he would find that that was precisely what was happening. What was the value of such courses? Not very high, judging by results. No doubt, if there had not been such courses, matters might have been worse. When I recall the divine offices which I attended in my childhood, I can merely say that they were very trying.

I can recall that some years ago Fernandel played the role of Don Camillo. Throughout the entire film his voice was admirably clear. But when he began to pronounce a liturgical blessing he always mumbled. I do not think that in this there was any intent to offend. Fernandel merely imitated what he observed in his childhood, and he did it perfectly. It was exactly the same impression that I got from ecclesiastics who celebrated the liturgy. One got the impression that the important thing was to make certain gestures and pronounce certain words, and the meaning did not matter. Nobody seemed to have any scruple if he swallowed half the words. I can recall a priest who, in other respects was very pious. But when giving Holy Communion he always used the strange formula: *"Ecce Agnus Dei; ecce peccata mundi!"*

In regard to the spirit of the liturgy, I would prefer not to speak. The pastor in my home town, a doctor in theology and a Roman prelate, author of a book about the Mass, advised his penitents to receive holy Communion before Mass, and to offer the latter in thanksgiving for the holy Communion they had received. Nevertheless, he was an intelligent and zealous priest who knew the rubrics perfectly, and celebrated the divine office with dignity. And he was one of the few who never mumbled!

I could say much more about singularities of this kind which I have met in the course of my life; but I am not interested in recalling memories.

As regards the people, they were deprived of any active part. The important thing was to fill up the time—with music, hymns, or any other means. The spirit of the time was best expressed by the author of a "method of entertaining children during Mass." His conclusion was, "In this way, Mass will be over before you know it."

Nobody will deny it if I say that the majority of priests of that epoch, no matter how zealous or pious, had no liturgical formation. They knew only the outside of the liturgy. They ignored its internal richness, its vital value, and its pastoral importance.[26]

The situation today, in the "classical" countries of the liturgical reform, Fr. Botte admits, is a little better. Nevertheless, he felt obliged to make the following comment:

> There is still a very great gap in the liturgical movement.... I think that the problem of the teaching of liturgy in the seminaries today is of the utmost importance for the future of the liturgical renovation.... We may introduce all the reforms we please, but unless there are well-formed priests to apply them they will not be of very much help.

This, too, is the experience of many other liturgists and pastors of souls. From among them, I shall take the liberty of quoting the author of the significant article, *"Former des célebrants,"* who writes as follows:

> ...We cannot expect any serious liturgical renovations in any diocese without an improvement in the manner in which future priests are initiated into the liturgy. We could carry out all possible reforms, we could publish directories, establish committees, encourage and prepare an active participation of the faithful; but if the seminary is to give the type of formation it was giving in 1930, it will be the surest way to destroy all our efforts.[27]

No doubt, among us the situation is more tragic than in France, Belgium, Holland, and Germany. How may we proceed to repair it?

Since on the one hand, the formation of priests is closely linked with the success of the entire Council plan in regard to the faithful, and on the other, pastors who are already in the ministry cannot go back to the seminary, there is no other solution but the following: Let everyone work at his best; and in addition, since there is a grave precept of the Council to do so, until the gaps are filled, recourse should be had to the study of books written for this purpose, and there are many, to participation in "liturgical weeks," and to congresses directed by competent persons. And to this end, everything else should be subordinated.

In this context, we should recall the grave responsibility placed by the Council on the consciences of bishops and major superiors. To them is applied the prescription of Article 18:

> Priests, both secular and religious, who are already in the Lord's vineyard are to be helped by every suitable means to understand ever more fully what it is they are doing when they perform sacred rites; they are to be aided to live the liturgical life and to share it with the faithful entrusted to their care.

In the case of bishops, it is prescribed that they are to establish, in addition, specialized committees on the diocesan and national level, specifically dedicated to the task of fostering the movement of liturgical formation and renovation in the diocese or the country. Obviously, the members of such committees should be entirely dedicated to the task, and not burdened with a thousand other occupations. In regards to this, it may be permissible to remind our very sincere and zealous diocesan pastors and major religious superiors that the sacrifice of giving a priest to this task—perhaps even leaving a parish vacant—will be amply rewarded by the work of the same priest within a diocesan or national committee.

The lack of priests cannot serve as a pretext or excuse, as so often happens, for overriding the demands of the pastoral needs of the community on the national or diocesan level. It is precisely this alarming lack of priests that urges us to use the choice and best available forces in key positions, in the nerve centers of the Church's organism, for on them depends all the success of her mission. It is time we gave thought to the amazing influence which a chosen group of zealous priests and laymen can have on the diocesan and national level, provided they are well prepared, with possibilities of adapting their knowledge to modern times and extending it more and more. Who does not know what the *Centre de pastorale liturgique* of Paris means for France, and the *Liturgisches Institut* of Trier for Germany? Why did the question of the "collegiality" of the bishops become such a clear issue at the Council if it was not due to the fact that the Church recognized in it the only possible and efficient method of facing the missionary tasks in the world of today? D. Ancel, Auxiliary Bishop of Lyon, thinks that it is very regrettable that the idea of "collegiality" has not yet taken sufficiently deep root. He writes:

> We lack a collegial sense, a sense of collegial consciousness. We have to convert ourselves. Some members of the Council want to convert others, instead. They speak as if their jurisdiction ends where their diocesan jurisdiction ends.[28]

The Council has already fulfilled its mission as regards the liturgy. Now it is our duty, as children of the Church, to give it effect.

It is obvious that the Council was preoccupied, in a special way, with the liturgical formation of candidates for the priesthood and religious life. That is the reason why it commands bishops and major superiors to assign to the teaching of the liturgy only men who are properly trained in institutes which specialize in this subject (Art. 15). This is also the reason why, from now on, liturgy will be one of the principal studies that will make up the theological course. With the same purpose in mind, the Council commands that the teaching of liturgy is to embrace not only rubrics and historical development, but also and above all the theological, spiritual and pastoral aspects of it. Further, the teachers also of the other disciplines are under obligation to stress, in every treatise where it is feasible, any connection with the liturgy which may exist. In fact, all such studies, each in its own way, point to the same reality, namely, the story of redemption, the center of all liturgical celebrations.

These comments convey an important message, precisely at a time when the Church is introducing a series of fundamental and even revolutionary reforms. These changes may create the illusion that with their simple application we shall reach the goal of the liturgical pastoral life, the participation of the faithful in the liturgical life. The truth is quite different. The pastor of souls who would think and act in this fasion would soon be the victim of a delusion that may be fatal. Very shortly before the Council began, Fr. Vagaggini made the shrewd observation:

> At this hour, the liturgical movement is over-optimistic, because of the reforms obtained and those sought. . . . However, judging by the results already obtained, it is becoming increasingly evident that the question of the reforms, and of the creation of new liturgical forms, although important, can never be more than a stage on the road to attaining the goal of liturgical participation, an instrument to help us reach that goal. . . . If the purpose of the liturgical movement is to bring back the liturgy, and in this context, to bring back Christ to the people. . .the decisive means to achieve it will always be that of understanding, or to use a better word, that of penetrating deeper into the inner spirit, of the movement. The reforms of structure. . .can be but a help, no matter how important, but no more than a help, to make people penetrate into the spirit of the liturgy. That such an aid was not decisive was well understood by a French priest who, during a discussion on the use of the vernacular, observed: "The liturgy, whether celebrated in French or Latin, will always be Hebrew for my people." And it always will be "Hebrew" not only for the people, but also for the clergy. Even after the reforms, when the first fervor of the novelty is over, we will notice how insignificant will be our progress in the direction of the goal if the clergy, in the meantime, did not grasp their "Hebrew" well and did not teach it to the people. And the "Hebrew," in this case, is the theological thought of the liturgy.[29]

No wonder, then, that the *Motu Proprio* of Paul VI, issued on January 25, 1964, insists so much on the necessity of preparing minds to receive the coming reforms. This concern is expressed in the pontifical decree concerning the liturgical formation of the clergy and faithful, the teaching and the living of the liturgy in seminaries, the establishment of liturgical committees, homilies during the Mass, and liturgical instruction within and without the Mass. The same concern is evident in the following words, following, as they do, a description of the nature of the liturgy:

> It should be immediately evident that in this area of concern nothing takes precedence for us over the need that all Christians, and especially priests, have to study the above-mentioned Constitution with care, with a view to observing its requirements with complete fidelity, once they have come into force. In view of the nature of the case, a knowledge and diffusion of the Constitution's liturgical prescriptions should be effected immediately. We earnestly exhort the bishops of the several dioceses, with the aid of their priests, "the dispensers of the mysteries of God," to act swiftly in promoting both the liturgical instruction of the faithful and their active participation in the liturgy, both externally and internally, taking into account their age and condition; their way of life, and standard of religious culture (cf. Art. 19).

On the day following the publication of the *Motu Proprio* of Pope

Paul VI (January 29, 1964), *L'Osservatore Romano,* the unofficial organ of the Holy See, published an article by D. Salvador Marsili, O.S.B., rector of the Liturgical Institute of the Pontifical Atheneum of St. Anselm, in Rome. From this article we quote the following passages, as a fitting conclusion to this section:

> The *Motu Proprio,* before mentioning the Council decisions that go into effect immediately, makes a strong appeal to the faithful and the clergy, and especially to the diocesan pastors, in order that, as of now, everyone may dedicate himself to a profound study of the same so that he may be ready afterwards to put it into practice, in the expectancy that the entire Constitution may be put into force.
>
> This appeal seems to us to be the most relevant element of the *Motu Proprio,* and we would like to see all making corresponding efforts. Before it can be applied, the Constitution must be studied. The liturgy is not the sum total of rubrics, as if all that would be needed would be to make gestures that were different from those made up to now. Instead of being a reform of ritual, the Constitution is a *reform of spirit and of mentality in ritual matters.* This is the reason why it presents us with theological perspectives that, in part, are intended to justify the reform, and, in part, are intended to create a new spirit of Christian worship precisely by means of the reform. In fact, it is not a matter of simply creating new external forms of worship; rather, it is one of creating mental categories that were either entirely new in the case of some, or declining or deficient in the case of others.
>
> Unless the spirit of the liturgy is assimilated, the reform movement runs the risk of ending miserably as an external show. It does not follow that because something is modern it has to be better.
>
> We believe that the Pope's appeal is very important, for the importance of the liturgical movement had been underestimated. This was sufficient reason for the voice of the Holy Father to be heard, just two months before the closing of the Council sessions.

B The Reform of the Liturgy

Now that we have considered the measures taken by the Council in regard to liturgical formation, we shall proceed to examine the reforms decreed in regard to the same liturgy.

It seems to us that Professor Balthasar Fischer, of the Liturgical Institute of Trier, in Germany, very aptly described the relation between the liturgical reforms instituted by the Council of Trent and those decreed by the II Vatican Council. He writes:

> Around the immutable nucleus of the liturgy there grew up, in course of time, prayers and ceremonies that do not have the same claim to immutability. In fact, in the first centuries they underwent continuous change and adaptation. If it is true that since the sixteenth

> century, also, these changeable parts have remained practically untouched, we should remember that such a state of things was supposed to be temporary, due to certain circumstances. In the event of a serious accident, we apply a plaster to an injured limb. In consequence of serious accidents suffered during the century of the Reformation, the Church was obliged to apply, as it were, a plaster to the liturgy. It was deemed necessary to impose, for some time at least, the same law to the whole world, and to determine the last word and the least gesture, so as to avoid a return to the chaotic situation that, in turn, was responsible for the divisions that occurred in the sixteenth century. A plaster cast can have salutary and beneficial results; but a person cannot spend all his life in a cast. The limb that is held in a cast needs to operate and move without hindrance.[30]

A little further on, the same author observes:

> When a person has been in a cast for a long time, and then one day the cast is removed, he realizes that at last he is back to his natural condition. Nevertheless, in the beginning he feels a little ill at ease and awkward. In a sense, the same will be true of the faithful, with the reform of the liturgy, when it begins to assume more definite form. But very soon the conviction and feeling that one is returning to a natural state that had been forgotten, will prevail. What was stiff and formal will become easy and natural, for that is what happens when normal conditions are reached.

We can state that the basic principle of the liturgical reform instituted by the Council is the fact that liturgy is the sum total of signs which signify and bring about grace in the soul, namely, the union between God and man. Here we have a very clear and evident principle which we can regard as the very nature of the liturgy. Here, however, it is more fitting to speak of a re-discovery, for today it is as clear as the noonday sun to what a slight extent the Roman liturgy of our time is the sum total of signs that really manifest the supernatural realities that are signified and conferred; how little the rites and the rest of the liturgical signs of today help the faithful of medium culture, in this day of atomic power and space travel, to understand as fully as possible the wonders of the divine mysteries. In fact, it would be more true to say that the rites and signs were more effective in concealing than revealing these realities. Persons who attended Council meetings will recall how often they heard in the very hall of the Council, Fathers who pointed to the advantages accruing to the faithful from the very fact that they did not understand the language, the rites, or the ceremonies. In contrast, the Council formulated the following principle. It is of capital importance for the contemplated liturgical reform, and for that reason was placed ahead of the other norms. It reads:

> In order that the Christian people may more certainly derive an abundance of graces from the sacred liturgy, holy Mother Church

> desires to undertake with great care a general restoration of the liturgy itself. For the liturgy itself is made up of immutable elements divinely instituted, and of elements subject to change. These not only may, but ought to be changed with the passage of time if they have suffered from the intrusion of anything out of harmony with the inner nature of the liturgy, or have become unsuited to it.
>
> In the restoration, both texts and rites should be drawn up so that they express more clearly the holy things which they signify; the Christian people, as far as possible, should be enabled to understand them with ease and to take part in them fully, actively, and as befits a community" (Art. 21).

The words quoted above indicate that the supreme test of the liturgy should be, that the rites will "express more clearly the holy things which they signify," and that in an atomic age, one of interplanetary travel. Who does not recognize that this principle contains a germ of revolution, using the words in the best sense, because it is a principle completely in line with the Church's tradition? We have said that people of our generation live in a world very different from that of the Bible and the old liturgy. There are certain elements which the Church will never be able to touch, like the essential elements in the sacrifice of the Mass, and the sacraments, as far as these are of divine institution. In these fields there is no possibility of adaptation of the liturgy to meet the needs of modern man; rather, it is he who has to adapt himself to such parts of the liturgy.

We can, at this time, envisage a wide range of reforms in accordance with the spirit of the Council if, as may be hoped, the post-conciliar commission takes seriously the principle of using in the rites only those symbols that have a meaning, and taking this to its logical conclusion.

We take the liberty here of reproducing an entire page from the writings of Fr. Gelineau, for it seems to us that it will be very useful in assisting us to understand how the Church can embark upon such an adventure without betraying her past, while remaining loyal to the spirit of tradition. He writes:

> For the Catholic who was born within the Church, received the normal instruction in the faith, was initiated into her traditional forms of worship, and was accustomed to find it in a response to his religious sentiments, the question arises: Why change the liturgy? For more than a thousand years, Christians have lived... with the ceremonies we know, with Latin, the Gregorian chant, a ritual for the administration of the sacraments that was endowed with an impressive stability, and in all that time they did not feel the need of a liturgical revolution. The liturgy was subjected to minor adaptations only, mainly because of the evolution of the arts. Why trifle with a building that has demonstrated its solidity and its value?

History itself gives us the answer. It is not the mission of the Church that has changed. It is the human and religious condition of men to whom she must communicate, through worship, the life of the Kingdom of God. There had to be a profound change in the liturgy when the Church passed from antiquity to the Middle Ages, for she was passing from her origins in a pagan world to a period in which Christian thought dominated. Today, too, the Church is face to face with a world of change. Christianity, in its sociological-religious meaning has disappeared, or is disappearing. Once again the Church is in the midst of a "diaspora," or dispersion. The extent of it is different, the form the same. A few examples will suffice to make this clear.

The liturgy contains, in its words and ceremonial, a constant appeal to faith, a constant announcement of the mysteries of redemption. In a world in which the faith was not challenged, in which the message of the Gospel reached the baptized in many ways, too much harm was not done if the liturgy remained a book that was practically sealed. In fact, in the Middle Ages Christian usages, the monastic and parochial life, the legends of the saints, the sculpture of the cathedral—all contained and transmitted a latent gospel message to men who were naturally religious. The Counter-Reformation developed the catechism and the missions to supplement any deficiencies in instruction. In short, Christian instruction remained for a long time, in spite of the growing unbelief of modern times, a constant part of our civilization.

It is not so today. The world of business, of work, of entertainment, of science, of art and culture, is laicized. Although a certain heritage of attitudes and usages still persists, it is no longer a sign of evangelical faith. One may visit a cathedral today, see a movie about Rome, or hear an oratorio without any reference to personal belief in Jesus Christ. Entire sociological groups, such as certain proletarian masses, may live completely outside the Church's influence. The faithful themselves, in the course of weeks and years, are submerged in a world where profane values and contemporary folkways do not imply any kind of orthodox religious life. That is the reason why it is a question of life or death for a baptized person, when he consecrates a half-hour or an hour to meet God in the church to partake in the liturgy, whether the celebration of the sacred mysteries will bring to him enough light and grace to resist the stifling influence of a laicized world, and, *a fortiori*, to give testimony of a faith living and clearly grasped.

If the word of God is announced in a language unknown to the hearer in whole or in part, if the prayer is said by the priest and the assembly in a form empty of meaning, if the community does not express the Church's faith so that everyone feels sustained and supported in his own faith, if the ceremonies which should translate and communicate visibly the invisible action of the Savior do not influence directly the sensibility of man, if the acts which should lead to super-

> natural realities are reduced to meaningless ornaments or to human values which result in imprisoning the spirit in a spell of esthetic enchantment—if, in a word, the sacred action does not appear as a totality of rites and ceremonies that affect the sensibility of those in whose favor they are performed, then such a form of public worship is lacking in fruit, no matter how "valid" it may be.
>
> Certainly, everything possible (and impossible) was tried, despite the difficulties, in order to find means to bring the message of the liturgy to those for whom it was intended. Missals for the faithful were multiplied, so that at least some could read the translation of the texts. A "commentator" was used during the celebration in order to clarify the meaning of the prayers of the priest, and the more obscure parts of the rites. Who does not see, however, that such palliatives merely reveal the lack of meaning in the words and ceremonies that needed to be interpreted before they could clarify the mystery they were intended to interpret.[31]

The II Vatican Council, therefore, gives us a great sense of security by decreeing that the main rule to guide the liturgical reform is to be the symbolic character of the rites and their vital meaning. Following the same Constitution, and without pretending for a moment that the treatment will be complete, we shall procede to illustrate first, the reforms that stem from the hierarchical and communal character of the liturgy, and then we shall discuss at greater length the reforms demanded by the teaching and pastoral character of the same. We shall accord due importance to two points which may be regarded as two seeds of revolution of primary importance, two sticks of dynamite hidden in the Constitution, namely, the principle of decentralization and of adaptation, and the rights of citizenship that have been conferred on the vernacular languages.

I Demands of the Hierarchical and Group Community Character of the Liturgy

We have noted above that the divorce between the masses of the people and the liturgical life is due in great part to the fact that in the minds of the faithful there was a failure to grasp the basic "community" character of the liturgy. And in the rites themselves this characteristic, too, was not made clear. This is the reason why the Council decreed a series of measures and reforms to emphasize the "community" character in the various rites, and at the same time sought to awaken the corresponding consciousness.

The community-hierarchical character of every liturgical celebration is recalled by the Constitution in the following words:

> Liturgical services are not private functions, but are celebrations of the Church, which is the "sacrament of unity," namely, the holy people united and ordered under their bishops. Therefore, liturgical services pertain to the whole body of the Church; they manifest it

and have effects upon it; but they concern the individual members of the Church in different ways, according to their rank, office, and actual participation.

From this dogmatic principle several dogmatic consequences stem, and these are enumerated in Articles 27-32, in a general way; in other scattered places through the Constitution there is further reference when the Mass, the sacraments, and so on, are spoken of.

As a general rule, it should be recalled that, in keeping with the essentially public and official character of every liturgical act, preference must be given to celebrations performed in a community pattern, whenever there is such a possibility. This is particularly true in regard to the Mass and the sacraments (cf. Art. 27).

Next, it is stressed that the community-hierarchic character of the liturgy demands that everyone—celebrant, ministers, singers, people—perform fully and exclusively those parts that pertain to their office (cf. Art. 28). Once more we are face to face with potent seeds of revolution in regard to the rites and our mentality concerning them. Fr. Gelineau comments:

> Common action does not mean that all do the same thing; rather, that only one thing takes place at any particular time, and that each one takes part in it according to the assignment he has received. What does this mean? It means that when a reader, invested with that authority by the Church, announces the word of God to the assembly, all those who are present hear it, and nobody, not even the celebrant, may take it upon himself to read it at the same time. It means that, if the celebrant addresses himself to the whole assembly in order to assure himself of their active participation before saying the Collect, or beginning the Preface, not one singer alone will make the response, nor the *"schola cantorum"* alone, but all the people together. It means that, in performing a choral part that concerns the whole assembly, such as the Introit or the Sanctus, neither the priest, nor the ministers, nor the faithful, will recite other prayers. It means that, if the reading of the Epistle pertains to the reader, and the Gradual to a chorist, neither will be done by the celebrant or the *schola*. It means that if a priest is present at the Eucharist, he will not take on the functions of a pseudo-deacon or a pseudo-subdeacon, or even of a simple layman. He will take on those of a priest.
>
> The list of violations of this principle of common action is very long. We are too accustomed in our churches to seeing everybody "keeping busy," each in his own way. The celebrant is concerned about what takes place at the altar; the master of ceremonies is busy with the personnel; the *schola* performs its functions in the organ gallery; and the rank and file of the faithful, in their place in church, busy in their own way according to their tastes and capacities.[32]

In the liturgy there is no distinction between official persons and private persons. All, including the commentator and the acolytes, perform a liturgical function in the same sense as the celebrant and the faithful, although on different levels. It is important to restore to our faithful, to our singers and to our acolytes a sense of dignity and responsibility proper to liturgical action, for this is nothing but a participation, "darkly and as in a mirror," in the liturgy of glory that awaits us when the Lord shall come in glory.

The present liturgical books, with rare exceptions, provide rubrics only for the celebrant, and in certain cases for the ministers. This is a further proof that so "clericalized" has the liturgy become that the official books accept as normal the mere "assistance" of the faithful at a liturgical celebration, performed as if the function pertained only to God and the priest. The Council now prescribes, in Art. 31 of the Constitution, that in the revision of the liturgical books due attention be given to the role of the faithful, and that this be expressly stressed in the rubrics.

The same consciousness of the community-hierarchical character dictates two other measures. First, the Constitution prescribes that, with the exception of differences due to hierarchical degree and the respect due to legitimate authority, there be no discrimination when the faithful take part in the liturgy. It should be borne in mind by everyone that with this article the Council seeks to do away with distinctions on the occasion of baptisms, marriages, burials, First Communion, and even Masses. It must be made clear that reasons of finance are not a sufficient motive for a pastor of souls to go against such evident principles of the liturgy, for such action would have consequences that would affect his pastoral work. It is important to bear in mind that this is not just a meaningless detail; it is a conclusion based on the very theological nature of the liturgy.

In Art. 30 it is prescribed that, with the exception of times when moments of silence are to be observed, everything is to be done in such a manner that the active participation of the faithful may be externally manifested through gestures, bodily attitudes, acclamations, responses, psalmody, antiphons and choral pieces, and through everything that is demanded in a sacred action between man and God. As happens in many cases, this is expressed in an article of just three lines. A superficial observer might say that there is no difficulty in carrying this out. Just teach the ordinary people when to stand, when to be seated, when to kneel, and then, all one has to do is to teach them to re-echo the voice of the celebrant.

The truth is very different. Anyone who has had experience knows how very difficult it is to induce the laity to take an active part in the liturgy, in view of the extreme individualism of the present generation, especially those who live in big cities. Who would fail to see behind the brief article of the Constitution on the liturgy, as a necessary requisite, an entire apostolate of catechizing, preaching, and theological formation around the great mysteries of God, Christ, the Church, the Mystical Body of Christ—all central truths of Christianity?

He who does not understand this will go his way unconcerned about the presence of the Holy Spirit in the Church, that is, he will be blind to the work of liturgical renovation. Or he will rush after a few "prescriptions" dictated by the letter of the Council, and possibly his congregation will give the appearance of people awakened from a secular slumber, when in fact all that has happened is that they have passed from inertia to formalism. In this case, it would be better to leave the congregation calmly praying during Mass, rather than to force them into an active participation in which harmony of spirit is missing.

What we have just said could bring into the minds of certain readers the following thought: My parishioners have no liturgical formation. They lack all the prerequisites for an active participation—some of them are actually illiterate. Now, a person who would think in this fashion would be lacking in the spirit of the Council. It is clear beyond doubt that what the Council demands is active participation in all cases, without exception. It is also obvious that in the minds of the Fathers the conditions required for such a participation do not yet exist, except in rare and selected cases. It is precisely because of this that the Council emphasizes the necessity for all pastors of souls to receive a good liturgical formation, so that in turn they may be able to educate the faithful. There is, therefore, no doubt that the absence of conditions conducive to an active participation does not constitute an excuse; rather, it should be an additional reason and stimulus for intensifying liturgical pastoral work.

Still another misunderstanding, hidden in the above-mentioned way of thinking, should be noted. It is the supposition that an active and full participation in the liturgy demands a special literary formation, or at least presupposes a community where the people are at least literate. This thought brings two observations to mind. The first is that, according to the very clear text of the Constitution, baptism is the only condition mentioned among the requirements for active participation in the liturgy, as a matter of right and duty, while there is no reference to intellectual culture as a requisite. A religion which reserved the most sublime form of communion with God to cultivated people alone, would be very unhuman and would have little of the divine in it. And let no one say that for simple people there is always open the possibility of direct communion with God through non-liturgical ways, for in this way they would have been deprived of the form of direct communion with God which is the center and apex of the whole life of the Church, the first principle of Christian life and spirit. The second observation would be this, that active participation is something very flexible and variable, something which will assume greatly diversified forms, according to the Constitution itself. For a Benedictine monastery, the ideal form of active participation may be a solemn performance in Gregorian chant, a form which evidently is not suitable for a community in the hills of Kentucky.

Keeping in mind the liturgy as it is today, one has to agree that in fact, the greater number of the ceremonies do not make provision for direct and active participation, not just on the part of the illiterate, but even on the part of well educated people, and even of the clergy, in case they lack special liturgical training. This is the precise reason why the Council has ordered a profound reform of the liturgy and of the rites, beginning with the language, a reform that will be so drastic that all may be able to understand, as far as possible, without any explanations. This is a necessary consequence arising from the nature of the liturgy, which is a sum total of signs which manifest and signify the realities they produce. In fact, the whole reform decreed by the Council should be directed by this norm:

The rites should be distinguished by a noble simplicity; they should be short, clear, and unencumbered by useless repetitions; they should be within the people's power of comprehension, and normally not require much explanation.[32a]

If the liturgy is essentially a community exercise, it is necessary that everything be done to awaken again in the faithful the consciousness of solidarity and community proper to the Mystical Body. That is the reason why Art. 42 prescribes that the sense of parish community life be fostered as much as possible, especially during Sunday celebrations. The consciousness of being one family around the bishop should be revived in the faithful. Once more we are faced with a herculean task, if it is true what a German pastor writes:

> A true Catholic parish is a community of a very special kind. It is vivified by the Holy Spirit and by grace, not by habit, or custom, or tradition. Every individual feels himself intimately connected with, and grafted onto Christ the Head, united with the Holy Spirit as soul, and with the whole community of the faithful. This concept, "to be in Christ," on the part of the individual and the community, was something that sprang spontaneously to the consciousness of the first Christians. This community spirit transformed them into powerful communities, active and eager to conquer, and this, without the support of customs, traditions, and such things that seem so essential to us.
>
> What we have today are isolated Christians. We have lost a sense of unity and community in Christ and with his Church, for prayer in common and sacrifice, for Christian solidarity in all matters of faith; or if we have not lost this spirit, at least it is very weak. This is our misfortune, the disease of our parishes. The disease is not of today or yesterday. Its causes were planted in the distant Middle Ages, and they are still operating. The century of the Reformation and Humanism, the influence of the Enlightenment and of Protestantism on Catholic life—these are all factors responsible for the progressive lack of a super-natural community spirit. Over and above, the highly educated circles were infested with the virus of subjectivism and individualism. This spirit, too, infected the lower levels of the simple people, and very soon extinguished in them the spirit of parochial community life, a fact which is confirmed by experience.[33]

Every wise pastor of souls realizes how immense is the task of Christian formation which the Church has imposed on us, so that we may be able to respond to her maternal appeal to bring the faithful to the abundant waters of the liturgy. The Church herself will do everything possible to bring about the fulfilment of this herculean task. Changes are expected even among the most "traditional" rites; a "prayer of the faithful" may be added; there may be Communion under both species on certain occasions; concelebration may take place more frequently than at present; and it is insistently recommended that the faithful receive Holy Communion during the Mass which they attend,[33a] and pastors are recommended to celebrate the divine office in common and with the faithful, especially the office of Vespers (Art. 99-100). It is emphasized that the divine office possesses a nobler form when celebrated "solemnly in song, with the assistance of sacred ministers and the active participation of the faithful" (Art. 113).

This decision, too, marks a notable innovation. Up to now the Solemn Mass in Gregorian chant was considered the most perfect form of worship. Yet it was a celebration in which the people could not fully participate. In regard to this matter, Fr. Schmidt further remarks:

> This document uses the word "noble." Now, the nobility of the liturgy resides first in the participation of the people, since they are elevated to a divine dignity: "a chosen generation, a kingly priesthood, a holy nation, a purchased people." We are dealing, therefore, with a "decayed nobility" if, in a Solemn Mass with music, the people are forbidden any kind of participation. If anyone is scandalized at this assertion, let him attend a Mass as a member of the faithful and not as an amateur in music. Will he not be disillusioned by all this empty external pomp that lacks a soul? What meaning can there possibly be in this public worship of the Mystical Body, the Divine Head and its members, in this concert hall atmosphere?[34]

He would be very wrong who would think that the chapter on sacred music and sacred art has little importance. The importance of the mentality to be created in regard to this is so great, and the transcendence of music to promote active participation of the faithful is such, that this very chapter, which contains only ten articles, mentions it expressly six times. Among other things, it is emphasized that the faithful should join in liturgical choral parts, even if, in order to achieve this, it should be necessary to reserve Gregorian chant to specially prepared groups. And this would be in accordance with this type of music.

The use of religious popular songs is also recommended in the liturgy, and it is expressly stated that new musical compositions should pay attention not only to art, but also, and above all, to making popular participation possible. To quote Fr. Schmidt once more:

> A notable improvement has been effected, since from now on religious popular pieces are now officially admitted in liturgical functions. It will now be possible to compose a "Mass for the people," one

> fully liturgical, in which the voice of the faithful will be heard without the danger of being criticized as non-liturgical.
>
> To the composers of sacred music, conscious of their liturgical vocation, an exceptional opportunity is now given to create, besides Gregorian chant, popular religious melodies inspired by the liturgy and worthy of it. Much is expected in this department, for it would be an unfortunate thing if it should happen that what we now know as popular religious pieces were introduced directly into the liturgy, without any criteria. The liturgical repertoire already contains more than enough pieces of low value, especially those known as "Mass with Music."...With the introduction of the vernacular, sacred composers will certainly have to resolve great problems, and will have to face them courageously.
>
> Only a loyal and open collaboration of sacred composers will make it possible for us to hear again, during the divine worship, the song of an assembly of the faithful, not only in a few model parishes, but everywhere.[35]

What is needed, in short, is a series of measures to make possible and to stimulate the active and conscious participation of the faithful in the sacred mysteries. Should we not have recourse to these new possibilities with gratitude and joy? Surely; but let us first be careful to revive the community consciousness of our people. A blood transfusion given to a sick and enfeebled person brings renewed life; but he will benefit only if the type of blood supplied corresponds to his own type. This is the law of vital harmony in nature. Something similar takes place in the spiritual world. The spirit of the Council, hidden in the Constitution on the liturgy, is the new blood which God injects into the veins of the Church. It would not be appropriate if an old organism which cannot harmonize with new energies were to receive new blood and spirit. The words of the Master spring spontaneously to mind: "Nobody uses a piece of new cloth to patch an old cloak; that would take away from the cloth all its pattern, and make the rent in it worse than before. Nor is new wine put into old wineskins; if that is done, the skins burst, and there is the wine spilt and the skins spoiled. If the wine is new, it is put into fresh wineskins, and so both are kept safe" (Mt. 9, 16-17).

2 *Demands of the Didactic and Pastoral Character of the Liturgy*

The second principle from which the Council derives a series of precepts and reforms, is the didactic-pastoral character of the liturgy.

The primary aim of liturgy is not to teach, but to worship God worthily and to sanctify man. It is obvious, however, that the didactic character of the liturgy is well accentuated in all religious celebrations. It will suffice if one glances at the first part of the Mass according to the Roman liturgy, even as it is celebrated today. The time devoted to biblical reading is quite considerable. We may say that among all methods of teaching, liturgy occupies first place, because, due to its very nature, it does not appeal to intelligence alone, but to the entire man, made up of soul and body, with all his internal and external powers and faculties. And when we speak of teaching, we are not restricting the word to the mere transmitting of knowledge; rather, we mean the imparting of a relish for the mysteries of faith.

Besides, the sacred atmosphere of the liturgical celebration is favorable towards fostering a perfect assimilation of the word of God at a time when every circumstance, and the entire context, gently invite the Christian to enjoy a vivid moment of the story of redemption—of what, in short, constitutes the *raison d'etre* and the end and purpose of all instruction and preaching.

What distinguishes the earthly liturgy from the heavenly one is this: in the earthly liturgy we reach the supernatural realities of each celebration not directly, but through a veil of signs; but in the case of the heavenly one, the same mystical realities will be possible for us directly, through the "light of glory" which will enable us to see and live the divine mysteries, face to face. The veil, in the case of the earthly liturgy, is the ceremonies, words—everything regulated by the rubrics. In this regard, we notice once again the perceptible signs that essentially integrate the liturgy from the coming of the Holy Spirit at Pentecost to the coming of the Lord in glory are not intended to hide; rather, they are intended to reveal the divine mysteries, to make them accessible to men as much as possible, but always safeguarding the transcendental character of such realities. If the liturgy had always had a clear consciousness that its rites should be symbolic and self-manifesting, it would not have come to the stage of rigidity and calcification that today makes the rites interpose themselves between the altar and the sacred assembly, like a veil that hinders the refraction of the mysteries of God in the spiritual retina and in the hearts of participants at the table of the Lord.

A GENERAL INDICATIONS

At the present time we do not know what the Mass of the future, what the ritual of the sacraments and sacramentals, and what the divine office of the post-conciliar era will be. That will depend on the work of the post-conciliar commission which is charged with carrying out the reforms according to the principles laid down by the II Vatican Council. Nevertheless, the Constitution itself gives a few suggestions which make it possible for us to anticipate, with some degree of accuracy, the direction which the Roman liturgy is going to take.

In addition to what has been said, in view of the attention given to it, it is clear that there will be much more emphasis on Sacred Scripture, and that the value attached to it will be greater than in the present Roman liturgy. Further, the renovation is to be made through a return to the primitive fonts, to the tradition of the primitive Church, where the eucharistic celebration was essentially the celebration of the Word and the Lord's Supper. In fact, even a person who knows little of the authentically liturgical spirit knows that the world and the language of the liturgy are the world and the language of the Bible. Nothing could be more natural than this, for what the Bible narrates, and what the liturgy celebrates under the veil of signs, the central theme of both, is the story of redemption. Pastoral experience demonstrates this fact, because progress in the biblical movement, at least when orientated to pastoral work, normally goes hand in hand with the progress of the liturgical movement. Biblical spirituality is the soil where liturgical spirituality flourishes, and vice versa.

The Church desires, therefore, that the Holy Scripture should become once again the Book of Books for the Christian, after so many centuries in which, under the influence of the Counter-Reformation, the reading of the Bible was forbidden to ordinary Catholics. This is the reason why the Constitution ordains that "in sacred celebrations there is to be more reading from the Holy Scriptures, and it is to be more varied and suitable" (Art. 35, 1); that "the sermon should draw its content mainly from scriptural and liturgical sources" (Art. 35, 2). This is also the reason why, especially in places where there are no priests, a "sacred celebration of the word of God" is to be introduced, in which devout reverence for God's word will have first place (Art. 35, 4); why Arts. 51 and 52 insist on the application of these principles in the new ritual of the Mass; why 91 and 92 insist on the same in regard to the divine office, stressing especially the need of a better biblical and liturgical formation; and finally why Art. 121 prescribes that the new musical compositions must be richly inspired by Biblical texts.

A few years ago a Protestant, who later became one of the official observers at the Council, remarked that the return of Catholicism to the liturgy, the Bible and the Fathers constituted a climax in a promising movement towards renovation which, in his judgment, was the greatest ecclesiastical event since the fourth century.[36]

In fact, the Constitution on the liturgy took seriously the motto under which Pope John XXIII wished to place the whole work of the Council:

> The work of the next Ecumenical Council is neither more nor less than that of restoring to the face of the Church of Christ all the splendor of the simplest and purest traces of her origin, in order to present her to the world exactly as her divine Founder has created her, without spot and without wrinkle.[37]

It is this natural instinct to return to the pure font, and not because of archeological dilettantism, that the Church has been led to look once more into the mirror of her primitive usages. It is specifically in regard to the place of the Lord's word in the liturgy that a well-known scholar testifies as follows:

> It constituted by itself almost the whole of the liturgical meeting. The prayer for the brethren that followed, and the thanksgiving of the president of the assembly, seem little more than a means of bringing it to an end.
>
> The number, selection, and extent of the biblical readings were

> left to the judgment of the president, but they certainly were numerous. This is clear from the twelve Lessons of the Vigil of Easter (today they are reduced to four), the only vestiges of the old structure of the Sunday worship that have survived to our day. As late as the fourth and fifth centuries, the Masses of the Saturdays of Quarter Tense had six readings, and in antiquity they were probably still more numerous. At all events, over a long period it would seem that the minimum number of readings was three, the first being taken from the Old Testament, the second from St. Paul, and the third from the Gospels.
>
> Besides, the psalms chosen to transform into prayer the content of the readings, today represented by the Gradual, Tract and Alleluia, were then sung in entirety, as still happens in some Masses during Lent. . . .
>
> Nobody in antiquity would have presumed to call the first part of the Liturgy such names as "Fore-Mass," "Preparation," or even "Liturgy of the Catechumens," as has been done in some of our best missals. Even though it is true that the catechumens were admitted only to this part, it is also true that this part of the Mass was destined also for the other faithful. Even if this was nothing but a preparation for the grace of baptism for the catechumens, an intellectual, moral and spiritual preparation for the faithful, it was already a sacrifice of praise and a communion with the Word.[38]

This is the reason why we may say with safety that as long as the Bible remains a sealed book to the laity, the missal, the ritual, and the breviary will also be closed to him. We must be under no illusions in regard to this. Concerning it, the Constitution imposes heavy burdens on the pastor of souls. The whole religious formation of children and adults has to be carried out against a background of biblical studies. Nothing of lasting value in the field of renovation, as sponsored by the Council, will be achieved unless a liturgical-biblical basis is given to the entire theological, ascetical, and catechetical work. Bible and liturgy must cease to be a specialty and must become, instead, the source of strength and inspiration which are indispensible for apostolic and missionary activity.

To what an extent the ideal envisaged by the Constitution is divorced from the present situation is stressed by Fr. Gelineau:

> For a long time the divine Word has been announced in a very imperfect way by and through the liturgy. . . . For centuries it has been solemnly proclaimed or read in a language incomprehensible to the faithful. . . . But could not people compensate, by reading in their own missal? No, because he who reads for himself does not *hear* the Word of God, since he does not receive it as a living message from God, who speaks to his people in the Church. Furthermore, the greater part of the Scriptures, and not infrequently the most beautiful parts, are not included in the Sunday Masses. The sermons,

in turn, are not sufficiently steeped in Scripture. The humble method of analyzing the Scripture step by step, after the manner of the Fathers, and explaining the words and phrases in order to make them clear, so that they might nourish the faith, is seldom practiced. Very often, the preacher takes the text of Scripture merely as a starting point, and then proceeds as he pleases. The catechism, which should give the child the very language of the Christian faith, does not speak the language of Scripture and does not prepare him for the liturgy.

Finally, private and personal prayers, usually founded on extra-liturgical devotions, fail to have recourse to the pleadings of the psalms and the invocations which pervade the liturgy. We have reached the stage when we no longer look on this as strange. There is no reason why we should find it strange, for the wonderful verses which the choral parts should bring to our lips and memory and heart are normally performed out of their context by a separate choir, and are sung in a foreign language.[39]

So great in extent and so profound is the liturgy in its didactic-liturgical role that the Council was led to prescribe a whole series of reforms. The aim was to bring about that each part of the liturgy, and the mutual relationship that binds them together, will become quite apparent to the faithful and will enable them to participate more fully in it, in accordance with Art. 50. The following lines will explain what the reform is going to be, without touching what is substantial. Parts that are repeated, or that are obsolete, should be omitted. Some elements of the primitive liturgy now no longer used, such as concelebration, Communion under both species, the Prayer of the Faithful, the catechumenate, the penitential elements of Lent, and so on, should be reintroduced.[39a]

At this point the reader may be inclined to ask why we have not yet mentioned other reforms, reforms which seem important and would foster active participation of the faithful in the Liturgy, such as the use of the vernacular, permission to adapt the liturgy to local ways and conditions, the role of the bishop in future legislation regarding the liturgy, and so on. These points were not dealt with, not because they are of lesser importance, but, on the contrary, because they are so important that they deserve to be treated separately. And this we now proceed to do.

B DECENTRALIZATION AND ADAPTATION

In a note published in *L'Osservatore Romano,* December 8, 1963, Fr. Antonelli, Secretary of the Liturgical Commission of the Council, wrote as follows:

> By a fortunate coincidence, the Constitution on the liturgy issued by the II Vatican Council was promulgated exactly four centuries after the closing of the Council of Trent (December 4, 1563). I call it a "fortunate coincidence," because as Trent opened a new

era in the history of the liturgy, so the II Vatican has closed it and begun another.

The same representative of the Roman Curia reminds us that the characteristic of Trent's reform and its merit lies in this, that it put an end to the emphasis on the individual, and ended, too, an abuse of freedom which threatened to transform the liturgy, the official worship of the Church, into a mass of human idiosyncrasies completely incompatible with dignity and sanctity in the celebration of the divine mysteries. After many centuries of liturgical decadence, the main cause of which had been the absence of a central authority, Trent reached "that unification of the liturgy. . .whose great merit was to eliminate so many 'singularities,' which were often unintelligible and decadent, which had been inherited from the Middle Ages." The popes who were elected after the Council, faithful to the directions of it, fixed once and for all the Liturgy of the Latin Church, successively editing the breviary (1568), the missal (1570), and the Roman Pontifical (1588).

Among the liturgical texts, now obligatory for the entire Latin Church, the "right of citizenship" was granted only to those rites which had a tradition of more than two hundred years, namely, the Ambrosian, Domican, Mozarabic, and that of Braga, Portugal.

In the year 1588 the Congregation of Rites was established, with the function of watching over liturgical unity and conformity in the West.

The New Code of Canon Law, promulgated by Benedict XV in 1917, in turn, reiterates the spirit of the Council of Trent when it declares, as in Canon 1257, that "it is the privilege of the Holy See alone to regulate liturgy and to approve liturgical books." By virtue of this prescription, the bishops were recommended, as a matter of right and duty, to watch over the due observance of liturgical laws as issued by Rome; but they were denied any legislative right in the matter. This prohibition was repeated many times. It appears even in the *Mediator Dei* of Pius XII, and in his allocution to the bishops of the world on November 2, 1954. The only possibility—and it was a slim one—was that of admitting legitimate customs, but this was governed, too, by severe clauses of the same Code.[40]

We have to admit frankly that the Congregation of Rites has fulfilled, to an admirable degree, its function as a centralizing and unifying organ. Nevertheless, the same Fr. Antonelli who makes the above admission does not hesitate to acknowledge that "we cannot enumerate among the benefits of that organ that of having tried to lead the faithful to an active participation in the liturgical life, something which had already been lost for centuries." Such a statement, coming from a person who in regard to this is definitely above suspicion, is in agreement with the following. The process of liturgical centralization, which killed at its source any further attempt to adapt the liturgy to new circumstances of time and place, was certainly a benefit to the Church. But the price paid was high. Four centuries later the II Vatican Council conceded that the substantial unity of the Church would remain untouched if provision was made, step by step, for adapting it to the new circumstances of time and place, circumstances which already exist, or will arise in different countries because of diversity. It is in this sense, and with good reason, that we may say that, at least in the domain of liturgy, the II Vatican Council marks the end of a movement established by the Council of Trent and known as the Counter-Reformation.

Anyone who knows the history of the Church will agree that the process of centralization that reached its climax, in the field of dogmatic pronouncements, in the solemn definition of the I Vatican Council on the primacy and infallibility of the Pope, was beneficial, and was almost a necessity imposed by adverse circumstances. Without the centripetal force of the papal primacy, humanly speaking we cannot see how the Church could have escaped unharmed and could have safeguarded her unity in face of the numerous centrifugal and disintegrating forces that have threatened her, such as the different new sects in the Middle ages, then the Reformation, the Enlightenment, Gallicanism, Laicism, and in later times, Modernism.

Today, as a result of so many centuries of living under a regime of growing centralization, and especially after the dogmatic principle of the primacy of the Pope, it has become evident that, wherever we turn, guided by the voice of the Pope and the pastors united with him, the Church sails buoyantly on the sea of the world, less troubled than before, and that she is engaged in correcting those defects that, against the will of the Fathers of Trent, unfortunately owe their origin to Roman centralization carried to its logical conclusion. Since the danger of internal division, which was so urgent in former centuries, is now no longer present, it is but right that the Church itself, which four centuries ago reserved to the Holy See the exclusive right to legislate in liturgical matters, should now begin to recognize, as in the first centuries, that local authorities have certain prerogatives. Bowing to local prerogatives, the primitive Church was Greek to the Greeks and Roman to the Romans; but an abuse of this led eventually to the chaotic condition which ended only with the Council of Trent.

Liturgy is the highest expression of the Church's life. Now, life is not a static or immobile reality; it is something essentially dynamic, always in process of becoming. To hinder this evolution means to stop the vital force which permeates the organism of the Church. It means to extinguish the Spirit who constantly renovates in his spouse the miracle of Pentecost, the miracle of the languages, and other charisms.

Mental outlooks, customs and cultures, diversified as they are from time to time and from place to place, make it necessary that the Church incorporate within herself forms and aspects which are variable, as are the diverse gifts of the Spirit which "breathes where it wills."

In European countries one of the factors responsible for the alarming defections from the Christian spirit among the rank and file of the faithful is certainly the abandonment of liturgical participation. And one of the causes of this is the extraordinary way in which ritual forms were permitted to congeal and become rigid, for this hindered that constant adaptation which is necessary in order to fight the nefarious tendency to place a wall of separation between the altar and the people.

The consequences of liturgical centralization, however, were even more fatal in the new Christian countries, in the so-called mission lands. We must not forget that the beginning of the great missionary work of the Church in modern times coincides exactly with the period of great centralization in ecclesiastical government. The missionaries of the primitive and apostolic era, inspired by the principles of the Council of Jerusalem made it their aim to *incorporate* into Christianity the new peoples they evangelized, and were always careful to respect local characteristics wherever they went. On the contrary, European missionaries who sailed for America, Asia, and Africa left Rome with the mandate to *implant* Christianity in its Roman and Western form, which was often totally at variance with the culture of the new people. Experiences such as those of Fr. Matthew Ricci in China, designed to incorporate Christianity with an old culture, have been very rare and have usually come to a violent end.

The results of missionary efforts, conceived and carried out under these conditions, are well known. Some people violently rebelled against any attempt to Christianize them, like an organism that instinctively expels something that is foreign to its nature. Others accepted Christianity, sometimes through force of circumstances, but they continued to groan under its weight, because they could not see in it the sublimation of all those authentically human values that the Good News of Christ should elevate, redeem, and supernaturalize, rather than repress, distort, and suffocate.

Under the pontificate of Leo XIII, and especially of Benedict XIV, a new era for the missions awakened. The encyclical *Maximum illud* of the latter remains the Magna Carta for the liberation of missionary Christianity from any stain of nationalism or colonialism, at least in regards to principles. This encyclical was followed by others, especially the *Rerum Ecclesiae* of Pius XI, and the *Evangelii* and *Fidei donum* of Pius XII, with which the missionary work of the Church was definitely freed from secular obstacles that hindered its vital vigor, such as nationalism, paternalism, Romanism and centralism.

Cardinal Constantini, former missionary in China and for eleven years Apostolic Delegate in that country, and subsequently Secretary of the Congregation for the Propagation of the Faith, characterized in this fashion the missionary work of the Church since the days of Benedict XV:

> Three great facts marked the great awakening and reform in the missions, namely, these latter are, or very definitely will be, free from the onerous protection of civil patronage; the foreign missions are planted in local churches, founded under an independent authority; and the character and traditions of each people are respected through an acceptance of everything which is naturally

good in the cultural and ethical patrimony of the various nations, through a Christianization of all that can be Christianized.[41]

In spite of all these facts, it is necessary to acknowledge that, in the field of liturgy, in European countries as well as in the missions, the principle of adaptation and decentralization, applied with excellent results in other sectors, such as the formation of a native clergy, continued to be almost unapplied here. Many years after Benedict XV, Pius XII on two solemn occasions insistently emphasized the principle that the Holy See alone was competent to legislate on matters of liturgy. All this, however, should not lead us to forget that the repeated insistence on the part of bishops, priests, and laity induced the Holy See to agree to local privileges, although the principle of centralization remained untouched.[42] It took a Council to establish liturgical centralization for the purpose of putting an end to unrestrained particularism; so, it took another Council to put its seal juridically on the principle of decentralization and of liturgical adaptation, thus correcting the excesses springing from an institution beneficial in itself.

The above comments seem to us to be opportune, even necessary, in order to show how the II Vatican Council is in the line of organic continuity in relation to Trent and the I Vatican. We shall now proceed to examine in more detail the new regulations in the Constitution on the liturgy.

In this regard, it would be well to keep before our mind the line of thought of the Fathers of the II Vatican. The moving and inspiring principle of the Council is: to make the faithful participate as fully as possible in the liturgy, the primary font of Christian spirit and life. In order to achieve the active participation of all without distinction—since everyone receives this right and duty in baptism — it is necessary to adapt the liturgy to the new circumstances of time, place, and persons. However, as only the local authority has the necessary knowledge of circumstances here and now, it follows as a consequence that the central authority should recognize this as a prerogative of the bishops—something, in fact, accruing to them by reason of their membership in the College of Bishops. In the absence of this, the liturgy cannot be adapted as it should be. Decentralization, therefore, is a step towards adaptation. The latter, in its turn, is a means to attain the goal sought by the Council, the participation in the divine mysteries.

The principles of decentralization and adaptation are expressed in Arts. 22-23, 37-40. The application of these principles in the case of the Mass, sacraments, and sacramentals, may be found in the corresponding chapters and articles. Let us first deal with the principles.

The first paragraph of Art. 22 asserts that the regulation of the liturgy pertains exclusively to the authority of the bishops. It is a consequence of the hierarchical nature of the Church. The authority contemplated is indicated by the words "authority of the Church," that is, the Apostolic See and, where Canon Law permits, the bishop. It is legislation of the Council of Trent which is included in Canon Law. It leaves to the bishops, taken individually, in addition to the right to watch over the observance of liturgical laws and books coming from the Holy See, the competence to declare if, in determined cases, a liturgical custom "beyond" or "against" a law may retain the force of law.

The preliminary text presented to the Fathers for discussion in the Council meetings granted the bishops precisely that right. There was something like a natural repugnance against legalizing, as a principle, the granting of further powers to bishops, for this would run counter to Trent and to the Code of Canon Law, which not a few Fathers considered untouchable. The Council discussions, fortunately, showed that the majority of those summoned there were not satisfied with concessions that may be given today and taken back tomorrow. They urged the introduction of decentralization as a juridical principle, to be endowed with the same vitality which Trent gave to centralization. If not, they feared that the old centralization would take over again.

In fact, the liturgical commission inserted a new paragraph, one of the utmost importance, Art. 22, Par. 2. This decreed that "in virtue of the power conceded by laws, the regulation of the liturgy within certain defined limits belong also to various kinds of competent territorial bodies of bishops legitimately established."

It should be noticed that this principle, in practice, abolishes Canon 1257 of the New Code of Canon Law, and those which depend on it. Beginning with February 16, 1964, the competent authority to *legislate* on liturgical matters is no longer exclusively the Holy See, but also "territorial bodies of bishops." How is this expression to be understood? Why was not the phrase "Episcopal Conference" used?

The preliminary text of the Council schema, when treating of the adaptation of the Liturgy, spoke in Articles 21, 22 and 24 of "Episcopal Conference." Many Fathers protested against this terminology, saying that the phrase designated solely a definite kind of episcopal meeting, when in reality such meetings assume different forms and structures from country to country, and from region to region. As a consequence, if this terminology were retained, the result would be that legislative rights might be denied to any episcopal assemblies that did not coincide exactly with the words "Episcopal Conference." In face of this, and also in view of the fact that episcopal conferences do not yet possess juridical statutes according to present legislation,[43] the Council decided in this Constitution which it issued to use a circumlocution. It spoke of "various kinds of competent territorial bodies of bishops legitimately established." According to an authentic interpretation by the spokesman of the commission on the liturgy established by the Council, the words designate not only episcopal conferences properly so called, but also plenary and provincial councils,[44] and, in certain circumstances even a group of bishops of different regions.

To this episcopal territorial authority, designated in such vague terms, situated, as it were, between the diocesan authority and the Apostolic See, the II Vatican Council gives a series of prerogatives. And it granted them even before giving a dogmatic statement on episcopal collegiality, and before deliberating on the juridical forms in which this collegiality will express itself. We shall consider the prerogatives granted.

In order to understand rightly the meaning of such a notable liturgical and juridical innovation, we should glance at the terms "under certain defined limits" and "the regulation of liturgical matters." The first means that a territorial authority depends on the Holy See in order to act. This dependence is apparent, among other ways, in the following. Their decisions have value only for their respective regions. Their decisions have value only if they do not go beyond the prerogatives sanctioned by the present liturgical Constitution, and by other documents that may be issued in the future. The decisions, finally, must be submitted to the Holy See before being put into effect.

The expression "the regulation of liturgical matters," in turn, indicates that the power of the territorial authority is *legislative* in the true sense of the word. What is granted is not the power just to *propose* reforms and adaptations, but the power to *decide,* within certain defined and safe limits, but with the duty to submit the decisions for the confirmation of the Holy See. According to an authentic declaration of the spokesman for the liturgical commission of the Council, the confirmation on the part of the Holy See is not for the purpose of giving the force of law to a decision that was lacking it, but to recognize such a force and to endow it with a new juridical stimulus.

An attentive consideration of these data enables one to realize that the II Vatican discovered a way of satisfying at the same time the concern of the Fathers of Trent, who determined to put an end to the arbitrary freedom of bishops in the official worship of the Church, and of the Fathers of the II Vatican, who were determined to do away with the immobility and fossilization of ritual forms. The liturgy of the future will avoid the second danger by the new principle of decentralization, which will allow a great deal of elasticity to the Roman liturgy, and will also avoid the danger of arbitrariness and of capricious particularism, for the recipients of the powers transferred from the center to the periphery are not bishops individually, but a determined group of them. If we are not mistaken, here we have a classical example of how a fraternal exchange of experiences and points of view may result in the discovery of a new solution, inspired by the same principles that have governed the whole history of liturgy. The liturgical life of the Church is today essentially that of the apostolic Church because, in addition to certain permanent and immutable features, she remains identical with herself, united and led by the same divine Liturgist of yesterday, of today, and of all time. In spite of this, the liturgical life itself assumes different forms, analogous to the vital forces which, in different ways, actuate the various potentialities of the seed buried in the ground, in the little plant as it puts forth its first sprouts, in the bush that reveals its first buds, in the big tree which offers the traveler the hospitality of its branches, the perfume of its flowers and the delight of its fruits.

Art. 22 gives a certain amount of legislative power to the territorial authority, but does not specify the extent of it. The same is true in Arts. 36, 54, 63 and 101, in regard to the use of the vernacular. The same applies to Arts. 37-40, 65, 113, 119, 120 and 128 where there is question of the adaptation of the liturgy to different circumstances of place and person.

Deserving of special attention are Articles 37-40 because of what they contain, as the spokesman for the liturgical commission admits. Art. 37 states the principle of adaptation as follows:

> Even in the liturgy, the Church has no wish to impose a rigid uniformity in matters which do not involve the faith or the good of the whole community; rather does she respect and foster the genius and talents of the various races and peoples. Anything in these people's way of life which is not indissolubly bound up with superstition and error she studies with sympathy and, if possible, preserves intact. Sometimes, in fact, she admits such things into the liturgy itself, so long as they harmonize with its true and authentic spirit.

The words quoted above are nothing else than an application in the field of liturgy of a principle that Pius XII, following the line of thought of Benedict XV, had established in regard to missionary work of the Church in general. By virtue of this principle, contrary to what has been the rule in the four centuries that have elapsed since the Council of Trent, the Roman liturgy of the future will have a flexibility which will make it possible for it to adapt itself to various countries and cultures, within the limits defined in Art. 38-40.

These limits will vary in different cases; and for this reason, too, the designation of the authority competent to legislate is not very definite. Art. 38 specifies the range of problems which the central authority itself, the Holy See, should leave for liturgical adaptation to local circumstances. Art. 39 indicates what adaptations, within the limits set by the authentic editions of the official liturgical books, are to be left to the competent territorial authority to decide according to their legislative powers. Art. 40, finally, indicates cases where there may have to be a wider adaptation of the liturgy. These are cases not foreseen according to the official books from Rome but which have been submitted to the Holy See. In these the territorial authority has merely the power to propose measures of adaptation. Let us examine each of these cases separately.

Art. 38 ordains that when the liturgical books, such as the missal, breviary, ritual, and so on, are being revised by the post-conciliar commission, the principle of adaptation should be kept in mind, namely, that "provided the substantial unity of the Roman rite is preserved,"[45] the ritual of Mass, of the sacraments, and so on, should be rebuilt in such a way that in the rites and the rubrics themselves there be provision for adaptation to local situations, above all—but not exclusively—in regard to mission territories properly so called.

Art. 39 is a continuation and a logical sequence to Art. 38. It asserts that, within the limits set by the liturgical books issued by the central authority, it shall be within the province of the competent territorial authority (not the individual bishops) to *decide* (in contrast to proposing to the Holy See) what adaptations are to be made, especially (but not exclusively) in regard to the administration of the sacraments, the sacramentals, processions, liturgical language, sacred music, and the arts, according to the fundamental norms laid down in the Constitution. In this Article, and in the preceding one, it is not difficult to see that the will of the Council is to adapt the liturgy to a diversity of situations, strongly insisting, however, that the substantial unity of the Roman rite is to be preserved—a reason why the rights to legislate within limits expressly laid down by the central authority is granted only to the territorial authority.

It is fortunate that the Constitution foresees cases of adaptation that may be more profound than those foreseen during the time when the liturgical books are being rewritten. What is to be done in such cases, for the margin left by the central authority is very restricted? Which authority will be competent to legislate in such cases? Art. 40, in order to safeguard the substantial unity of the Roman liturgy, decides that the Apostolic See alone is competent there. Since this authority, however, does not have the necessary knowledge of local circumstances, the territorial authority should diligently and prudently investigate what local adaptations are opportune, and then it should request permission from the Holy See to act in the matter. If there should be doubts as to whether or not the adaptations requested are opportune, the Holy See will permit them to be carried out for a specified length of time, by way of experiment, and afterwards, if they are found to be helpful and opportune, the permission may be made permanent.

Finally, to ensure a good reception for suggestions made by the territorial authority, the Council decreed, in paragraph 3 of Art. 40, that the Roman commission is to be made up of persons who are really competent.

These are the general norms concerning the range of local adaptations. Such norms are evidently valid for all parts of the liturgy treated in the various chapters, and they must be applied with the pastoral prudence and daring which pervade the Constitution itself. In some cases, however, a more concrete application is made. Thus, Art. 65 anticipates that in the rite of baptism elements of local initiation may be integrated, within the norms laid down in Art. 37-40, and provided such additions are compatible with Christian faith and tradition. Concerning the sacrament of matrimony, the Council goes to the extent of allowing the territorial authority the right to draw up its own ritual, thus making possible the widest adaptation to local usages and customs.[46] Art. 107 gives the territorial authority power to decree, or to suggest to the Holy See, as the case may be, local adaptations concerning the liturgical year. Art. 113, 120, and 128 do the same in regard to sacred music and sacred art in general.

There is no doubt that in this section the Council acted with so wide a range of vision that it surpassed the most optimistic expectations. Fr. B. Fischer remarks:

> The absolute uniformity of the liturgy in all parts of the world may have been necessary and beneficial for a long period of time, but it also had its dangers. Was it not, perhaps, a mistake to bind the people of Asia and Africa at the present time to our European norms in regard to liturgical colors, when everyone knows that colors, for these people, have a different meaning? In China, for instance, white is a sign of mourning. Why, for instance, was the Hindu priest forbidden to touch the altar with his forehead, according to local custom, instead of requiring him to kiss the altar, which is something very distasteful to Hindu sensibility? There is little doubt that the heavy, "steamroller" effect of a liturgy that remained unchangeable, and was carried out in European fashion, hindered greatly the progress of the Church in the far fronts of God's kingdom.[47]

Fr. Vagaggini, in turn, remarks:

> Here is a challenging prospect. Let us consider, for instance, the seriousness of the problem in certain mission lands of Asia and Africa. With prudence, but also with apostolic freedom, the path is now open to a slow, but deep, adaptation of the Roman rite to the local needs of peoples to whom the Roman liturgy can offer nothing, no matter how noble or glorious it may be, because of the level of culture they have attained, and because of their way of thinking.[48]

The Church, after centuries of centralization, in part beneficial and in part harmful, has rediscovered the principle of vital flexibility that allowed the missionaries of primitive communities to be Jews with the Jews, Greeks with the Greeks, and Romans with the Romans. In the wake of the II Vatican, European Christianity will never more be transplanted; instead, what will be preached will be the Christianity of Christ, in its full dimension of catholicity and universality, in which there will be no longer "Jew or Gentile, slave and freeman, no more male and female" (Gal. 3, 28).

C USE OF THE VERNACULAR

One of the pioneers of the liturgical movement wrote a few years ago: "Among all the questions of liturgical reform, the most important, the most decisive for active participation of the people in the rites and solemn prayers of the Church, the most difficult, is the one of liturgical language."[49]

That the language is one of the most important and decisive factors for active participation of the faithful is so clear that further proof is not needed. An *a priori* argument in favor of it could be expressed in this form: Only a person who understands the signs which put us in communion with the realities signified and produced can intelligently participate in a celebration. Now, among liturgical signs, the spoken word undoubtedly occupies first place, because it is found everywhere in the liturgy. This fact is especially apparent in the sacraments, for there the rites are necessarily things that you see and words that you hear, and the latter are the more important, for they fix the meaning of the former. This would be enough to show that a Council such as the II Vatican, whose aims were so clearly pastoral, could not help facing with prudence, and also with an open and clear mind, the question of the use of the vernacular in the Roman liturgy, the most widespread in the Church.

Another way of proving this is to appeal to history. In that way we face it from the opposite angle. It is a negative argument, to show that the language of the liturgy is a factor of primary importance to bring the people to the altar and the altar to the people. It is this. Historical studies show that the establishment of Latin as the official liturgical language, one that was untouchable in the liturgy of the West, was one of the factors most responsible for the divorce of the populace from the liturgical life. There is no need of further documentation, for we have discussed the matter in preceding pages. But we can invoke again the testimony of Fr. Schmidt, who is specially competent in the matter. He writes:

> If we place in the mouth of the faithful answers formulated in a strange language, no effect is produced. Since the people do not understand, they cease to hear, and keep silence, and the result will be that they invent a worship of their own, deriving it from books, from the commentators, or from their own sentiments. Thus the people who should sing and pray are transformed into a mute people, and the announcement of God's word, no matter how solemn, has become an empty formalism. A vital liturgy is impossible unless it is received as a living word, unless there is direct spoken contact, a vital dialog, an immediate contact between clergy and people. In the process of teaching, even in universities, the direct hearing of the lecture is much more efficacious than the reading of a manual or the explanation of a commentator. In radio and television, attention fades quickly, or at least is diminished, when a commentator has to translate the words of the speaker. The same is true in the church. The mute presence of the faithful is the most palpable proof that we have reached a crisis in the way of accepting God's word.[50]

And this, incidentally, is the lesson we learn from a study of historical development in the field of liturgical language.

For the early Christians it was a self-evident principle that the language of the liturgy should be the language of the people. This is the reason why Christ did not speak to the people in ancient Hebrew, and did not teach the people to pray in it; he spoke Aramaic. This was the reason why the writings of the New Testament were not written in classical Greek, but in the so-called *Koine,* a language then spoken throughout the entire Roman Empire. This was also the reason why all Eastern liturgies maintain the principle of adopting the home language in the liturgy, except in rare cases, and these only temporarily. The same principle was in vogue in the primitive Roman liturgy. The liturgical language was not Hebrew or Aramaic, but Greek. If by the third or fourth century it was changed to Latin, this was precisely because in the meantime Greek had become unknown among the people, and Latin was increasingly taking its place.

Due in part to circumstances beyond the control of the Church, the later Roman liturgy, with very rare exceptions,[51] unfortunately ceased to follow this wise precedent, and as a consequence created, little by little, within the liturgical celebration itself, a form of bilingualism, with the fatal result that it brought about a separation between altar and nave, between the priest and the faithful; and because it was sanctioned in official books, it has remained a reality to this day. The result is that today the priest addresses his official prayers to God in a language understood only by a privileged few, and the ordinary people have nothing else to do than to "assist" at what is happening between the priest and God, sometimes having the "privilege" of following in their missals the prayers said by the priest.

Throughout the entire West, from the beginning of the Middle Ages, national languages began to appear, little by little. The Church continued to maintain Latin usage unchanged, either because these new dialects took a long time to become cultural dialects, or because it was believed, and at the time there was reason for it, that Latin constituted a powerful unifying factor in an era in which the first symptoms of a great centrifugal and disintegrating movement were beginning to appear. Then came the Reformers, who fought against Latin and demanded the translation of the Bible, and the celebration of the liturgy in the vernacular.

The Church now faced another painful alternative. On the one side it was clear that the accusations of the Reformers had their *raison d'être,* because for the lower uneducated classes the Bible and the liturgy were no longer fonts of life as they had been in the early Church. On the other hand, a pure and simple adoption of the vernacular might seem to favor the Protestant heresy which denied that the Mass and the sacraments, by themselves, had value, and attributed all the efficacy to the work of the individual, especially the psychological efficacy of the word of God rightly understood. The Fathers of Trent decided to make Latin obligatory. They clearly foresaw, however, that this would mean a separation from the people, and this was a matter of deep concern to them. So they issued stern admonitions to the pastors of souls to solve this problem by giving instructions in the liturgy, during and outside of Mass.[52] Unfortunately, as was true of several similar projects, this prescription of Trent remained a dead letter until the rebirth of a liturgical movement in this century. The exclusive use of Latin served to aggravate the sad spectacle of the alarmingly increased numbers who turned their backs on those pure fountains, the Bible and the liturgy.

Ever since Pius X issued his plaintive plea for active participation, the question of Latin never ceased to be a source of concern, a growing concern, with the liturgists, especially from 1947 on, when the liturgical movement began to take on an increasingly pastoral aspect. While the Church continued to maintain the old principle of Latin as the sole liturgical language of the West, there was no alternative for lovers of the liturgy but to put in force the prescription of Trent concerning the teaching of the liturgy, a project which has produced splendid results. They also had recourse to the translation of the missal and ritual, in an effort to put into the hands of the cultivated faithful some of the venerable liturgical texts, so that they at least could follow in the vernacular what the priest was saying in Latin.

It is easy to see that the translation of the liturgical books represented only a partial and provisional solution, especially because, as we have already emphasized, the use of two languages in the same celebration results in a liturgical duality that is almost fatal and certainly unacceptable. The Holy See gave indications that it was willing to concede an increasingly wider margin to the vernacular, in case this was requested by the bishops. Hence the concession of a ritual that was totally, or at least partially, bilingual, the privilege of the so-called "*Hochamt*" to the dioceses of Germany, Austria and the German parts of Switzerland. Privileges were granted, but the principle in regard to Latin remained unchanged. Pius XII was insistent on this. The only door open to the liturgists and pastors of souls was to urge "in season and out of season." Only a few months before the meeting of the Council, an author revealed:

> An examination of the present literature concerning liturgical pastoral life gives the impression that for not a few authors the obstacle . . . to the active participation of the people is to be found in the fact that the language of the liturgy is one thing, and the language of the people another.[53]

In an article which would seem daring to those who were not present at the meetings of the general congregations of the Council, we read the following in regard to this duality:

> This duality can be remedied, really and definitely, only through a larger use of the vernacular. The translation of the liturgical texts does nothing more than make subjectively still more evident the divorce between priests and people in the community which offers the sacrifice. Only on the above hypothesis will we achieve an immediate understanding of the sacred action, and the participation in the same by those present, in the measure allowed to them, even though the sacrificial part of the Mass remained, for the present, in Latin.[54]

In the United States there was formed among Catholics an association which required, as the sole condition for membership, a solemn promise to pray daily for the bishops, so that they might give to the Church what it should normally have—a liturgy in the vernacular.[55]

The Fathers of the II Vatican Council actually found circumstances more favorable than did the Fathers of Trent; but anyone who considers the courage with which the Fathers of the II Vatican faced this particular problem, and the conclusions they reached in their deliberations, cannot help agreeing whole-heartedly with the opinion of Fr. Vagaggini:

> The II Vatican Council, by officially introducing bilingualism into the life of the Latin liturgy, took a historic and memorable step.[56]

We have also to agree with Fr. H. Schmidt, when he says:

> Although abandoning something really beautiful and of cultural value, the Church feels that it is her duty to take this course, especially in the vast world outside Europe, where Latin does not find points of contact with old and independent cultures, and where it is, for that reason, something foreign and imported. The Church is again conscious of her universal mission, and so she has rid herself of a tradition that was dear to her, but which, nevertheless, had become an obstacle.
>
> This step may prove painful for many, and for others incomprehensible. But the Spirit which gives strength and vigor inspired the Fathers of the Council to solve, with prudence and courage, a problem which had been in existence for a long time.[57]

Such a result was not accomplished without a long and sometimes painful clash of opinions and a meeting of contrasting views, in both the pre-conciliar committee meetings and in the plenary sessions. Of all the matters discussed, this was the one which provoked the most lively discussions in the Council. No less than eighty-one spoke officially at the first session of the Council, either for or against the use of the vernacular, furnishing the Secretary General with a folder of material comprising over a hundred large and crowded pages. Up to this point, no other subject, not even the discussion on the collegiality of the bishops or the establishment of the deaconate as a permanent state, has surpassed that record.

Even in the pre-conciliar commission, three tendencies had already begun to appear. One group maintained that the position of Latin remain absolutely unchanged, another favored the immediate use of the vernacular in the whole of the liturgy, and a third party advocated the view that Latin should be the principal language, but that in certain parts of the liturgy a vast and increasing use of the vernacular be permitted. In the pre-conciliar meetings, it was the third view which eventually prevailed, and in its discussions and balloting the plenary sessions took substantially the same view, but, as we shall see, they opened a still wider door for the vernacular.

The principles concerning the use of the vernacular in the liturgy of the future are contained in Art. 36, which includes four items. The first asserts that the use of the Latin language is to be preserved in the Latin rites, without prejudice to any particular law. According to this general principle, then, the II Vatican determines that Latin will continue to be maintained in the Latin rites; but it does not specify for how long, and to what extent. This is the expression that was chosen in preference to others that were more categorical and restrictive, such as the term "Western liturgy," which appeared in the original schema. The official spokesman for the theological commission made clear that under the term "Latin rites" would be included the Roman, Ambrosian, Toledan, Dominican and others. It should be noted, too, that the reference to "particular laws" was not included in the original text. Hence, concessions granted in the past remain untouched, and the door was not closed to similar concessions in the future. These words acquire an increased importance for they create a wider breach in the principle regarding the maintenance of Latin in the future. As a consequence, the bishops of a designated area may petition the Holy See for the faculty of celebrating the entire liturgy in the vernacular, without in any way running counter to this paragraph.

The Council itself, however, although it is not opposed in principle to the celebration of the entire liturgy in the vernacular, does not go to the extent of positively conceding it. The concessions, for the moment, extend to the cases specified in paragraphs 2 and 3 of Art. 36.

The second paragraph asserts that the mother tongue *may* receive more ample use in the Mass, the administration of the sacraments, and other parts of the Liturgy, and this will apply, *in the first case,* "to the readings and directives, and to some of the prayers and chants, according to the regulations in this matter to be laid down separately in subsequent chapters." We should pay particular attention to the word "may" and "in the first place." The word "may" indicates that the Council was not imposing the mother tongue, on the hypothesis, real or pretended, that it was not necessary, or served no useful purpose, or that it was not practical. The words "in the first case" indicate that the use of the mother tongue is not necessarily limited to the cases mentioned, but may go far beyond them, if pastoral needs require it. The Constitution does not forbid that the Canon of the Mass may be celebrated in the mother tongue. This follows very clearly from the words of the official spokesman for the liturgical commission, words approved in the plenary session: "As regards the different parts of the Mass in which the mother tongue may be used—and we do not exclude any part expressly, although consideration should be given to those Fathers who would exempt the Canon—we lay down these regulations. . . ."

The third section of Art. 36 is more liberal, too, than the original draft. It designates the competent authority which is to decide on the matter. As we have seen, the original text spoke of "episcopal conferences," an expression which finally gave way to one that was more generic. The territorial authority is competent to decide whether and to what extent the vernacular is to be used. The original text merely granted the right to propose to the Holy See measures to be taken. The revised text stresses the intervention of the territorial authority as a decisive and legislative force. The decisions of the territorial authority have to be submitted to the Holy See; but this intervention of the Holy See, according to an authentic declaration of the official spokesman of the commission, is not for the purpose of giving juridical power to a law which lacked it, but is a form of acknowledging such a power and lending new juridical force to it, as we have stressed already.

Worthy of attention is another detail in the same paragraph. By virtue of it, the territorial authority is competent to authorize the use of the vernacular language in the liturgy. Every ordinary, however, retains the right to use or not to use this faculty, depending on local needs and opportunities. In other words, the decision of the collective territorial authority is necessary so that the ordinary, individually, may proceed to introduce the vernacular language; but the use of that faculty is not imposed on the diocesan authority. This is what the official spokesman for the liturgical commission expressly declared in regard to the Mass.[58]

The fourth section of Art. 36, which was not included in the original text, decrees that translations from the Latin text into the mother tongue, intended for use in the liturgy, must be approved by the supra-diocesan territorial authority.[59] This measure is meant to forestall a multiplicity of liturgical texts in neighboring regions, and at the same time constitutes a guarantee, in the sense of hindering the circulation of inexact versions.

These are the general norms of the first chapter of the Constitution. The subsequent chapters determine in greater detail the extent to which the vernacular languages may be used in the different parts of the liturgy.

In what pertains to the Mass, Art. 54 has the following regulations: (1) In Masses in which the congregation participates, a suitable place should be allotted to the mother tongue. This could be achieved primarily, but not exclusively, by the reading of the Epistle and Gospel, and by the Prayers of the Faithful, for these are parts that refer more directly to the people. (2) When a more extended use of the mother tongue is desirable, the following must be observed: (a) in regard to those parts recited or sung by the faithful (such as the Proper and the Ordinary), the territorial authority may allow such a use, in accordance with Art. 54 b; (b) in regard to parts recited or sung exclusively by the celebrant, the norm of Art. 40 is to be followed. That is to say, the territorial authority, after careful and prudent consideration, should submit a request to the Holy See for such a more ample use. The latter will grant the permission sought, and also, if circumstances require it, permission to explore further. As may easily be seen, the same rule is here applied for the adaptation of the liturgy, when this goes beyond the limits foreseen in liturgical books.

It is worthy of note, too, that, according to Art. 54, steps should be taken, too, so that the faithful may also be able to say or sing together in Latin those parts which more directly concern them. This provision was absent from the original text, but was requested by certain Fathers. This measure does not mean that Latin enjoys a lordly superiority over the vernacular. Rather, it has in mind such things as pilgrimages, or international congresses, and it seeks to make it possible for groups composed of various languages and nationalities to enjoy full participation in the Liturgy which, in the circumstances, could not be held in the vernacular, due to the differences in language.

Art. 63 regulates the use of the mother tongue in the sacraments and sacramentals. As is well known, except for privileges granted here and there, prior to the Council the maximum the Holy See had conceded was permission to use a bilingual ritual, in which certain parts could be said in the vernacular, usually with the obligation of repeating them in Latin. And, in general, these parts were usually accidental ones.

The liturgical schema, in its original form, said nothing about the use of the vernacular in the administration of the sacraments and sacramentals, with the understanding that this matter would be regulated by what was determined in the discussion on the use of the vernacular in the liturgy in general, and in the Mass in particular. As was anticipated, many of the Fathers asked for a clearcut decision on this matter also. Some advocated that little or no space be allowed to the vernacular, and some wanted nothing but the vernacular, even in the essential parts of the sacraments. A third group wished to see generous usage of the mother tongue, but with the obligation of retaining Latin for the sacramental formula. To accommodate all of these wishes, the commission decided to insert a new article, granting permission for the vernacular, except in the essential part of the sacraments. Only in matrimony, and in other cases expressly approved, may the vernacular be employed in the essential formulary of the sacrament.

When so amended, the text obtained the necessary two-thirds majority in the balloting at the plenary session; however, since more than six hundred Fathers expressed a wish that this faculty be extended still further, the commission submitted to the plenary session a new formulary in which the use of the vernacular was permitted without any reservation whatever. This proposal received more than a two-thirds majority, and for this reason was accepted in the definitive formula.

Article 101 regulates the use of the vernacular in the recitation of the divine office. Section one asserts, as a general principle, that "in accordance with the centuries-old tradition of the Latin rite, the Latin language is to be retained by clerics in the divine office." The original text did not make provision for any exception for clerics, except in the case of sections two and three of the same article, namely, when clerics participate in the divine office conducted in the vernacular language by nuns, or by members of institutes dedicated to acquiring perfection, or by others of the faithful who are authorized to use the vernacular. The liturgical commission, by suggesting such a ruling, did not ignore the fact that many of the clergy did not have sufficient knowledge of Latin. It believed, however, that this consideration should yield place to one which it considered to be superior, the real or hypothetical situation that the unity of the clergy and the Church would be favored and strengthened if Latin were retained as the one and only language. There was also a fear that if a concession were made here, the study of Latin in the seminaries would deteriorate still more—and love for Latin had been inculcated repeatedly, even in recent documents from the Holy See. A considerable number of the Fathers believed, however, that such arguments could not be maintained to the point of hindering large numbers of clerics who were not endowed with a deep knowledge of Latin from receiving from the daily recitation of the divine office the fruits desired by the Church, fruits to which they have a right.[60] This would be in accordance with Arts. 86 and 90. Hence, the liturgical commission decided to maintain the general norm that, in principle, clerics must recite the divine office in Latin; but to the original text it added a clause which opens the door to the use of the vernacular whenever its use becomes necessary. The clause is as follows: "In individual cases the ordinary has the power of granting the use of a vernacular translation to those clerics for whom the use of Latin constitutes a grave obstacle to their praying the office properly." This text was accepted by the Council.

In order to understand the above text, we should keep in mind two observations made by the official spokesman of the commission. The first makes it clear that, when determining whether or not the reasons given are weighty enough to justify the use of the vernacular, the ordinary is to incline towards the side of generosity, and in every case to consider the "physical, moral, intellectual, and spiritual condition" of the person who makes the request.[61] The second observation is that the use of such permission should not result in negligence on the part of others to acquire mastery of Latin in the seminaries.

Section 2 of Art. 101 wisely stipulates that the "competent superior" may authorize nuns and members of lay institutes to use the vernacular without reservation, and they may do this even in choir recitation, provided their office has been approved.

Finally, section 3 of the same article states that any cleric who, together with the faithful, or with persons mentioned in section 2, prays the divine office in the vernacular, fully satisfies his obligation, provided an approved text has been used. This is of special interest to those who have not received from their ordinary a general permission to use the vernacular.

The reader who has followed us to this point should now be in a position to judge whether or not we have been correct in asserting that the Constitution on the liturgy has an eminently pastoral goal in keeping with the whole character of the Council. In the center of all the deliberations is the "people of God." The II Vatican seeks to popularize the liturgy in the best sense of the word by transferring to the popular domain of the faithful what, up to now, was little more than a privilege to a chosen elite of the clergy. All its deliberations and decisions have no other goal. They are all inspired by no other principle than this: to make sure that all take part more actively, more consciously, and more fully in the precious treasures of the liturgy. The ideal picture that has inspired and has permeated every one of the articles and sections of the Constitution on the liturgy of the II Vatican Council is none other than this: Christ glorious, Mediator and Head of the redeemed human race, Christ intimately united in the Spirit with the body of the faithful, on earth and in heaven.

5 CONCLUSION

"In the name of the Most Holy and Undivided Trinity, the Father, Son, and Holy Spirit. The decrees that have now been read in this sacred and ecumenical II Vatican Council, legitimately convened, meet with the approval of the Fathers. And we, by the apostolic authority which Christ has granted to us, together with the venerable Fathers, approve, decree, and institute them in the Holy Spirit. We also ordain that what has been determined by the Council be promulgated for the glory of God."

These were the solemn words with which His Holiness Paul VI, on December 4, 1963, gave to the world this most cherished gift of the Father of Lights, the Constitution on the sacred liturgy called *Sacrosanctum Concilium*. This was a historic moment in the long pilgrimage of the Church towards the Coming of the Lord. It was a moment of intense emotion. After a lapse of two thousand years, one could hear, resounding through the Church, an echo of the apostolic college gathered around the rock of Peter in the Council of Jerusalem, "For it hath seemed good to the Holy Spirit and to us" (Acts 15, 28).

If it has been our fortune to have found a reader who has followed us so far, we should like to see the solemn text of the Council impressed on his consciousness as a warning to remind him how great is the responsibility which each pastor of souls, and each devoted child of the Church, is now assuming in virtue of this most precious gift which has been entrusted to us by our Mother the Church.

This magnanimous gesture of Mother Church, regenerator of her children, comes to us under the seal of the Most Holy and Undivided Trinity, confirmed by the authority of Christ who said, "All that you bind on earth shall be bound in heaven" (Mt. 18, 18). But the same Christ, who poured the effusions of his Spirit upon the assembly gathered around his Vicar, brings to us a severe warning, "Much will be asked of the man to whom much has been given; more will be expected of him, because he was entrusted with more" (Lk. 12, 48).

More than precious is the gift of a new liturgy for a Church that is preparing to begin a new stage in her pilgrimage towards the Lord of Glory and towards returning to the Father. The precious talents, contained in fragile human vessels, should bring returns, with the grace of the Spirit, so that the curse fulminated against the avaricious and unfaithful administrator, mentioned in the parable, may not fall on us.

We, bishops and priests, are administrators of God's possessions, workers in his vineyard. In virtue of a grave law issued by the supreme authority on earth, we are charged with distributing to the faithful those treasures of the spirit and of Christian life which issue forth from the liturgy. And this we are obliged to do with generous hands, not as a concession, but by virtue of the most sacred of duties. Great is the responsibility of diocesan pastors, for they have bound themselves before God to act with prudence, and especially with apostolic daring, so that they may make it possible to achieve the enormous possibilities revealed by the Council. Great, too, is the responsibility placed on the shoulders of priests, secular and regular, of fulfilling the letter, and above all the spirit, of this new Council document, in loyal subjection to, and cooperation with, our diocesan superiors. Never should it be said of us, "the children begged for bread, and there was no one to break it for them" (Lam. 4, 4). In front of us, whether we be bishops or priests, stands a multitude of the children of the kingdom. They are not asking for the paltry crumbs that fall from the rich table of the lords. They are demanding full participation in the abundant table furnished by the Divine Liturgist, and we are waiters at that table. We are servants of those who sit at table with Christ, and in this consists our greatness and all our responsibility.

Shortly before his death, D. Lambert Beauduin, the great pioneer of the liturgical movement, expressed this conviction:

> As long as the people do not think with the Church, do not live along with her in the mysteries of Christ, do not pray with her, nothing will happen. The Council should have as its objective to give value once more to the great prayer which is the liturgy. This is my deep conviction.[62]

The II Vatican has fulfilled its mission, for it has opened to us splendid and unsuspected possibilities. The faithful stand eagerly waiting to be granted full access to the Mass, the sacraments and sacramentals, and the divine office. However, in accordance with an unchangeable law of divine economy, Christ has placed mediators between the multitudes who hunger for the bread of the liturgy and the Council itself. It is essential that the breath of life from the Spirit should awaken our consciences, therefore, and pervade our souls as pastors, and produce in us the transformation needed so that we may break from habits inherited from a faulty formation and a routine pastoral life. Above all, we must be conscious of our function as instruments of grace, and of our mission to reflect the light which comes from the Father, through the Son, and in the Holy Spirit, as we resume our task of leading our flock to the Father, through the Son, and in the Holy Spirit.

NOTES TO CHAPTER 5

1 A.S.S. (1903-1904), 329-339; 387-395; *Ephemerides Liturgicae* 18 (1904), 129-149.

2 H. Schmidt, *"Il popolo cristiano al centro del rinnovamento liturgico,"* in *La Civilta Cattolica* 115, Vol. I (1964), 123.

3 Cf. J. Gelineau, *"Réforme liturgique, renouveau de l'Eglise,"* in *Etudes* 320 (1964), 15.

4 St. Cyprian, *De Oratione dominica,* 23, in P. L. 4, 553.

5 C. Vagaggini, *Il senso teologico della Liturgia* (2nd. ed.; Rome: 1957), 653.

6 Cf. A. Bugnini, *Documenta pontificia ad instaurationem liturgicam spectantia—1903-1954* (Rome: 1953), 65, n. 9.

7 *Rivista Liturgica* 42 (1955), 189.

8 *La Maison-Dieu* 66 (1961), 3.

9 I. Roatta, *"Catechesi della Messa,"* in *Rivista Liturgica* 42 (1955), 271.

10 *Etudes de Pastorale liturgique* (*Lex Orandi* (*I*) Paris, 1944), 8 ff.

11 *Informations Catholiques Internationales,* Sep. 15, 1962, 17.

12 Gelineau, *art. cit.,* 9.

13 J.A. Jungmann, *Missarum sollemnia;* G. Dix, *The Shape of the Liturgy* (Westminster, 1945).

14 Vagaggini, *op. cit.,* 221 ff.

15 Thus, only to quote an example, in the sung Mass the choir sings the *Kyrie, Sanctus* and *Agnus Dei,* while the celebrant says other prayers.

16 On the contrary, the particularist character of today's Mass, of the prayers at the foot of the altar, of various prayers of the Offertory, as well as of those which follow the *Agnus Dei.*

17 St. Augustine, *De doctrina christiana,* 3, 9, 13.

18 Gelineau, *art. cit.,* 15.

19 *Op. cit.,* 657-658.

20 W. Duerig, *Die Zukunft der liturgischen Erneuerung* (Mainz, 1962), 9.

21 H. Jenny, *Constitution de la Sainte Liturgie* (Paris: Ed. du Centurion, 1964), Introduction, 24.

22 Cf. Jenny, *"Problemes de méthodes de l'enseignement liturgique,"* in *Les Questions Liturgiques et Paroissiales* 37 (1956), 206-207; also Duerig, *op. cit.,* 91-92.

22a In the Congress of Pastoral Work in Assisi (1956), the Apostolic Vicar of Ruteng, Indonesia, William Van Bekkum, made the following statement: "We missionaries, did not receive a liturgical education in our childhood. Unfortunately, the formation received in the seminary could not fill this gap, since under the name of liturgical instruction we had an introduction to the rubrics or, at the most, a summarized and supplementary glance at the history of the liturgy. The majority of our missionaries was never able to assimilate and make their own the true, internal and external participation in the Mass and in the liturgical life. However, as long as we do not achieve this, we cannot grasp the full value, nature and richness of the liturgy; we cannot have a clear idea of the missionary value of an authentic liturgical celebration." *"Il rinnovamento liturgico al servizio delle missioni,"* in *La restaurazione liturgica nell'opera di Pio XII* (Atti del Congresso di Assisi, 1956), 121.

23 R. Guardini, *"Ein Wort zur liturgischen Frage,"* in *Unser Gottesdienst, apud* Duerig, *op. cit.,* 92.

23a Duerig, *op. cit.,* 90.

24 J. Hild, *"Die aktive Teilnahme des Volkes an der Liturgie als Angelegenheit des Seelsorgers,"* in *Anima* 9 (1954), 344.

25 F. Vandenbroucke, *"Problèmes du Bréviaire,"* in *Questions Liturgiques et Paroissiales* 37 (1956), 169-172.

26 B. Botte, *"A propos de la formation liturgique dans les Séminaires,"* in *La Maison-Dieu* 66 (1961), 70-71.

27 *Ibid.,* 77.

28 *La Croix,* Nov. 14, 1963.

29 Vagaggini, *op. cit.,* 11-12.

30 B. Fischer, *"Was hat das Konzil über die Liturgie beschlossen?"* in *Katholisches Sonntagsblatt,* Jan. 1, 1964, 1.

31 Gelineau, *art, cit.,* 13-14.

32 *Ibid.,* 22.

32a Much is implied in Art. 34. And how much truth there is in what Fr. Gelineau says! "How numerous are the rites and ceremonies that can be understood only at the cost of explaining the historical origins of usages that have lost their meaning and are now but a subject of wonder. The numerous borrowings made by the Ceremonial of the Bishops from the Roman-Germanic court, the many accessory ceremonies of the Canon of the Mass, the prayers of devotion prescribed for the celebrant—all the entire accumulation of external details that were introduced in olden times to portray in outward and impressing manner what is a mystery. Today they serve but as veils to conceal the essentials.... What man of good will who reads the New Code of the Rubrics, published in 1960 as a preliminary sketch, will conclude that this vast labyrinth is the answer to what the Council has in mind? Thanks be to God, other achievements, such as the marvelous and restrained office of Good Friday, give us grounds for confidence.... The Roman Mass itself is not so far from this ideal as one might think. A few eliminations and arrangements will be all that are needed to make it possible for the original and eloquent forms to reappear. For instance, the structure of the Mass, and the characteristics of each of its two forms will be better understood—the Liturgy of the Word and the Liturgy of the Eucharist—if, during the Liturgy of the Word, the celebrant remains seated, listening to the readings, answering the psalms, and leading the prayers. He should arise and return to the table of sacrifice only after the offerings have been placed on it, at the moment of initiating the great eucharistic prayer that accompanies the Lord's Supper."

33 Duerig, *op. cit.,* 148-149. The author has excellent pages on the problem of educating Catholics for the liturgy.

33a In the chapter on the Eucharist, Fr. Schmidt uses the expression "Mass of the people," as if every Mass had not been that! Today we have to speak that way, even if some day (and we hope it will be in the near future), others will prefer to avoid such an expression. Why, then, does the Constitution use it? To awake the astonishment of the reader? To say something surprising that will startle him? Or to provoke opposition? In fact, it is loyally admitted that the sung Mass, in its present form, is so little the "Mass of the people" that not even the good and pious faithful feel any attraction for it. It is freely acknowledged that the low Mass, in its present form, corresponds so poorly with the demands of the faithful that, according to a very widespread opinion, the person who serves the Mass is considered the representative of the people. The Constitution itself is convinced—and this is very important—that the low Mass, although for the present it should be celebrated in accordance with the rubrics, will never be able to constitute an assemblage of the faithful in the liturgical sense (Art. 123-124).

34 Schmidt, *art. cit.,* 127.

35 *Ibid.*, 128.

36 R. Schutz, *Vivre l'aujourd'hui de Dieu* (Les Presses de Taizé, 1960), 19.

37 *La Documentation Catholique,* t. 57, n. 1341, Dec. 4, 1960, col. 1474.

38 C. Charlier, *"Réforme liturgique et renouveau biblique,"* in *La Maison-Dieu* 66 (1961), 18-19.

39 Gelineau, *art. cit.* 17-18.

39a See *Rite to be observed in the Concelebration of Mass and the Rite for Communion under both kinds* issued by the Congregation of Sacred Rites and *De oratione communi seu fidelium* prepared by the commission on implementation of the Constitution on Sacred Liturgy.

40 M. Noirot, *"Le droit du Saint Siège, des Evêques et des fideles en matière liturgique,"* in *La Maison-Dieu* 42 (1955), 34-35.

41 C. Constantini, *Va'e annunzia el Regno di Dio,* Vol. II, 25.

42 Cf. A. Rétif, *Was heisst katholisch?* (Aschaffenburg, 1958), 110.

43 The matter constitutes subject of a counciliar schema entitled *"De episcopis et de regimine Dioceseon,"* not issued yet.

44 Such information, as well as other we shall provide in the following pages, is still under conciliar seal, properly speaking. We use this material for the sole reason that without it we could not rightly understand the very text of the Constitution.

45 We should notice that nowhere is it explained what exactly is the substance of the Roman rite.

46 By the way, Art. 63 allows the territorial authority to elaborate, on the basis of the Roman Ritual, a particular ritual for all sacraments.

47 Fischer, *loc, cit.*

48 Vagaggini, *"I principi generali della riforma liturgica approvati dal Concilio,"* in *L'Osservatore Romano,* Dec. 8, 1962.

49 Vagaggini, *Il senso teologico della Liturgia,* 713.

50 Schmidt, *loc. cit.* 126.

51 The privilege, for instance, given to the Slav peoples, of celebrating the Roman liturgy in their native language. To the missionaries of China a privilege was granted in 1615 of saying the whole Mass in the vernacular language, except the Canon. To the priests of the Latin rite in Israel was granted the faculty of concelebrating in Hebrew.

52 Denz., 946.

53 Duerig, *Die Zukunft der liturgischen Erneuerung,* 39.

54 *"Der Schritt in die Zukunft,"* in *Wort und Wahrheit* 13 (1958), 247.

55 B. Kaemper, *Lateinischer oder deutscher Gottesdienst?* (Köln, 1959), 10. The above-mentioned association, according to information furnished by Fr. Vaggini, publishes a magazine with the suggestive title *Amen,* and subtitle: "How can he who assists as simple faithful say Amen to your thanksgiving, if he does not understand what you are saying?" (1 Cor. 14, 16). The Vernacular Society was disbanded in 1965, after announcing that it felt its general aims had been accomplished.

56 *L'Osservatore Romano,* Dec. 8, 1962.

57 Schmidt, *loc, cit.,* 125.

58 Here are the exact words of the Relator, which we transcribe because they seem necessary to us in order to understand the meaning of the counciliar text: *"Voluimus ita loqui ut... qui in quibusdam Missae partibus lingua vernacula uti volunt, ad*

suam praxim priores — sc. qui desiderant totam Missam latina lingua celebrare — non coerceant ... Nemini ergo porta clauditur ut, si velit, totam missam latina lingua celebret; et nemini clauditur porta ut in quibusdam partibus Missae vernaculam linguam adhibeat."

59 As it is known, the *Motu proprio, Sacram Liturgiam,* of Paul VI (Jan. 25, 1964) —at least according to the non-official text of *L'Osservatore Romano,* Jan. 29, 1964— ordains that versions of any liturgical text be submitted for the approval of the Holy See before being used. This in fact represents a disposition not foreseen by the conciliar Constitution.

60 Cf. Arts, 86, 90.

61 A little before, the Relator had said in the same sense: *"Singuli casus, quoad gravitatem impedimenti, sunt humaniter considerandi et expendendi a nostris Ordinariis pro caritate erga presbyteros nostros."*

62 Cf. *La Maison-Dieu* 66 (1961), 2.

6
The priesthood of the baptized realized in the sacred liturgy

Joao de Castro Engler C.M.F.

1 Scriptural basis

2 The priesthood of Jesus Christ

3 The Church's participation in the priesthood of Christ
  A The priesthood, a hierarchical ministry
  B The priesthood of all Christians
    1 The priesthood, a spiritual sacrifice
    2 Priesthood, conferred by baptism and exercised in the liturgical Sacrifice

4 The priesthood of the faithful according to the Constitution
  A The Eucharistic celebration
  B Active participation in the sacraments and the sacramentals
  C The divine office and liturgical prayers

5 Conclusion

Father De Castro Engler of Brazil is rector of the international college *Claretianum* in Rome. His article was translated into English by Father Tarcisio Beal of Washington, D.C.

His Holiness Paul VI, in an address at the close of the second session of the II Vatican Council, recalling what had already been accomplished, declared that the liturgical theme, in some respects, was "of most significance, by reason of its intrinsic value and its importance in the life of the Church."[1] These words of the Pope are in complete agreement with the declaration of principles and purposes made by the Constitution itself from its very first lines, lines which throw light on all its subsequent content. It asserts:

> This sacred Council has several aims in view: it desires to impart an ever-increasing vigor to the Christian life of the faithful; . . . it sees particularly cogent reasons for undertaking the reform and promotion of the liturgy (Art. 1).

To intensify Christian life is one of the main tasks of the liturgy, as is made clear in the next article proclaimed by the Constitution:

> For the liturgy, through which the work of our redemption is accomplished, most of all in the divine sacrifice of the Eucharist, is the outstanding means whereby the faithful may express in their lives, and manifest to others, the mystery of Christ and the real nature of the true Church . . . (Art. 2).

And in another place:

> The liturgy is the summit towards which the activity of the Church is directed; at the same time it is the font from which all her power flows (Art. 10).

In order to carry into effect among the faithful this vast and varied program of life and Christian activity in the world, it is essential that the faithful acquire a clear understanding of what is meant by proper participation in liturgical life. This does not mean a passive participation; rather, it calls for an active role in liturgical worship. A simple reading of the text of the Constitution will make clear how insistent were the Fathers, as they pleaded again and again, for an active participation of the faithful in the liturgical life of the Church.[2] "To take part actively," "active participation" and similar synonyms or their equivalents are expressions that are repeated again and again.[3]

This active participation of Christians in liturgical activities implies and manifests their participation in the priesthood of Christ. As the Constitution asserts:

> Rightly, then, the liturgy is considered as an exercise of the priestly office of Jesus Christ. In the liturgy the sanctification of man is signified by signs perceptible to the senses, and is effected in a way which corresponds with each of these signs; in the liturgy the whole public worship is performed by the Mystical Body of Jesus Christ, that is, by the Head and his members.

Almost identical expressions may be found in *Mediator Dei:*

> The sacred liturgy is consequently the public worship which our

> Redeemer, as Head of the Church, renders to the Father, as well as the worship which the community of the faithful renders to its Founder, and through him to the Heavenly Father. It is, in short, the worship rendered by the Mystical Body of Christ in the entirety of its Head and members.[4]

Before we consider the reflections which the Constitution sets before us in regard to the priesthood of the faithful, let us say something about the traditional theological doctrine on this matter. In order to get a more exact idea of the priesthood of the faithful, let us consider what sacred scripture has to say on the subject. It will afford us a good starting point.

1 SCRIPTURAL BASIS

As regards sacred scripture, we shall do no more than transcribe the sacred texts, and in connection with them we shall then give briefly the teaching of tradition and theology. The texts of scripture:

> Draw near to him [Christ]; he is the living antitype of that stone which men rejected, which God has chosen and prized; you too must be built up on him, stones that live and breathe, into a spiritual fabric; you must be a holy priesthood, to offer up that spiritual sacrifice which God accepts through Jesus Christ. . . . You [however] are a chosen race, a royal priesthood, a consecrated nation, a people God meant to have for himself; it is yours to proclaim the exploits of the God who has called you out of darkness into his marvelous light (1 Pet. 2, 4-5; 9. [Knox trans. throughout]).

He [Christ] has proved his love for us, by washing us clean from our sins in his own blood, and made us a royal race of priests, to serve God, his Father; glory and power be his through endless ages, Amen (Apoc. 1, 5b-6).

> Then I saw in the midst where the throne was, amid the four figures and the elders, a Lamb standing upright, yet slain (as I thought) in sacrifice. . . . He now came, and took the scroll. . .and . . .the four living figures and the twenty-four elders fell down in the Lamb's prescence. . . . And now it was a new hymn they sang. Thou, Lord, art worthy to take up the book and break the seals that are on it. Thou wast slain in sacrifice; out of every tribe, every language, every people, every nation thou has ransomed us with thy blood and given us to God. Thou hast made us a royal race of priests, to serve God; we shall reign as kings over the earth (Apoc. 5, 6-10).
>
> Then I saw thrones prepared for those to whom judgment was committed; I saw the souls of all those who went to execution for love of the truth concerning Jesus, and of God's word, and all who would not worship the beast, or its image, or bear its mark on their foreheads and their hands. These were endowed with life, and reigned as kings with Christ for a thousand years; but the rest of

> the dead remained lifeless while the thousand years lasted. Such is the first resurrection. Blessed and holy is his lot who has a share in this first resurrection; over such the second death has no power, they will be priests of God, priests of Christ; all those thousand years they will reign with him (Apoc. 20, 4-6).

As regards these texts, Father J. Coppens observes that those from the Apocalypse—especially 5, 10 and 20, 6—are to be interpreted in the light of the Final Judgment, and seem to refer to a situation which will take place only at the end of time. This would leave only the First Epistle of St. Peter, 2,9. Congar, and also Cerfaux, think that the texts from the Apocalypse have relevance, too, in the present period of the earthly life of the Church.[6]

We now proceed to other passages in which the reference to priests and priesthood is more explicit, and still other passages that have reference to the priesthood, especially to its most characteristic act, namely, sacrifice.

> And now, brethren, I appeal to you by God's mercies to offer up your bodies as a living sacrifice, consecrated to God and worthy of his acceptance; this is the worship due from you as rational creatures. And you must not fall in with the manners of this world; there must be an inward change, a remaking of your minds, so that you can satisfy yourself what is God's will, the good thing, the desirable thing, the perfect thing (Rom. 12, 1-2).
>
> Remember what you once were, the Gentiles, according to all outward reckoning. . . . You were outlaws from the commonwealth of Israel, strangers to every covenant, with no promise to hope for, with the world about you, and no God. But now you are in Christ Jesus; now, through the blood of Christ, you have been brought close, you who were once so far away. He is our bond of peace; he has made the two nations one. . .united in the same spirit, we have *access through him to the Father.* You are no longer exiles, then, or aliens; the saints are your fellow-citizens, you belong to God's household. Apostles and prophets are the foundation on which you were built, and the chief corner-stone of it is Jesus Christ himself. In him the whole fabric is bound together, as it grows into a temple, dedicated to the Lord; in him you are being built in with the rest, so that God may find in you a dwelling-place for his Spirit (Apoc. 2, 11a; 18-22).
>
> Let us hold fast, then, by the faith we profess. We can claim a great high priest, and one who has passed right up through the heavens, Jesus, the Son of God. It is not as if our high priest was incapable of feeling for us in our humiliations; he has been through every trial, fashioned as we are, only sinless. *Let us come boldly, then, before the throne of grace,* to meet with mercy, and win that grace which will help us in our needs (Heb. 4, 14-16).
>
> Why, then, brethren, we can *enter the sanctuary* with confidence

> through the blood of Christ. He has opened up for us a new, a living approach, by way of the veil, I mean, his mortality. A great priest is ours, who has dominion over God's house. Let us come forward with sincere hearts in the full assurance of the faith, our guilty consciences purified by sprinkling, our bodies washed clean in hallowed water [of Baptism] (Heb. 10, 19-22).
>
> It is through him, then, that we must offer to God a continual sacrifice of praise, the tribute of lips that give thanks to his name. Meanwhile, you must remember to do good to others and give alms; God takes pleasure in such sacrifice as this (Heb. 13, 15-16).

In regard to the sacrificial and priestly value of the italicized expressions "access through him to the Father," "let us come boldly, then, before the throne of grace," "enter the sanctuary," keeping in mind the fact that they are taken from the Epistle to the Hebrews, Spicq has this comment:

> The entrance into heaven and the "access" under the form of an entrance into the temple acquire a still deeper significance by reason of the seven-fold use of the verb *prosérchomai,* to which the Epistle to the Hebrews gives an exclusively religious meaning. In the Old Testament it was already a technical expression to indicate the action of the priest in coming to the temple to fulfil his ministry, approaching the altar to offer a sacrifice. . .the march of the people is not only a journey to a place of rest, but also a liturgical procession towards the throne of grace. . . . The Christians are those who approach, who come close, *hoi proserchómenci.* The *laós tou Theou* (people of God) is a community of religious who walk towards the Holy of Holies where God lives.[7]

We have, therefore, in the texts above mentioned, an affirmation of the priesthood of the Christians, of the people of God, in explicit or equivalent terms. What is the meaning of this expression, and to whom does it apply? To answer this, we must first consider the priesthood of Jesus Christ, the sole and highest Priest of the New Law (Heb. 7, 23-25; 27-28; 9, 12; 10, 10-14) from whose priesthood all Christian priesthood derives.[8]

2 THE PRIESTHOOD OF JESUS CHRIST

The priesthood of Christ is expressed in terms of his sacrifice. We were redeemed by the "precious blood of Christ; no lamb was ever so pure, so spotless a victim (1 Pet. 1, 19), who, however, "on the cross, his own body took the weight of our sins; we were to become dead to our sins, and live for holiness; it was his wounds that healed you" (1 Pet. 2, 24), because he "died as a ransom, paid once for all, on behalf of our sins, the innocent for us the guilty, so as to present us in God's sight; in his mortal nature he was done to death, but endowed with fresh life in his spirit" (1 Pet. 3, 18). Christ offered himself in sacrifice for his disciples so that they might be sanctified through the truth (Jn. 17, 19). "The purpose for which any high priest is chosen from among his fellow-men, and made a representative of men in their dealings with God, is to offer gifts and sacrifices in expiation of their sins (Heb. 5, 1; 8, 3). Thus, Jesus was the High Priest, and "it is his own blood that has enabled him to enter, once for all, into the sanctuary" (Heb. 9, 11-14; 10, 11-14).

St. Augustine says very truly: "Christ is priest because he assumed our body, because he offered himself as a victim for us."[9] "Christ was anointed king and priest. . . . Why priest? Because he offered himself for us."[10] And St. Thomas, in his commentary on the Epistle to the Hebrews writes: "Christ is called priest because he offered himself to the Father."[11] No less explicit is the Council of Trent when speaking about the priesthood of Christ, who has "offered himself on the altar of the cross" by a bloody sacrifice.[12] Finally, *Mediator Dei* speaks in terms of sacrifice, thus:

> The august sacrifice of the altar, then, is no mere empty commemoration of the passion and death of Jesus Christ, but a true and proper act of sacrifice, whereby the High Priest by an unbloody immolation offers himself as an acceptable victim to the Eternal Father, as he did upon the Cross.[13]

St. Augustine defines sacrifice as anything that is done in search of holy union with God, a definition which St. Thomas accepts in several passages of his works.[14] This concept is borne out by sacred scripture, for the Apostle presents Jesus to us at the moment of his entrance into this world as offering to his Heavenly father the oblation of himself:

> No sacrifice, no offering was thy demand; thou has endowed me, instead, with a body, thou hast not found any pleasure in burnt sacrifices, in sacrifices for sin. See then, I said, I am coming to fulfil what is written of me, where the book lies unrolled; to do thy will, O my God (Heb. 10, 5-7).

This voluntary offering was the redeeming sacrifice of Christ, although it would be fulfilled only on the Cross.[15] St. Thomas distinguishes clearly between the internal and the external sacrifice. He writes:

> There are two forms of sacrifice. One, the principal, is the internal sacrifice, to which we are all obliged, for all are obliged to offer God a devout spirit.[16]
>
> The external sacrifice consists in offering externally to God something as a manifestation of subjection and dependence, and this offering may be regulated by positive law. Instead of some particular thing, one may also offer some external act of virtue, either one that is prescribed, or one that is an act of supererrogation.[17]

We have two sacrifices in Christ, or, to be more correct, two elements of one and the same sacrifice, namely, the internal, the union and conformity with the will of the Father, and the external, the accepting and the living of his entire life according to the will of God, with its consummation in his passion and death, with all their humiliating and painful accompaniments.

But Christ did not offer just a private sacrifice, internal and external, of himself to the Father. Rather, he had and he exercised an official and liturgical priesthood; and because of this he is called the eternal Priest according to the order of Melchisedech. In the Epistle to the Hebrews, St. Paul compares the priesthood of Christ with the levitical priesthood, and shows the superiority of that of Christ. Moved by his love for the Father, Christ not only offered him the sacrifice of a holy life, consummated on Calvary, but, in addition, his death was the sacrifice determined and accepted by God as perfect reparation for the sins of the world ("He was the Lamb of God who takes away the sins of the world" Jn. 1, 29); the reconciliation of mankind with God ("Yes, God was in Christ, reconciling the world to himself" (2 Cor. 5, 19); the full justification and sanctification of men ("he has completed his work, for all time, in those who he sanctifies" (Heb. 10, 14); and the perfect glorification of the divine Majesty. His death was the true sacrifice of the New Law, the sole and perfect sacrifice of which all the preceding sacrifices of the Old Testament were symbols and images. And because it was the sole and perfect sacrifice, it was offered only once, thus consummating the entire work of divine reparation and the reconciliation of man with God. Precisely because of this, the passion and death of Christ were not in themselves a ritualistic sacrifice in the sense that they could be and should be repeated in religious manifestations of the worship due to God; rather, they were "supra-ritualistic," the sole drama, destined, because of their excellence, to take place only once and for all.[18]

On the eve of its bloody realization on the cross, Jesus wished to celebrate his passion and death in a mystic way, by a ritual sacrifice, to commemorate the paschal sacrifice of the chosen people, a sacrifice that was about to cease with the death of the new Lamb. This sacrificial rite was instituted and celebrated at the Last Supper, with the unbloody offering of his body and blood under the species of bread and wine, which he gave to the apostles with the command that they repeat that act through the centuries.[19] This Easter sacrifice of the law of grace is thus described by St. Paul:

> The tradition which I received from the Lord, and handed on to you, is that the Lord Jesus, on the night when he was being betrayed, took bread, and gave thanks, and broke it, and said, Take, eat; this is my body, which is to be given up for you. Do this for a commemoration of me. And so with the cup, when supper was ended. This cup, he said, is the new testament, in my blood. So it is the Lord's death that you are heralding, whenever you eat this bread or drink this cup, until he comes (1 Cor. 11, 23-26).

A little earlier the same apostle had written:

> We have a cup that we bless; is not this cup we bless a participation in Christ's blood? Is not the bread we break a participation in

> Christ's body?. . .Or look at Israel, God's people by nature; do not those who eat their sacrifices associate themselves with the altar of sacrifice? I am not suggesting that anything can really be sacrificed to a false god, or that a false god has any existence; I mean that when the heathen offer sacrifice they are really offering it to evil spirits and not to a God at all (1 Cor. 10, 16; 18-21).

This doctrine has been confirmed by an uninterrupted tradition from the beginning of the Church to our day.[20]

3 THE CHURCH'S PARTICIPATION IN THE PRIESTHOOD OF CHRIST

A The Priesthood, a Hierarchical Ministry

Our divine Lord, by instituting the Eucharist as a sacrifice, also instituted a priesthood in his Church, a priesthood destined to renew the same sacrificial rite of the Last Supper by the authority of Christ and in virtue of power conferred by him. This has been the constant Christian tradition, a tradition accepted by the Council of Trent and recalled in *Mediator Dei* in these words:

> Christ the Lord, the eternal High Priest according to the order of Melchisedech . . . at the Last Supper offered his body and blood under the species of bread and wine to God the Father, and under the same species allowed the apostles, whom he at the same time constituted priests of the New Testament, to partake thereof, commanding them, and their successors in the priesthood, to make the same offering (par. 67).

The priesthood of the ministry is communicated only through the sacrament of holy orders, and it is not, therefore, a prerogative of all Christians. The Church was constituted by her divine Founder after a hierarchical pattern, and in the Church the distinct roles of those who should serve the faithful always existed, as is evident from the writings of the New Testament[22] and from what we know of early Christian life.[23] However, if this hierarchical and ministerial priesthood is possessed only by those who have received sacred ordination, it is also the priesthood of Christ, and, in a measure, is shared in by all Christians. This is the teaching of sacred scripture, as we have seen. What is the meaning, and what is the extent, of this priesthood common to all the faithful?

B The Priesthood of All Christians

Let us take as a starting point a statement made by Pius XII, with the precise intention of limiting the concept and avoiding equivocations. He says:

> The main and proper office of the priest has always been that of "sacrificing," in such a way that when there is not a true and proper

> power of sacrificing there is not a true and proper priesthood.... It was the apostles, and not the faithful in general, that Christ constituted and made priests, and to whom he gave the power of offering sacrifice.... On the other hand, we cannot deny or doubt that the faithful have a certain priesthood, and neither can we underestimate or despise that fact.... However, no matter what is the true and full meaning of this reality and this honorable title, we must say that this "priesthood" of all Christians, great and mysterious though it is, is essentially distinct from the priesthood properly so called, for this power is the power to perform, as representative of the person of the High Priest who is Christ, the sacrifice of Christ himself.[24]

Two things are evident from these documents. Taking as a basis for comparison the act of sacrificing, or the Eucharistic immolation of Christ in the unbloody renovation of the sacrifice of the Cross, only those who have received priestly power through the sacrament of Holy Orders are competent to perform it, and therefore they alone are properly priests. Consequently, under this aspect, the ordinary faithful are not priests, except in a metaphorical or improper sense, and this we have to acknowledge.[25] On the other hand, Pius XII affirms the existence of the priesthood of the faithful, declaring it to be something "high and mysterious," not merely a "title of honor" but a "reality," something of "real and full meaning" which "cannot be denied or doubted."

We have, therefore, a priesthood in its full meaning, and we should add, a meaning as complex as is the reality it expresses.

We have seen that the priesthood of Christ must be considered above all in terms of sacrifice. And it is also in relation to sacrifice that the priesthood of the laity exists. It is a priesthood because of the sacrifice made of one's self by the renunciation of sin, and the observing of a holy life, and a priesthood through participation in the Eucharistic sacrifice of Christ. These are two real aspects, or two realities, which constitute the common priesthood of the faithful.

1 *The Priesthood, a Spiritual Sacrifice*

This spiritual sacrifice is, first of all, the sacrifice of one's own life, by living a holy life, by fulfilling one's earthly purpose according to the designs of God. This individual sacrifice, united to that of Christ, makes the total sacrifice of the Head and members of the Mystical Body. St. Peter says:

> Indeed, you are engaged to this by the call of Christ; he suffered for our sakes, and left you his own example; you were to follow in his footsteps (1 Pet. 2, 21).

Or, as St. Paul expresses it:

> Yours is to be the same mind which Christ Jesus showed. His nature is, from the first, divine, and yet he did not see, in the rank of Godhead, a prize to be coveted; he dispossessed himself, and took

> the nature of a slave, fashioned in the likeness of men, and presenting himself to us in human form; and then he lowered his own dignity, accepted an obedience which brought him to death, death on a cross (Phil. 2, 5-8).

It was of this constant realization of Christ's immolation in his members that St. Paul spoke when he wrote:

> I help to pay off the debt which the afflictions of Christ leave still to be paid, for the sake of his body, the church (Col. 1, 24).

In the Epistle to the Hebrews he has further comments on this form of sacrifice to which all the faithful are called by virtue of their Christian vocation, when he speaks about the priesthood of Christ. He reminds us of the holy life of Christ by reason of his sufferings, prayer, and obedience until death, and how Christ, in this manner, won "eternal salvation for all who render obedience to him, a high priest in the line of Melchisedech" (5, 7-10). And he goes on to say that "it is hard to make ourselves understood in the saying of it, now that you have grown dull of hearing" (5, 11). In the sixth and twelfth chapters he has further comments to make, and in the thirteenth he advises the faithful to imitate the example of Christ:

> . . . let us rid ourselves of all that weighs us down, of the sinful habit that clings so closely, and run, with all endurance, the race for which we are entered. Let us fix our eyes on Jesus, the origin and the crown of all faith, who, to win his price of blessedness, endured the cross and made light of his shame, Jesus, who now sits on the right hand of God's throne. Take your standard from him, from his endurance, from the enmity the wicked bore him, and you will not grow faint, you will not find your souls unmanned (Heb. 12, 1-3).
>
> Let us, too, go out to him away from the camp, bearing the ignominy he bore; we have an everlasting city, but not here; our goal is the city that is one day to be. It is through him, then, that we must offer to God a continual sacrifice of praise, the tribute of lips that give thanks to his name. Meanwhile, you must remember to do good to others and give alms; God takes pleasure in such sacrifice as this (Heb. 13, 13-16).[26]

This is also the sacrifice of which St. Peter speaks in the texts already cited (1 Pet. 2, 4; 5; 9), and one could almost say that everything which this apostle writes in the Epistle, in which he calls Christians a "royal priesthood," is neither more nor less than an exhortation to virtue as an expression of the spiritual sacrifice which, by imitating Christ, they have to offer to God.[27] In order to understand the extent of this spiritual sacrifice we should also compare the Epistle to the Romans 12, 1-2 and 6, 1-14.[28]

In addition to what sacred scripture teaches, we have also an abundant and constant fund of traditional teaching in regard to the same matter. Thus, St. Augustine writes that "Man, consecrated in the name of God and dedicated to him, is a sacrifice." "We are the whole sacrifice ourselves."[29] This spiritual meaning is the one most clearly and explicitly shown by tradition, as has been shown by the exhaustive work of investigation done by P. Dabin and J. Lécuyer.[30] The latter has this to say:

> This is the spiritual sacrifice demanded from the Christian. It would be superfluous to enumerate all the virtues that would stem from this fundamental attitude of soul; the Fathers delighted to enumerate them. . . .[31] All Christians are called to this priesthood; there is not, therefore, a family privilege, as in the Old Testament when it was necessary to be the son of a priest in order to share in the priesthood. All Christians now enjoy the privilege.[32]

To the baptized, and only to them, writes St. Cyril of Alexandria, is it allowed to enter the interior sanctuary and to offer spiritual sacrifices to God, presenting to God, as incense, the perfume of a life lived according to the Gospel.[33]

Father Congar, with these studies in mind, comes to the conclusion that there is an impressive and continuous chain of tradition in favor of it. He writes:

> Tradition is constant in regard to this, and its continuity ranges from the Apostolic Fathers and the Apologists to the classical epoch, and from there to the high Middle Ages, to the early scholastics, and to the scholastics of the great era. . . . The priesthood of the faithful corresponds, without a doubt, to the spiritual worship which is the offering of a holy life. Thus, it is frequently asserted that every saint is a priest; that we are priests by faith and charity, by the fact of belonging to the Mystical Body of Christ.[34]

It is interesting to observe how the Angelic Doctor expresses this thought. He is a writer who gives clear and fundamental formulation to the second aspect of this question, the reality of the common priesthood of the faithful, something we shall presently discuss. In answer to the objection that every Christian has the power to consecrate the Eucharist, seeing that he is a priest, in view of the teaching of St. John Chrysostom that "every saint is a priest," and every soul united to God by charity is a priest, St. Thomas says:

> A just man is united to God by the spiritual bond of faith and charity, but not by the sacramental power. Because of this, the spiritual priesthood offers spiritual hosts, about which sacred scripture says: A penitent spirit is a sacrifice to God (Ps. 50, 19). And in another place: Offer up your bodies as a living sacrifice (Rom. 12, 1); and still another: You must be a holy priesthood, to offer up that spiritual sacrifice (1 Pet. 2, 5).[35]

This is a priesthood common to all, whether they be simple faithful, or members of the hierarchy, for all are united in Christ, incorporated into him by sanctifying grace. In this respect there is no essential difference between the sanctification of the faithful and that of priest, bishops, and religious. The manner will be different; there will be different degrees of responsibility; but the ideal of Christian perfection will always be the same.[36] The priest, as well as the ordinary layman, must offer to God the sacrifice of a life lived according to evangelical self-denial. He must present the oblation of himself, both during Mass and at other times. As Pius XI expresses it:

> This is the reason why the immolation of the ministers and of the other faithful must be united in the holy sacrament of the Eucharist, in order that they may offer themselves as hosts, holy, living, and agreeable to God.[37]

And as regards this personal immolation:

> . . . this offering, in fact, is not confined merely to the liturgical sacrifice. For the Prince of the Apostles wishes us, as living stones built upon the cornerstone Christ, to be able as a "holy priesthood, to offer up spiritual sacrifices, acceptable to God by Jesus Christ."[38]

It is a spiritual priesthood. This does not mean a metaphorical, an unreal priesthood. This is not a metaphor, and this becomes clear whether we consult scripture or tradition.[39] With Father Congar, we should call it a real-spiritual priesthood,[40] a real-spiritual sacrifice of one's self, united with the sacrifice of Christ; and in this sense, it is a real priesthood, not a metaphorical one.

2 *Priesthood, Conferred by Baptism and Exercised in the Liturgical Sacrifice*

This doctrine was clearly formulated by St. Thomas Aquinas,[41] and was recalled by Pius XII in *Mediator Dei*. He writes:

> Nor is it to be wondered at, that the faithful should be raised to this dignity. By the waters of baptism, as by common right, Christians are made members of the Mystical Body of Christ the Priest, and by the "character" which is imprinted on their souls, they are appointed to give worship to God; thus they participate, according to their condition, in the priesthood of Christ (Par. 88).

The aspect of real priesthood and spiritual sacrifice, of which we have been speaking up to now, did not pertain to the liturgical life of the Church; it did not have a *direct* relationship with the celebration of the Eucharistic immolation.[42] This is not true of this second reality, the priesthood of the faithful. It is implicit in the scriptures, and appears less frequently in tradition,[43] despite the fact that it has a firm basis in revelation. St. Thomas Aquinas writes:

> The Christian has a double destiny. First and principally, he is destined to enjoy the life of glory, and for this he is marked with the sign of grace. . . . Secondly, every Christian is destined to receive, or to communicate to others, what concerns the worship of God. And the sacramental character is intended specially for this. For

> every rite of the Christian religion has its source in the priesthood of Christ. It is thus apparent that the sacramental character is especially the character of Christ. The faithful acquire a resemblance to this priesthood through the sacramental character, which is nothing but a participation in the priesthood of Christ which has its source in Christ himself.[44]

The character prepares and disposes the Christian to receive and to communicate to others whatever pertains to divine worship. St. Thomas goes on to say that "the faithful have an active potency to impart, a passive potency to receive."[45] Active potency corresponds to the priestly character received in holy orders, and the passive potency is the baptismal character.[46] Having established these two points, it merely remains for us to classify in accordance with them. However, the character of baptism, considered in itself, is not a mere passive potency. As Congar expresses it: "We would translate the thought of St. Thomas more adequately if we spoke of the priesthood of the faithful as a capacity to participate and receive, to perfect oneself by receiving,"[47] and in this sense the observation is justifiable. However, the great Thomist, Father Penido, observed already in 1944:

> The theologians who lived after the days of St. Thomas took this thought a step further, for they ascribed to the baptismal character the power of actively participating in the offering of the eucharistic sacrifice.

And Penido recalled that this doctrinal development had received the approval of the supreme authority in the Church when the encyclical *Miserentissimus Deus* was issued.[48] Today we could add *Mediator Dei* and the Allocution of Pius XII to the cardinals and bishops on November 2, 1954, and the present Constitution on the liturgy of the II Vatican Council.

We may say that, in accordance with tradition and with Thomistic doctrine, when speaking of the common priesthood of the faithful, we should distinguish between the real-spiritual aspect and its sacramental-liturgical aspect.[49] In fact, it is an accepted doctrine that the baptismal character, which is imprinted on the soul only with the actual reception of Baptism, gives to the faithful the capacity validly to receive the other sacraments, and therefore to take part in the liturgical sacrifice, a capacity which a soul which is justified without the reception of Baptism does not have. Nevertheless it can and must offer to God the spiritual sacrifice; and therefore it already possesses the real-spiritual priesthood. This is what Father Lecuyer says, and what he says has a basis in scripture:

> . . . a non-baptized person, who does not possess faith, a catechumen, for instance, may take part in the public prayers of the Christian community; but he has to be excluded from Mass and from the reception of the sacraments. In order to participate in the liturgical life of the Church, which is a social and visible body, interior holiness

> is not enough. It is necessary to be incorporated, by an external rite, into the new priestly people. . . . This is what St. Cyril of Alexandria says, echoing the practice of earlier centuries.[50]

We have, therefore, in this tradition the two real elements of the common priesthood of the faithful. Speaking on the same theme, Father Penido says elsewhere:

> One line of tradition is constituted by the teaching of the Fathers in regard to the metaphorical priesthood[51] . . . [but] a second line of tradition insists on the participation of the faithful in Eucharistic worship.[52]

4 THE PRIESTHOOD OF THE FAITHFUL ACCORDING TO THE CONSTITUTION

We cannot hope to find in the Constitution on the liturgy a doctrinal treatment of the common priesthood of the faithful, because the Constitution does not have a doctrinal purpose. Instead, it gives merely principles and an orientation to guide the liturgical life of the Church. In the preparatory schema of the Constitution on the Church there was a section on the priesthood of the laity,[53] but since this document has not been issued we must have recourse frequently to *Mediator Dei,* which was relied on in great measure as a basis for the present Constitution, as will be evident to anyone who studies both documents.[54]

A formal and explicit reference to the priesthood of the faithful is found only once in the entire Constitution. Thus:

> Mother Church earnestly desires that all the faithful should be led to that full, conscious, and active participation in liturgical celebrations which is demanded by the very nature of the liturgy. Such participation by the Christian people as "a chosen race, a royal priesthood, a holy nation, a redeemed people" (1 Pet. 2, 9; cf. 2, 4-5) is their right and duty by reason of their baptism" (Art. 14).[55]

As we see clearly in the above-quoted passage, there is reference to the priesthood of the faithful, which is based on the character received in baptism; a liturgical priesthood, a priesthood of worship. This is made more evident in *Mediator Dei:*

> By the waters of baptism, as by common right, Christians are made members of the mystical body of Christ the Priest, and by the "character" which is imprinted on their souls they are appointed to give worship to God; thus they participate, according to their condition, in the priesthood of Christ (Par. 88).[56]

We call this the only "formal and explicit" reference. However, it should be noted that in the Introduction, and especially in Chapter I (Art. 2, 5-13) the faithful are presented in their quality as "people of God," consecrated to God in the sense of a "consecrated nation" to which there is reference in the First Epistle of St. Peter (2, 9); and the expressions should be read, too, in the light of the Epistle to the Hebrews and of the Apocalypse, where the priestly character of the faithful is apparent, in the sense of a spiritual priesthood as we have explained it above. In the opening verses of the Constitution, when illustrating the reasons why the liturgy is so important in intensifying the Christian life, we are told that the liturgy

> is the outstanding means whereby the faithful may express in their lives, and manifest to others, the mystery of Christ and the real nature of the true Church. It is of the essence of the Church that she be both human and divine, visible yet invisibly equipped, eager to act and yet intent on contemplation, present in this world and yet not at home in it; and she is all these things in such wise that in her the human is directed and subordinated to the divine, the visible likewise to the invisible, action to contemplation, and this present world to the city yet to come, which we seek (Art. 2).

This entire descriptive definition of the genuine nature of the Church, or the society of the faithful, brings to our minds the picture given by St. Paul in the Epistle to the Hebrews of the People of God as a society of pilgrims in this world journeying towards a future land, towards a heavenly sanctuary, a society on pilgrimage, a religious and liturgical society united with its Chief and Leader, Jesus Christ, High Priest and center of worship in heaven as well as on earth.[57]

The Constitution goes on to say:

> While the liturgy daily builds up those who are within into a holy temple of the Lord, into a dwelling place for God in the Spirit (Eph. 2, 21-22), to the mature measure of the fullness of Christ (Eph. 4, 13), at the same time it marvelously strengthens their power to preach Christ, and thus shows forth the Church to those who are outside as a sign lifted up among the nations (Is. 11, 12) under which the scattered children of God may be gathered together (Jn. 11, 52) until there is one sheepfold and one shepherd (Jn. 10, 16).

This is to remind us of what St. Paul wrote in his Epistle to the Ephesians (2, 18-22) and what St. Peter wrote in his First Epistle (2, 4-5), passages which speak about the spiritual priesthood. Under the expression "it strengthens their power to preach Christ" we may see the duty and right imposed on every Christian by the sacramental character.

The Constitution, based upon the work of salvation accomplished by Christ, reminds us that as God has sent his Son incarnate, anointed by the Holy Spirit, for the redemption of the world, "therefore in Christ the perfect achievement of our reconciliation came forth, and the fullness of divine worship was given to us" (Art. 5). We are further reminded that "In the liturgy the whole public worship is performed by the Mystical Body of Jesus Christ, that is, by the Head and his members" for "liturgy is considered as an exercise of the priestly office of Jesus Christ (Art. 7).

The divine worship is exercised, not only by "realizing" or "effecting" the sanctification of man through signs perceptible to the senses, but also, as St. Thomas teaches us, "by receiving or imparting" these effects of sanctification. Man participates in the priesthood of Christ through all the sacraments, and receives some benefits from this priesthood.[58] The Constitution itself recalls the fullness of the priestly power given to the apostles, thus:

> Just as Christ was sent by the Father, so also he sent the apostles, filled with the Holy Spirit. This he did that, by preaching the Gospel to every creature, they might proclaim that the Son of God, by his death and resurrection, has freed us from the power of Satan and from death, and brought us into the kingdom of his Father. His purpose also was that they might accomplish the work of salvation which they had proclaimed, by means of the Mass and the sacraments, around which the entire liturgical life revolves (Art. 6).

Almost immediately after this, the participation of the faithful is mentioned:

> For that reason, on the very day of Pentecost, when the Church appeared before the world, those who received the word of Peter "were baptized, and they continued steadfast in the teaching of the apostles and in the communion of bread and in prayers . . . praising God and being in favor with all the people" (Acts 2, 41-47). From that time onwards the Church never failed to come together to celebrate the paschal mystery: reading those things "which were in all the scriptures concerning him" (Lk. 24, 27), celebrating the Eucharist in which "the victory and triumph of his death are again made present" and at the same time giving thanks "to God for his unspeakable gift" (2 Cor. 9, 15) in Christ Jesus, in "Praise of his glory" (Eph. 1, 12), through the power of the Holy Spirit (Art. 6).

The real elements of the spiritual priesthood and of the sacramental-liturgical priesthood of the faithful are closely united: any religious act performed by a baptized person, if instituted by Christ or the Church as an official act, provided it is performed in a manner legitimately approved and the faithful have received delegation to perform it, has all that is needed for the exercise of the spiritual and liturgical priesthood.

Beginning with the sacramental-liturgical priesthood received by the faithful in virtue of their baptism, the Church expects from them "a full, conscious, and active participation in liturgical celebration" (Art. 14). The reason for this is that:

> liturgical functions are not private functions, but are celebrations by the Church, which is the "sacrament of unity," namely, the holy people united and ordered under their bishops. Therefore, liturgical services pertain to the whole body of the Church; they manifest it and have effects upon it. But they concern the individual members of the Church in different ways, according to their different rank, office, and actual participation (Art. 26).

The whole Church performs the liturgical action; and therefore all those who are members of it take part in it—but according to the degree of participation which is assigned to each person. To the hierarchical priesthood, which has been conferred by the sacrament of holy orders, a full liturgical participation is granted: they are ministers legitimately commissioned by Christ himself to participate in the entire divine worship in his name, in his place, and representing the entire Church, his Mystical Body. Participating to a lesser degree, next in order, come those who have been legitimately commissioned for the things that pertain to divine worship. What part of this commission pertains to the ordinary faithful? Let us examine what the Constitution has decided, and let us follow the same division and procedure of the different liturgical acts as they are presented.

A The Eucharistic Celebration

In the second chapter, after speaking of the mystery of the Eucharist, and after recalling how Christ instituted it at the Last Supper and entrusted it to his Church to celebrate it throughout the centuries (Art. 47), the Constitution speaks immediately of the participation of the faithful in this celebration, thus:

> The Church, therefore, earnestly desires that Christ's faithful, when present at this mystery of faith, should not be there as strangers or silent spectators; on the contrary, through a good understanding of the rites and prayers, they should take part in the sacred action conscious of what they are doing, with devotion and full collaboration (Art. 48).

Pius X had already expressed his concern for "an active participation of the faithful in the most sacred mysteries and in the public prayer of the Church."[59] Pius XI was even more explicit. He writes: "It is absolutely necessary that the faithful do not assist at the divine functions as strangers and silent spectators."[60] And Pius XII: "It is, therefore, desirable that all the faithful should be aware that to participate in the eucharistic sacrifice is their chief duty and supreme dignity, and that they should do so, not in an inert and negligent fashion. . . ."[61]

The new Constitution gives specific directions regarding the active participation of the faithful:

> They should give thanks to God by offering the immaculate Victim, not only through the hands of the priest, but also with him (Art. 48). They should learn also to offer themselves; through Christ the Mediator, they should be drawn day by day into ever more perfect union with God and with each other, so that finally God may be all in all (Art. 48).
>
> They should be nourished at the table of the Lord's Body (Art. 48); the more perfect form of participation in the Mass, whereby the faithful, after the priest's Communion, receive the Lord's Body from from the same sacrifice, is strongly recommended (Art. 55).

> [So that the faithful may pray in common] there is to be restored, after the Gospel and the homily, the "common prayer," or the "prayer of the faithful," especially on Sundays and feasts of obligation (Art. 53).

That the faithful, in union with the priest, should offer the sacred Victim. In *Mediator Dei,* Pius XII clearly explained this participation by saying:

> Let the faithful, therefore, consider to what a high degree they are raised by the sacrament of baptism, and . . . let them further, in keeping with the spirit of the sacred liturgy, be most closely united with the High Priest and his earthly minister, at the time of the consecration of the sacred host, and especially at the moment when the solemn words are pronounced: "By him and with him and in him, is to thee, God the Father Almighty, in the unity of the Holy Spirit, all honor and glory for ever and ever. . . .[62]

Thus it is clearly taught that there is a true and active participation in the liturgical action, in union with Jesus Christ and his representative, the celebrant. The Constitution is clear in regard to this, for it speaks of the participation demanded by the nature of the liturgy itself as well as by virtue of baptism, something which is the right and duty of the faithful as a "chosen people, royal priesthood, holy nation, redeemed people" (1 Pet. 2, 9; cf. 2, 4-5). *Mediator Dei* is still more explicit, and Pius XII, after recalling expressions taken from tradition and from the liturgy itself in regard to the participation of the faithful in the offering of the Sacred Victim, goes on to say:

> Nor is it to be wondered at, that the faithful should be raised to this dignity. By the waters of baptism, as by common right, Christians are made members of the Mystical Body of Christ the Priest, and by the *character* which is imprinted on their souls, they are appointed to give worship to God; thus they participate, according to their condition, in the priesthood of Christ.[63]
>
> Nothing is lacking, therefore, in order that the offering made by the faithful be an active participation in the liturgical action: they take part in an act of the public worship of the Church by virtue of a duty and a right received through baptism.
>
> [After recalling that the unbloody immolation at the words of consecration is performed by the priest, and by him alone, as representative of Christ and not as representative of the faithful, *Mediator Dei* concludes, however:] The faithful not only offer the sacrifice by the hands of the priest, but also, to a certain extent, in union with him. It is by reason of this participation that the offering made by the people is also included in liturgical worship.[64]

They should learn to offer themselves. This is the union of our own sacrifice with that of Christ. As *Mediator Dei* says:

> In order that the oblation by which the faithful offer the Divine

> Victim in this sacrifice to the Heavenly Father may have its full effect, it is necessary that the people add something else, namely, the offering of themselves as victims.[65]

This spiritual immolation of oneself is not restricted to the time of the celebration of Mass; rather, it is that of which St. Peter speaks: "You must be a holy priesthood, to offer up that spiritual sacrifice which God accepts through Jesus Christ" (1 Pet. 2, 5), and St. Paul adds: "I appeal to you to offer up your bodies as a living sacrifice, consecrated to God and worthy of his acceptance" (Rom. 12, 1). The encyclical, however, goes on to say:

> But at that time especially when the faithful take part in the liturgical service . . . it is then, with the High Priest and through him they offer themselves as a spiritual sacrifice, desiring to become as like as possible to Christ in his most grievous sufferings.[66]

Such an immolation of oneself, when united with that of Christ in the liturgical action, becomes in some manner a liturgical act, something which it could not be were it performed outside of the liturgy.

They should be nourished at the table of the Lord's body. The Constitution asserts:

> That more perfect form of participation in the Mass whereby the faithful, after the priest's Communion, receive the Lord's body from the same sacrifice, is strongly recommended (Art. 55).

Participation in the sacred Victim immolated on the altar, although not essential to the sacrifice of the Mass, is an integral part of the same sacrifice for the priest who celebrates, and for that reason is essential on the part of the priest. As regards the faithful, it is highly recommended in order that they may have a fuller part in the sacrifice of the Mass. Although this participation may be achieved by receiving hosts consecrated at another Mass, it would be more perfect if the hosts were concrated at that Mass. *Mediator Dei* had already taught this, and given reasons why it is possible to receive holy Communion with hosts consecrated at an earlier Mass.[67]

These are the three main elements in the active participation of the faithful in the liturgy; and as regards holy Communion, we merely add the words of St. Paul in the Epistle to the Corinthians (2, 23-27) which we have quoted above.

Finally, we come to the *liturgical prayer which accompanies the eucharistic sacrifice.* Obviously, there are many prayers during Mass; but the new Constitution restores especially the so-called "Prayer of the Faithful" or the "Common Prayer." What we shall say later on in regard to the recitation of the divine office by the faithful may be applied to this paragraph.

B *Active Participation in the Sacraments and Sacramentals*

The universal priesthood of the faithful, received by virtue of the baptismal character, is exercised in the reception of all the other sacraments, which, without this character, could not be validly received, and the reception of the sacraments "disposes the faithful to worship God duly" (Art. 59). The Constitution seeks to give the liturgical act of administering or receiving the sacraments the utmost importance, and for this reason prescribes the introduction of a special Mass for the conferring of baptism on adults (Art. 71), decreeing that confirmation may be given within the Mass (Art. 71), and that matrimony be normally celebrated within the Mass (Art. 78).

The new Constitution emphasizes in various passages the sanctification and consecration of the events and circumstances of one's life to God, and of material things, in virtue of the sacraments and sacramentals (Art. 60, 61, 81).

The sacramentals, sacred signs which bear a resemblance to the sacraments, which signify effects particularly of a spiritual nature (Art. 60), should undergo a revision which will take into account the primary principle of enabling the faithful to participate intelligently, actively, and easily (Art. 79). Special mention should be made of this prescription of the Constitution:

> Let provision be made that some sacramentals, at least in special circumstances and at the discretion of the ordinary, may be administered by qualified lay persons (Art. 79).

The latter is a truly liturgical act, for which the faithful will receive official delegation. Father E. Schmidt, S. J., explains this happy new departure, and foresees its application in the Christian life of the families in which the custom exists of blessing the children before they retire and when they rise, the custom of praying at table, and that of making the sign of the Cross over food. The Constitution provides that special liturgical formulae should be composed to be recited by laymen under such circumstances. This is a surprising extension of the popular liturgy which has as its starting point the celebration of the sacrament of matrimony, of which the bride and bridegroom (and it therefore includes the woman) are the ministers.[68] Evidently, the prescription of the Constitution should not be limited to this case.

C *The Divine Office and Liturgical Prayers*

The Word incarnate, Jesus Christ, High Priest of the new and eternal covenant, brought into the world and performed during his earthly life that worship of praise which is continually being offered to God in heaven. He

> continues his priestly work through the agency of his Church, which is ceaselessly engaged in praising the Lord and interceding for the salvation of the whole world. She does this, not only by celebrating the Eucharist, but also in other ways, especially by praying the divine office (Art. 83).

According to *Mediator Dei,* the divine office is

> the prayer of the mystical body of Jesus Christ, offered to God in the name and on behalf of all Christians, when recited by priests and other ministers of the Church, and by religious who are deputed by the Church for this.[69]

Pius XII urged the laity to take part in this public prayer, especially in Vespers for the Sundays and holydays of the year.[70]

The new Constitution not only repeats this desire on the part of the Church that the faithful take part in this public prayer, but also expressly proclaims the liturgical character of it. Thus:

> Therefore, when this wonderful song of praise is rightly performed by priests and others who are deputed for this purpose by the Church's ordinance, or by the faithful praying together with the priest in the approved form, then it is truly the voice of the bride addressed to her Bridegroom; it is the very prayer which Christ himself, together with his body, addresses to the Father (Art. 84).

These are expressions which, if they do not declare official the recitation of the divine office by the faithful when it is prayed "together with the priest in the approved form," at least greatly favor this interpretation. They accentuate, in a manner never done before, the active participation of the faithful in the official prayer of the Church. The same thought is repeated in the succeeding article of the same Constitution:

> Hence, all who render this service are not only fulfilling a duty of the Church, but also are sharing in the greatest honor of Christ's spouse, for by offering these praises to God they are standing before God's throne in the name of the Church, their Mother (Art. 85).

There are two other references, unequivocal references, to the official character which the Church gives to the prayers of lay persons. We quote:

> Members of any institute dedicated to acquiring perfection who, according to their constitutions, are to recite any parts of the divine office are thereby performing the public prayer of the Church. They, too, perform the public prayer of the Church who, in virtue of their constitutions, recite any short office, provided this is drawn up after the pattern of the divine office and is duly approved (Art. 98).

Since no limitation is placed on these expressions, we may assume that they refer to private as well as public recitation of the office. The *Motu Proprio* of Pope Paul VI indicated how explicit the Constitution was by determining that the prescriptions should be carried out from the First Sunday of Advent on. With respect to the office, he states that "members of any institute . . . are to be considered performing the public prayer of the Church."[71]

The novelty of this prescription becomes clear when we compare it with what Pius XII stated in his Constitution *Sponsa Christi,* namely:

> Among religious women, the Church delegates only nuns [meaning those dedicated to the contemplative life, with solemn vows, and papal enclosure] for the public prayer which is performed in her name, in choir or privately.[72]

5 CONCLUSION

Pius XII has said that the liturgical movement of the previous decades constituted a "passage of the Holy Spirit through his Church."[73] The present Constitution must be considered the ripest fruit of this movement. It opens a new era in the liturgical life, and therefore in the supernatural life of the faithful who are members of the mystical body of Christ. St. Paul, in the Epistle to the Ephesians, speaks of the "unfathomable riches of Christ" (Eph. 3, 8) and directs to Christ a fervent prayer: "May he, out of the rich treasure of his glory, strengthen you through his spirit with a power that reaches your innermost being"; that "Christ may find a dwelling-place, through faith, in your hearts"; that "your lives [may] be rooted in love, founded on love" (Eph. 4, 14-17).

We believe that one of the things which contains an unfathomable treasure of spiritual richness for Christian life is the consciousness and experience of this participation in the royal priesthood of Jesus Christ in the liturgy, which is nothing but "an exercise of the priestly office of Jesus Christ" (Art. 7).

St. Paul says of Christ that he would be "all, and in all" (Col. 3, 11). In fact, by virtue of the hypostatic union of the human nature with the divine, and also by reason of the purpose of the incarnation, Christ was primarily a Priest in order that, on behalf of the entire human race, he might give God the glory which is due to him, and reconcile man with God.

How was this task achieved? The author of the Apocalypse says: he made us a royal race of priests, to serve God, his Father (Apoc. 1, 6).

The sacred character of the Christian people, their participation in the fulness of Christ as Priest. (Jn. 1, 16), which received so much emphasis in ancient tradition, was eclipsed for a long period as a reaction against the inroads of heresy. Now that adverse circumstances are past, it has been revived in the Church. The new Constitution is destined to make fruitful these real values of the supernatural life of union with Jesus Christ, and this goal is admirably expressed in its fourteenth Article, which should be studied prayerfully again and again:

> Mother Church earnestly desires that all the faithful should be led to that full, conscious, and active participation in liturgical celebrations which is demanded by the very nature of the liturgy. Such participation by the Christian people as a "chosen race, a royal priesthood, a holy nation, a redeemed people (1 Pet. 2, 9; cf. 2, 4-5), is their right and duty by reason of their baptism.

This is the goal: a full, conscious and active participation.

A profound consciousness of their supernatural union with Christ, High Priest in relationship to his Father, will bring the faithful to this full and active participation in the liturgical life.[74]

NOTES TO CHAPTER 6

1 *L'Osservatore Romano,* Dec. 5, 1963. On Dec. 11, 1963, when receiving a large number of faithful in a general audience, Paul VI insisted on the same subject: "This audience seems to us to bring back the spiritual echoes of the Ecumenical Council that a week ago solemnly concluded its second session. And what is its main echo? The one that manifests the voice of the Council on the sacred liturgy.... Let us hear the voice of this great assembly of pastors of the Catholic Church which says to us: the first duty, the first reform, the first message to the world is this—it is necessary to pray well.... The authority of the Church in her most solemn expression thus gives preference to prayer above all other manifestations of her life, that is, to the colloquium with God, to religious and spiritual activity properly so called, to her interior life in the act of entering into communication with the world of the supernatural through Jesus Christ and his priesthood" (cf. *L'Osservatore Romano,* Dec. 12, 1963).

2 In the Constitution, *"revient sans cesse, comme une hantise la nécessité d'une participation active, intelligente, consciente, fructueuse, de tout le peuple a l'action liturgique,"* says D. H. Jany, member of theounciliar commission (*La Maison-Dieu* 76, 1963, 23). *"Tutto mira ad uno scopo: far si che i fedeli comprendano facilmente i riti, li possano sequire e possano tornare ad essere attori e non semplici spettatori delle azioni liturgiche,"* comments Father Antonelli, Secretary of the Conciliar Commission, *L'Osservatore Romano,* Dec. 8, 1963). This participation of the faithful *"viene ripetuta cosi spesso nella Constituzione, che quo considerarsi il suo ritornello..."* (E. Schmidt, *"Il popolo cristiano al centro del rinnovamento liturgico," La Civiltá Cattolica,* 1964, Vol. I, 123.

3 Cf. Art. 11, 14, 21, 26, 27, 30, 31, 33, 41, 48, 50, 53, 54, 79, 83, 84, 85, 87, 90, 100, 113, 114, 118, 121, and 124.

4 Pius XII, *Mediator Dei,* para. 20.

5 About the relation between 1 Pet. 2, 9 and other biblical texts, especially Ex. 9, 16, cf. L. Cerfaux, *"Regale Sacerdotium,"* in *Recueil Lucien Cerfaux* II (Louvain, 1954), 283-298.

6 J. Coppens, "Le sacerdoce des fideles," in Eph. Théol. Lovanienses (1963), 699-701; Y. Congar, *"Priestertum,"* in *Lexikon f. Theol. und Kirche,* 2nd. ed., 754; L. Cerfaux, *"Regale Sacerdotium,"* in *Rev. Sc. Phil. et Théol.* (1939), 5-39.

7 *L'Epître aux Hébreux* I, Paris, 1952, 281-283. About the parallelism of the quotations of Rom. 13 and Eph. 2 with 1 Peter 2, cf. Cerfaux, *"Regale sacerdotium," loc. cit.,* 303-305; about the Apoc. and Hebrews, cf. *ibid.,* 305-307.

8 St. Thomas says: "Christ... origin of all priesthood" (*Summa Theol.,* III q. 50, a. 4, ad 3.

9 St. Augustine, In Ps. 109, ML 37, col. 1459.

10 *Op. cit.,* 149, ML 37, col. 1592.

11 St. Thomas Aquinas, *Super epist. ad Heb.,* V, lect. 1, 252 (Ed. Marietti, 1952).

12 Denz., 938.

13 Para. 68.

14 Summa Theol., II-II, q. 81, a. 4; q. 48, a. 3, in c. F. Bourassa observes: *"Il est remarquable que St. Augustin et St. Thomas considerent comme le sacrifice véritable, le sacrifice intérieur et spirituel de la créature, le sacrifice visible et rituel étant l'expression sensible du sacrifice intérieur"* (*"Verum sacrificium,"* in *Sc. Ecclés,* 1950, 147). The same author remarks as "less interesting" the change among modern theo-

logians, who emphasize as true and proper the external and ritualistic sacrifice (*Ibid.*, 148).

15 *"L'insistence mise sur la spontaneité et le caractere résolu de l'offrande personelle du Sauvueur ... suggere que c'est cette volonté d'oblation de la victime et la sainteté du prêtre qui la présente a Dieu qui ont valeur rédemptrice"* (C. Spicq, *"Introduction a l'Epître aux Hebreux," La Sainte Bible* (ed. of Jerusalem), 32.

16 II-III, q. 85. a. 4, in c.

17 *Ibid.*

18 F. Bourassa, *"Verum sacrificium,"* in *Sc. Eccles.* (1950), 150 f.

19 Denz., 938.

20 *Didaché,* 14, 1-3. Clement of Rome, *1 Cor. 40, 2-4; 44,4.* Ignatius of Antioch, *Epistle to the Ephesians,* 5, 2; *To the Philadelphians,* 4. Cf. F. X. Funk, *Die Apostolischen Väter* (Tübingen und Leipzig, 1901); Justin, *Dialogue against the Jew Triphon,* 41 (cf. MG 6, col. 563-564).

21 Para. 67.

22 C. Spicq, *Les Epîtres Pastorales* (Paris, 1947), p. L, note 6: *" ... les Padotrales sont le document le plus important du N.T. concernant les origines de la hiérarchie ecclésiastique..."*

23 *"L'examen de la tradition révele ... la répudiation radicale et constante de toute espece de confusionisme entre le sacerdoce d'ordre et le sacerdoce royal des fideles ... distinguent nettement le sacerdoce entendu au sens large, du sacerdoce proprement hiérarchique"* (P. Dabin, *Le Sacerdoce Royal des fideles dans la tradition ancienne et moderne* (Paris, 1950), 33, 37.

24 Allocution to the cardinals and bishops on November 2, 1954, in A.A.S. 1954, 667 f. Already in 1944, Msgr. Penido wrote: "The 'priesthood' of the laymen, therefore, will be essentially different from the hierarchical or sacramental priesthood; the first will be just a "participation" in the second. The difficulty resides in defining precisely the meaning of this participation" (*O Corpo Místico* (Petrópolis: Ed. Vozes, 1944).

25 So says Y. Congar in *Jalons pour une Théologie du Laicat* (Paris, 1954), 245; cf. also 238-245, in which he uses a great variety of expressions to designate the priesthood of the faithful, and to distinguish it from the priesthood received through the sacrament. None of these expressions is satisfactory. Also in the second session of the II Vatican Council, on the schema *De Ecclesia,* there were many conflicting opinions in regard to the word to be adopted. We follow almost completely the terminology of Congar.

26 L. Cerfaux observes in regard to this epistle: *"Par certains traits, le epître aux Hébreux se rapproche de l'Apocalypse. Comme la vision de Jean, et plus didadctiquement, elle expose la these du sacerdoce céleste du Christ (4,14) ... En dépendence du theme principal s'esquisse timidement une théorie du sacerdoce des chrétiens. Ceux-ci suivent la voie ouverte par le Christ purifiés par son sacrifice, ils ont acces au ciel. LEUR ROLE SACERDOTAL CONSISTERAIT DANS UNE VIE DE SINCERITE ET DE PURETE, DANS L'EXERCICE DE LA FOI, DE L'ESPERANCE, DE LA CHARITE..,* (10, 19-25). Cf. *Recueil Lucien Cerfaux;* 29-30.

27 Cf. 1 Pet. 4, 1.

28 M. J. Lagrange comments this way on Rom. 12, 1-2: "St. Paul begins with a summary of what Christian life should be like, that is, a sacrifice offered to God and an interior transformation" (*Saint Paul: Epître aux Romains,* (3rd ed.; Paris: 1922), 291; cf. also Lyonnet, *"Deus cui servio in spiritu meo (Rom. 1, 9): De cultu spirituali in N. T.,"* in *Verbum Domini* (1963), 52-59.

29 *The City of God,* 10, 6; cf. ML, vol. XLI, col. 283.

30 Paul Dabin, *Le Sacerdoce Royal des fideles;* J. Lécuyer, *"Essai sur le sacerdoce des fideles chez les Peres,"* in *La Maison-Dieu* 27 (1951), 7-50.

31 Lécuyer, *art. cit.,* 20.

32 *Loc. cit.,* 15, 16.

33 *Loc. cit.,* 16.

34 *Jalons pour une Théol.,* 187 f.

35 *Summa Theol.* III, q. 82. a. 1, answer to the 2nd. obj.

36 H. de Lubac, *Méditations sur l'Eglise* (3rd. ed.; Paris: 1954), 122.

37 Pius XI, *Miserentissimus Redemptor,* A.A.S. (1928), 165-178.

38 *Mediator Dei,* para. 99.

39 *"De ce que Saint Pierre déclare que la maison est 'spirituelle' et que les hosties offertes par le sacerdoce royal sont 'spirituelles,' il ne suit pas que le sacerdoce soit spirituel aus sens d'exclusivement métaphorique. Car 'pneumatique,' en grec néo-testamentaire, ne signifie pas métaphorique, au sens de symbolique, d'impropre, de figuré ou de non-réel"* (P. Dabin, *op. cit.,* 38.

40 *Jalons pour une Théologie,* 243.

41 Cf. Paul Dabin, *op. cit.,* 31; Congar, *Jalons. . .,* 183 f.

42 L. Cerfaux, *Recueil* II, 310 f. and 315; H. De Lubac, *Méditations,* 117; Congar, *Jalons . . .,* 180 ff.

43 Congar, *Jalons . . .,* 176 f., especially note 48 and pp. 246 f.

44 *Summa Theol,* III, q. 63, a. 3, in concl.

45 *Ibid.*

46 Speaking of the character proper to the sacrament of confirmation, St. Thomas calls it an "active potency," but not in the sense that it gives a faculty to dispense spiritual things to others, but rather to confess faith publicly" (Comment, to the IV Book of the Sentences, Dist. 7, q. 2, a. 1. s. 1, ad 3ium). Because of this, in the present article we are referring only to the character of baptism.

47 *Jalons . . .,* 242. Cf. also J. M. Alonso. *"Santo Tomàs y el llamado 'sacerdocio de los fieles,'" XII Semane Españolo de Teol,* 1953, 144.

48 Cf. A.A.S. (1928), 165-178.

49 St. Thomas explains the texts of Pet. 2,5 and Rom. 12,1 as referring to a spiritual priesthood and sacrifice; and when he speaks of the baptismal character as a participation in the priesthood of Christ which is directed to divine worship, he never mentions these texts of the Scriptures. Cf. Congar in *Lexikon f. Theol. und Kirche* VIII, 1963, col. 754.

50 *"Essai sur le sacerdoce des fideles chez les Peres,"* in *La Maison Dieu* 27, 35.

51 *O Corpo Místico,* 263. By saying "metaphoric" he does not mean unreal (cf. pp. 260 ff.). Father Penido, on speaking of these two aspects, asks the question: "How, then, establish the relation between 'metaphorical priesthood' as a fruit of the incorporation into the High Priest?" We think it would be more exact to say, by changing the terms: "a metaphorical priesthood as a fruit of baptism." Incidently, the same Penido says, immediately, quoting the words of St. Thomas on the baptismal character as participation in the priesthood of Christ: "Consequently, in baptism we do not receive merely a metaphorical priesthood so that we may offer an internal and private sacrifice, but also a participation in the hierarchical priesthood, so that we may take part in the external and liturgical worship" (*loc. cit.,* 264).

52 Lécuyer, *art. cit.* Cf. also Congar: "There is, therefore, only one common basis for

the common priesthood: union with Christ, which, however, may be achieved through two ways. This priesthood is complete in the life of the baptized who, by virtue of this sacrament performs the worship of the New Testament." *Lexikon f. T. und K.* VIII, 1964, col. 755.

53 Cf, the information given by the *Ufficio Stampa* about the II Vatican Council, published in *L'Osservatore Romano, Civiltá Cattolica, La Croix, Informations Catholiques Internationales,* etc.

54 P. M. Gy, consultant for the counciliar commission, says about *Mediator Dei: "... la constitution prend largement appui sur la grande encyclique de Pie XII et en répete une fois ou l'autre les termes mêmes, sans guillemets ni références: seuls sont allegués explicitement les textes bibliques, liturgiques et patristiques"* (*La Maison-Dieu* 76 (1963), 13.

55 We shall give the articles of the Constitution in parenthesis, without further indication.

56 Para. 88.

57 Cf. C. Spicq, *L'Epître aux Hebreux* (Paris, 1952), 269-283.

58 The divine worship consists in receiving divine benefits or in imparting them to others" (Summa Theol, III, q. 63, a. 4, in concl.). "All sacraments make man a participant in the priesthood of Christ, because he receives some benefit from it" (III, q. 63, a. 6, ans. to the 2nd. obj.). We should also keep in mind what has been said in the foregoing pages about active and passive participation in the priesthood of Christ. Thus, the intervention of Cardinal Jaime de Barros Câmara, of Rio de Janeiro during the 51st meeting of the Second Session of the II Vatican Council: "The chapter on the priesthood of the faithful should include a reference to the sacraments of confession, anointing of the sick and of orders, in order to express more completely through the various sacraments the plenitude and exercise of the priesthood." Cf. *La Civiltá Cattolica,* Nov. 16, 1963, 400.

59 *Motu proprio, Tra le sollecitudini,* Nov. 22, 1903.

60 Apostolic Constitution *Divini Cultus.* A.A.S. (1929), 39-40.

61 *Mediator Dei,* para. 80.

62 A.A.S. (1947), 559 f., or n. 104.

63 Para. 88.

64 Para. 92.

65 Para. 98.

66 Para. 99.

67 Para. 118.

68 *"Il popolo cristiano al centro del rinnovamento liturgico," La Civiltá Cattolica,* Jan. 18, 1964, 120-131.

69 Para. 142.

70 Para. 150.

72 *Motu proprio,* Jan. 25, 1964, n. 8.

72 Const. *Sponsa Christi,* Nov. 21, 1950, A.A.S. (1951), 5-24.

73 Speech at the closure of the International Congress of Liturgical Pastoral Work, in Assisi, Sept. 22, 1956.

74 For a better understanding of this Christian counsciousness, the book by Father J. Desplanques, S. J., *The Mass of Those Who Are Not Priests,* may be of help.

7
Liturgical piety and pious exercises

Constantine Koser O.F.M.

1 Exposition of the theme
2 Meaning of the liturgy and pious exercises
3 Subjectivism and the liturgy
4 Objectivism and pious exercises
5 Errors to be avoided
6 Christian spirituality according to the Constitution
  A Liturgical spirituality
  B The need of supplementing the liturgy with other pious exercises
7 Conclusion

The Most Reverend Father Koser, of Brazil, previously definitor general for South America at the headquarters of the Order of Friars Minor in Rome, is now the vicar general of the order. His article was translated into English by Father Tarcisio Beal O.F.M.

Sacrae Liturgiae fovendae atque instaurandae studium merito habetur velut signum providentialium dispositionum Dei super nostra aetate, veluti transitus Spiritus Sancti in sua Ecclesia; et vitam ipsius, immo huius nostri temporis universam rationem religiose sentiendi et agendi, nota propria distinguit.[1]

Anyone who has an appreciation for the niceties of Latin will find this sentence rather strange and may be inclined to think that it savors a little of barbarism. Yet when translated into a modern language[2] it can be expressed in a form that is meaningful and at the same time a symptom of the up-dating in which the Church is so courageously engaged. The Fathers of the Council, together with the Pope, determined as they were to "bring into better harmony with our times"[3] those functions of the Church which admit of adaptation, went so far as to abandon the traditional Latin style of ecclesiastical documents. They chose, instead, a new style, despite the risk of being regarded as mediocre Latinists. Had they succumbed to the urge to employ nothing but the traditional style, they would have found it hard to express today's requirements in the language of yesterday.

In the *Constitution on the Sacred Liturgy* there is implied more than an adaptation of expression. There is an adaptation in content. In keeping with this is the basic declaration that for all Christians an active participation in the liturgy, an intensive liturgical life, and a spirituality steeped in the liturgy, are unavoidable obligations.[4] In this manner the Church has solemnly accepted a doctrine which, until now, was the subject of spirited controversy.

When we compare what is defined and determined in this Constitution with the thought contained in the vast majority of books on spirituality and devotion published since the invention of printing, we cannot help thinking that here there is a victory, the triumph of a viewpoint opposed by vast multitudes. We must conclude, too, that this new orientation will have a most profound and decisive effect on the spiritual life. With good reason, then, we shall devote some thought to this new sense of direction given to the Catholic world.

The Constitution is new. There is, at the moment, no vast store of studies to which it has given rise. We walk through virgin territory, and the tenderfoot must not rush in before the scout has yet returned.

1 EXPOSITION OF THE THEME

In 1909, when L. Beauduin, O.S.B., delivered in Malines his famous commentary on the plea of Pope Pius X for "active participation" of the faithful in the official worship of the Church,[5] a new phase of liturgical renewal began. For decades efforts had been made to promote that renewal; but from the date of this particular address these efforts grew in momentum, and developed into a force of great power and influence which we now know as the "liturgical movement." Spiritual life within the Church had tended to move in a unique direction. There had been a great development in the forms of piety, but they tended to be independent of the Church's official form of worship. The *Medulla Missae* of Martin Cochem may be cited as an example.[6] His book brought the Mass back into the center of the spiritual life for hundreds of thousands of the faithful. It was a work that powerfully nourished the life of prayer in the souls of innumerable persons. Yet the author, although holding the Mass in the highest esteem, never fostered the use of the missal. He taught ways of devoutly hearing Mass independently of the prayers and official rites of the Church. It was against the "method of hearing Mass," so far removed from the approved method, that the liturgical movement reacted. This latter was an attempt to bring back to the faithful not only an esteem for the Mass, for the sacraments, and for other liturgical acts, but it also encouraged them to participate actively in such functions in ways that were approved.

D. Prosper Guéranger, O.S.B., through the medium of his *L'Anée Liturgique*,[7] had exercised a powerful influence in the same direction, for he had taught the faithful how to take an active part in the liturgy, and how to build up an entire spirituality on the basis of the rich data of the Roman Liturgy. Liturgy ceased to be a foreign body in the Church, a book closed with seven seals. Instead, it was to become like a fountain full of interior life, of a new character, less individualistic, less subjective, more Catholic, and more in accord with the sublime realities of the Mystical Body.

The liturgical movement had several objectives. It aimed at making the faithful understand the liturgy. It sought to bring them into active participation in it: to transform liturgy into a source of Christian life; to create a new type of Christian life, one inspired by a form of worship that had official approval; and to create a liturgical spirituality.

These efforts could not fail to create a new way of life, a new type of Christian. Along with the expansion of the movement there arose a new flood of ideas, a change of mentality and conduct, new ways of participating in the divine office, a new influence even on modes of speaking. As a result, there was a renewed and invigorated interest in the Church as the Mystical Body, in the diocese and parish as living communities, in the Communion of Saints as a reality that could serve as an ideal—in a word, a "new" concept of Christian life, one in which emphasis is placed not on what pertains to the individual but on what is shared with others.

These splendid realities, strongly influencing the faithful, could not help bringing into contrast the former manner of life, set as it was in a secular tradition and crystalized in a great variety of "spiritualities." Those who were devotees of these older methods, those who had dedicated themselves to such forms of spirituality, could not immediately foresee in the new realities something which undermined the very basis of their own spiritual life. The "tidings" brought by the new movement were, in fact, a series of threats to the forms of piety which had heretofore held sway.

Among the promoters of the liturgical movement there were not lacking from the beginning those who foresaw the inevitable problem, and who attempted to avoid clashes and to obviate misunderstandings. Neither did it lack its hotheads, those who, no doubt in perfect good faith, did what they could to exaggerate the contrasts. On the other hand, too, on the side of those devoted to "popular devotions" the same thing happened. The cry of the hotheaded prevailed for the moment over the voices of the wise and prudent, with the result that a bitter controversy arose in many countries; and the war of words was fought, sometimes with greater and sometimes with lesser intensity.[8] It must be kept in mind, however, that there were not lacking on both sides persons endowed with lucidity and discretion, and these succeeded in maintaining truth as well as charity in the forefront. Uninfluenced by prejudice, they traced the line of development of the liturgical movement and of the popular devotions. However, the few who were engaged in the controversy attracted most of the attention, and the many, as usually happens, lacked the sense of balance and moderation necessary to obviate mistakes and exaggerations on both sides.

In the effort to oppose the pious exercises and to promote the liturgical movement, the superior value of the liturgy was frequently and energettically emphasized. Preeminence was also given to the esthetical value of liturgical forms in contrast with the rather questionable features of the pious exercises in themselves, and with their manifestations in architecture, in the plastic arts, and in the various modes in which prayer and the interior life find expression. Emphasis on points of contrast such as these gave rise to irritation.

Another element which gave rise to noisy conflicts was the insistence on the objective values of the liturgy in contrast with the subjectivism associated with the pious exercises. The answer from the opposition was, that the "objectivism" of the "liturgists" could not give rise to a spiritual life; that it was, in fact, conducive to decadence of the spiritual life, to formalism and ritualism. When one side urged that there was an obligation to follow the liturgical pattern, the other replied that, while there was no question about the superiority of liturgical forms, this very superiority did not make liturgical participation an obligation. What was of obligation, they urged, was the Mass and the sacraments, not liturgical participation in them. Such participation pertained to the celebrant and the ministers, not to the faithful.

Another ground for conflict arose. The promoters of the liturgical movement referred to their movement as "liturgy"; but actually what they were fighting for—and nothing else was possible—was participation in the official ceremonies and, to a certain point, acknowledgment that there was an obligation in regard to this. And because the upholders of the pious exercises were not willing to accept the type of piety that was being imposed, they were accused of being adversaries of the liturgy. The latter defended themselves by pointing out how widespread was the practice of hearing Mass frequently, of daily Communion, of confessions of devotion—practices which the other party regarded as somewhat out of harmony with liturgical practice.

These controversies, entered into with vigor by both sides, produced an amazing flood of publications. Books appeared, specialized reviews, articles in general magazines, theses, conferences, courses, meetings – a veritable mountain of literature. No inventory of all of this has yet been made, not even by specialized writers who are usually quite prolific when compiling such bibliographies.[9] The disputes have not yet come to an end, and so the great library of literature on this subject continues to expand.

The liturgical movement, due in great part to lucidity and discretion on the part of many of its promoters, and to the increasingly open protection afforded by the Holy See, continued its forward march. At first, the liturgy as it existed was regarded as worship at its highest perfection. Little by little, however, due to the internal dialectics of truth, a conviction began to form that the official modes of worship as they existed did not allow enough margin to the sentiments awakened in the souls of the faithful, and did not correspond to the ideal that was aimed at. With the aid of thousands of publications, research in the history of the liturgy confirmed the theory on which the movement was based; it refuted many others. In particular, it showed to what an extent, in olden times, liturgical forms were in constant search for adaptation, and how moribund crystalization set in when this was not present. Gradually the need was felt not only for adaptation, but also for profound modification, in order that active participation on the part of the faithful could be attained in the measure desired. As a result, many ceased to believe in the "myth" that the existing liturgy was the most perfect–something which had encouraged the efforts of, for instance, Prosper Guéranger.

From grasping the need for reform to formulating proposals for it was but one step. And from formulating proposals to proceeding to experiment on one's own initiative–this was but another step. As a consequence, many promoters of the liturgical movement found themselves in conflict with the competent authorities in regard to matters of official worship, and a new and mighty problem came into being. During this phase, strenuous efforts also were made to arrive at an exact definition of the liturgy and of popular devotions.

Things had now reached the point when papal intervention became a necessity. The German bishops, represented by the Archbishop of Breslau, sent a "memorandum" to Pope Pius XII, objecting to certain abuses pertaining to the liturgy, and certain doctrinal errors stemming therefrom. These errors pertained to doctrines concerning the nature of the Church.

Pope Pius replied to the memorandum by issuing the encyclical *Mystici Corporis* in 1943. It did not follow closely the theme of the memorandum, but in general it took a position on the side of the popular devotions and in opposition to the strictures of the liturgical movement. The movement once more was on trial.

Again from the German hierarchy came a document in opposition to the movement, this time from the Archbishop of Freiburg. Pius XII answered with the encyclical *Mediator Dei* in 1947. This was the first papal encyclical that took liturgy for its theme. And once again the movement was on trial.[10] This latter document, however, already accepted the idea of reform, and the efforts begun during the reign of Pope Pius X with an orientation towards the past now received a new sense of direction.

The first result was the decree *Musicae Sacrae Disciplina* of 1955; then the instruction of the Sacred Congregation of Rites in regard to this document (1958), followed by the *Novus Rubricarum Codex* of 1960, in the wake of the fruitful reform of the Holy Week liturgy and the introduction of what is called the Psalter of Pius. The great international congresses on liturgy, too, played their role in bringing about these reforms.

So great was the effect of these decrees that the conviction, entertained by many, that the Roman liturgy was immutable quickly vanished, and the idea of a profound reform began to gain ground. The II Vatican Council, anticipating an adaptation and reform of the liturgy, brought hopes that positive results along the same lines can at last be achieved. The discussions in the Council, moreover, and now the constitution *Sacrosanctum Concilium,* assure us that this is just the beginning of a road of reform that promises to be long and painful.

The victory of the liturgical movement, in regard to the elements in it that are sound, was complete in the Council; but it would be a mistake to speak about the defeat of the pious exercises. These retain their rights; but they are duly restricted by the superior excellence of the sacred liturgy. Not everything was definitely clarified; but the light which glows from the first Constitution of the II Vatican Council is abundant enough to illumine almost all the points that up to now had been subjects of bitter controversy.

2 MEANING OF THE LITURGY AND PIOUS EXERCISES

In order to make clear in theory as well as in practice the relationship between the Liturgy and pious exercises it is important to know precisely what each means. Most authors act on the assumption that there is no question about meanings; they begin *in medias res.* Unfortunately, however, the meaning of the terms is not clear. And perhaps the greatest difficulty in the present instance is the lack of clearness in defining the terms that must be compared. Despite the appearance of *Mediator Dei* in 1947, the difficulties remain, although that encyclical was a big step towards a solution of the controversy about the meaning of terms.[11]

Mediator Dei says that the liturgy is "the entire public worship of the body of Christ, of its Head as well as its members."[12] Vagaggini, although recognizing the authority of this pontifical document, prefers another definition. He considers liturgy as "the assemblage of perceptible and efficacious symbols and of worship in the Church."[13] He considers that liturgy is not only worship, but that it implies, also, the attitude on the part of God towards his Church, its sanctification.[14] Balthasar Fischer declares that the definition of *Mediator Dei* was maintained by later official documents and that its application was further restricted in the decree *Musicae Sacrae Disciplina.*[15] This decree does, in fact, repeat the definition,[16] and then proceeds to offer an explanation, adding several elements which restrict its scope. Thus, it states: "Liturgical acts are sacred acts, instituted by Jesus Christ or by the Church, which, in the name of both, and in accordance with the liturgical books approved by the Holy See, are performed by legitimately chosen persons in order to give God, the saints, and the blessed the type of worship that is their due."[17] It could be argued that the "entire public worship" is the one that is in accordance wiih the "liturgical books approved by the Holy See" and that the same books indicate who are the "legitimately chosen persons" who may take part in public worship in the name of the Church. Understood thus, it would not be a restriction on the application of the term; it would, in fact, be nothing but an obvious explanation of its meaning. Be that as it may, the explanation is official and has to be taken into consideration.

The Constitution on the sacred liturgy combines in a single formula the two points of view: the view of those who place emphasis only on the aspect of official worship, and the view of those who would include in the definition the note of divine and sanctifying action. According to the mind of the Fathers, there was no intention of defining a doctrine or solving a controversy; nevertheless, because of the presence at the conciliar session of practically the entire hierarchy, and in view of the fact that all attached their signatures on December 4, 1963, the document is equivalent to an expression of the "unanimous consensus of the ordinary magisterium" and for that reason has supreme significance. The Constitution declares: "Rightly, then, the liturgy is considered as an exercise of the priestly office of Jesus Christ. In the liturgy the sanctification of man is signified by signs perceptible to the senses, and is effected in a way which corresponds with each of these signs; in the liturgy the whole public worship is performed by the Mystical Body of Christ, that is, by the Head and his members."[18]

The elements that enter into this definition of the liturgy, and the different aspects of them, must be carefully kept in mind, for they serve as a safe test to distinguish "liturgical acts" from all others. They are, then, significant words, and they will shed light on the following pages.

In the Constitution there are other topics, too, which deserve close attention if we are to reveal, as clearly as possible, the concept of the liturgy which is here under consideration. Thus, it is asserted that "the work of our redemption is accomplished" through the liturgy.[19] So, too, the liturgy is called an expression of Christian life,[20] an action in which Christ who is present takes part,[21] an action in which Christ associates the Church with himself for the sanctification of man and the worship of God[22]; and because "no other action of the Church can equal its efficacy by the same title and to the same degree,[23] it is the aggregate of public worship, the *integer cultus publicus* in such wise that outside the liturgy there is no public worship.[24] It is a foretaste and a prefiguring of the heavenly celebration.[25] Liturgy is an activity of the Church,[26] and although it does not exhaust all the activity of the Church, it is, however, "the summit towards which the activity of the Church is directed and at the same time the font from which all her power flows."[27] Furthermore, it is the end towards which "all other activities of the Church are directed."[28] The public character of the liturgy is of such a nature that in order to win a place in that category the mere fact that the Church has given approval to some particular exercise of devotion is not enough[29]; and neither will it suffice if the exercise is in accord with the laws and norms of the Church.[30]

Furthermore, liturgy is an action of the Church, of such a nature that all its members may take an active part in it.[31] Because of this, liturgical services are not "private functions, but are celebrations of the Church, which is the 'sacrament of unity,' namely, the holy people united and ordered under their bishop."[32] Hence these services "pertain to the whole body of the Church; they manifest it and have effects upon it; but they concern the individual members of the Church in different ways, according to their differing rank, office, and actual participation."[33] And liturgy is not restricted merely to worship, for it likewise contains "much instruction for the faithful. For in the liturgy God speaks to his people and Christ is still proclaiming his gospel. And the people reply to God both by song and prayer."[34] The action of the ministers is performed in the name of all the people present,[35] and has a special efficacy.[36] Liturgy is "the public prayer of the Church,"[37] the "voice of the Church, that is, of the whole mystical body publicly praising God."[38]

What, then, are "pious exercises"? The uncertainties to be found in the definition of the liturgy are naturally reflected in any effort to define "pious exercises," for both notions are correlated. There is still another difficulty. It is the difficulty we meet when we attempt to define the term "layman." We are forced to express ourselves in negatives; yet the reality signified is definitely positive.

Vagaggini does not help at this point.[39] *Mediator Dei,* although it frequently speaks of "popular devotions," defends them from attack but never defines them. The encyclical follows the procedure of defining what is meant by liturgy, and then referring to "other religious exercises," or words of that nature, or circumlocutions. The instruction *Musicae Sacrae Disciplina* repeats the definition of liturgy given in *Mediator Dei,* and after explaining it, continues: "The other sacred acts, whether performed within or without the Church, even with the presence of the priest or presided over by him, are called exercises of piety."[40] This is obviously not a definition.

A. M. Roguet, analyzing the words of the instruction, comes to the conclusion that they do not constitute a definition that is wholly negative.[41] He points out, as positive elements, the reference to "sacred acts" which may be performed "within the church" and "presided over by the priest."[42] It should be kept in mind that the only words that could be regarded as part of a definition are "sacred acts," and this merely indicates the category to which they belong. The note that would characterize them is lacking. Here, too, Roguet does not go beyond a list of traits that are negative. Thus, such services are inferior to the liturgy; they were not instituted by either Christ or the Church, even though directly or indirectly they are under the control of the Church and approved by it; the norms of the liturgical books do not apply to them; they are not performed by persons legitimately delegated by the Church; they are not a form of worship that is obligatory for all; they are not imposed unconditionally on all Christians, but, instead, resemble forms of worship that are added over and above.[43] Next, when the author attempts to determine in a more positive way what is meant by "popular devotions" he has recourse, instead, to a discussion of their content, style, and outlook—matters which, for the most part, are open to question, and which do not specify the inner reality.

There is no doubt that the elements presented in negative form are sufficient to make it possible to identify "pious exercises." But the truth is that they do not constitute a definition of the essence, for they lack the "specific difference" which constitutes them, which distinguishes them from liturgical actions with which they are classified under the heading of "sacred acts." Something specific is added when they are declared to be "private sacred acts." But this term has been deliberately avoided in pontifical documents, and with good reason. In the Mystical Body there is no place for strictly private acts, because of the Communion of Saints. When we attempt to identify more accurately what is meant by "private" we are dealing with negatives once more. They are acts in which the Church as such does not take part; acts which are not "official," and so on. These difficulties have caused serious embarrassment to authors who attempt to determine the relationship between liturgy and "popular devotion."

The Constitution *Sacrosanctum Concilium* is no improvement over former documents in regard to this concept. It is quite reticent in its treatment. However, by maintaining the right of existence for a form of worship that is not liturgical and even by emphasizing its necessity, by repudiating again and again any form of liturgical exclusivism, it indirectly indicates elements concerning the nature of the popular devotions. Thus, when it says that, in order to accomplish the work of Redemption, Christ is present in the Church, it does not say that he accomplishes it exclusively, but only that he does it especially in her liturgical celebrations.[45] Hence it can be concluded that Christ operates also through pious exercises, and that this fact, besides adding dignity to them, belongs to their nature. In like manner, too, these exercises are an "activity of the Church; and if the liturgy is this in a preeminent way so that it is its very "summit,"[46] it is not so in an exclusive or all-embracing way, for the sacred liturgy "does not exhaust the entire activity of the Church."[47] Actions of the Church which are not liturgical acts, but are, or at least contain, pious exercises can be found in its missionary activities,[48] in its work of evangelizing catechizing, in charity, in prayer, in the apostolate.[49] By being what it is, liturgy certainly constitutes the *raison d'etre,* the end, culmination, origin, and efficient cause of all of these.[50] But the restriction still remains: liturgy does not exhaust the entire activity of the Church.[51]

The same restriction is laid down, in general, in regard to the interior life. "The spiritual life, however, is not limited solely to participation in the liturgy."[52] Outside the liturgy, the spiritual life is nourished by prayer, prayer said in private,[53] and there is the injunction to "pray without ceasing."[54] Mortification, or the practice of asceticism, is also mentioned.[55]

At this point the Constitution speaks explicitly about popular devotions. They are highly recommended, especially if performed under obedience to a decree of the Holy See or the bishop.[56] The superiority of the liturgy demands, however, that these popular devotions be organized in accordance with official forms of worship, that they spring in some way from it, and that they lead the people to it.[57] The Constitution makes two more references to popular devotions, namely, the manner in which they are to be performed in seminaries,[58] and religious popular hymns,[59] and then closes its comments on the subject.

The following particulars pertaining to pious exercises should be kept in mind: They are a sacred function, a function of Christ who is present, a function of the Church, a function of the Mystical Body; they are a truly divine form of worship, and they promote sanctification when duly performed. These are the positive elements that can be noted. We can see, however, that none of them is distinctive; all are common to the liturgy and are found in it in a superior way. The distinctive elements indicated by the Constitution are all negative. They are not "public worship"; they are not the "public prayer of the Church"; they are inferior to the liturgy; they are, so to speak, incidental to the liturgy, to the life of the Church, and to the life of the faithful.

From these negative traits we cannot derive a positive formula that will point out the distinctive element proper to pious exercises. These traits, however, serve as a criterion to distinguish such devotions from liturgical ones. We have not reached a definition, then, but we have a number of identification marks that are sufficiently clear.

More importance was attached to pious exercises in the encyclicals *Mystici Corporis* and *Mediator Dei,* and in the instruction *Musicae Sacrae Disciplina* than in the Constitution. We may note that Articles 12 and 13 are a summary of the documents mentioned, but we cannot fail to observe that Article 13 is in striking contrast with what was written in *Mediator Dei.* Pius XII wrote: "He would do something very wrong and dangerous who would dare to take on himself to reform all these exercises of piety and reduce them completely to the methods and norms of liturgical rites. However, it is necessary that the spirit of the sacred liturgy and its directives should exercise such a salutary influence on them that nothing improper be introduced nor anything unworthy of the dignity of the house of God or detrimental to sacred functions or solid piety."[60]

Liturgy, therefore, serves as a negative norm without denying that its spirit must influence them. In the Constitution *Sacrosanctum Concili-*

um, however, we read: "But these devotions should be so drawn up that they harmonize with the liturgical seasons, accord with sacred liturgy, are in some fashion derived from it, and lead the people to it."[61]

It is one thing to say that liturgy must exercise such an influence that nothing prejudicial to official worship can be introduced; but it is a very different thing to say that popular devotions must "accord with sacred liturgy."

This regulation of the Constitution is intimately bound up with the concept of pious exercises. According to *Mediator Dei,* there is a vast field of Christian life which is more or less independent of the liturgy, one which is only negatively influenced by it, but one on which liturgy does exercise some influence by reason of its spirit and way of acting. The existence of a Christian life of a non-liturgical character was thus admitted and upheld. According to the Constitution, however, popular devotions do not have an autonomy; they have no such importance in Christian life; and besides, the liturgy must be their focus. The rule is not just a negative one but a positive one, that they must be in accord with the liturgy. It is asserted that Christian life by itself and necessarily has a liturgical character, although this character is not everything, and neither does it absorb into itself all other elements.

Thus, it would be in accordance with the Constitution to say that pious exercises are actions of Christ and the Church; that, without being liturgical, they have had their origin in the liturgy; that they derive from it whatever strength they have; that they must conform to the character and spirit of liturgical actions; and that they must carry Christians forward to a spiritual life of a liturgical character. They are, therefore, actions of worship and sanctification different from liturgical actions, because they are not "public worship, the public prayer of the Church." Nevertheless, they are intimately related to the liturgy. In their relationship to official worship, they can be looked on as a preparation, a spiritual atmosphere, an effect, an auxiliary element, an action which collaborates with the due performance of a liturgical action.

We can all agree, therefore, that this is a notion quite different from the one proposed by the encyclicals *Mystici Corporis* and *Mediator Dei,* and even from the instruction *Musicae Sacrae Disciplina.* We are now dealing with a very different notion. In order that the first Constitution of the II Vatican Council may be carried out, much will have to be changed in the practices of piety on the part of the faithful, of religious, of the clergy—of everyone in the Church.

3 SUBJECTIVISM AND THE LITURGY

The first charge against pious exercises is that of subjectivism. This subjectivism is usually explained as a cause of an effect of anthropocentrism. Deep-rooted in everyone is the vice of selfish religiosity, in which the "salvation" of the individual becomes the criterion for everything, the one thing that has supreme value. In contrast with the subjectivism of popular devotions, emphasis is placed on the character and the objective value of liturgy and liturgical piety, its objectivity of content and attitude, of style and form, of efficacy and value.[62]

The insistence on the objective character of the liturgy had, as a result, a tendency towards "objectivism," sometimes to a greater, sometimes to a lesser degree. As in the case of all "isms," there was exaggeration in regard to ideas and attitudes, true enough in themselves, but separated and isolated from the context of which they were part. This went so far that efforts towards asceticism, mortification, the achieving of self control, vigilance in moments of temptation, custody over the senses, and self abnegation were actually frowned upon and discouraged. In order to emphasize the value of the work itself (the *opus operatum*), the value of the acts of the person concerned (the *opus operantis*) was overlooked.

These errors, and the fatal consequences of them, found a fertile soil. This reached such a stage that, in order to safeguard souls from danger, Pius XII had to intervene on several occasion, and not through encyclicals alone. In *Mediator Dei* he faced the problem specifically. He declares that the dogma of the "objective" power, the *opere operato* of the liturgy, erroneously interpreted, led "some" to conclude that Christian piety means that no regard be had for "what is 'personal' or 'subjective,' as they would have it."[63] He insists that "in the spiritual life . . . there can be no opposition or incompatability between the action of God . . . and the tireless collaboration of man in cooperation with others."[64] It is essential, then, that the "objective" efficacy of the liturgy be intimately, ceaselessly linked with the "subjective" activities of the participants. The efficacy of the liturgy is no substitute for continuous cooperation on the part of the faithful, and neither is cooperation, when emphasized and active, a negation of the objective efficacy of the liturgical action.

The encyclical insistently emphasizes that in the liturgy there is a part that is interior, a part that is exterior. "The worship rendered by the Church to God must be, in its entirety, interior as well as exterior."[65] The interior element is not just a supposition, or a concomitance, or even just a consequence; rather, it is a constituent element in the liturgy as an act of worship—its principal element, in fact. Thus, "the chief element of divine worship must be interior. . . . The sacred liturgy requires, however, that both of these elements be intimately linked with each other. This recommendation the liturgy itself is careful to repeat, as often as it prescribes an exterior act of worship."[66]

It is a grave error, therefore, to define liturgy only through its external, juridical, and ritual elements.[67] Now, although liturgy has an objective efficacy as regards the graces which it signifies, it does not give rise to a psychological response, the interior element which is the principal one. Hence, in order that a liturgical act be truly an act of divine worship, there is required, on the part of the person concerned, a subjective, individual effort, a collaboration on the worshipper's part. An "objectivism" that would presume to dispense with this would become one of the gravest errors.

The subjective aspect of the liturgy, this cooperation in the act itself on the part of the person concerned, receives special and frequent attention from the Constitution on the liturgy. The question is not discussed specifically as it is in *Mediator Dei;* but the correct doctrine, and the law stemming from it, are proposed and imposed in an explicit manner, the objective efficacy of the liturgy is frequently emphasized. "Rightly, then, the liturgy is considered as an exercise of the priestly office of Jesus Christ. In the liturgy the sanctification of man is signified by signs perceptible to the senses, and is effected in a way which corresponds with each of these signs; in the liturgy the whole public worship is performed by the Mystical Body of Jesus Christ, that is, by the Head and his members."[68] It is emphasized that this efficacy is not restricted to the form of worship alone; it extends to sanctification. It produces in souls the grace which it signifies[69] and also the grace of cooperation.[70]

Cooperation itself, however, does not spring from the liturgy considered as an act; rather, it demands a subjective, human effort. "In order that the liturgy may be able to produce its full effects, it is necessary that the faithful come to it with proper dispositions, that their minds should be attuned to their voices, and that they should cooperate with divine grace lest they receive it in vain."[71] Giving the full measure of needed attention is not sufficient, in order that the liturgical action be licit and valid. It is required, in addition, that the faithful take part in it, "fully aware of what they are doing, actively engaged in the rite, and enriched by its effects."[72]

Contrary to what the "objectivists" assert, the subjective element is so important and so essential that its presence is an ardent wish on the part of the Church. "Mother Church earnestly desires that all the faithful should be led to that full, conscious, and active participation in liturgical celebrations which is demanded by the very nature of the liturgy."[73]

Furthermore, this is to be taken as a basic rule in the process of liturgical renovation. "In the restoration and promotion of the sacred liturgy, this full and active participation by all the people is the aim to be considered before all else; for it is the primary and indispensible source from which the faithful are to derive the true Christian spirit."[74]

The Constitution then indicates rules to achieve this cooperation as regards pastoral life in general,[75] the formation of the clergy,[76] the clergy engaged in pastoral work,[77] the faithful,[78] servers, lectors, commentators and members of the choir,[79] and the training of those who take part in the divine office.[80]

The Constitution places great emphasis on the subjective element, but at the same time it does not neglect the objective efficacy of the liturgy. It proposes, and at the same time imposes on all a synthesis of the two elements, in accordance with the nature of liturgy. Fidelity to this Constitution, especially to the part that emphasizes that the faithful take part in the liturgy "fully aware of what they are doing, actively engaged in the rite, and enriched by its effects,"[81] will make the liturgy not in theory only, but in practice, too, "the primary and indispensible source from which the faithful are to derive the true Christian spirit."[82] Thus will flourish an intense and varied Christian life, liturgical in character, the "liturgical life" of which the Council speaks.

4 OBJECTIVISM AND PIOUS EXERCISES

The accusation made against pious exercises is that they lack an "objective" element and cultivate "subjectivism" and "individualism" in opposition to the reality of the Mystical Body. From these errors, which have been imputed to pious exercises, stems, it is said, a lack of interest in the liturgy. And this lack of interest, according to *Mediator Dei,* is a sad reality in many places. "We are sorely grieved to note," the Holy Father writes, "that there are places where the spirit, understanding, or practice of the sacred liturgy is defective, or all but non-existent."[84] We cannot help seeing in this, as the encyclical does, a very pernicious obstacle to Christian life. Neither can we deny that subjectivistic and individualistic tendencies are prominent in many forms of pious exercises, and that in books of spirituality as well as in the practice of the interior life, grave and numerous distortions arose in the past and still continue, despite the fact that they have been denounced with good reason, and opposed. It happens, however, that neither in *Mediator Dei* nor in *Mystici Corporis* were these errors subjected to scrutiny, for these great documents were intended to oppose the mistaken "objectivism" of those who vehemently and virulently were denouncing the errors of "subjectivism" in pious exercises.

The errors of subjectivism and individualism are certainly grave and widespread, and are a serious distortion of the Christian life. Why they did not receive from ecclesiastical authorities the same treatment accorded to the errors of objectivism is an interesting question, one that deserves attentive study!

Within certain circles it was the pious exercises themselves, and not just the errors found in them that were and are opposed. It was this especially which caused concern and forced the ecclesiastical authorities to go to the defense of what is a legitimate Christian patrimony, and also an unavoidable necessity of Christian interior life. Pope Pius XII did this in the two encyclicals mentioned. The theory of the objectivists was that pious exercises are irremediably subjectivistic and individualistic, with the result that they not only fail to fit into a liturgical pattern, but they are in unavoidable conflict with Christian truth. Against an orientation necessarily "theocentric," these exercises would have to be classified as "anthropocentric." In contrast with the divine causality of the action itself (the *opus operatum*), these exercises would be concerned only with the activities of the person concerned (the *opus operantis*), reminiscent rather of the opportune helps supplied by actual grace, and not the supernatural life of the soul, the result of sanctifying and habitual grace. In contrast with the whole dogma of the Mystical Body of Christ and the Communion of Saints, these exercises seemed to be hopelessly individualistic and personalistic, creating and nourishing a mentality which makes a "communitarian" attitude impossible—and such an attitude is essential for all who live by faith and within the "mystery" of the Church.

All these generic accusations were specifically rejected by Pius XII. From his documents we conclude that subjectivism, anthropocentrism, and individualism are errors, and must be eliminated wherever found. Pious exercises, however, are not necessarily in this category, and the elimination of such errors would leave them untouched in their essence. Furthermore, it would purify and fortify them, making them pious exercises to a greater, not to a lesser degree. But the elimination of subjectivism and individualism would not result in objectivism; and neither would the elimination of the individual lead to "communitarianism." The correct doctrine, in opposition to all these mutually conflicting errors, is priority of the individual over the community, because this is based on the nature of things; and precisely because of this it has validity in the service of the Church.

Contrary to what happens in the case of a physical body, the members of the Mystical Body have their own individual, personal identity, and this individuality must be given priority over everything else. This, in consequence, is the goal of the Mystical Body. It reaches its goal only if each individual who makes it up, reaches his.[85] By reason of this, the individual, the person, does not exist for the community, but the community, for the individual. Priority pertains to the individual, not to the community, a doctrine explicitly taught, too, by Pius XII in *Mystici Corporis*.[86]

Here we have a doctrine of immense depth, and it must be kept in mind when there is question of public worship. Because of this, Pius XII explicitly emphasized it in *Mediator Dei* in these words: "It is unquestionably the fundamental duty of man . . . to offer due worship to the one true God by practicing the virtue of religion. This duty is incumbent, first of all, on men as individuals. But it also binds the whole community.[87] This is also true of the public worship of the Church, the liturgy. As a result, the action itself (what is *ex opere operato*) depends on the activity of the person concerned (the *ex opere operantis*) who, in this case, is Christ, varying according to the different aspects of the activity; and as regards the balance, it depends on those who take part in the liturgical action. This is the fundamental and essential order of things, and it needs to be reestablished, for it has been inverted by the objectivists.

From this order of things, however, subjectivism and individualism do not follow; that is to say, the action of the individual is not all that matters. The "objective" action is not excluded from the action itself, the *opus operatum,* and least of all is the value of public worship excluded. This is something that has a value superior to the individual action because of the special intervention of Christ, and because of the convergence of all the members of the Mystical Body in the same act.

Neither is the individual, the personal, the subjective wrong, for they, too, constitute the basis of the public worship, the Liturgy. Individualism, personalism, and subjectivism, however, are excesses in a direction which, in itself, is right. They are the result of ignoring the "objective" elements, and of failing to incorporate them, in due measure, in the religious-moral life of the individual. Hence, wherever in pious exercises these "isms" exist—and unfortunately they do exist and proliferate—they must be corrected by giving proper attention to what is objective so as to secure a proper balance.

Another pernicious error, often deeply rooted in pious exercises, is "anthropocentrism." It is a problem that cannot be ignored. God must be the center of our religious life whether on the natural or the supernatural level. This holds true for all times, for all places. This order of things is denied in theory and in practice by anthropocentrism. Elimination of this error would not result in the elimination of the creature and of his legitimate interest as determined by God. What would be eliminated would be religion itself, for this can exist only if the creature attains the end for which it was made, subject to God, of course, and with that end in mind. "Theocentrism," rightly understood, can never mean the elimination of rights that properly pertain to human beings. Condemnation of the doctrine of "completely disinterested love" in the seventeenth and eighteenth centuries has already made clear this facet of Catholic doctrine.[88] By metaphysical necessity, theocentrism is the only correct doctrine; but this should not result in the destruction of the rights of the creature.

There are rights of an inferior order which are not concerned directly with the final end. Provision must be made for them, and they have a place in the interior life. But they are not opposed to theocentrism, and neither can they be classified as anthropocentrism.

It is of supreme importance that anthropocentrism be avoided in pious exercises. As *Mediator Dei* warns: "It is unquestionably the fundamental duty of man to orientate his person and his life towards God."[89] To place one's self above God is such an act of foolishness that one rarely meets a person who would do it consciously. But so strong and so subtle is the force of self-love, in the heart of all of us, that secretly and without advertence on our part it can often exercise influence. This is a shortcoming found, in particular, in pious exercises, and efforts to eliminate it will often fall short.

Even though we agree that anthropocentrism exists, when we consider pious exercises, we cannot at the same time assert that it is essentially inherent in them and inseparable from them. The shortcoming in question is due to an error on the part of the individual; it does not spring from the essence of these acts considered in themselves. It can, therefore, be removed. Usually the danger is found in the attitude or the intention of the person. But there are exercises and set forms of devotion that are vitiated in themselves. These cannot be included among the pious exercises, for they lack the note of "devotion" [*pietas*]. They must be rooted out radically.

Pious exercises have also been accused of being "individualistic" of their nature, and consequently opposed to the doctrine of the existence of the Mystical Body, and diametrically opposed to the mystery of the Communion of the Saints. This would be equivalent to attributing supernatural efficacy to the action of a creature, independently of Christ and the Church. It has to be conceded that in the last century the mystery of the Mystical Body, as well as that of the Communion of the Saints in all its extension, were almost forgotten in the exercises of piety. A highly accentuated form of religious individualism spread over almost the entire world. Its influence was particularly strong in many pious exercises. It was undoubtedly a vice.

Once more, we do not have here an error necessarily inherent in all pious exercises. The Communion of Saints continues to operate not only in liturgical actions but also in the other actions of a Christian. If liturgical actions alone were actions of the Mystical Body, and all others were purely private, the vice would be incurable. In reality, all the actions of a Christian, whether liturgical or not, are done under the influence of the Communion of Saints and exercise an influence through it. In principle, therefore, nothing can be urged against pious exercises. The encyclical on the Mystical Body explicitly teaches this in many passages.[90] *Mediator Dei* applies this doctrine directly to pious exercises. Individuals should practice personal piety not merely because of the fruits they produce in the individuals alone, "not simply for their own advantage, but for that of the whole Church, where whatever good is accomplished proceeds from the power of her Head and redounds to the advancement of all her members."[91] It is beyond doubt that liturgical prayer "is superior in excellence to private prayers."[92] But this is not due to the fact that what is liturgical comes from Christ and pious exercises do not. Both come from Christ, but in a different way. If one has a correct notion of the meaning of the Mystical Body and of the Communion of Saints, it is easy to understand how mistaken are those who fail to see in pious exercises the action of Christ and his Church or who think that such exercises are outside the direct influence of the Communion of Saints.

The Constitution on the liturgy does not discuss at great length the objective and subjective qualities of pious exercises, but it does give expression to a clear and definite doctrine in regard to certain points. It teaches that they can be utterly vitiated by individualism, but they are at the same time correct and justifiable, for they are actions of Christ and the Church. The activity of Christ and the Church is not limited to liturgical rites, although in them it is exercised in a special way. Thus, in accomplishing his great work, "Christ is always present in his Church, especially in her liturgical celebrations."[93] It should be noted that the word is "especially," not "exclusively." Concerning the Church's action, we read: "The sacred liturgy does not exhaust the entire activity of the Church."[94] The Fathers of the Council are here referring to the conversion of the heathen, to the preparation of catechumens for baptism, to the conversion of sinners, to the preaching of the divine Word to the faithful, to deeds of charity, piety, and the apostolate in general, to the "consecration of the world," and to movements in favor of peace among Christians.[95] Wherever this "action of the Church" is not exercised in liturgical functions, we do actually have pious exercises, such as missions among the faithful, the preaching of novenas, different kinds of retreats, and so on. Evidently, not all non-liturgical functions are pious practices, but a great number of them belong to that category. And they are "actions of the Church," activities of the Mystical Body, actions in which the Communion of Saints is present.

As regards the interior life, which, according to the Constitution, must stem from the liturgy and grow with its strength,[96] it is explicitly taught that not everything in it is reduced to participation in liturgical functions.[97] In this article there is express mention of "prayer in secret," "praying without ceasing," mortification, and imitation of Christ in daily life.[98] As functions of the Church, "popular devotions . . . are to be highly commended,"[99] with preference for those "ordered by the Apostolic See,"[100] with a special recommendation for those of a regional character, provided they are approved by the respective ecclesiastical authorities.[101]

Pious exercises, therefore, far from being functions intrinsically vitiated by an anti-Christian individualism, are "actions of Christ" and "actions of the Church," springing from their relationship with the Mystical Body and influenced by the Communion of Saints. As such, it is evident that they cannot be essentially vitiated by anthropocentricism and subjectivism. Their function is to be theocentric and objective in the proper sense. That is the doctrine taught by Pius XII. That is Catholic teaching.

Pious exercises, however, are not objective, theocentric, and in accord with the doctrine of the Communion of Saints, as it were, automatically. To reach such a high plane of quality, value, and supernaturalism, a human effort is demanded. Subjectivism, anthropocentricism, and individualism are vices too frequently found in the realm of these exercises but can be healed after a brief effort. To a greater extent than is the liturgy, such exercises are exposed to human limitations – and the three items mentioned above are very human. This is exemplified in the history of man's spiritual life, strikingly and frequently. It is necessary that the hierarchy responsible for making adaptations in the life of piety of the faithful, as well as the faithful themselves, reach the high levels which are made possible and are demanded by the nature of the Mystical Body.

What is needed, on the part of all, is a conscious, intense, persevering, and energetic effort against subjectivism and in favor of what is objective, against anthropocentrism and in favor of what is theocentric, against individualism and in favor of the Communion of Saints, of its role in life, and of our conscious realization of it.

To achieve this, it is necessary that the truths of the Mystical Body be preached again and again, that they be grasped by all, and that they exercise a strong influence on our lives. It is necessary that our mental outlook be molded by the truths of the Faith, especially by the mystery of the Church. It is a sacred duty to see that not only one's mental outlook, but also the formulae and the ceremonials of pious exercises are inspired by these truths, and find in them their measure and rule.

If we keep in mind these requirements and compare them with the pious exercises as they now exist – recalling, for instance, those cited by Pius XII, such as meditation, examen of conscience, spiritual exercises (retreats), Eucharistic devotions, prayers and devotions to the Blessed Virgin, and other practices that are not liturgical[102]–two observations immediately suggest themselves. The first has regard to the number and diversity of non-liturgical functions, and the effort they involve. The second is concerned with their style and content. We notice that in certain environments there is a reformation, for theocentrism and the mystery of the Church are receiving a greater role. In general, we have to agree, however, that these mysteries have not been exercising the influence that they should. In order that Christian life and practice, which up to now had been so completely molded by these exercises, may be conformed to a life of faith in the mystery of the Church, many changes will be necessary.

The difficulties that will hinder the carrying out of these changes stem rather from mental outlooks than from any other cause. The individualism, subjectivism, and anthropocentrism of the Modern Age, which were so strong from the seventeenth to the nineteenth century – the periods when popular devotions were born and received their present character – have exercised far too powerful an influence. If, in a calm moment, we readily admit that there is need of adaptation and reformulation in the liturgy, it is far more necessary to demand the same in the case of pious exercises. In their case, too, the requirements of modern times are very different from what sufficed when they had their origin and took on a characteristic form. The same concern for a sound and fervent Christian life should, in this case also, lead to an energetic movement in favor of adaptation, new orientation, reformulation, and renovation.

At this point, the Sacred Council gives us a rule of deep significance. "...These devotions should be so drawn up that they harmonize with the liturgical seasons, accord with the sacred liturgy, are in some fashion derived from it, and lead the people to it, since, in fact, the liturgy by its very nature far surpasses any of them."[103]

It would be possible to select a stronger motivation. The fact that the liturgy is, beyond doubt, superior is not in itself a premise from which we can derive a conclusion that will serve as the basis for formulating the real reason, which is this. Liturgy, by divine institution, contains the sacraments and the Mass, and for that reason, the most important elements in Christian life, its source, its essential structure, and its goal. The Constitution asserts: "Nevertheless the liturgy is the summit towards which the activity of the Church is directed: at the same time it is the font from which all her power flows. For the aim and object of apostolic work is that all who are made sons of God by faith and baptism should come together to praise God in the midst of the Church, to take part in the sacrifice, and to eat the Lord's supper. ... From the liturgy, therefore, and especially from the Eucharist, as from a font, grace is poured forth upon us; and the sanctification of men in Christ and the glorification of God, to which all other activities of the Church are directed as towards their end, is achieved in the most efficacious possible way."[104]

Since liturgy is all this, it necessarily follows that pious exercises which do not stem from the liturgy and do not lead to it, have no claim to existence – as the Constitution declares and prescribes.[105]

This is a doctrine which can be utilized extensively in the formulation and the structure of pious exercises, in their style and content. If carried into effect faithfully, it will transform them and give them a new character, one derived from the Mystical Body and the Communion of Saints. But at the same time it is a doctrine and law which, if not put into effect with judgment and understanding, with a certain largeness and flexibility, may suffocate that strong element in the Christian life which is composed of non-liturgical pious exercises.

Nevertheless, the very nature of Christian life, which is the life of a member of the Mystical Body, demands that these exercises should have a content and structure capable of overcoming the vices of subjectivism, anthropocentrism, and individualism, and should be able to manifest, strongly, in all circumstances of time and place, the spirit of the Communion of Saints. A mentality in accord with the mystery of the Church and nourished by it, which of course must be that of all Christians, will certainly produce a spiritual life that will be in marked contrast with the type that had its origin in souls strongly influenced by the subjectivism, anthropocentrism, and individualism of the modern age.

5 ERRORS TO BE AVOIDED

From the encyclicals *Mystici Corporis* and *Mediator Dei* and from the Constitution *Sacrosanctum Concilium* it is possible to assemble an array of errors and dangers to be avoided in liturgical functions and pious exercises, matters that did not receive sufficient consideration in past decades. It was this fact in particular that gave rise to a conflict that at times was acrimonious and often harmful to souls. We shall here enumerate these errors and dangers so that conscious efforts may be made to avoid them.

When all efforts are concentrated on liturgical piety and efforts are made to inculcate it, in the hope that all may participate actively in the liturgy, the first danger and the immediate threat is exclusivism. Liturgy contains the essential elements of Christian life to such an extent, and the concrete expression of it can be so soul-stirring, that there is grave danger that in the realm of piety it may be given, not merely priority, but a monopoly. This danger and threat have been the occasion of many controversies in the past, and they have been energetically rejected in *Sacrosanctum Concilium*. "The sacred liturgy does not exhaust the entire activity of the Church."[105] "The spiritual life, however, is not limited solely to participation in the liturgy."[106] Therefore, the efforts to establish a liturgical piety must be conducted with the awareness that it is not everything, that there is another field of action for the Church and for spiritual life.

A second danger resides in formalism and ritualism. Liturgy, in its nature as a public cult intended for men and women, must needs have recourse to symbols and rites, to formulae that are pre-established and somewhat durable. The custom of participating in all this can easily give rise to routine. From this could spring a fatal threat to piety: the tendency to forget the spirit of the liturgy and to concentrate only on the letter of it. The nature of litury itself, as defined in the Constitution, is fundamentally opposed to formalism and ritualism, because in it is found the action of Christ and of his Church which is so efficacious in the worship of God and the sanctification of man.[107] Neither can operate with effect if form and rite are permitted to occupy first place in the mind and soul of the worshipper. Still less will be the effect if these latter are given exclusive control. This is the reason why the Constitution lays down the rule: "In order that the liturgy may be able to produce its effects in full, it is necessary that the faithful come to it with proper dispositions, that their minds should be attuned to their voices, and that they should cooperate with divine grace lest they receive it in vain. Pastors of souls must therefore realize that, when the liturgy is celebrated, something more is required than the mere observance of the laws governing valid and licit celebration; it is their duty also to ensure that the faithful take part fully aware of what they are doing, actively engaged in the rite, and enriched by its effects."[108]

Estheticism is another threat. It is related to formulism and ritualism. These three must be regarded as things to be avoided. They are constantly present; and because we can grow accustomed to them, they are a threat. Therefore we must be ever on the alert, with a strong determination to battle against them and to overcome them.

As the situation has developed, the error that has attracted most attention has been objectivism. This consists in paying undue attention to the value of the activity itself (the *ex opere operato* effect), and forgetting the indispensible role played by the person concerned (the *opus operantis*). The same passage in the Constitution, quoted against formalism and ritualism, contains also a condemnation of this error.[109] There are many other references, too.[110] In fact, the frequency with which it has been discussed shows how much attention it has received.

Another danger in liturgical piety is to be found in what may be called "immobilism." Liturgy, being a form of public worship, has to be regulated by laws, and these bring in their train a tendency towards immutability, which is a characteristic of laws. And when we are dealing with laws for the universal Church, the tendency towards stability is greater, and it becomes difficult to bring about such modifications and transformations as are demanded by environment and human psychology. In order that it may influence human life and achieve its main objectives, liturgy must adapt itself frequently; it must even take the lead in the process of change. If it fails to do so, it will lag behind and no longer exercise the influence that it should.

This partiality for stability, a by-product of laws, may easily captivate those who cultivate the liturgy. This could give rise to a cult of the archaic, a preference for what is old just because it *is* old. This tendency was certainly present in the liturgical movement. It was considered at length in *Mediator Dei* and was formally rejected.[111]

At the other extreme of the movement was a group who understood the need of adaptations and was filled with grief and anguish when they experienced difficulty in obtaining them from ecclesiastical authority. Many of them on their own initiative proceeded to introduce reforms, thus going beyond their own competence. This tendency, too, received attention in *Mediator Dei* and was condemned.[112] However, the errors, abuses, and exaggerations of some had the merit of making ecclesiastical authorities conscious of the urgency of adaptations in the liturgy, and as a result, the process of renovation, which in fact had never ceased completely, was accelerated. The Holy See entered so courageously on the path of modification and reform that a certain feeling of instability resulted. In quick succession came the New Psalter of Pius XII, the reform of the Holy Week services, the introduction of vernacular languages into the ritual, evening Masses, the decree *Musicae Sacrae Disciplina,* a preliminary revision of the Calendar of the Saints, a *Novus Codex Rubricarum,* a reorganization of the catechumenate and of the rite for the baptism of adults.

The Constitution on the liturgy owes its origin to an impetus in opposition to immobilism, and by its authority it sanctions the principle of successive and permanent adaptations. In its Introduction it emphasizes the purpose of renovation, safeguards fidelity to the principle of divine institution, and declares that the "Council sees particularly cogent reasons for undertaking the reform and promotion of the liturgy."[113] In the third section of the first chapter, principles of adaptation are established, so formulated that they will always serve to curb immobilism. "The liturgy is made up of immutable elements divinely instituted, and of elements subject to change. These not only may but ought to be changed with the passage of time if they have suffered from the intrusion of anything out of harmony with the inner nature of the liturgy or have become unsuited to it."[114]

"Modifications have to be made, tradition respected as much as possible and convenient, but the needs of the time have to be provided for. Again: "That sound tradition may be retained, and yet the way remain open to legitimate progress, a careful investigation is always to be made into each part of the liturgy which is to be revised. The investigation should be theological, historical, and pastoral."[115] From this doctrine and law, the Church receives a mandate that will never be carried out in full. As long as the human race remains what it is, the need of adaptation and reform will always remain.

The widespread propagation of the Latin Church brought an impressive manifestation of the unity of the Church. Travelers were quick to notice it. Wherever they went, they could always feel "at home." They could be present at the "same Mass," receive the "same sacraments," take part in the "same ceremonies." They received so much spiritual comfort from all of this that they were loud in their praise of it. But there was a hidden danger—that of bringing unity down to the level of uniformity. There was a further danger: the danger of creating a chasm between liturgy and life. Before the Council of Trent there was so much diversity that it gave rise to many problems. Then Trent began a movement towards unification. It ended in uniformity. The Oriental rites were always conceded the right to existence; but in the West, and in mission territories, the Latin rite was imposed. It was brought to the extreme of uniformity by a system of very detailed legislation and by a centralization of the only authority competent to legislate in liturgical matters.

The Constitution on the liturgy, in order to forestall any tendency towards uniformity and its evil consequences, proclaims the right, even the duty, to differ, and at the same time sets limits so as to prevent excesses that would be as prejudicial as uniformity. It asserts: "Even in the liturgy, the Church has no wish to impose a rigid uniformity in matters which do not implicate the faith or the good of the whole community; rather does she respect and foster the genius and talents of the various races and peoples. . . . Provided that the substantial unity of the Roman rite is preserved, provision shall also be made, when revising the liturgical books, for legitimate variations and adaptations to different groups, regions, and peoples, especially in mission lands. And this should be kept in mind when drawing up the rites and devising rubrics.[116]

But here must be a limit; even pastoral requirements demand it. "As far as possible, notable differences between the rites used in adjacent regions must be carefully avoided."[117] In this way the Constitution faces the problems which could arise from the opposite pole of uniformity, the dangers and evils resulting from excessive variety.

There is also the threat of "religious isolationism," the danger that liturgical forms may become so abstract, sublimated, and stylized, that contact with the concrete life of the faithful is lost. If liturgy is to be a source of Christian life for all, it cannot take "academic" forms. Rather, it must be capable of partaking in the life of the majority of the faithful. The need of refining its form and expression will not, of course, be neglected. But celebrations of this kind cannot be liturgy in the sense so ardently desired by the Church. "Mother Church earnestly desires that all the faithful should be led to that full, conscious, and active participation in liturgical celebrations which is demanded by the very nature of the liturgy.[118] [Hence] full and active participation by all the people is the aim to be considered before all else."[119] The result of this will be that liturgy will not be that supreme work of art which is desired in certain circles. Instead, it will contain elements derived from the lower and more popular level.

These articles of the Constitution, quoted in relation to immobilism and uniformity, show that the Council not only laid down general principles, but also descended to particulars so as to remove any doubts regarding their meaning. Thus, certain popular rites that up to now would be classified as "popular devotions" will probably be included in the liturgy. To a greater extent, prayers, expressions of sentiment, ceremonials that express the needs of the faithful, their aspirations, their daily tasks—all these, no doubt, will be included. We cannot remain wedded to the obscure symbolism of olden times and to comparisons taken from the past; for, to persons living in the world of today, the older world is becoming more and more incomprehensible, and its needs very different. It will be difficult to achieve an "active participation" on the part of the faithful if liturgical forms continue to reflect, in a stylized and sublimated way, the atmosphere of a world that has ceased to be. Unless liturgy is brought down from the detached and abstract level in which it has been, and unless it is brought into contact with daily life which is far from the refined, it will be difficult to make it in practice what it is in itself, "the primary and indispensible source from which the faithful are to derive the true Christian spirit."[120] There are still dangers to be avoided in liturgical piety so that it may be, in practice as well as in theory, "the primary and indispensable source" of Christian life. The Constitution has pointed this out repeatedly. The dangers mentioned, however, seem to be the principal ones. But if we are conscious, attentive, and watchful in our efforts, and if we keep pastoral needs in mind, the threats and dangers will be overcome and eliminated.

Let us now turn our attention to the dangers associated with religious exercises. And such dangers are real. First of all, there is a tendency towards exclusivism. Psychologically, this is quite similar to what is found in liturgical piety, but it is never so radical. The reason is, that in non-liturgical devotions, despite their exclusivism, one cannot live without recourse to Mass and the sacraments—and they are the center of the liturgy. The failing, in general, pertains more to forms of expression, to lack of conformity with "liturgical style." In regard to this, the Constitution is much more severe than *Mediator Dei,* for it declares that, up to a certain point, liturgical "form," too, is to be the rule for non-liturgical devotions. "These non-liturgical devotions should be so drawn up that they harmonize with the liturgical seasons, accord with the sacred liturgy, are in some fashion derived from it, and lead the people to it."[121] In such exercises, therefore, exclusivism must be eliminated with more vigor and determination than in liturgical acts. It is more pernicious, and is more basically opposed to the fundamental principles of the Christian life.

Pious exercises must not be permitted to become predominant in the life of anyone; they must not be allowed to determine his standard of judging; they must not prevail over forms of liturgical piety. The text of the Constitution just quoted makes this explicit.[122] If liturgy has to be in itself, and in the lives of the faithful, the "primary and indispensable source from which the faithful are to derive the true Christian spirit,"[123] if Christian life and Christian spirituality have to bear a liturgical character,[124] although not an exclusive one,[125] it is evidently a mistake to give predominance to pious exercises. This becomes clear from the general tone of the Constitution rather than from isolated passages.

The greatest danger in pious exercises, however, is subjectivism. We have already discussed this in the preceding pages.[126] The mere mention of it here will suffice. Because of its seriousness and of the constant threat that it represents, it calls for a persevering vigilance on the part of the ecclesiastical authorities as well as of the faithful. Let us not deceive ourselves: unless there is enduring effort, no one is likely to avoid subjectivism in his spiritual life. The tendency is too human to be overcome by mere decree. The same holds true for two other grave errors: anthropocentrism and individualism. It will bear repetition. These dangers do exist. They are grave; and for that reason they cannot be ignored. In this domain there is need of a serious, profound, energetic revision of the forms of prayer so as to remove the presence of traits that are diametrically opposed to the Christian spirit. And there is much to remove.

If there exists, in the case of liturgical piety, a danger of formalism and ritualism, of immobility and uniformity, of empty detachment, they all have corresponding dangers to balance them in the case of pious exercises. These are as follows: lack of discipline in form, a tendency towards constant change, exaggerated individualism, lack of reverence, lack of decorum, excessive multiplicity, a thirst for innovation, and arbitrariness and lack of good style. The Church, through the vigilance of the various Roman Congregations, and by a series of laws emanating from diocesan authorities and even from the Holy See, has always tried to prevent these errors. However, errors in mental outlook and in an individual's forms of piety cannot be remedied by ecclesiastical authorities at the higher level; this is a task for the individual pastor. The Constitution tries to prevent these errors by giving an orientation that stems from the mystery of the Church, namely, by focusing attention on the action of Christ and of the Church, and on the consequences of the Communion of Saints—for, these are principles which will help to eliminate these abuses. Unlike its procedure in regard to liturgical piety and the errors affecting it, the Constitution in regard to pious exercises does not give further details. Following its example, we, too, bring the subject to a close.

6 CHRISTIAN SPIRITUALITY ACCORDING TO THE CONSTITUTION

The Constitution on the liturgy is a program of Christian life rather than a document of juridical character for the restoration, reform, and adaptation of the liturgy. In the conciseness that one would expect from a Constitution issued by a Council, it gives something resembling a spiritual theology of a very special character. It gives a brief summary of a liturgical type of spirituality and declares it to be of obligation to all.[127] What is the nature of this spirituality? How do liturgy and pious exercises fit into it?

First of all, there is the question of terminology. Spirituality is the sum total of ideas and motives, of outlook and behavior, of techniques, methods and procedures, of psychic constitution and reaction, all of which constitute the outlook, rule, and character of the life of an individual or a group. In any Christian spirituality, ideas and motives must stem from the Gospel. The Christian message, however, gave rise to many different types of spirituality. Against an immensely rich background, it allows for a wide range of variations. One is not at liberty to pick out some elements and to reject the rest. It is essential that the sum total of revealed truth be accepted and put into practice in all types of spirituality. There is room for variety, however, and one may pay special attention to certain portions of the Gospel without denying the rest. This may be due to historical background, or the appeal these portions have for certain groups, or to certain circumstances, or to reasons such as national, family, social, or educational milieu, all of which have much influence on life. It is evident that a force as powerful as the liturgy will and must inevitably exercise profound influence. The same holds true for pious exercises. What has the Constitution on the liturgy to say on the matter?

A Liturgical Spirituality

Of profound and decisive influence is the doctrine that Christian spirituality in its core and in its inspiration must be liturgical. This can be clearly deduced from the following words: "For the liturgy, 'through which the work of our redemption is accomplished,'[128] most of all in the divine sacrifice of the Eucharist, is the outstanding means whereby the faithful may express in their lives, and manifest to others, the mystery of Christ and the real nature of the true Church."[129]

In any Christian spirituality these elements must be the core, basis, substance, principal and determining element, the one from which stems all inspiration for life. And if this element springs from the liturgy, a Catholic and Christian spirituality cannot avoid being liturgical. Let us recall, too, a further paragraph from the Constitution: "While the liturgy daily builds up those who are within into a holy temple of the Lord, into a dwelling place for God in the Spirit, to the mature measure of the fullness of Christ, at the same time it marvellously strengthens their power to preach Christ to those who are outside as a sign lifted up among the nations under which the scattered children of God may be gathered together, until there is one sheepfold and one shepherd."[130] Here it is plainly stated that liturgy is the source of Christian life, even such life at its highest development, "to the mature measure of the fullness of Christ," without, at the same time, neglecting the apostolic and missionary activity of the Church.

Although the Constitution asserts that the liturgy "does not exhaust the entire action of the Church," it still insists that "liturgy is the summit towards which the activity of the Church is directed; at the same time it is the font from which all her power flows."[131] In the light of this, the prescription which follows appears as a simple consequence: "[Popular] devotions should be so drawn up that they harmonize with the liturgical seasons, accord with the sacred liturgy, are in some fashion derived from it, and lead the people to it."[132] That is to say, all Christian and Catholic spirituality has to be liturgical. The Constitution speaks even more clearly.

It asserts that the liturgy is "the primary and indispensable source from which the faithful are to derive the true Christian spirit."[133] It does not call the liturgy "a" source; it calls it the "first" and the "necessary" one, so that without liturgy, Christian life cannot exist. The Constitution is not speaking of supernatural grace. It is speaking of "the true Christian spirit."

There can be no doubt, then, that, according to the Council, *a liturgical spirituality not only exists, but is of obligation for everyone.* This assertion might be regarded as the *Leitmotiv* of the Constitution. It is found in all its articles and is the source from which stems all its prescriptions. It is a doctrine that, under this form, was not a part of the patrimony of Catholic teaching; rather, it was a highly controversial subject.

It is true that the Constitution, according to the "mind of the Fathers," does not contain any new definitions, any new dogmas; and so we cannot classify this doctrine as a "dogma" or a "Catholic truth." We may be permitted to ask, however, where, if not here, can we come upon a "consensus, morally unanimous, of the ordinary teaching magisterium of the Church?" We cannot close our eyes to the words "morally unanimous consent of the ordinary magisterium!"

There is a liturgical spirituality, and it is of obligation. This is clearly the "mind of the Fathers"; and if further proof is needed, it becomes clear from the fact that it is among the prescriptions in the first chapter of the Constitution. A liturgical spirituality presupposes "full and fruitful participation" in liturgical ceremonies; and the achievement of this participation is given as the supreme norm for the reform and restoration of the liturgy.[134] In order to achieve this participation, it is necessary that the clergy understand the liturgy, liturgical life, and liturgical spirituality.[135] It is essential, too, that in seminaries there be teachers of liturgy who are competent, and the Constitution prescribes that there be such.[136] Liturgy must be considered, not just as a study that is necessary, but one of the principal ones, and all the others must make their contribution to the liturgical life.[137] The education of the seminarian, whether he is intended for the secular or regular clergy, should be carried out according to the regulations for liturgical spirituality, and this, too, should dictate the spirit of the pious exercises.[138] Priests, both secular and religious, who are already engaged in pastoral work, should receive suitable aid so that they may understand "ever more fully what it is they are doing when they perform sacred rites; they are to be aided to live the liturgical life and to share it with the faithful entrusted to them."[139] This type of spirituality will serve as an indispensable guide in the work of the apostolate among the faithful.[140]

Thus, the doctrine and law that there is such a thing as liturgical spirituality, that it is a matter of obligation to all, is clearly established in the Constitution. It is a statement of the Council, far-reaching in extent, and weighted with vast and significant consequences for the life of the Church and of every member of the faithful—a declaration of striking novelty in the field of spiritual doctrines.

One is justified, therefore, in seeking a very careful answer to the question that arises here: What is to be understood by "liturgical spirituality" according to the Constitution on the liturgy? More specifically, since it is a matter of obligation, is liturgical spirituality limited to the immutable core of the liturgy, or does it include also the changeable elements of ecclesiastical institutions?

If the obligation is limited to the unchangeable elements, to the essence of the liturgy, we could sum it up in this fashion: All Christian spirituality must possess a sacramental, sacrificial, and ecclesiastical character, including everything they imply, and not forgetting that under "ecclesiastical" is included Christ as Head of the Mystical Body, the one and triune God, the origin and end of everything. In practice, however, liturgy comprises a very complex body of elements of ecclesiastical institution that are not, strictly speaking, identical with the Christian message. It represents a definite, clearly defined type of spirituality, one among a group, all of which are Catholic. This implies a human expression of the Christian message, the essential element in liturgy. It involves a choice in the placing of emphasis when there is more than one aspect to something, an attaching of more importance to one, less to another, and almost forgetting the third one. It is a way of understanding the Christian message as determined by the ideologies of a certain era, of ethnical background, cultural and civilizing influences, the personal preferences of those who propagated the movement, and so on. It comprises a certain style, which is not simply that of the New Testament, and neither is it that of all people, as the Constitution admits. It includes the responses and reactions of a conditioned esthetic taste and the preferences inculcated by schools of art. If what is of obligation must comprise these elements, then the doctrine and regulations of the Constitution extend over a much wider range and exercise a much wider influence.

In regard to all of this, what is the "mind of the Fathers?" There is no clear-cut and explicit passage in the Constitution which gives a complete and satisfying answer. There can be no doubt that, from the beginning, the Fathers of the Council were conscious of the problem, for they included in the opening section of the Constitution a passage that makes clear the distinction between the two components in the liturgy,[141] and this distinction is afterwards repeated.[142] Besides, they prescribed principles and laws which, if consistently applied, will result in a liturgy of a completely different type, for the norm will be "complete and active" participation of the faithful,[143] use of the vernacular language,[144] attention to the manners and customs of the time,[145] and the inclusion of variations that are in accord with usage and regional customs.[146] It is not the "mind of the Fathers" to prescribe for all people a liturgical form of piety in the sense of a way of life, wedded to a changeless liturgy to be observed by everyone, wherever the Church is established. At least it has to be admitted that an obligation which is so sweeping and that affects so many in so many ways, is not imposed in such a way as to stifle discussion. The least that can be said is, where there is doubt there is freedom of action.

On the other hand, neither can we establish beyond dispute the conclusion that the Fathers of the Council wished to restrict what is of obligation to the essential elements in the liturgy. This is clear from the fact that, on more than one occasion, when speaking of liturgical spirituality they were dealing with more than the essential elements. There is evidence of this, for instance, when they state that popular devotions should harmonize with the liturgical seasons, and, in general, that they should accord with the sacred liturgy.[147] The same can be deduced from what is prescribed for the instruction of those who are already ordained priests,[148] and for the training of seminarians,[149] and for the general orientation of pastoral work.[150] In these, and in other matters, "liturgical life" comprises elements which go beyond the core of the liturgy.

In a matter as important as is this, greater clearness and exactitude would be welcome. Is the Constitution at fault? Possibly. But it is also clear that, in a case like this, the dividing line is such that theoretical and juridical formulae will not help us to arrive at a clear-cut and precise definition. What is clear is this, that according to the Constitution, a liturgical spirituality binding on all is not restricted to the essential elements; rather, it comprises elements which give expressions in concrete form to the liturgy. The extent to which this can be extended is not specified, and neither is stress placed on details. One should be guided by prudence and broadmindedness in each case, in accordance with the "mind" of the Council, for the aim is a full liturgical life, and that cannot be said to be achieved if attention is paid only to essential elements. And it cannot be achieved, too, unless efforts are made to avoid liturgical exclusivism, so often condemned in the Constitution. Here is an opportunity to diversify liturgical spirituality, and to exercise the virtue of tolerance and understanding, according to the principle that "no one should demand from another more than what our teacher and mother, the Church, demands of all."[151] In any case, this is a question that is still open to controversy, one that demands further explanation on the part of the ecclesiastical authorities.

This is a question that is teeming with consequences. It is even more important to know what is the sum total of the ideas and guiding lines in the spirituality that has been prescribed. The Constitution is very clear in regard to it. The fundamental idea is the dynamic presence of Christ,[152] a reality too often forgotten. In the doctrine and practice of the spiritual life we find many references to "seeking" Christ in the desert, under cover of darkness, in the midst of trials. Language such as this presumes that Christ is "absent." As a figure of speech this is just and proper. In reality, however, there is no "absence" of Christ. But there is a psychological problem. Men "have the impression" that Christ is absent because they themselves have failed to cooperate with grace. The absence is psychological; it is on the part of men, not of Christ. The psychological and subjective experience is interpreted as an "absence"; and so, this subjective experience of "absence" is attributed to Christ, who is "present." There is nothing wrong with this. The error begins when language conveys a false image of reality, and when, because of it, the great reality is forgotten, namely, the mysterious presence of Christ in the soul, the supernatural, intense, dynamic, constant presence brought about by grace, and strengthened by the sacraments.

There can be no doubt that the influence of Christ's presence in the soul has often been lost sight of and liturgical renewal deserves credit for having emphasized it and transformed it again into the wonderful reality that it is. There were some who confused this real presence of the mystical Body, which is something spiritual and mystic, with the physical presence. Pius XII recalled this in *Mystici Corporis*[153] and corrected the error. The false notion just mentioned, however, does not cancel the credit that is due; for, the renewal and development of the theology of the Mystical Body in many ways is bound up with the liturgical movement. At least, it coincides chronologically with it, and as a general rule the same persons promoted both renewals.

It is the mystery of the Mystical Body that brings to mind and heart the truth of the dynamic presence of Christ. In the atmosphere of the popular devotions and of the types of spirituality associated with them, if the idea of the Mystical Body was not entirely absent, it was at least very vague and never developed into a "dynamic" idea. In liturgical spirituality, on the contrary, the reality and the idea of the action of Christ present in the soul, of our cooperation with Christ, for Christ, and in Christ is everywhere. It occupies first place among ideas that are constantly recalled. This truth influences the soul and brings it into a very definite, a very close relationship with Christ—a relationship of love, confidence, fidelity, of loving and effective repentance, of humility, of legitimate pride, initiative, and happiness.

We must not forget that we are still "wayfarers"; we have not reached our destination, and this union, presence, and action can be destroyed by sin. Therefore they have to be cultivated and watched over with care. Liturgy, in fact, is replete with such sentiments. It brings them repeatedly to the mind of those who take part in it "fully aware of what they are doing, actively engaged in the rite, and enriched by its effects."[154] This is the reality which shapes the outlook and response of the soul. It is the core of liturgical spirituality.

The relationship between the soul and Christ is individual and personal; but it is also, so to speak, "Church-centered." The soul is never alone with Christ and in Christ. It is always in integral and dynamic union with many brethren. That is because Christ is present in the soul by the mystery of the Church, and in no other way. "Christ always associates himself with the Church, his beloved Spouse."[155] In all his actions, he functions as Head of the Church, his Mystical Body. Rightly, then, the liturgy is looked on as "an exercise of the priestly office of Jesus Christ and of his Body."[156] He who cultivates the liturgy after the right manner, with the right dispositions of soul, with mind attuned to voice, and cooperating with grace "consciously, actively, and fruitfully,"[157] will come to realize that he is a member of the Church, an individual incorporated into the Communion of Saints, and one among many brethren. The resplendence and supernatural reality of the Church as the Mystical Body will become a "dynamic idea" in his soul, will shape his mentality, and will give its character to his behavior.

When this stage has been reached, personal interests will not lose their value, and just and necessary worldly tasks will not be eliminated. Rather, the honor and glory of God in the mystery of the Redemption will become all-important and will become the dominant interest.[158] In this way the "paschal mystery" will be called to mind and brought to life, embracing as it does the passion, death, resurrection, and ascension of Christ, and of all persons united "with Christ, for Christ, and in Christ."[159] Thus the soul is free from the prison of subjectivism and individualism, without losing its identity, while integrating itself in the mystery of the Communion of Saints. It is freed from the humiliating chains of temporal preoccupation and left free to wander in the wonderful world of supernatural grace among the unspeakable treasures of the spirit, without losing sight of its earthly duties or losing interest in their smallest details. There is room for all of this in the liturgy, and there is provision for it; but at the same time, all of this will be transfigured by the light and the glory that emanate from the paschal mystery.

Within the mystery of the Church, man finds the mystery of the "objective" efficacy of things. Accepting this with living faith, he is rewarded with strength and courage; for, he realizes that Christ and the Church act in his soul by means of the Mass, the sacraments, and all liturgical rites.[160] This joyful certainty gives the strongest impetus and stimulus to spiritual life.

Liturgy constantly reminds us, at the same time, of the need of cooperation on the part of the doer, a cooperation that must be steady and continuing.[161] In the case of minds shaped by reliance on the value of the activity of Christ and the Church (those who emphasize the worth of the act itself, the *ex opere operato* effect), there is need of much emphasis on the importance of the value of the activity of the doer (the *opus operantis* effect), and this is all the more important since it has to be directed against discouragements that arise, against difficulties encountered, trials to be endured, and even in face of lamentable weaknesses and infidelities.

In liturgical spirituality, all one's thoughts, attitudes, and responses are constantly nourished with the potent and health-giving food derived from scripture, from the contents of tradition, and from the treasurehouse of formulae, rites, and ceremonies, and from the strong psychological response which springs from active participation.[162] Liturgy is a true school, an intensive and efficacious school, of prayer, of love of God, and of one's neighbor, of zeal for souls, of Christian "irradiation," of dedication, of cultivation of virtues, a place where one learns to fight against sin and evil tendencies. It is a whole spiritual theology, with lessons for the day, and for the whole span of life. He who surrenders himself to it, listens to it, learns from it, and obeys it will see, from the change that takes place in himself, that liturgy "is the outstanding means whereby the faithful may express in their lives, and manifest to others, the mystery of Christ and the real nature of the true Church."[163] He will feel that "from the liturgy. . .and especially from the Eucharist, as from a font, grace is poured forth upon us; and the sanctification of men in Christ and the glorification of God, to which all other activities of the Church are directed as towards their end, are achieved in the most efficacious way possible."[164]

Liturgy has the power to lift man to the highest perfection, "to the mature measure of the fulness of Christ."[165] It forms a spirituality which molds all the stages of spiritual ascent, from the humblest beginnings to luminous culmination in Christ and in the mystery of the Church.

We must not fear that the obligation to embrace a spirituality such as this will result in a deadening uniformity, in contrast with the words of sacred scripture which remind us that "star differs from star."[166] The essential elements of liturgy, the Mass and the sacraments, are so rich in the potentialities they offer for growth in the spiritual life that nobody could carry all of them into effect. Even if everyone were to decide to introduce into his life something different from the fund of liturgical spirituality, there would still be some left over. There is no danger of a deadening uniformity, for, although there is an obligation to embrace a liturgical form of piety, it includes not only the essentials, but also other elements of expression and rite which are by no means clearly defined. First, there is no attempt to determine all the different modes of expression, for there is left a wide margin of potentialities of undetermined riches even as regards essential elements. And secondly, the liturgy, for instance the Roman liturgy, is very rich in content and no attempt is made to descend to particulars in giving expression to it—for, these are left to the discretion of individuals, with the result that they will differ widely.

There will, therefore, be a wide scope for differences, and these differences can be not only numerous but profound. Hence we can say, that in his interior life no individual will be able to exhaust all the possibilities. Inevitably he will be compelled to make a choice, to set a limit to what he will select within the rich field of liturgy. One group will differ from another, one individual from another; and the differences between them may be vast and profound.

The Roman liturgy, as it exists, is a repository of elements of different and to some extent contrasting origins. Some, like the passages from the Old and New Testament, are of divine institution, others had their origin in the synagogue, and still others are of Roman or Hellenic origin. Some had their source in the Byzantine rite, and there is an amazing array of ideas, ceremonies, and rites which found their way in during the course of the migrations. And in the course of the centuries, all this has been affected by modifications, restorations, innovations, new feasts and rites, new sacramentals and prayers, new saints, and new ideas of the spiritual life.

To all these elements of differentiation, already quite numerous and seemingly inexhaustible, the Constitution adds others, more numerous and with more potential for change. First of all, it is probable that a new liturgical style will be created, little by little, as a consequence of the adaptation and accommodation to the realities and manners of the modern world.[168] The principles established in regard to adaptations may not have very profound consequences immediately. However, like all axioms, once they are announced and accepted, they pursue their course until they modify reality in the direction fixed for them. They are also principles that will maintain liturgy in a constant state of reform; for, time marches on, and its pace is quickening. What is good enough today may be old-fashioned tomorrow. In its changeable parts, liturgy will have to submit itself to a sustained and ceaseless process of modification, and the same will apply to the spirituality associated with it.

The new style which will result from a consistent application of the principles enunciated in the Constitution probably will not be uniform for all. There is stress on the participation of the people in a real and intensive way, and this will give rise to diversity; for there is diversity among people.[169] Admission of the vernacular will give rise to perceptible differences.[170] Words cannot retain indefinitely the meaning assigned them in dictionaries. Words can acquire strong emotional overtones, and changes will be necessitated because words can acquire new meanings, and the same word, in different languages, can have different meanings. Still stronger as a basis for diversity is the principle of adaptation to usage and customs, to the culture and civilization of different peoples. "Provision shall also be made, when revising the liturgical books, for legitimate variations and adaptations to different groups, regions, and peoples, especially in mission lands, provided that the substantial unity of the Roman rite is preserved; and this should be borne in mind when drawing up the rites and devising rubrics."[171]

Thus we see that it would be a mistake to hold that liturgical spirituality, although prescribed, will result in a uniform type of interior life. There will be room for endless diversity, and all will be at liberty to find and choose their own way, provided the essential elements of the liturgy are respected, and provided the principle that there is a certain degree of obligation in regard to expressions and rites as forms of the interior life is maintained.

B The Need of Supplementing the Liturgy with Other Pious Exercises

If the liturgy is the "primary and indispensable source from which the faithful are to derive the true Christian spirit"[172] there is no room for non-liturgical spiritualities in which the dominant element, the one which impresses the character, comes from pious exercises. In the interior life, these at most can play but a secondary role, never an essential or fundamental one. This is particularly true since they must be so drawn up that "they harmonize with the liturgical season, accord with the sacred liturgy, are in some fashion derived from it, and lead the people to it."[173]

This doctrine and law, explicitly set forth in the Constitution is a principle of spirituality, a doctrine expressed in strong and novel terms, by the Church. It modifies in striking fashion the rules given by Pius XII on this matter.[174] Many pious exercises existing within the Church will be affected by it, and will have to undergo essential changes. On the surface, some of these changes may seem insignificant, but in reality they affect the core, the dynamic idea, the dominant element in the religious exercise.

It sometimes happens that the boundaries between the liturgy and pious exercises are fluid. At present the liturgy includes many elements that, in olden times, were regarded as pious exercises, but now, by decree of the Church, they have been absorbed into the public cult, without undergoing change in form or content. The same Constitution has decreed that "any (approved) short office" drawn up "after the pattern of the divine office," and recited "in virtue of their constitutions" by "institutes dedicated to acquiring perfection" have the "status of public prayers."[175] The divine office itself was a pious exercise at the time of its origin. Others, too, may become part of the liturgy through the same juridical process; and this will certainly be done, to a greater or lesser extent, when there is question of establishing cultural and ethnical traditions proper to certain regions.[176] Since in this case pious exercises do not change form and content, they will be absorbed into the liturgy by becoming part of its expression, rite, and style. A spirituality, built up in accordance with these elements, is not outside the range of the liturgy; rather, it is part of it. Nevertheless, this is not to be regarded as a change in what constitutes the core, substance, and essence of liturgical spirituality.[177]

If, therefore, pious exercises cannot in any legitimate way be the core of a Catholic spirituality, they can be but secondary, additional, or accidental elements. This must be taken into account in the mind and attitude, the esteem and the efforts of those who cultivate and propagate them. It should be kept in mind, and emphasized.

This, however, does not give us the right to despise or deprecate pious exercises; for, they have a value and a legitimate function within the totality of Christian piety. The Constitution, as has been said,[178] does not favor any form of liturgical exclusivism. It expressly states that the "sacred liturgy does not exhaust the entire activity of the Church,"[179] and that the "spiritual life . . . is not limited solely to participation in the liturgy."[180] If the passages which speak of the necessity and the obligation of a liturgical form of spiritual life have to be respected and accepted, taken seriously, and carried out earnestly and consistently, the same must apply to the passages which forbid exclusivism in liturgical spirituality.

The Constitution does not unfold and disclose aspects of the spiritual life which are constituted by non-liturgical elements; it indicates them briefly, but in an explicit and categorical manner. In regard to this matter, the encyclicals *Mystici Corporis* and *Mediator Dei* give data that are more abundant and more specific. The teachings of the two encyclicals should continue to be respected, with the limitation, however, that they are to be interpreted in accordance with the new orientation given by the Council when it imposed on all the obligation of embracing liturgical spirituality, and in accordance with the rule that pious exercises must be organized to fit into the background of the liturgy, so that they "accord with the liturgy."[181] This rule is certainly an orientation quite different from that of the encyclicals,[182] for it implies a very different attitude and outlook. Even so, not everything will be modified.

Among the non-liturgical elements of the spiritual life, the Constitution mentions only "praying in secret" "praying without ceasing," mortification, and exercises of piety prescribed by the Holy See or approved by episcopal authority.[183] Elsewhere there is mention of such things as missions, preaching, religious instruction, charity, social work, and the apostolate;[184] for, in fact, many times these take the form of pious exercises. In all of this, according to the doctrine of the Constitution, there are certain elements that are necessary, and without them liturgical spirituality cannot subsist. Here, too, are found elements that are of obligation, as well as others which are left to the free choice of the individual.

According to the Constitution, liturgical spirituality needs to be complemented by elements borrowed, at least in part, from pious exercises. This is the function of pious exercises: to be complementary. This does not mean that, of their nature, they are necessary or obligatory. Certainly, all of them are not; and, least of all, are all of them intended for all. It means that in liturgical spirituality, which has to be the spirituality of everyone, some things will be accepted provisionally, some will be by-products, and some will be consequences, in regard to what constitutes the spiritual life.

7 CONCLUSION

The Constitution on the Liturgy is not a treaty to decide the relations between the liturgy and pious exercises. In regard to some points it has too little to say; in regard to others it is silent. The study of this document, therefore, cannot result in a complete exposition of these relations. Nevertheless, the doctrine and law it lays down is very rich, profound, and far-reaching in its effects on Christian spirituality. It is important to understand that in the Constitution it is explicitly and forcefully taught that, within the Church, a liturgical form of spirituality is indispensably necessary. Having established this, following the same document, it is necessary to study carefully and attentively what is liturgical spirituality, what constitutes its essential elements, what elements are of secondary importance, and what are the limits. It is particularly important to determine how far the obligation to embrace this type of spirituality extends. As regards the core of the liturgy, there is no question, for that is within the limits. The problem will arise in regard to concrete expressions, to rite, mode, form—to everything in the liturgy that is not of divine, but of ecclesiastical institution—for that can be changed by competent authority.

This doctrine, that there is an obligation incumbent on all to conform to a spirituality that is liturgical and to build up a spiritual life in accordance with it, must be recognized and duly respected. But it is important, too, to keep in mind that the Constitution expressly teaches that liturgy does not enjoy a monopoly in the spiritual life; on the contrary, it needs to be supplemented. Pious exercises are part of this supplementary aid that is needed, and so are other ecclesiastical exercises. These exercises must be built up in accordance with the liturgy, stem from it, and lead souls to it—but they will still remain "pious exercises." This Council document does not specify any particular pious exercise, when it speaks of the need of supplementary aid; it merely states that such help has to come from that field.

Such being its doctrine and law, the Constitution *Sacrosanctum Concilium* will certainly remain, in the spiritual history of the Church, an epoch-making document. The expression may be trite, but its meaning is significant; and for that reason it is used here.

NOTES TO CHAPTER 7

1 Zeal for the promotion and restoration of the liturgy is rightly held to be a sign of the providential disposition of God in our time, as a movement of the Holy Spirit in his Church. It is today a distinguishing mark of the Church's life, indeed of the whole tenor of contemporary religious thought and action.

2 The extracts in this article are based on the translation supplied by the National Catholic Welfare Conference, Washington, D.C.

3 Constitution on the sacred liturgy, *Sacrosanctum Concilium,* Art. 1. Hereinafter referred to as Con.

4 Cf., for instance, Art. 14.

5 Cf. *Motu proprio, "Tra le sollecitudini."*

6 First published in 1697, it has appeared in many editions and many languages.

7 The first French edition appeared over a century ago. Under the title of *The Liturgical Year,* it has appeared in at least two English versions.

8 Cf. M. T. L. Penido, *"Corpo Místico, 'Liturgicismo' e Piedade Liturgica,"* in *Revista Ecclesiastica Brasileira* (REB) 4 (1944), 517-540. Also *"Em Tôrno de Liturgicismo,"* REB 5 (1945), 482-494.

9 Cf. *La Maison-Dieu* 72 and 73, containing papers read at the national congress of the *Centre de Pastorale Liturgique,* held at Angers in 1962.

10 Cf. A. M. Roguet, *"La Liturgie et les dévotions,"* in *La Maison-Dieu* 73 (1963), 29-30.

11 Cf. C. Vagaggini, *Il senso teologico della liturgia* (2nd ed.; Roma: 1957), 30 ff.

12 Cf. Pius XII, *Mediator Dei* (Vatican Library trans.; Washington, D. C.: N.C.W.C., 1948), 20.

13 *Ibid.,* 32.

14 *Ibid.,* 33.

15 Cf. *"Liturgie,"* in *Lexikon für Theologie und Kirche* 6 (1962), col. 1085.

16 Cf. A.A.S. 50 (1958), 632.

17 *Loc. cit.;* cf. C.I.C., can. 1265.

18 Art. 7.

19 Art. 2.

20 *Ibid.*

21 Art. 7.
22 *Ibid.*
23 *Ibid.*
24 *Ibid.*
25 Art. 8.
26 Art. 9.
27 Art. 10.
28 *Ibid.*
29 Art. 13.
30 *Ibid.*
31 Art. 21.
32 Art. 26.
33 *Ibid.*
34 Art. 33.
35 *Ibid.*
36 Art. 2; 7; 10; 33; 61.
37 Art. 90; 98.
38 Art. 99.
39 Cf. Vagaggini, *op. cit.,* 131 f.; 615 ff.; 722 ff.; 778; 851.
40 A.A.S. 50 (1958), 632.
41 Roguet, *art. cit.,* 30.
42 *Ibid.*
43 *Loc. cit.,* 30-32.
44 *Loc. cit.,* 33.
45 Art. 7; cf also Art. 35.
46 Art. 10; 41.
47 Art. 9.
48 *Ibid.*
49 *Ibid.*
50 Art. 10.
51 Art. 9.
52 Art. 12.
53 Art. 12; cf. Mt. 6, 6.
54. Art. 12; cf. 1 Thes. 5, 17.
55 Art. 12.
56 Art. 13.
57 *Ibid.*
58 Art. 17.
59 Art. 118.
60 *Mediator Dei,* 184.

61 Strictly speaking, this prescription refers only to what this same Art. 13 calls "popular devotions of the Christian people" and "devotions proper to individual churches." It does not include what Art. 12 says about "entering into one's chamber to pray," "pray without ceasing," and about mortification. As a result, it could be understood that a strictly private life of prayer, which is discussed in Art. 12, would not be subject to the rule of having to "accord with the sacred liturgy." Popular devotions or "devotions proper to individual churches" would thus be distinguished from a strictly private life of prayer, and there would be three great factors to consider: "liturgical action," "popular devotions," and a strictly private life of prayer. We soon notice, however, that in Art. 12 the Constitution ceases to use a word that could serve as a common denominator for the elements to which it is referring. These could be merely examples of what later on are called "popular devotions." Art. 13, therefore, could be understood as a continuation of Art. 12, adding to it the observation that among non-liturgical acts of piety, those that have received some form of legislative approval from the Holy See or from a diocesan authority warrant special attention. Jungmann-Wagner hold a different opinion. Landersdorfer, Jungmann and Wagner, *"Anmerkungen zum Text der Konstitution..."* in *Konstitution des II Vatikanischen Konzils über die heilige Liturgie: Lateinischer Text und deutsche Uebersetzung* 2nd ed.; Münster, Achendorff, 1964), 93. They say that Art. 13 supersedes [*überwunden*] the distinction between "liturgical acts" as forms of worship and "popular devotions," a distinction that had been introduced by the *Musicae Sacrae Disciplina* of 1958. The sacred non-liturgical acts referred to in Art. 13 would form a special category and would constitute a distinct form of worship [*gottesdienstlicher Eigenwert*]. The constituents of a life of prayer, spoken of in Art. 12, would also be "popular devotions," but "simple" [*blosse*] devotions; while those of Art. 13 would be the same, but with a value peculiarly their own.

Jungmann-Wagner's comment possibly reflects the idea of the committee that wrote the text of the Constitution. The prescription of Art. 13, 3, consequently, according to the mind of the committee, possibly refers only to the "popular devotions" mentioned in paragraphs 1 and 2 of the same article, and not to the constituents mentioned in Art. 12. This conclusion is drawn from the letter of the document and the mind of the committee when drafting it. It seems, however, that by applying the principles given by the Constitution concerning the obligation placed on all to conform to a liturgical form of spirituality, this distinction practically annuls itself. It would seem to be impossible to cultivate a liturgical spirituality in the degree required by the Constitution and, at the same time, to live a strictly private life of prayer, isolated from any liturgical character. By definition, spirituality dominates the interior life to an extent too great to allow, psychologically, the distinction described above; and this is still more true in view of the intensiveness here postulated. It seems that we must conclude that, from a juridical point of view, we cannot apply Art. 13, 3 to all "popular devotions." Understanding it thus, it has no validity over a private life of prayer. From a practical point of view, however, in the light of what is psychologically possible, and what can be deduced from the aforesaid principles, a strictly private life of prayer cannot help following what paragraph 3 indicates, although this is not demanded by any law.

The line of distinction between Articles 12 and 13, as indicated by Jungmann-Wagner, actually exists, and has received sufficient attention in the present treatment. It does not modify, however, the conclusion already reached. Since this matter attracted our attention only after this work was first published, we could not emphasize it sufficiently. In such a case we would have placed less emphasis on Art. 13, 3 and given more emphasis to the principles which actually lead to the same conclusion. We beg our readers to bear this in mind in regard to the context corresponding to Notes 103, 121, 122, 132, 173, and 181.

Jungmann-Wagner, judging from their comments (*loc. cit.*, p. 93) on Art. 118 where there is reference to "devotions and sacred exercises" seem to identify the "sacred exercises" with what is said in Art. 12. We say "seem," for their comment is so brief that we are not justified in being more specific. Contrary to what Jungmann-Wagner suggest, the same Constitution uses these words in Art. 13, and in Art. 118 it presents them rather as synonyms.

The above-mentioned observation leads us to believe that in drawing up the Constitution these two words were considered at length and were the subject of discussion. The text of the Constitution, however, seems not to give sufficient basis for the distinction. Quite the contrary. The following is a possible explanation. In their notes, Jungmann-Wagner refer more than once to items which, if not of a strictly personal character, must have come to their knowledge as writers of the Constitution. Several times they mention the intention, the "mind" of the committee; yet this intention is not made explicit in the conciliar document. One well may ask: To what extent is it permissible to use these items in the actual interpretation? It must be kept in mind that it was the Council, not the committee, that issued the decree. The "mind" of the committee, therefore, is valid only insofar as it reflects the "mind" of the Council, and of the pope who promulgated the decree. In order, then, to take advantage of items coming from the committee, and in order to give them a decisive value, it is necessary to prove first that it was the mind of the committee that prevailed in the mind of the Fathers.

62 Cf. footnote 8, the two articles by Penido, together with the bibliography to which they lead. Roguet, *loc. cit.* (footnote 10) is a demonstration of the persistence of this objection. Cf. p. 18 of his article.

63 *Mediator Dei,* 25.

64 *Ibid.,* 36.

65 *Ibid.,* 23.

66 *Ibid.,* 24.

67 *Ibid.,* 25.

68 Art. 7.

69 *Ibid.*

70 Art. 1.

71 Art. 11.

72 *Ibid.*

73 Art. 14.

74 *Ibid.;* cf. also Art. 50 and 90.

75 Art. 14.

76 Art. 14, 15, 16, 17.

77 Art. 18.

78 Art. 19.

79 Art. 29.

80 Art. 90.

81 Art. 11.

82 Art. 14.

83 *Ibid.*

84 *Mediator Dei,* 8.

85 Cf. *Mystici Corporis,* A.A.S. 35 (1943), 221-222.

86 *Ibid.*

87 *Mediator Dei,* 13; 14.

88 Cf. Denz.-Schoenm., 1351-2374 (Denz., 1327-1349).

89 *Mediator Dei,* 13.

90 *Pia exercita,* A.A.S. 35 (1943), 201-202 *et passim.*

91 *Mediator Dei,* 35.

92 *Ibid.,* 31.

93 Art. 7.

94 Art. 9.

95 Art. 9, 10.

96 *Ibid.*

97 Art. 12.

98 *Ibid.*

99 Art. 13.

100 *Ibid.*

101 *Ibid.*

102 Cf. *Mediator Dei,* 172-185.

103 Art. 13.

104 Art. 10.

105 Art. 13.

105a Art. 9.

106 Art. 12.

107 Art. 7.

108 Art. 11.

109 *Ibid.*

110 Cf., for instance, the following articles: 14, 17, 18, 19, 29, 48, 50 59, 61, 90, 94, 99.

111 *Mediator Dei,* 63-65.

112 *Ibid.*

113 Art. 1.

114 Art. 21.

115 Art. 23, 37, 40, 49, 62, 79, 87, 107.

116 Art. 38; cf. Art. 39, 40, 107, 118, 119, 123.

117 Art. 23.

118 Art. 14.

119 *Ibid.*

120 *Ibid.*

121 Art. 13; cf. above.

122 Art. 13.

123 Art. 14.

124 Art. 12, 17, 19, 42, 61.

125 Cf. above.

126 *Ibid.*

127 Art. 14, 17, 18, 19.

128 Secret of Ninth Sunday after Pentecost.

129 Art. 2.

130 *Ibid.*

131 Art. 10.

132 Art. 13.

133 Art. 14.

134 Art. 21, 33, 41, 43.

135 Art. 14.

136 Art. 15.

137 Art. 16.

138 Art. 17.

139 Art. 18.

140 Art. 19.

141 Art. 1.

142 Art. 21, 49, 50.

143 Art. 14, 21, 34, 41.

144 Art. 36, 54, 63, 79, 101.

145 Art. 21, 62, 79.

146 Art. 37, 40, etc.

147 Art. 13.

148 Art. 15, 18.

149 Art. 16, 17.

150 Art. 10, 19, 41, 42, 43, 49, 50, 59, 9.

151 Denz.-Schoenm., 3667 (Denz., 2192).

152 Art. 7.

153 *Mystici Corporis, loc. cit.*

154 Art. 11.

155 Art. 7.

156 *Ibid.*

157 Art. 11.

158 Art. 2.

159 Art. 106.

160 Cf. Art. 2, 7, 11, 59, 83, 85, 99.

161 Cf. Art. 11, 14, 16-19, 21, 41.

162 Cf. Art. 24, 33-35, 37-40, 51, 56, 59, 60, 92.

163 Art. 2.

164 Art. 10.

165 Art. 2.

166 1 Cor. 15, 41.

167 Cf. as above.

168 Art. 1, 21.

169 Art. 14, 21, 34, 48, 50, etc.

170 Art. 36, 54, 63, 101.

171 Art. 38.

172 Art. 14.

173 Art. 13.

174 Cf. as above.

175 Art. 98.

176 Art. 37-40.

177 Cf. as above.

178 Cf. as above.

179 Art. 9.

180 Art. 12.

181 Art. 13.

182 Cf. as above.

183 Art. 12, 13.

184 Art. 9.

185 *Ibid.*

8
The liturgy, center of theological studies and pastoral activity

Evaristo Paulo Arns O.F.M.

1 The teaching of liturgy in seminaries
   A The training of teachers
   B Importance of liturgy in the theological curriculum
2 Forming a liturgical mentality in the other branches
   A Exegesis
   B Sacred eloquence
3 Liturgical life in the seminaries
4 Preeminent role of liturgy in pastoral work
   A Obstacle to liturgical renewal in parishes
      1 Our formation and resources
      2 Level of instruction of the faithful
      3 Independence on the part of the faithful
      4 Lack of means
   B Pedagogical principles and the liturgical renewal through pastoral work
5 Conclusion

Father Arns is professor of Patristics and of liturgy in the clericate of the Franciscans at Petropolis in Brazil. His article was translated into English by Father Tarcisio Beal of Washington, D.C.

The tenth week of studies for teachers of liturgy, held in the monastery of Mont-Cesar, Louvain, July 15-20, 1963, discussed the theme *Liturgy and Theology*. Four leading subjects were proposed for discussion by leaders in the liturgical movement in Europe, namely, *Liturgy and Patristics,* by B. Botte, O.S.B., *Liturgy and Christology,* by P. M. Gy, O.P., *Essential and Accidental Rites in the Sacraments,* by Houssiau, and finally *Theology of the Sacred Season,* by J. Gaillard.

On reading the reports of the above, it is evident that there is an intimate connection between theology (from its historical studies up to dogma) and liturgy. The teacher of theology, preoccupied with the task of conveying to the students a vivid realization of what he is presenting to them, naturally reconstructs the schema proposed by St. Justin,[1] namely, to listen to the divine message, to pray, and to make an offering to God and to receive something in return.

This is the psychological approach, employed by the theologians of antiquity, who were at the same time pastors of souls, such as St. John Chrysostom, St. Augustine, and St. Gregory the Great. To listen to, and to draw attention to, what God says means to prepare the atmosphere for the divine message [the *kerygma*]. To try to speak to or answer the divine revelation is to pray. To become convinced of one's dependence on the Almighty and his mediator means to offer this sacrifice and to receive Communion from the divine table.

Would not this be also the underlying schema in the entire revelation of the Old and New Testament? In the creation, for instance, God reveals himself. Adam speaks to him. He refuses, however, to offer the sacrifice implied in the order that he is not to touch the tree of knowledge of good and evil. In the flood, God revealed his destructive power; Noe maintains contact with God by obeying his orders. Soon after he leaves the ark he offers a holocaust. We could not even imagine the revelation of Christ in regard to the profound concept that God is our father if he had not already taught us to pray "Our Father" and the attitude we should take in prayer, and if we had not the sacrifice of the Son, together with our communion in this sacrifice.

The purely theoretical theologian, who seeks to reduce theology to an abstract science, never gets beyond the borders of the way that leads to God. On the other hand, the teacher of theology who restricts himself to convey to his students just the explanation of the rubrics, and their practical application, will never be anything but a fossil.

The liturgical renewal, especially since *Mediator Dei,* should have taught us that when all unite their efforts, all benefit. Teachers of theology, as well as students, benefit.

Nevertheless, the *Revista di Pastorale Liturgica* I, 1 (November, 1963), p. 51 (its very first issue) reproduces the following observations of two rectors of seminaries; these observations may read like a joke, and for that reason we reproduce them in the original: *"Ma que cosa se ne fanno i nostri giovani del sacramentario gelasiano o pelagiano o che so io! Che imparino a dir bene la loro Messa e conoscano con esatteza le cerimonie.*

Questo e lo scopo della scuola di liturgia." ("What have our boys got to do with the sacramentaries of Pelagius and Gelasius, or whatever their names are? Let them learn how to say Mass and to observe the ceremonies. This is what liturgy should be.") The other knows still better what we need today: "*Bisogna far vivere la vita cristiana, e no stare a insistere sulla partecipazione alla Messa.*" ("You're here to live the Christian life and not to be always talking about participation in the Mass.")

Even serious books of great influence, such as the one by G. Martil, *Los Seminarios Hoy,* which was translated into Italian,[2] mention art and liturgy only incidentally as food for piety and not as the best form of it. Although this book does not ignore the liturgical movement, it is satisfied to give just a few items of pastoral advice, and does not seek to transmit to future liturgists the key to the problem.

Many among the priests of today will recall advice such as that given by a Roman prelate, who actually had the title of Doctor of Theology, namely; receive Holy Communion before Mass, and then you can make your thanksgiving during it.[3]

How different is the attitude of Pope Paul VI, expressed in his allocution at the closing of the second session of Vatican II: "The first theme to be examined, and the first, too, because of its *intrinsic value and its importance for the life of the Church* is the one which deals with the sacred liturgy which has just been happily concluded."[4] Professors of theology might have rejoiced because of the incentive which came from the Roman Pontiff, namely:

> It would be well for us to accept this treasure as the fruit of our Council and *to look on it as something which must characterize and animate the life of the Church.* In fact, the Church is a religious society, a community of prayer, a people redolent with interior and spiritual life which springs from faith and grace. . . . We perceive that, in the Constitution on the liturgy, there is respect for the scale of values, and duties, namely, God in the first place; prayer as our first obligation; the Liturgy as the primary font of divine life which is communicated to us, and the first school of our spiritual life. . . .[5]

1 THE TEACHING OF LITURGY IN SEMINARIES

Two main causes contribute to the discredit of the teaching of liturgy in our seminaries, namely, lack of specific training of the teachers, and the small number of class periods.

Special preference was given to those who had graduated from a university, or a faculty recognized by the Holy See, when there was a question of appointing someone to teach in the fields of theology, canon law, and philosophy.[6] One or several specialized professors were provided for the teaching of sacred scripture, dogmatic theology, moral theology, and church history.[7] The teacher of liturgy was usually assigned about fifteen classes a semester, and the course was regarded as of secondary importance.

It should not be wondered at if each professor of liturgy followed his own bent and confined himself to commenting on a manual of rubrics which supplied him with satisfactory information on the history of the liturgy.

Art. 15 of the Constitution on the liturgy puts an end to this improvization when it ordains that "Professors who are appointed to teach liturgy in seminaries, religious houses of studies and theological faculties, must be properly trained for their work in institutes which specialize in this subject."[8]

Do such specialized institutes already exist? At the present time there are two Pontifical Institues of Liturgy for the training of professors, namely, the Pontificium Institutum Liturgicum of San Anselmo, in Rome, and the Institut Superieur de Liturgie, in Paris, attached to the faculty of theology of the Institut Catholique. Both grant the same degrees and follow similar programs. At the close of four semesters, with examinations and thesis completed, a qualifying diploma for the teaching of liturgy is granted to those who lack a licentiate degree in theology. One who holds a licentiate degree, according to the Constitution *Deus Scientiarum Dominus,* must defend a thesis on a subject dealing with liturgy, if, at the conclusion of the four semesters prescribed, he is to be admitted to the degree of Doctor of Theology.[9]

A faculty of liturgy does not exist so as not to multiply titles, but in these institutes, a doctorate in theology is equivalent to a doctorate in liturgy.

A The Training of Teachers

The primary aim of these institutes is to prepare teachers of liturgy and assistants to the bishops in the liturgical commissions. Their scientific method provides the student with a complete panorama of the liturgy, since, in the teaching of this subject, theological, historical, spiritual, cultural, pastoral, and juridical aspects are all integrated. There is no doubt that the Constitution on the liturgy will influence the program of these institutes by requiring from them in the future more class periods to provide adequate training for teachers of this subject.[10]

In addition to these two pontifical institutes, there are others, such as that of Trier for the German dioceses. It is designed to support, foster and orient the liturgical movement in Germany. It sponsors students who select a liturgical thesis for their degree in sacred theology. The course of the *Année Pastorale Liturgique,* founded in 1958 in the Abbey of St. Andrew, Bruges 3, Belgium, has been highly recommended. The course lasts for only one year, the number of students is restricted to twenty, and the formation has an eminently pastoral character. The Pontifical Pastoral Institute of the Lateran also offers specialized courses in liturgy. Its aim, evidently, is not the formation of teachers in liturgy. The same is true of the higher courses in catechetics and liturgy established in 1964 at the Pontifical University of Salamanca for priests and religious who wish to be specially trained in such pastoral studies.[11]

We are convinced that, in addition to schools or academies of sacred music, recommended by Art. 127 of the Constitution on the liturgy, and of higher institutes of sacred music, inspired by Art. 115, we shall also witness the early establishment of institutes for pastoral liturgy in all countries (Art. 44).

B *Importance of Liturgy in the Theological Curriculum*

In the *Ordinationes S. C. Seminariis et Studiorum Universitatibus* of June 12, 1931, liturgy was placed among the secondary, not among the necessary, studies.[12] The present Constitution thus decrees in Art. 16:

> The study of sacred liturgy is to be ranked among the compulsory and major courses in seminaries and religious houses of studies; in theological faculties it is to rank among the principal courses. It is to be taught under its theological, historical, spiritual, pastoral and juridical aspects.

One of the Fathers of the Council, in his *"placet juxta modum"* (or provisional approval), felt that this article should be eliminated, together with those that are close to it, on the plea that they descend to details. The Commission took advantage of this to emphasize the article, saying that in its own opinion these principles are most important because they are the basis for the entire reform, namely, for pastoral work and for requisites for its efficacy. Thus, in the opinion of the Council, the teachers of liturgy help to lay the foundations for the entire structure of liturgical renewal. Incidentally, the Preparatory Liturgical Commission had already furnished the reasons why liturgy should necessarily be included among the main studies, saying that

> This is a consequence of the nature of liturgy itself, because it is a vital action of Christ and of the whole of his mystical Body, and the source and culmination of the spiritual and pastoral life of the Church.[13]

On the same occasion, however, the Commission warned against misinterpreting the Constitution in such a way as to make the courses in liturgy as extensive as those in dogmatic theology and sacred scripture. One class a week throughout the entire theological course would be sufficient.

The teachers of liturgy, therefore, have an internal motive, mentioned above in the words of the Commission, and also an external motive based on the fact that the II Vatican Council has considered liturgy as a synthesis of theology and the principal goal for the life of the Church. Thus: "Liturgy is the summit towards which the activity of the Church is directed; at the same time it is the font from which all her power flows" (Art. 10). The teachers, in turn, have the obligation of resolving the problem of harmonizing the teaching of liturgy with the other studies. A Declaration in regard to Art. 16, 2, recommends:

> The study of sacred liturgy should not be treated merely under its juridical or rubrical aspects, and neither should it be viewed from a

merely historical point of view, but a scientific, integral basis should be provided for it, by revealing it under its theological-historical aspect, as well as its spiritual, pastoral, and juridical aspects.

Fortunately we do not have to await the elaboration of manuals on the liturgy portraying the aspects above-mentioned. We have them already, and they are magnificent, drawn up by the same experts who took part in the liturgical Commission of the Council. As an example, we could indicate *L'Eglise en Prière: Introduction à la Liturgie,* by A. G. Martimort,[14] which is the result of the joint effort under the supervision of the director of the Institut Supérieur de Liturgie of Paris. Evidently, a work such as this could not attain all the objectives. However, it gives safe directions. Teachers of liturgy must conform to the regulations found in Art. 44 and 55. They will be notable aids towards pastoral-liturgical work. . . .

The dynamism of the students, the daily experience of the liturgy itself, and scientific demands will compel the teachers to lay aside the easy trappings of the manual and to take on the heavy equipment of research. Since, however, they were especially trained and endowed with a feeling from the mission of the Church, they will unite prudence with vigilance, docility under instruction with application to research, theory in class with practice in pastoral problems, faith with ritual, personal prayer with community prayer—in brief, they will display their love for Christ and the liturgy.

Dom Botte, who devoted his marvelous talent to research in the field of liturgy, warns teachers, in this regard, against the dangers of anarchy and pseudo-history.[15]

The fact, however, is that liturgists are the persons most responsible for this anarchy. Rather, those who despised and ignored the rubrics were responsible, by daring to exhibit at the altar "what they considered good."

How may we prevent our future priests from adopting and improvising such methods which lead them to conclude that "all's well that ends well"? Dom Botte answer that in such a case, Christ would not have died. Christ was put to death because the leaders and people did not "see eye to eye with him"; therefore, not everything that wins the approval of the people is necessarily right. To such empiricists, the liturgical spirit is lacking. Who is to blame? From 1955 on, not all who were engaged in pastoral work could regard themselves as sufficiently prepared for radical changes such as those of Holy Week, sacred music and liturgy, the new code of rubrics, and modifications in the missal. In the midst of their missionary labors, without a religious community and round table discussions to support them, the priest, even if fully aware of their duty, will often have to depend on the occasional illuminations that light up their pathways in the country. Meanwhile, the teacher of liturgy, as he looks at his class, asks himself the question: How many of these, my students, will find themselves in such situations three years from now?

The liturgical spirit includes, *in addition,* a knowledge of the rubrics, and a respect for them.

A second danger, pointed out by Dom Botte, is also mentioned in Art.

16 of the Constitution, namely, pseudo-history. However, I would like to meet the first teacher of liturgy who, in the past, has not succumbed to this temptation. The rites and prayers had their origin in the past. Even those who are born today, tomorrow will have passed into history. Any man who is in a hurry resembles a public recorder. What is his job? He writes down the name of the child, the date of its birth, the names of its parents, and whatever the law demands in addition. In the certificate he indicates the books and page in which the information may be found. This was the method of liturgy. From now on, how would the teacher of liturgy, after the manner of the recorder, bring the child to speak, to manifest his personality, to give expression to his ideals? The answer is: through the texts of the liturgy. And how eloquent they are! But eloquent texts are like eloquent men. They need time. The teachers of church history, sacred scripture, and dogma have time to quote and comment on their sources. The teacher of liturgy, however, even if he were to restrict himself to what is of bare obligation, would never be able to comment on the main texts of the Mass, to say nothing of the divine office, the sacraments, and those texts which provide the basis for the ceremonies, acclamations, and hymns of the liturgy.

In order not to endanger the very basis of the reform, the teacher should have enough time to conduct the class, not by means of reports, imparting of information, and by little prescriptions, but, rather, with the purpose of training the students to understand the texts so that they will be able progressively to continue their work of self-perfection. I would venture the opinion that the few classes allotted to liturgy are intended to be reserved to liturgy alone, leaving sacramental theology to be dealt with elsewhere. The same teacher could treat of the dogmatic questions, which in this case are more positive than speculative, as well as of the moral and juridical questions, always aiming at the practice of liturgy and the pastoral norms for the administration of the sacraments. The teacher of canon law could assign him the task of treating of the canons of the third book, namely Canons 726-1551; that is, a third part of the code. The teacher of morals could do the same.

Such a procedure would reshape the entire program of theological studies, and possibly put an end to traditional norms which still exist in houses of study. On the other hand, a series of boring repetitions of correlated treatments, in addition to being a waste of time, can be avoided. The priest who had pursued such an integrated course, when presiding over a parochial committee called to participate with him in the responsibilities of the liturgical life of the community, will merely need to consult his manual and his notes, since he lacks time to specialize in law, morals, and dogma. Only thus will it be possible for the teacher to carry out the recommendations of Art. 16 of the Constitution, namely, that the study of sacred liturgy is to be taught "under its theological, historical, spiritual, pastoral, and juridical aspects." The II Vatican Council has opened our eyes to so many realities, and will lead us to a revision of many points which before we took for granted. Perhaps this is one of those.

As long as we leave the study of liturgy within the framework of a weekly class, the students will pay much more attention to theological insights, to the apostolate of the masses, and to topical sermons; but they will not regard the "altar of the Mass as the heart of the household, where we listen to the words of the Father, and where the children are nourished at the table of the Eucharist." And neither will they realize that we are trying to form pastors of souls who know how and are willing to introduce the people of God to the mysteries of the liturgy. Willingness on the part of the students must greatly increase if we wish to be sure that the future pastors of souls, when they leave the seminary, will become "imbued with the spirit and power of the liturgy and undertake to give instruction about it" (Art. 14).

2 FORMING A LITURGICAL MENTALITY IN THE OTHER BRANCHES

Art. 16 establishes that: "The study of sacred liturgy is to be ranked among the compulsory and major courses in seminaries and religious houses of studies. It also adds the following rule for the benefit of the other teachers of theology: "Moreover, other professors, while striving to expound the mystery of Christ and the history of salvation from the angle proper to each of their own subjects, must, nevertheless, do so in a way which will clearly bring out the connection between their subjects and the liturgy, as also the unity which underlies all priestly training."

Holy Church has inherited from her Divine Master this preoccupation with unity in priestly formation. She maintained it even in dark days, such as those of St. Gregory the Great, when he wrote his *Liber Regulae Pastoralis*.[16] We believe that from the Middle Ages (which was the period for the systematic organization of higher studies) up to the present, no faculty has appeared that could claim to possess a common objective that could unify the mystery of Christ and the history of salvation as the modern faculty of theology does.

Theoretically, all is well. The Council now proposes another practical goal, making everything converge on the liturgy, without impoverishing the studies or introducing artificiality into the methods.

The teacher of dogma, since he is required to delve deeply into truths which, in many cases, constitute the very core of worship, will become a-religious if he fails to arouse in himself and in others a profound respect and gratitude for the wonders of God. Respect and gratitude seems to us to be fundamental qualities for a liturgical as well as for a theological attitude.

Preparation for liturgy is not to be taught, *ex professo,* either in classes of dogmatic theology, or moral theology, or even in canon law. The conditions for true culture must continue to be respected. Utilitarianism, the hankering after ferverinos, although these be attractive to some types of students, only lead to false piety and to the distortion of love and intelligence. Liturgy will produce its ripest fruits only if based on a plenitude of truth and on the profound needs of modern man. If studies are permitted to be less intellectual, less scientific, less rigorous, less traditional, in regard to God and the Gospel, they will supply answers that are apparent, but not true, and they will not satisfy the deep-felt wants of pious souls and the Church's missionary spirit today.

A Exegesis

The repeated insistence of the Constitution on the celebration of the Word of God, which is an essential part of the liturgy, by itself would make the teacher of exegesis the person primarily responsible for the success of the new liturgical movement in the seminaries, and consequently in the parishes. In addition, liturgy transforms the revelation of God into an act of worship, and this is precisely what it is in the first place. As a consequence, the understanding of revelation is no less important in regard to the second part of the Mass, namely, the liturgy of the Eucharist. This can be deepened progressively if the biblical meaning of sacrifice and communion and of community participation (cf. the Epistle to the Hebrews), in addition to the actions and attitudes recorded in the Bible, are also deepened. *A fortiori,* the same is due in regard to the breviary and preparation for Mass. . . .

Art. 24 recommends the teacher of exegesis "to promote that warm and living love for scripture" which is necessary "to achieve the restoration, progress, and adaptation of the sacred liturgy." If he does this, he will have the consolation of seeing his students, throughout their lives, engaged in the practice of what he is now teaching. In fact, it is still too soon to foresee the consequences that will derive from Art. 35 in favor of studies and of the formation of a biblical mentality, if "in sacred celebrations there is to be more reading from holy scripture and it is to be more varied and suitable," and if "the sermon should draw its content mainly from scriptural and liturgical sources" (art. 35, 2), and if "Bible services should be encouraged" in all kinds of situations (35, 4).

God grant that the reefs of pseudo-history and pseudo-philology can be avoided, and that we may have true biblical theology instead. We shall then have the prospect of reviving the golden epoch of preaching and of exegetical literature of the fifth century, now aided by all the devices of modern science. We may then hope to see, in addition to the flowering of exegetical literature, the formation of academies of interested and educated laymen, such as that of the Aventine in the days of St. Jerome. Among these laymen, religious women will certainly be awarded their rightful place.

Of greater significance to us, it seems, is the popular hunger for the Bible. In order to satisfy this hunger, we shall be welcoming easier exegetical commentaries, new explanatory books dealing with liturgical celebrations, and appropriate editions of all kinds of liturgical texts.

B Sacred Eloquence

In an allocution to the pastors, assistants and Lenten preachers of Rome on February 12, 1964, the Holy Father spoke of the necessity of returning to the genuine ministry of the Word in the life of the Church. The Church is engaged in the task of restoring the Word to its former place of honor, by returning to the popular presentation of it, and to the purity, sincerity, and strength proper to the Christian tradition, as well as to the profundity and simplicity of the liturgical homily.

We know that "the sacred liturgy does not exhaust the entire activity of the Church" (Art. 9), neither does it constitute the sole mission of man in the world. The homily, therefore, is not always to be restricted to liturgy. But here, too, we can look forward to a style reminiscent of St. Cyril of Jerusalem, of St. Leo the Great, and, in some measure, of St. Gregory the Great. We know, through St. Justin, that the majority of the Fathers of the Church, after reading the recollections of the apostles and the writings of the prophets, when presiding over the congregation, were accustomed to speak in order to warn and exhort the faithful to follow these inspiring teachings.[17] Or, they directly explained the ceremonies of Mass, of the sacraments, and of the mysteries which are celebrated in the course of the liturgical year.[18] Incidentally, this is a matter which deserves the attention of the experts.

The study of patrology, perhaps to a greater extent than in the past, should place emphasis on liturgical sources. The exegesis of these texts, which are rich in content and expressive in form, would create an atmosphere favorable to the liturgical mentality, as well as many occasions for the study of pastoral needs, of the spirituality of the Christian people, of the currents of ideas which, in every epoch, reveal elements that are stable and elements that vary.

Here we shall pause, for we are still in the midst of the first rays of dawn. How many surprises will the new day bring to those who work together in the vast field of liturgy within the seminaries!

3 LITURGICAL LIFE IN THE SEMINARIES

At the Last Supper, Jesus was surrounded by only twelve. This was his first seminary. There he celebrated the liturgy of the Word and the sacrificial action.

There is, therefore, no more fitting way to celebrate the Memorial of the Lord than to assemble around his table those whom he no longer called "servants" but "friends," those whom he has "chosen" and whom he has destined to "bear fruit" (Jn. 15, 15 f).

This is the reason why the Constitution recommends that seminarians "shall be given a liturgical formation. . .so that they may be able to understand the sacred rites and take part in them more wholeheartedly; and they will also need personally to celebrate the sacred mysteries, as well as popular devotions, which are imbued with the spirit of the liturgy" (Art. 17).

After the seminarians have received fruitful instruction on the psalms and on the meaning of the *Sacrifice of Praise* which is offered in the name of the whole of creation, morning and night prayers should be replaced, even in the last years of the minor seminaries, by lauds and compline, prayed in common and in the vernacular. Naturally, recourse will be had to pedagogical aids, and to a progressive spiritual formation, so that the warlike songs of David may prevent the soldiers of the new covenant from falling asleep. Routine, which in seminaries is the lowly custodian of discipline, could in time hinder the ways of the spirit of Christ. Other canonical hours, recited in common, could also be numbered among appropriate means for solemnizing anniversaries, festive commemoratives, and meetings for purposes of study.

In seminaries, over a period of years, it has been the custom each month to plan the community Masses for certain days. There cannot be ideal schedules. The repertory of hymns must be constantly varied, but it is silence which will deepen meditation and understanding.

Short and well-prepared homilies, during certain Masses, will certainly be more effective than long conferences in the course of which everyone is trying to determine for whom the allusions of the speaker were intended. The important thing is that Christ be in our midst.

In addition to personal formation, the living observance of the liturgical year requires a community incentive. Spiritual reading in common, spiritual direction and conferences continue to be our greatest weapons. We will not achieve anything, however, unless the seminarians themselves do their part during the period of Lent, the ember days, Pentecost, the feast of Christ the King, and so on. Since liturgical ceremonies had their origin and development in centers of higher spirituality, seminaries cannot be unmindful of them. If well prepared, the ceremonies will give a "foretaste" of that "heavenly liturgy which is celebrated in the holy city of Jerusalem" (Art. 8) and will always associate the Church with Christ (cf. Art. 7).

Easter and Christmas are wonderful opportunities for intense pastoral activity on the part of the seminarians. The mystery of Christ will evoke increasingly resounding echoes in the souls of those who feel themselves responsible, during Easter and Christmas, for the announcing of the Good Tidings (*kerygma*).

And what is to be said about Sundays, those dreary days in certain seminaries?

Do the seminarians have a special liturgy of their own? Will they be content to rest in the seminary, observing, perhaps, the Jewish regulation of a maximum of 1,500 paces? Do they go to the cathedral? Do groups of them accompany their teachers in visits to chapels?

Innovation is a great temptation for young people. Give them a limited field of action in any suburb, and they will soon want to take over the entire city. On the other hand, traditionalism is the weak point for those who are no longer young. Nevertheless, when some demand more openings and more action, we may bring to their attention the many concessions made to seminarians, so numerous that they themselves feel stunned. However, any pedagogical system that refuses to review its method and relive its experiences has already built up its own funeral pyre.

Pius XII was much preoccupied with the pastoral, progressive formation of seminarians: *In toto institutiones et probationes tempore ne omittant Moderatores et Magistri animos alumniorum ad apostolatum allicere, quin etiam in eodem moderate eos excercere.*[19] This, naturally, without injury to their formation as would happen in cases of *"immoderata servitia ministerialia in paroeciis tempore quadragesimae aut missionum et similia."*[20]

Assuming that provision has been made for Sunday rest, when preparation affecting mind and heart has been provided and when there has been practical preparation in reading, commenting, singing, leading the congregation, then the seminarians, if the authorities deem it fitting, may accompany a priest, (and in this case monthly rotation is recommended), not for the purpose of preaching during Mass, or of instructing the people, but to participate in the liturgy with them, after the manner of a commentator, or, possibly, of a deacon. If direction is provided for such seminarians by the priest in charge of them, if the prefects often promote round tables, and if psychological and technical instruction is supplied, step by step, then we would have fulfilled the injunction of Pius XII, namely: *"Haec vero pastoralis alumnorum conformatio, ab ineunte studiorum curriculo inchoanda, progrediente vero aetate gradatim perficienda.*[21] Over many years we have made these experiments and we have had no regrets, provided the priests, or others who are assisted by seminarians, did not treat them as assistants or as altar boys, but rather as their new helpers.

And this final observation of Art. 17 should not, by any means, be allowed to pass unnoticed: "[Seminarians] must learn how to observe the liturgical laws, so that life in seminaries and houses of religion may be thoroughly influenced by the spirit of the liturgy." Some time ago, an expert in liturgy pointed out that Fernandel, in the role of Don Camillo, had a beautifully clear diction throughout the play, but when he had to pronounce the words of a Latin blessing he automatically began to mumble the words; and this he did, not with the purpose of offending, but of reproducing what he had always observed. If the criticism leveled against our pronunciation comes from persons who do not understand Latin, our carelessness may be due in part to the fact that we realize that we are not understood, anyway. Perfect pronunciation, as well as dignity in gestures and accuracy in performing the ceremonies, show that our spirit is attuned to them. This should be a matter of concern to us in our capacity as liturgists, or as individuals responsible for the formation of future liturgists.

St. John Chrysostom, speaking of the formation of priests, placed liturgical training in the center of everything. He writes: "Let us center our attention on those mysteries we celebrate these days. So admirable are they that we never can esteem them too highly. Behold the priest where he stands. He brings with him, not a fire, but the Holy Spirit. . . ."[22] From that time, the monks, who were the principal promoters of the liturgy, were invited to bring their treasures to the missions and to the care of souls. St. Gregory the Great repeated the dramatic appeal to monks versed in liturgy to become missionaries and pastors of souls. Ever since the Council of Trent, there has been a constant appeal to the effect that seminarians pay special attention to the riches of the sacraments. However, we have never witnessed such a unity in desiring a liturgy worthy of God and at the same time within the reach of all men as we are now witnessing in the II Vatican Council. The Church is today providing *"nova et vera"* for the seminarian in preparation for his future work in the Kingdom of God.

4 PREEMINENT ROLE OF LITURGY IN PASTORAL WORK

Pope Paul VI, in his Apostolic Letter of November 30, 1963, granting special faculties and privileges to the bishops of the world, explained that "the pastoral ministry embraces the office of teaching, sanctifying, binding and loosing."[23]

This triple office is carried out in a continuous and unsurpassable manner in the liturgical actions. It is no wonder, then, that the Holy Father, in his allocution at the closing of the second session of the II Vatican Council, praised the Constitution on the liturgy in words full of poetry and hope, as follows:

> Liturgy is the first gift we can offer to the Christian people. It is an opportunity for the world to express its sentiments in happy and authentic prayer, feeling, at the same time, that ineffable regenerating power we experience when, all together, we sing the divine praises, and express our human hopes through Our Lord Jesus Christ in the Holy Spirit.[24]

The following words of Msgr. Spada have been repeated many times in Italy: *"O la liturgia diventa pastorale, strumento convinto e vissuto di cura d'anime, o restera una Rubricaria che ne lodera il Signore ne salvera le anime."*[25] ("When something has become a mere rite, it adds nothing to, and changes nothing in, the lives of those who practice it.")[26]

In many churches and chapels, it may have happened in the course of the centuries that pastors attempted to fill the void in Sunday services with music, hymns and announcements, so that the time for Mass could pass without notice.[27]

A Obstacles to Liturgical Renewal in Parishes

1 Our Formation and Resources

If, on the one hand, it is true that the Church has never been indifferent to the liturgy and its reform, which enjoyed varying degrees of success through the centuries, it is undeniable that the initiative of Dom Prosper Guéranger (d. 1876) in favor of Gregorian chant and the liturgy, took place a century ago; on the other hand we all know that the liturgical movement, which aims at reapproaching the Christian people through the liturgy and the Mass, had its beginning only in 1909, with Dom Beauduin.[28] It was then that Cardinal Mercier gave his valuable support to the effort of translating the missal, and centering all piety in the liturgy.

The pioneers were self educated. What can be said about our teachers and about ourselves? What did we do in face of the ignorance of the people, or lack of literature, of scarcity of trained helpers? Chained to the altar, and to Latin, we consoled ourselves with the unfailing efficacy of the sacraments (for they worked *ex opere operato*), and with the docility of our people who came to pray and to meet God. Some encouraged the recitation of the Rosary, for it was within the capacity of the common people; others forbade it. So everybody, from his own point of view, was right. People often wondered about certain changes, but they felt that the priest must know what he was doing; and even if he did not, God did, anyway.

The liturgical movement, however, continued to expand, and those in responsible positions in the Church called attention to practical points with the result that all this converged into a decisive pastoral action which was summarized by Art. 17 and 18 of the present Constitution. Art. 18 states:

> [Those] who now are already working in the Lord's vineyard are to be helped by every suitable means to understand ever more fully what it is that they are doing when they perform sacred rites; they are to be aided to live the liturgical life and to share it with the faithful entrusted to their care.

2 *Level of Instruction of the Faithful*

The Catholic religion, which the Mohammedans respectfully call the Religion of the Book, as they call their own, presupposes a certain level of culture, that is, noble sentiments and a mental formation. The vigils, the long Sunday gatherings, and the pervading influence of religion on everyday life, gave to the early Christians an adequate preparation for the liturgy, which, incidentally, found expression in the *popular* Greek (*Koiné*), or in the *Christian* Latin. However, let us not over-estimate the Christians of those days. The complaints of St. Augustine resemble those of pastors of our day, and those of Caesarius go far beyond them in many respects.

The liturgical studies of the last century, prior to the movement of Dom Beauduin, presupposed a good academic formation; but even after Dom Beauduin, in order to regain the masses in a country of culture and full of apostolic initiative such as France—how much effort was required, how much dead weight had to be moved![29]

By ordaining that "the rites should be distinguished by a noble simplicity; they should be short, clear, and within the people's powers of comprehension, and normally should not require much explanation" (Art. 34), and moreover, by allowing the use of the vernacular, the Constitution gives us a well-founded hope that liturgy itself, from now on, will instruct the people, raising their level, and ceasing to be just another established form of instruction.

But we must not be too optimistic. Despite all the instruction given to servers, lectors, and members of the choir (Art. 29), and despite the introduction of acclamations, responses, psalmody, antiphons, songs, actions and gestures (Art. 30), the liturgical education of the people is far from complete.[30]

We are still far from the goal. The Fathers of the Council realized it. Thus, in order to save us from discouragement, they state in Art. 19:

> With zeal and patience, pastors of souls must promote the liturgical instruction of the faithful, and also their active participation in the liturgy both internally and externally, taking into account their age and condition, their way of life, and standard of religious culture. By so doing, pastors will be fulfilling one of the chief duties of a faithful dispenser of the mysteries of God; and in this matter they must lead their flock, not only in word, but also by example.

3 Independence on the Part of the Faithful

For centuries the celebrant united himself spiritually with the faithful in the highest degree, but only internally. As regards the external relation, which was also necessary, this has been promoted by the introduction of the missal, of different dialogue Masses, and by the aid of commentators; but all this has been a growth of recent decades. The Fathers of the Council, however, were of the opinion that all this was insufficient, and that more was needed in order to transform mere assistance at Mass into participation in it.

An inquiry, conducted in France by the magazine *Ecclesia* (March, 1960, pp. 125 ff.) indicates that community Masses elsewhere are also unappealing to the majority of the faithful. It would be an over-simplification of the problem if one were to think that, with a text in the vernacular in their hands, people will immediately engage in dialogue with us during the celebration of Mass and the administration of the sacraments. The majority of men [in certain countries] will continue to crowd the rear of the church merely waiting for the end of the service. Others, and they will not be few, will prefer to meditate in silence on the inspiring texts rather than to unite their voices in the communal celebration (Art. 27). Still others, and they will be numbered in the millions, will not understand liturgical versions either because they are insensible to aesthetical appeal, or little acquainted with biblical terminology.

Should we, then, grow discouraged? By no means. First, because we have seen marked progress in matters which had seemed impossible. We know that, as Art. 7 states: "every liturgical celebration, because it is an action of Christ, the priest, and of his body, the Church, is a sacred action surpassing all others; no other action of the Church can equal its efficacy by the same title and to the same degree." We have been happy to cooperate in this unequaled and unsurpassable action. Secondly, because an atmosphere favorable to liturgical renovation will be created if the episcopacy, the clergy and the faithful labor positively for a common liturgical ideal, something which would have been looked on with disfavor not many years ago. Press, radio and television brought the activities of II Vatican Council to the attention of the world.[31]

A report by C. Michenneau on a community Mass in a Nazi concentration camp in which Protestants participated, shows to what an extent public opinion can be molded. After they had prayed in common with Catholics, on a few occasions, they received an invitation to attend a Mass. They accepted it. In this way the idea grew up of establishing a sort of "pilgrimage" to Christ. The Mass was organized in this fashion: The priest clothed himself in the garb of a pilgrim, which symbolized at the same time the tunic of the Greeks and the chasuble of the Romans, since, according to St. Paul, there is no longer a distinction between Greek and Roman, but only Christians. Now the priest, as the first pilgrim, is at the front of the altar; his task is to show the way to the others. From time to time he turns to the people, asks questions, and receives answers, thus satisfying himself that all are following him, and that he is not alone. Simple explanations in the course of the ceremonies were all that were needed to make the non-Catholics accept the Mass of the Catholics. "After this memorable Mass, Catholics and Protestants formed but one group."[32]

4 Lack of Means

In many places we are satisfied if there is available an altar boy to help the priest at the altar, and if there is a person to pray and sing with the people.

There are always persons with the courage and talent to take the place of a commentator. Courses in seminaries, or personal and more elaborate instructions are not available for such persons, as Art. 29 prescribes in regard to servers, lectors, and commentators. Hence, in many cases their tasks must be simplified.

The Council, too, foresaw this by providing that "the revision of the liturgical books must carefully attend to the provision of rubrics also for the people's parts" (Art. 31). This provision will make participation easier, especially in regard to the sacrificial part of the Mass when the celebrant no longer can direct the faithful. However, other provisions, still more practical, should be made in favor of our unaided pastors so that at the moment when they enter the Holy of Holies they will not be abandoned by their congregations. In fact, this part is relatively short, and interrupted by acclamations and ceremonies easy to understand, if brief notifications are given by an authorized person. However, this part is so important that everybody should devote full attention to it. In this case, the *permanent* deacon could establish in a very clear and impressive way the necessary identification between the action of the priest and that of the faithful. For this, however, we shall have to wait.

Help that can be supplied by religious women is deserving of special attention. The rare occasion on which they assume control of liturgical celebrations should not lead us to despise this reservoir of good will and idealism which can be utilized in favor of the liturgical renewal.[33] Courses in theological initiation and other means of formation make many of them capable of leading the parochial liturgical committee, of conducting rehearsals for celebrations, and of encouraging, in a discreet manner, the participation of all in the liturgy. Feminine qualities, the religious habit, and the high esteem which so many religious women enjoy in our midst open to them many possibilities which are closed to us. If we complain so loudly about the lack of suitable laymen, why do we ignore those who are so easily available for the service of God?

Space does not permit us to discuss the appeal made by the Constitution in regard to pious lay societies. Their founders, in regard to this matter, can find a wide field in which to put their ideals into practice, by giving integral education to youth, while they themselves grow in the plenitude of Christ.

Leaders in Catholic Action, too, will be available to take the initiative in communal activities, and they will be at hand when work for Christ is most needed.

How many new horizons would appear if our Catholic schools transformed individuals into authentic leaders! We should like to discuss this matter at greater length.

More than once we were told the following: "In olden times Catholic boarding schools insisted on the sanctification of the Sunday by assistance at Mass; today we tolerate the custom on the part of students of not complying with this precept." The director of a boarding school even admitted candidly: "Upper class people are our clients, and they do not identify themselves with their own parish. "But," he added, "if I ever become a pastor I may change my mind."

Without going into detail, and especially without blaming our heroic educators, we could point out, as a reason for this apathy, the fact that the boarding school was a temporary arrangement and has become an *abnormal* means. Separatism seems to be a consequence of this, although not a necessary one. Good teachers of religion should, for instance, promote, with the participation of the entire class, or even with a larger group, the celebration of the word of God, as foreseen by Art. 35, 4. The examples proposed by *Paroisse et Liturgie* (Nov. 1960, 6, pp. 454 ff.) are perfectly adapted to all situations. We shall here indicate the schema without the texts:

Sacred Celebration of the Word of God

Entrance:	Hymn
	Invocation - Response
Parts:	Readings from the Bible
	Explanation
	Hymn for Meditation
	Silent Prayer
	Prayer in Common
Conclusion:	Acclamations
	Pater Noster in common
	Final Hymn

If a priest is present, Benediction with the Blessed Sacrament

The community sense, however, will be the characteristic note of everything.

Formation according to the mind of the Church will be achieved by awakening the spirit of faith and generosity in young people, and by entrusting to them certain activities and responsibilities. To profess the Christian faith publicly and to convince others to do the same leads to a new conception of the Word, and of the life of prayer.

B Pedagogical Principles and the Liturgical Renewal through Pastoral Work

Despite our few resources, or perhaps because of them, our possibilities seem incalculable. It is rightly said that necessity is the mother of invention.

However, in order not to discuss methods of empiricism and personalism, which usually promote the glory of the protagonists rather than God, we shall now formulate a few pedagogical principles in the light of the new Constitution on the liturgy.

(a) An attitude in accordance with the mind of the Church will make it possible for us to make progress without harmful deviations. The new Constitution is a work of the Church and must be studied in the spirit in which it was originated. Obedience to it and to the many documents and texts which from now on will come from competent authorities guarantee that we will remain united with the Church and Christ.

Before we act, we must be humble enough to consult the documents, to re-examine our points of view, to modify our habits, and to take the advice of experts. Despite our shortcomings, we work for God and his people. The magazine *La Maison-Dieu,* No. 66, reports that from a region as urgently in need of priests as is Africa, twenty priests left for the monastery of St. Andrew in Bruges to study liturgy for one year. Among these there were some who could claim that for twenty years they had been working for the care of souls.

(b) Liturgy by itself must preach to the people. If the diction is correct, clear, and, as far as possible, pleasing in the vernacular, it will resound in the ears and hearts of those who esteem their language. The ceremonies, for their part, will become a varied form of teaching, that is, the people will see, feel, understand, and participate in them. Besides Mass, the sacraments and sacramentals, from now on, will be celebrated before the eyes of the people and in union with them, always with the objective of securing their full participation.[34] To achieve this, the thoughts and feelings of the people must be respected. They are not present in spite of us; they constitute "our people," and they come to meet Jesus. It is the family of God which is gathered together.

(c) Progress should be in due measure. When the Instruction on sacred music and sacred liturgy appeared in 1958, it was greeted as a pedagogical document, because it presented an ideal, but it presupposed that the achievement of it would take time. The present Constitution repeatedly uses such words as "foster," "promote" and similar words. Pastoral solicitude demands that we give to the sheep of our flock food that is in accordance with their age and their needs. This, in any other field, would be self evident. In the liturgy, however, this does not happen, for its rules are usually formulated without any distinctions for the entire Church, and issued in a positive, obligatory form. We get the impression that the same rites and duties are to be observed in little country chapels no less than in the abbeys of Benedictines. The mystery is the same, and the fruits will appear, as the phrase goes, *ex opere operato*. However, the Constitution warns us against formalism when it says: "With zeal and patience, pastors of souls must promote the liturgical instruction of the faithful, and also their active participation in the liturgy, both internally and externally, taking into account their age and condition, their way of life and standard of religious culture."

(d) Dynamic and patient action. The people have been following the activities of the Council with obvious interest and with high hopes. Despite warnings that a revolution was not to be expected, the expectations of the people increased from the day when the Fathers of the Council decided to give priority to the liturgy in their schedule. Inertia received a shock. We miss a golden opportunity if, when authorized, we fail to act. To say to the faithful, "This fad will pass," is like canonizing immobility, and this is the worst enemy of the pastoral and missionary spirit. Were we to do so, we would resemble that European pastor who, after the reform of Holy Week, decided to celebrate a Mass of Requiem on Good Friday, because his people knew that some changes had been introduced, and because, as he understood it, a Requiem would dispose his people better to share in the grief for the death of Christ. It should not be our aim to mislead our people by the use of journalistic phrases, by "eye-catching" headlines, and by new items weighted with standardized terminology. Fortunately, much has been given to us, and much more is promised to us, by the Constitution.

On the other hand, the history of liturgy teaches us that sudden and ill-timed innovations are never assimilated. Piety, *par excellence,* is traditional, for we pray through concepts deep-rooted in our soul. When alone with God, the most profound and enlightened theologian is like little Samuel in the Temple, trying to find out what the Lord desires of him. Prudence and patience are virtues characteristic of the traveler or pilgrim who, throughout liturgy and life, is in search of the Lord (Art. 9).

5 CONCLUSION

At the threshold of a new era, the Church comes to our aid so that we may walk the right road resolutely. She has undertaken the task of renovating herself and no one of her members can excuse himself from this urgent task.

The liturgical movement will have more repercussions in seminaries, and its immediate consequences will be felt in the methods employed in the care of souls. As the Spirit of God has perceptibly guided the work of the Council up to now, so we have the certainty that, if he finds us docile and disposed, the same Spirit will make us "faithful dispensers of the mysteries of God" (1 Cor. 4, 1-2), and perfect man of God "instructed in all good works" (2 Tim. 3, 17).

NOTES TO CHAPTER 8

1 St. Justin, *I Apologia,* c. 65, PG 6, 420.

2 G. Martil, *I Seminari Oggi* (Milan: Editrice Ancora, 1956).

3 *La Maison-Dieu* 66 (1963), 71.

4 *Revista Ecclesiástica Brasileira* (REB) 23, 1075-1076.

5 *Ibid.,* 1076

6 Canon 1366, par. 1.

7 Canon 1366, par. 3.

8 The popes and the Holy See have been insisting, throughout recent decades, on the liturgical formation of the clergy: in 1945, an encyclical letter of the Sacred Congregation on Studies in Seminaries, *De Institutione clericorum deque Officii divini recitatione;* in 1947 the encyclical *Mediator Dei;* in 1954 an allocution of Pius XII on Nov. 2.

In addition to preoccupation about liturgical formation, the Holy See has frequently given rules for training in music. Thus: Pius X, *Tra le Sollecitudini,* A.A.S. 36, 1903-04, 329 339; Pius XII, *Musicae Sacrae Disciplina,* A.A.S. 48, 1956, 17, 23, 24; *Instructio S. R. C. de Musica sacra et sacra Liturgia,* A.A.S. 50, 659-663.

9 For further information, cf. *Ephem. Liturg.* 76 (1962), 53-55.

10 We are indebted to Dom Augustine Mayer, O.S.B., Rector Magnificus of Pont. Atheneo Anselmiano, for the detailed information he has furnished us.

11 Cf. *Ephem. Liturg.* 77 (1963), 440.

12 The Constitution *Sedes Sapientiae,* of 1956, did not change anything in the curriculum of studies for religious houses in this regard. Cf. Art. 37, 40, and 45.

13 Declaration on Art. 16, (REB) 1963, 999.

14 Cf. REB, 1962, 790 f.

15 *La Maison-Dieu* 66 (1963) 175.

16 See how this pope portrays the calamitous condition of the Church in his time in *Ep. to John of Constantinople,* I, 4: PL 76, 1010.

17 St. Justin, *op. cit.,* c. 67, PG 6, 429.

18 Dom Augustine Mayer, O.S.B. states that through sermons, preaching, and instruction a liturgical, sacramental, ecclesiastical, and communal mentality will emerge among the people.

19 Const. Apost. *Sedes Sapientiae,* May 31, 1956, Art. 47.

20 *Ibid.* Art. 40, par. 6.

21 *Ibid.* Art. 20.

22 *On the Priesthood,* 3, 4 PG 48, 642.

23 REB 23 (1963), 1080.

24 *Ibid.,* 1076.

25 *Apud* M. Farina, *Terra e Seme. Premesse alla vita liturgica parrocchiale* (Milan: Opera della Regalità, 1961), 8.

26 C. Michonneau, *apud* Congar, *Sacerdoce et Laïcat: Pour une Liturgie et une Prédication réelles* (Paris: Les Editions du Cerf, 1962), 171.

27 Cf. *La Maison-Dieu* 66 (1963), 71.

28 Cf. *"Dom Lambert Beauduin, O.S.B., Liturgia e Ecumenismo,"* REB (1960), 378-382.

29 Some time ago a congress on liturgy was held in Jugoslavia in which there was a discussion on the active participation of the laity in rural parishes. Incidentally, from 95 to 98 per cent of the people live in rural areas. Cf. *Ephem. Litur.* 77 (1963) p. 415.

30 Cf. D. Hildebrando P. Martins, O.S.B., *Renovemos a Paróquia* (Rio de Janeiro: ed. Lumen Christi).

31. Cf. Decree on the means of social communication, REB (1963), 1049.

32 C. Michonneau, *Parroquia Comunidad Misionera* (Spanish trans.), 1957, 354.

33 Cf. *Aujourd'hui, La paroisse* (Fleurus, 1963). Especially *"Participation de la ré-ligieuse à la liturgie paroissiale,"* as well as *"Formation liturgique de la réligieuse,"* 146-154.

34 Cf. Farina, *loc. cit.* in footnote 25; and J. A. Jungmann, S. J., *Tradition Liturgique et problèmes actuels de pastorale,* (Le Puy: Mappus, 1962).

9
Celebration of the Word of God without a priest

The Most Rev. Bishop Jorge Kemerer S.V.D.

1 Reasons for the Sunday service without a priest

2 Arrangement and content of the Celebration of the Word of God (Bible service)
   A Celebration of the Word of God
   B The prayer of the faithful
   C Sacramental rite

3 Manner of carrying out the Celebration of the Word of God

4 Conclusion

Bishop Kémérer is the ordinary of the diocese of Posadas in Argentina. His article was translated into English by Father Barton Korn O.F.M.

Editor's Note: Confer Art. 37 of the "Instruction" (1964) which was published after Bishop Jorge Kémérer's article was written.

The theme indicated in the title has, for some time, been of special interest to missionaries in non-Christian lands. Proof of this interest are the International Congresses of Nijmegen (1959) and Eichstätt (1960) which treated this theme.

The II Vatican Council was taken up with the same restless spirit, and, in Article 35, 4 of the liturgical Constitution, approved a "celebration of the sacred word of God" with the following words:

> "Bible services should be encouraged, especially on the vigils of the more solemn feasts, on some weekdays in Advent and Lent, and on Sundays and feast days. They are particularly to be commended in places where no priest is available; when this is so, a deacon or some other person authorized by the bishop should preside over the celebration."

We will have the opportunity to return to this decision of the Council which encourages the celebration of the word of God in general terms.

The present exposition takes into account, first of all, the conditions in Latin America, where the scarcity of clergy and the enormous distances which sometimes separate Christian communities demand a definitive solution which would supply for the absence of the priest.

As both factors—the scarcity of priests and the forbidding distances—are equally real in mission lands, a very similar situation presents itself in each case, allowing for a common solution to the problem.

1 REASONS FOR THE SUNDAY SERVICE WITHOUT A PRIEST

With this brief introduction in mind, it might be proper to ask: On what do we base the value and necessity of the Sunday celebration? I believe that the first reason can be accredited to the fact that by the Sunday celebration the community achieves a primary and fundamental end of human creation, that is: the manifestation of public worship to God, by fulfillment of the grave Christian obligation of sanctifying the Lord's Day.

Christians belonging to the Catholic Church know that the primary and fundamental end of man and the sanctification of Sunday are fully achieved by the celebration of the sacrifice of the Mass. However it is erroneous to think that the sanctification of the Sunday is only possible by the celebration of the Mass. This would be to limit that sanctification to the presence of a priest, so that, if he were absent, such sanctification would not be possible. It is necessary to oppose such a line of thought.

The priest, through celebration of the Mass, and the Christian people, by their active and profitable participation in the same, render to God the cult which he merits, and certainly, in the most perfect form. Nevertheless, for lack of the priest, the community does not become exempt from the obligation of offering worship to God; this duty always binds, and with the same gravity, the only difference being in the form of fulfilling it. This means then that the community, in the absence of the priest, will have to render to God that cult which circumstances permit.

And not even the dispensation which is at times conceded for work on Sunday is able to exempt one from the obligation of rendering public worship to God on that day. On the contrary, one must insist more on the fulfillment of the Sunday precept in that case; the Christian who in certain seasons of the year does servile work and does not sanctify the day of the Lord in a positive manner runs the risk of forgetting his supernatural destiny and of losing himself more and more in the materialism of the present life.

The "celebration of the sacred word of God" does more than assure the fulfillment of that essential obligation of the human creature, to pay the homage owed to God; over and above this, it is an apt means, and in a certain sense, the most apt, for providing catechetical instruction of the Christian people.

Ordinarily, our Catholics—and this holds especially for Latin America—reach an adult age with a minimum of religious ideas, and these are almost always highly imprecise and confused; baptized as young infants, only initiated in the rudiments of the Christian faith, they are admitted to reception of the sacraments of Penance, Holy Communion and Confirmation. There follows upon this initiation into the Christian life, almost always terminated before the age of ten, a youth of ignorance and abandonment of religious practices. How is the priest to reach these lambs of his flock, who are always so numerous and dispersed across vast expanses and who are so much in need of the Truth of God?

Much importance is usually given to religious instruction in the schools. We must, however, ask ourselves: If we assure them a religious instruction in the schools, can we then perhaps remain content with that and consider the problem of the Christian formation of children and youth as already resolved? Are we not aware that, in countries where religious instruction in the schools is authorized by law, the practice of religion leaves much to be desired? Religious instruction in the schools becomes one more subject in the curriculum, and, even when it is taught with efficiency, it works more on the intellect than on the will, not reaching the real life of the pupil or influencing it only at great effort on his part. It must be agreed that religious formation of the individual is only accomplished in the family which lives its faith and in the Christian community which exercises in a vital manner the divine cult.

A "Sunday celebration" constructed with a truly catechetical finality, worthily promoted and enacted with perseverance, makes possible an announcement of the Gospel which reaches the most needful of the faithful, that is, those who live farthest from their priest and who ordinarily constitute the majority of the parish.

2 ARRANGEMENT AND CONTENT OF THE CELEBRATION OF THE WORD OF GOD (Bible service)

If it is important and necessary to understand the value of the Sunday celebration without a priest, it is equally important and necessary to construct that religious service and to give it its true content. To a great degree, the secret of everything that one could hope for from the celebration of the Word of God without a priest lies here.

The structure of the celebration of the sacred Word of God corresponds fundamentally with the following traditional scheme of the liturgy:

Celebration of the Word of God
Prayer of the Faithful
Sacramental Rite

The religious act should be preceded by a rite of preparation, in which is announced the character of the Sunday or liturgical feast with thoughts which vary according to the season in which the Church is living; the choice of the hymn with which the celebration will begin should likewise be taken into account.

A Celebration of the Word of God

The liturgical Constitution of the Ecumenical Council calls that rite the *Sacra Verbi Dei Celebratio,* and indeed it constitutes a true cult of the Divine Word. So that such veneration attributed to the Word of God may receive its visible expression, it is advised that in the middle of the altar, besides the crucifix, there be the Bible, or at least, the Gospels, sufficiently large, open, and placed between two lighted candles. This arrangement is meant to express that in the absence of the Eucharistic Christ, he may be felt and venerated in his Divine Word. If the Blessed Sacrament should be in the tabernacle, the candles would express a double veneration: the Eucharist and the Word.

It is to be emphasized that the Bible readings (*celebratio Verbi Dei*) constitute the heart of the Sunday celebration without the priest, and for this reason, they should be presented with a greater dignity and with a certain solemnity, without, however, inciting shocking pathos. Special care should be taken so that the reading may be easily understood; the best translation of scripture should be on hand, one that really lends itself to public reading.

Which biblical texts should be read? I am of the opinion that, for various reasons, the biblical readings of the Sundays and of the liturgical feasts should be preferred, especially if, as the liturgical Constitution prescribes, the forthcoming reforms of the Missal are to improve and enrich the pericopes in such a way that a reading cycle during the course of various years may make possible the proclamation of all of the themes of the New Testament and a large part (the most appropriate) of the Old Testament.

Following the reading of the biblical text, at least after the epistle, an appropriate popular hymn might be sung, or, a psalm which lends itself to meditation and a more profound assimilation of the message of God might be chanted in order to highlight the entire mystery.

After the hymn would follow the commentary of the biblical text; this commentary might be written or at least outlined *by the bishop*. Nothing would be more appropriate at that moment than the words of the spiritual father; he would thus maintain permanent contact with his children, supply them with the breads of Truth, and exercise towards all the faithful of his diocese the essential function of his ministry: to be master of the Truth. It would be expedient that he be solicitous concerning the wording of that commentary, accommodating it to the mentality of the people to which it is destined.

The commentary of the Word of God having been read, there should be a profession of faith with the recitation of the creed. It would be opportune to have the guide of the celebration introduce that act of faith with some biblical text which has relation with that which is to follow.

As a coronation of the Word of God, the following ritual might take place: the external expression of his veneration for the Word by each one present. This might be accomplished by kissing the sacred text or bowing one's head before the Book and touching it with one's hand.

With this would be concluded the celebration of the Word of God, which –as has already been said–should be considered the heart and center of the entire Sunday celebration.

B The Prayer of the Faithful

There is no doubt that, having listened to the Word of God in a spirit of faith, one would be most disposed to communicate with God in the intimacy of his soul. The son who received the Word of the Father should direct himself to him with a heart full of humility and confidence. The prayer of the faithful begins. It might be noted here that one should beware of any and all exaggeration. "*Non multa sed multum.*" There should be neither an accumulation of prayers nor an abundance of words; "Not he who says: Lord, Lord. . ." That which is said should reveal simplicity, clarity, and thus, in as far as one prays, he may be taught to pray. We think that it suffices to reduce the ritual of prayer to two forms: the "litany of supplication" and the "thanksgiving."

The litany of supplication can include the principal general intentions, similar to those of the prayer of the faithful of Good Friday or those inspired by the litany of the saints. Other more up-to-date petitions which are called forth by the concrete necessities of the universal or local Church might be added to those already suggested. Each of these supplications might be followed by the expressive community response: "We beseech you, hear us" or a similar one. At the end of the petitions, one might conclude with a triple invocation to the Lamb of God and with the proper oration of the day, if a fixed oration should not be preferred.

This form of prayer which we have called the litany of supplication corresponds with the ancient prayer of the faithful (or "common prayer") of the Mass.

The second form of prayer of the community would be the thanksgiving which terminates with the praise of the *Sanctus,* recited or sung; this thanksgiving corresponds to the preface of the Mass. At the end of that prayer a memento should be made of the material and spiritual benefits which God has bestowed upon men, and, following the remembrance of each of those benefits, all present should express their gratitude to God in the form of a refrain.

C Sacramental Rite

The ritual of prayer is concluded by what we call the "sacramental rite," a formula which ought to stand out from the previous forms of prayer and which ought to be recited more slowly and with a rather solemn intonation. In this formula the "memory of the Lord" is made; that is, recalling the mysteries of the passion, death, resurrection and ascension of Jesus, the community is united with the pope, with its bishop and with all the priests of the world who on that day renew in the Mass that which Christ himself enacted at the Last Supper.

The community then makes the offering of the sacrifice of the Mass and expresses the desire to approach the table of the Lord: to this offering it unites that of its life, of the coming week with its joys and sorrows, its labors and its hopes. It closes with a doxology similar to one which terminates the Canon of the Mass.

The guide now invites all to spend a few moments in *silent prayer* before concluding the fraternal celebration. Afterwards, the president of the assembly calls upon all to repeat the prayer which Jesus taught us, the Our Father. This recitation should be made with particular fervor.

When there is a deacon in the Christian community, he distributes holy Communion at this time.

Before the assembly disperses, some biblical text might be recalled, preferably one which highlights the practice of charity. In this way the assembled would be taught to practice what has just been celebrated.

In the absence of a priest to give the blessing, all should kneel before leaving and implore the blessing of the most Blessed Trinity. A closing hymn would follow.

In conjunction with this Sunday celebration, certain other popular devotions recognized by the Church for their value and seriousness might be employed. We refer principally to the rosary and the way of the cross which can easily be allied to the ritual of preparation and especially with one or the other of the Bible readings and with song, whether a popular melody or a psalm.

In this way much profit will be gained from the various parts of the service and it will be given a new value, especially by the proclamation of the Word of God.

These celebrations are fitting for certain seasons or feasts, and sometimes might substitute for the first type of celebration, which will nevertheless always remain fundamental.

3 MANNER OF CARRYING OUT THE CELEBRATION OF THE WORD OF GOD

Having described in a succinct form a type of Sunday celebration, I would like to add a word or two about the manner of carrying out the liturgical act.

On this point we have the orientation of the II Vatican Council which voted to consider the celebration of the sacred Word of God where it speaks of the "deacon" and the "episcopal delegate."

While it will be the task of the deacons to prepare the environment and the candidates, the "episcopal delegate" will exercise the function of president of the assembly. Much importance should be attributed to the preparation of this delegate, and, so that he may dedicate himself to his function, it would be very much in place to make his a true "canonical mission."

Whenever possible the delegate should be accompanied by an assistant who would exercise the function of "guide" for the Sunday celebration.

It would be up to this guide to announce the celebration, to make brief reference to the Bible readings, to indicate the hymns, to invite those present to assume postures which correspond to the various parts of the celebration and to introduce appropriately to the community the prayers which the delegate recites with those assembled.

The guide, as his title indicates, assures the smooth running of the action or cult; the delegate presides over the assembly, is entrusted with the biblical readings and the commentaries, and recites the formulas of prayer, that is, he is charged with the liturgy of the celebration.

So that both the delegate and the guide may carry out their functions better, it is suggested that they place their materials on lecterns, one on each side of the altar.

Whenever the delegate reads a passage from scripture or gives his commentary, he should look at the assembly; the guide should do likewise when speaking. The delegate, on the other hand, should look to the crucifix when reciting a prayer.

The biblical readings and the recitation of the prayers should be made in a grave and solemn tone, with due deliberation and clarity. The altar and the necessary objects should be prepared well in advance. The arrangement of the altar should be dignified and should correspond with the spirit of each day and liturgical season. Fifteen minutes should be reserved before the beginning of the celebration so that the hymns may be adequately practiced.

4 CONCLUSION

1. It is hoped that the Sunday celebration without a priest may be-

come, in time, a regular event for those Christian communities which may lack a priest on Sundays.

2. Given the importance of the Sunday celebration without a priest and its recognition by the II Vatican Council itself, the task of establishing a basic form for this celebration becomes imperative.

3. In order to achieve this end, it seems necessary that the task be entrusted to a group of liturgists who, in collaboration with various pastors, might carry the work to its fulfillment.

Editor's Note: We have learned that His Excellency, the Bishop of Posadas, has already elaborated a series of leaflets for the different Sundays of the year. Requests can be addressed to:

Editorial "BONUM"
Maipú 859
Buenos Aires, Republic of Argentina

10
The instruction for the implementation of the Constitution

Ferdinando Dell'Oro S.D.B.

1 *Introduction*
  A History of the Instruction
  B Restatement of some principles
  C Application of the Instruction's norms

2 *Liturgical formation, authority, and celebrations*
  A Liturgical formation
  B The competent authority
  C The liturgical commissions
  D Liturgical celebrations
    1 Simplicity and clarity of the individual rites
    2 The use of the national language
    3 Celebration of the Word of God

3 *The Mass, the other sacraments, the sacramentals, and the office*
  A The Eucharistic Mystery
    1 Simplifications and innovations in all Masses
    2 Masses in the vernacular with participation by the people
      a Proclamation of the Word of God
      b The Prayer of the Faithful
  B The other sacraments and the sacramentals
    1 Confirmation
    2 The rite of matrimony
    3 Continuous rite of the sacraments for the sick
  C The divine office

4 *The arrangement of the church*

Dom Ferdinando Dell'Oro was a *peritus* of the II Vatican Council and a consultor in drawing up the Constitution on the Sacred Liturgy. His article was translated into English by Fr. Armand Padula O.F.M.

1 INTRODUCTION

A History of the Instruction

The Instruction, promulgated by the Sacred Congregation of Rites (SRC) on September 26, 1964, is the first document worked on by the Commission,[1] to which the Holy Father has entrusted the task of effecting a literal application of the Constitution on the sacred liturgy according to the spirit of the Council which approved it (December 4, 1963), and the function of preparing the general liturgical reform on the basis of the norms contained in the same Constitution.[2]

At the beginning of its delicate and complex activity, the Commission was expresssly called upon to prepare an Instruction to clarify the conciliar Constitution and the *Motu Proprio* of Pope Paul VI.[3]

Submitted for study on March 5, 1964, the Instruction passed through five successive schemata. After having been examined by about forty consultors and then by the members of the Commission, it was given its conclusive form on June 20. Then the schema was ready to be consigned to the Holy Father.[4] The Supreme Pontiff, after having given due consideration to this Instruction, with the help of the Commission and of the Sacred Congregation of Rites, "approved it in a special way as a whole and in its parts, confirmed it by his authority, and ordered it to be published,"[5] determining, at the same time, a convenient interval of time for the faithful to be instructed and prepared for their observance (ICL, n. 10).[6]

The Instruction is composed of five chapters, with titles corresponding to the Constitution of the Council, and follows its order and arrangement.[7] The purpose and nature of the document are outlined in the Introduction.[8]

B Restatement of Some Principles

(1) The finality and scope to which the document, the faithful and authoritative interpreter of the liturgical Constitution, openly calls the attention of the pastor of souls and toward which it directs its practical action is twofold:

a) To stir up that formation of the faithful and to promote that pastoral activity which has the sacred liturgy as its summit and source (ICL, n. 5)[9];

b) The power of this pastoral activity centralized in the liturgy must aim at expressing the paschal mystery in that fulness of divine life which flows from this mystery of salvation: so that men, dead to sin and conformed to Christ, "may live no longer for themselves but for him who died for them and rose again" (2 Cor 5, 15), (ICL, n. 6).[10]

By means of the liturgical formation – for which the pastors of souls must strive diligently and patiently, measuring such action according to the age and condition, the way of life, and standard of religious culture of the faithful (CL, Art. 19) – the Church aims at bringing the faithful to a full, conscious, active and fruitful participation in the liturgy,[11] hence enabling them to live it. The practical directives established recently by the Instruction are based on this aim (ICL, n. 4). It follows that the full, conscious, active participation of the faithful fulfills in them – in different ways – the paschal mystery which each one of us must express in his life. Essentially, however, and vitally the conformity to Christ though the re-lived paschal mystery (the second end referred to by the Instruction) is obtained through faith and through the sacraments of the faith, principally baptism (cf. CL, Art. 6) and the mystery of the Eucharist (cf. CL, Art. 7), to which the other sacraments, the sacramentals (cf. CL, Art. 61) and the cycle of celebrations, whereby the Church unfolds the paschal mystery in the course of the year, are ordained (cf. CL, Art. 102-107), (ICL, n. 6).[12]

These, in their concise formulation, are the highest aims and ends of the Constitution of the Council, which the Instruction strongly emphasizes – clearly and repeatedly. And not without reason. Animated by a certain journalistic and commercialistic spirit, an attempt has been made to focus excessive attention on the part of the clergy and also on the part of the faithful on the reform – better on the renewal – of the liturgy,[13] with the prospects of imminent, proximate and remote practical changes. As a result, in certain sectors there has been created an ever-increasing uneasiness and an obstacle to the understanding of and participation in liturgical celebrations in which is expressed the worship of the Church, the Mystical Body of Christ: this instead of exposing in its true light the doctrine, the new spirit and the renewed ritual mentality proclaimed by the Constitution, in which the two fundamental features of the liturgy, theological and pastoral, are harmoniously expressed in their fullness.[14] In its fifty years of slow but profitable action on different levels and in different countries, the liturgical movement is to be accredited with the effecting of very precious results in the Church, now "in the state of Council."[15]

The liturgical reform, understood in its full expression, recalls to us the theological vision of human destinies, the primacy of the action of grace and therefore of the sacramental life and of prayer. The Holy Father, in his address to the bishops of Italy convened in General Assembly (Rome, April 14, 1964), said that the liturgical reform offers us the means of achieving the religious re-education of our people, of purifying and restoring their expressions of worship and of piety, and of restoring dignity, decorum, simplicity and good taste to our religious ceremonies; without this interior and exterior restoration there is no hope for a survival of full Christian life in the modern era of change.[16]

A positive result in this pastoral action, which proves difficult to attain, requires:

1) A serious, meditated study of the liturgical Constitution.[17]

2) An easy, interesting and renewed catechesis for the faithful, opportunely carried out during the liturgical year and corresponding to the various times which compose it.[18]

3) And finally, a docile and unanimous acceptance of the instructions, the norms and the practical accomplishments of the Commission[19] in a disciplined, common and harmonious action and collaboration with the competent territorial authority.[20]

With this done, the general reform of the liturgy, realized gradually and by stages by the competent authority, and opportunely presented and explained by the pastors of souls to the faithful by means of the required catechesis, will not fail to find the faithful prepared and well disposed to accept it (cf. ICL, n. 4).[21]

First of all, however – as the document emphatically states – it is necessary that all be persuaded of the intention of the Constitution on the sacred liturgy of the II Vatican Council: not so much to change liturgical forms and texts, as to realize the ends referred to above.[22] In fact the changes thus far introduced and to be introduced into the sacred liturgy in the future are directed toward this end (ICL, n. 5). N. 60 of the Instruction confirms this.

(2) The Document rightly stresses that it has already been affirmed that this pastoral action, centralized in the liturgy, does not express and does not exhaust the entire activity of the Church (cf. CL, Art. 9). But the principle of the unity of action realized in the differentiation of the forms for the purpose of a sole and common end – that, namely, to which the action of the Church here on earth tends[23] and toward which all the efforts of her multiple apostolic activity converge – points to the need:

a) Of exercising all pastoral works . . . in just connection with the sacred liturgy. And at the same time:

b) Of exercising the pastoral-liturgical action . . . in intimate union with the other pastoral activities (ICL, n. 7).

Hence we have not merely a pastoral liturgical action[24] exercised in a separate and abstract manner (ICL, n. 7), to be placed side by side with numerous other pastoral activities and having a determined field or sector of action: but rather it is that all pastoral activities and works be animated and pervaded with a liturgical force, with an open communal spirit and with a variety of expression visibly reflecting the meaningful moments of the liturgical year. This multiform but harmonious and unified action must lead to, converge on and culminate in the liturgy. From this, as from a font, grace is poured forth upon us; and the sanctification of men in Christ and the glorification of God, to which all other activities of the Church are directed as towards their end (CL, Art. 10).

The document emphasizes that it is especially necessary that there be a close union between the liturgy and catechesis, religious formation and preaching (ICL, n. 7). Occupying an eminent position in this pastoral activity of the word is the homily, the integrating part of the eucharistic celebration (cf. CL, Art. 52).[25]

From this multiple and harmonious pastoral action centralized in the liturgy, the bishops and their assistants in the priesthood can well hope for consoling fruits. From a perfect participation in the sacred celebrations[26] – the document repeats – even the faithful will derive the divine life in abundance and, made the ferment of Christ and the salt of the earth, will proclaim the divine life and communicate it to others (ICL, n. 8).

C *Application of the Instruction's Norms*

From these premises, on which we have willingly spent time, there has developed the entire Instruction, which gives the directive norms for the literal application of the Constitution in the spirit of the Council and establishes practical changes (II) already possible even before the reform of the liturgical books. To these are added opportune directives (III) so that in its structures the temple – the convening place of the holy assembly – may render possible or facilitate the active participation of the faithful in the sacred and solemn liturgical celebrations.

To put in action what is contained in the Instruction one must keep in mind that:

1) The practical dispositions of the Constitution and of this Instruction the innovations or modifications permitted or established by the present Instruction and to be introduced now[27] pertain only to the Roman rite (ICL, n. 9).

2) The other Latin rites[28] can adopt as their own the practical dispositions of the Constitution and of the present Instruction[29] upon the initiative and the deliberation of the competent ecclesiastical authority.[30]

3) Some norms and dispositions of the Instruction are directly entrusted to the competent territorial ecclesiastical authority. The practical putting into effect of such norms and dispositions depends only on this authority, which can and must put into action these dispositions by means of legitimate decrees.

4) In the decrees of the competent territorial ecclesiastical authority, the time and the circumstances in which these decrees will take effect shall always be defined (ICL, n. 10).

In the document, by "competent territorial ecclesiastical authority" is meant in the first place every territorial episcopal authority legitimately constituted[31]; in the second place (and this is deduced also from CL, Art. 22, p. 1, and ICL, n. 22) the ordinary of the place,[32] upon whose consent or judgment or permission depends the putting into effect of certain practical norms established in the document itself.[33]

The expression "ordinary of the place" understood in the strict sense in the document acquires afterwards a wider meaning, that of Canon 198, Par. 1 of the CIC, in the application of Articles 97 and 101 of the same liturgical Constitution[34]; by far wider because the SRC has extended this special faculty also to major superiors of non-exempt religious institutes and of societies of clerics who live the common life without vows.[35]

Therefore the expression "competent territorial ecclesiastical authority" in the document has not just one meaning: the meaning differs according to the nature of the practical dispositions which emanate from the document.

Between the promulgations of the decrees of the territorial competent ecclesiastical authority – here understood in the strict sense (cf. ICL, n. 22) – and their being put into effect, there must always elapse a reasonable interval of time,[36] so that in the meantime – here there reappears the principle enunciated in n. 4 of the Instruction – the faithful can be informed and instructed as to their observance (ICL, n. 10); this interval should never be knowingly ignored in any way or by any priest (cf. ICL, n. 20).[37]

To achieve an orderly and gradual liturgical reform it would be much more profitable to communicate timely information through a convenient instruction given to them on different levels – which assures a positive result for the innovation – and to effect a pastoral preparation of their minds[38] in order that they might heartily accept certain new ways expressed in the worship, rather than the lack of discipline and preparation found in many impatient members,[39] too confident perhaps in the magical effect of the innovation recently promulgated.

A ready example of putting into effect the interval of time for the decrees which regulate the gradual liturgical reform, has been given by the same SRC which, applying Canon 9 of the CIC, had established that the norms contained in the Instruction would go into effect on March 7, 1965, the First Sunday of Lent.

2 LITURGICAL FORMATION, AUTHORITY, AND CELEBRATIONS

A *Liturgical Formation*[40]

(a) The liturgical Constitution – as the Holy Father Paul VI has said – intends to establish in the Christian people a new religious pedagogy[41] the fundamental lines of which and the ends to which it is directed being well delineated both in the Introduction of the same Constitution and in the Introduction of the present Instruction.

The knowledge and assimilation of this new religious pedagogy, effected through the participation of the faithful in the liturgy,[42] demands an adequate formation above all in the pastors of souls, who, imbued . . . with the spirit and power of the liturgy, will become in their turn teachers of the faithful (cf. CL, Art. 14), through understanding and becoming enriched with this spirit. A prime need, therefore, affirms the Constitution (Art. 14), is that attention be directed first of all to the liturgical instruction of the clergy.

It is with this above all that the Instruction[43] is concerned when it gives practical norms for the liturgical formation of the young clergy, principally of clerics in seminaries and in religious houses.[44]

Such formation[45] aims:

a) At bringing the seminarian to full awareness of the place which liturgical piety occupies in the personal search for God.[46]

b) At rendering the future priest capable of establishing a union between his liturgical ministry and other pastoral activities.[47]

c) At preparing the future priest for his responsible role in liturgical prayer.

This formation is developed in a threefold level, thus outlined by the Instruction:

1) intellectual	n. 11-12 =	liturgy as knowledge (teaching of the liturgy)[48]
2) pertaining to worship or ritual	n. 13 =	liturgy as worship by means of liturgical celebrations
3) spiritual	n. 14 =	liturgical formation (integral)

The formation on the intellectual and worshipping level, through which the clerics (both in seminaries and in religious study houses) are rendered capable of participating fully in liturgical celebrations, will render possible that integral and always active liturgical formation, from which the candidates for the priesthood will draw nourishment for their own spiritual life, so that afterwards they might communicate it to others on one condition: that the Constitution on the sacred liturgy . . . be fully applied according to the dispositions of the Holy See, by means of the unanimous and harmonious action of all superiors and teachers (ICL, n. 14).

The document indicates clearly the component parts of this liturgical spiritual formation (or integral liturgical formation): one pedagogical, the other sacramental; the first is external, varied and gradual, and aims at effecting in the clerics the capacity of embracing and of allowing themselves to be formed by this characteristically liturgical pedagogical action; the second, the sacramental, by means of sensible and efficacious signs (in a manner proper to them), aims directly at the internal, i.e., to everyone's spirit, transfusing in them that power which makes them participants of the sacred mystery which they celebrate and in which they participate, and renders them capable of expressing it in their life.

The external, pedagogical component, as a suitable introduction to the sacred liturgy through the harmonious and unanimous actions of all superiors and teachers, is effected in the ways indicated in n. 14 of the Document[49]; the sacramental component,[50] so to speak, which aims at one's interior (that is, to the spirit of the candidate for the priesthood) is centralized in the Eucharist and in the divine office.

(1) The Eucharist — sacrifice and sacrament — the center of the entire spiritual life, shall be celebrated daily with the use of different and appropriate forms which best correspond to the condition of the participants (ICL, n. 15).[51] The Instruction determines that on Sundays and on other major feast days,[52] a sung Mass shall be celebrated with the

participation of all who are in the seminary or house of studies, with a homily and, as far as possible, with the sacramental communion of those who are not priests (ICL, n. 15).

And to render this solemn liturgical celebration (the only one in the morning) more expressive, in which the active participation of those present is truly expressed in the internal, external and sacramental participation,[53] the priests,[54] when the service of the people does not require that they celebrate individually, can – especially on the more solemn feast days – concelebrate, as soon as the new rite of concelebration has been published (ICL, n. 15).[55]

No one can overlook the fact that the liturgical spiritual formation, which is outlined by the Instruction, reaches here and in the form indicated in n. 16 its fuller expression and its interior efficacy.

(2) The second centralizing element of the sacramental component[56] – always directed toward the interior or the spirit of the candidates to the priesthood – is given by the divine office. By means of the divine office the Church praises God incessantly and intercedes for the salvation of the world (CL, Art. 83); and at the same time, makes the whole course of the day and night holy (CL, Art. 84).

For the clerics who are not yet obliged to the recitation of the divine office the Instruction proposes – it is most fitting – the breviary as the book for common daily prayer, referred to by Canon 1367, n. 1 of the CIC.

It is most fitting, the document affirms, that the clerics . . . should recite or chant (ICL, n. 16):

LAUDS in the morning = as MORNING PRAYER
and VESPERS in the evening = as EVENING PRAYER[57]
or COMPLINE at the end of the day

The directors themselves shall take part in this common recitation, as far as possible.

The common character, an outstanding note of the liturgy (cf. CL, Art. 27), finds in the Eucharist and in the common recitation[58] of the *Opus Dei* not only its fullest expression of worship and of sanctification, but gradually communicates to those who take part and transfuses in them this ecclesiastical and communal spirit,[59] which in turn afterwards leads to the multiple expression of that love which unites all in Christ.

There must not be any lack of this communal spirit, renewing itself in the seminary and in the religious house, among the clerics in sacred orders for whom there shall be provided in the order of the day – besides the recitation of Lauds and Vespers or Compline with the entire community, to which reference was made above – sufficient time to pray the divine office (ICL, n. 16).[60]

(3) The spiritual life, however, as the Constitution of the Council well teaches (Art. 12), is not limited solely to participation in the liturgy. There are also many forms or exercises of piety in which – to use the expression of the encyclical *Mediator Dei* – the inspiration and action of the Holy Spirit cannot be extraneous; in fact some of them are highly

recommended to the clergy and to religious by the Church herself.[61]

These are greatly useful – although in different ways – to vivify, purify and strengthen spiritual life in the faithful and for disposing them, so *Mediator Dei* teaches, to participate in the sacred functions with greater fruit and avoid the danger of liturgical prayers becoming a vain ritualism.[62] Now, such exercises of piety arranged according to the laws or customs of each place or institute (ICL, n. 17) in no way disturb, do not burden and do not divert from that liturgical spiritual formation of which the Instruction treats, provided they are correctly ordained to the proper end.[63] Nevertheless, care should be taken (and the prescription of the document is understood and accepted in all of its expression and clearness) especially if these exercises are celebrated in common, that they be in harmony with the sacred liturgy, according to the purpose of Art. 13 of the Constitution, and that they be related to the seasons of the liturgical year (ICL, n. 17).

The document gives only a short reference at the end of n. 14 to the celebration of the entire mystery of Christ distributed in the course of the year (cf. CL, Art. 102-104), and this reference is evident: the liturgical year is (or should be) the natural and vital ambient in which the integral liturgical formation, which has the Eucharist as its center, receives its form, proportion and development.

Whatever has been said concerning the liturgical spiritual formation of the clerics in n. 14-17 of the Instruction must be applied also to the members, both men and women, of institutes dedicated to acquiring perfection, with the necessary adaptations (ICL, n. 18).[64]

A first result which the Instruction expects from this integral liturgical formation given the clerics in seminaries and in religious houses will be that of having afterwards priests and pastors of souls capable – precisely because they are prepared – of understanding ever more fully what it is that they are doing when they perform sacred rites . . . of living the liturgical life and to share it with the faithful entrusted to their care (CL, Art. 18).

Secondly, the Church will have in these priests, thoroughly imbued with the genuine Christian spirit inherent in the liturgy (cf. CL, Art. 14), zealous and patient collaborators in unsealing the very many mute lips of the people, who can no longer remain silent and indifferent.[65] Guided by them toward the liturgy not only in word but also by example (CI, Art. 19), the Christian people will find, by means of an active and intelligent participation in liturgical celebrations (cf. CL, Art. 14) – to use the words of the Holy Father – the way of opening their soul, pouring out their sentiments, their sufferings, their hopes, and will know how to make their own the divine words which aim at beautifying and sanctifying their spirit.[66]

(b) Concerning the liturgical education of the faithful, the document limits itself to exhorting and encouraging the pastors of souls to strive diligently and patiently to carry out the command of the Constitution, in Art. 19 (ICL, n. 19).[67]

Similar education of the people takes place in conjunction with constant action in determining – gradually, by means corresponding to the age and condition, the way of life and standard of religious culture of the faithful – and stimulating in those engaged in liturgical action their active participation, both internal and external (cf. ICL, n. 19).[68] It presupposes on the part of the pastors of souls a concrete plan of harmonious pastoral action to be put into practice during the year, seeing to it that the various liturgical times are taken into account.

In such a picture of action one shall keep in mind what has been recommended in the Instruction.[69]

So that this collective education, the education of the people as a whole, might penetrate, slowly permeate and gradually elevate the spiritual life of the parochial community, the Instruction strongly recommends concern about the liturgical formation and the active participation of those who are engaged in religious associations of the laity, keeping in mind that it is the latter's duty to share more intimately in the life of the Church and also to assist the pastors of souls in properly promoting the liturgical life of the parish (ICL, n. 19).

To secure, as the Holy Father says, in the Christian people the new religious pedagogy by means of the liturgical Constitution, it is desired that the pastors of souls, and principally the young clergy, shall have in the diocesan liturgical commissions (ICL, n. 47) or in the liturgical commission of the body of bishops (cf. ICL, n. 45) a coordinating center in common action and a strong assistance.[70]

B The Competent Authority

Regulation of the sacred liturgy depends solely on the authority of the Church,[71] that is, on the Apostolic See and, as laws may determine, on the bishop (CL, Art. 22).[72]

Such a principle, set down in the Constitution in three paragraphs, receives a clearer definition by the present document (cf. ICL, n. 3).

Having reaffirmed the general principle (cf. ICL, n. 20) enunciated by the Constitution (cf. MP, XI), the Instruction clearly determines the individual competencies:

a) of the Apostolic See (n. 21) over the whole Church;
b) of the bishop (n. 22) in his diocese;
c) of the territorial episcopal conferences over the territory of their competence.

In n. 23-31, the document in a particular way determines with greater clarity the tasks of the episcopal bodies or conferences[73] in liturgical matters.[74]

Having established what is meant, for the interim, by the various kinds of territorial bodies of bishops and which prelates compose it (n. 23), the Instruction determines the formalities, that is, the procedure to be observed in the conventions (n. 24-26) and in the drawing up and approval of the Acts (n. 27-28): particularly of those acts in which there are decrees concerning the use and extent of the vernacular language to be admitted in the liturgy (n. 30, cf. ICL, n. 40-42). Finally it indicates the formalities to be observed in the transmission of these Acts to the Holy See for the necessary confirmation (n. 29) and in the promulgation and putting into practice of the decrees of the territorial ecclesiastical authority (n. 31, cf. ICL, n. 10).

The Instruction, in very explicit terms, then calls for the exact observance of Par. 3 of Art. 22 of the Constitution and of n. XI of MP, with these words: "No other person shall proceed in this matter on his own authority to the detriment, as may often happen, of the liturgy itself and of its restoration by the competent authority" (ICL, n. 20).[75]

In concluding his summary report of the six months' activity of the Commission – the work of attentive study and patient research, done with circumspection, with a constant sense of veneration for the past and of understanding for the pastoral exigencies of the present[76] – the secretary, Fr. A. Bugnini, expresses himself in the following manner: "It is necessary to moderate dangerous anxieties and harmful intemperances. Of all the articles of the Constitution, there was none perhaps, of all the matter that was legislated upon, on which there was such unanimous accord [on the part of the members of the Commission itself] as on Par. 3 of Art. 22. Therefore, no other person, even if he be a priest, may add, remove, or change anything in the liturgy on his own authority. To be noted is the parenthetical clause: *even if he be a priest.* No foolish ambition for a greater good or for an infallible pastoral remedy could justify personal will or initiative in the sphere of worship."[77]

Equal concern and an authoritative appeal are culled from the words (Oct. 29, 1964) by the Holy Father to the members of the Commission, whose principal task is that of preparing the reform of the liturgical books.[78]

C *The Liturgical Commissions*

To encourage and increase liturgical pastoral action[79] or to set it in motion where it has not yet begun, the Constitution of the Council, in Art. 44-45, treats of the liturgical commissions: national (or territorial) and diocesan.

The Instruction assigns or indicates to these commissions their functions:

a) The territorial or national liturgical commission is not obligatory nor is it imposed by the document (to be desirably established: ICL, n. 44; CL, Art. 44); it is only highly recommended and practically indispensable. It will be established by the competent territorial ecclesiastical authority (CL, Art. 44; ICL, n. 44) and will consist normally of bishops (a specification added by the Instruction), with the addition of some priests expert in liturgical and pastoral matters, who are designated by name for the office.[80] Moreover, members of the institute of pastoral liturgy as well as individual experts can be called to assist the liturgical commission (ICL, n. 46. Cf. n. 11, c). N. 45 gives a list of the specific functions of the commission.

b) However, every diocese is to have a commission on the sacred liturgy[81] under the direction of the bishop, for promoting the liturgical apostolate (CL, art. 45).[82] What the diocesan commission is now obliged to do – and by both word and action, as is desired – is indicated in detail by n. 47 of the document.

As regards Art. 45 of the Constitution, the MP of Jan 25, 1964 reads: "At times it may be advisable for several dioceses to have one commission in common." What must be said of this?[83] The same MP, from Feb. 16, 1964, had also put into effect Art. 46 of the Constitution, establishing that in every diocese, besides the liturgical commission, two other commissions should be set up: one on sacred music and the other on sacred art. It may prove convenient in many cases for these three diocesan commissions to be merged into one (MP, 2). On this point the Instruction has not defined anything further (cf. ICL, n. 3).

D Liturgical Celebrations

The Constitution of the Council teaches that the liturgy is above all things the worship of the divine majesty; but at the same time it exercises on the faithful, who participate in it actively, a didactic-formative function, whose multiple action is clearly spelled out in Art. 33 of the same Constitution. For in the liturgy God speaks to his people and Christ is still proclaiming his gospel. And the people reply to God both by song and prayer. This marvelous dialogue, internal and external, takes place in (or through) this complexus of sensible, efficacious signs of the sanctification and worship of the Church[85] – manifested in various ways – consisting of liturgical celebrations.

So that these rites can really produce an educative effect upon the people, the Constitution in the general plan of reform has determined to restore the sacred actions to their native function, by expressing them with more simplicity, clarity and intelligibility (cf. CL, Art. 34).

Such a task concerns principally the Commission entrusted with the restoration of the liturgy: to effect the restoration in such a way that the liturgical cult – as the Holy Father has authoritatively repeated (Oct. 29, 1964) – really becomes a school for the Christian people:

"A school of piety, whereby the faithful might learn to foster intimate union with God.

"A school of truth, whereby through visible signs their spirit might be led to the knowledge and love of invisible things.

"A school finally of Christian love, whereby everyone might feel more and more united to the other members of the Church by the bonds of fraternal communion."[86]

At present, as far as we are concerned, we can begin to achieve this purpose by an orderly and decorous performance of the sacred rites, properly prepared, in which there cannot be lacking that exterior pomp (cf. ICL, n. 13c) required by the very nature of the rite and suited to dispose the spirit for a better participation. Such celebrations should have that form (solemn or simple, with or without singing) determined by the liturgical books and mirroring the peculiar nature of the celebration (cf. CL, art. 11-27), with care taken to avoid arbitrary additions. In these celebrations everyone (ministers, servers, members of the choir and people) should know how to perform his part suitably and worthily (cf. CL, Art. 28, 29); not excluded is the commentator,[87] to whom is entrusted the delicate task – accompanied by a healthy discretion – to see to it that the attention of the entire assembly is directed to the liturgical celebration by their actions, responses, prayers and song, the common and harmonious expression of a conscious and active participation in the mystery being celebrated.

On its part the Commission, through the present Instruction, has begun this external and ceremonial (so to say) restoration of the liturgical celebrations: this can be put into effect even before the general liturgical reform.

This restoration concerns the structure of the rites, liturgical language and the partial simplifying and restoring of the individual rites which can be put into practice now (ICL, n. 3).[88] These will be treated in the second part of this commentary.

1 *Simplicity and Clarity of the Individual Rites*

The restoration of the rites, for the purposes indicated above, always begins first with the act of simplification,[89] whereby whatever burdens, changes (or even disfigures) the rites themselves is removed, thereby making it possible to perform a second action: that of making them a living and intelligible expression of that which they signify. This is the method used in the present Instruction:[90]

By eliminating useless repetitions (doubling) in liturgical celebrations[91]	n. 32-33	it has reserved to the individual ministers the office pertaining to each one (cf. CL, Art. 28)
By reducing frequent signs of honor, little in harmony with the mentality of our times	n. 35	it has restored a simple and short form to the rites (cf. CL, Art. 34)[92]
By proposing to gradually eliminate the distinction of persons in the sacred rites[93]	n. 34-35	it has made the communal character proper to the liturgical celebrations evident (cf. CL, Art. 32)
And by proposing to remove all appearances of money-making from these rites[94]	n. 35	it has thrown light on the peculiar nature of the sacred actions: the sanctification and worship of the Church (cf. CL, Art. 32)

The putting into effect of the conciliar prescription recalled in Art. 34 of the Instruction – because of its peculiar nature, the diversity of place and the variety of customs – is entrusted to the individual bishops or to the regional or national conferences of bishops.

To the pastors of souls, however, and not only to them, the document in n. 35 commits a pastoral-formative action – among themselves and among the faithful – to be effected with prudence and charity, but untiringly. This will indirectly contribute (and not a little) to that liturgical renewal which cannot consist only in the restoration of the forms of worship, but which also aims at an interior assent and participation, to express in our lives and to manifest to others the mystery of Christ and the real nature of the Church (CL, Art. 2), which we proclaim by means of renewed and more expressive rites in liturgical celebrations.

2 *The Use of the National Language*[95]

Associated with the simplification and restoration of the rites is the renewal of the liturgical language. Rites and words in the liturgy are intimately connected (CL, Art. 35). The Constitution of the Council, recognizing the great advantage which the mother tongue offers in the rites, has officially accepted it in the liturgy (CL, Art. 36, 2).

The mother tongue translates, so to speak, in living words the meaning which the sign manifests in the sacred rites; likewise these rites can thus better assume the role of the school of the Christian people.

Having indicated how the mother tongue can be given a greater part in liturgical celebrations (cf. CL, Art. 36, 2), the Constitution openly affirms that it is for the competent territorial ecclesiastical authority (cf. ICL, n. 23) to decide whether, and to what extent, the vernacular language is to be used: a decision which must be confirmed by the Holy See (CL, Art. 36, 3).[96]

The Instruction now lists which parts of the individual rites can be expressed in the vernacular, with the previous decision of the competent ecclesiastical authority, mentioned above. These concern:

1) Masses, whether sung or read,[97] which are celebrated with the people: n. 57 (here n. 59 must be kept in mind)

2) The administration of the sacraments[98] and sacramentals: n. 61.

3) The recitation of the divine office and of the short offices: n. 82, 86-88.

It pertains solely to the Apostolic See to allow the vernacular language in other parts of the Mass which are chanted or recited by the celebrant alone (ICL, n. 58). New melodies for parts to be sung in the vernacular language by the celebrant and the ministers must be approved by the competent territorial ecclesiastical authority.

With the introduction of the vernacular languages in liturgical celebrations, there begins (or perhaps is resumed) in the history of Latin Christian euchology the chapter on the bilingual liturgy, which poses, as a fundamental problem, that of translation (in the new language: the vernacular) of texts up until now expressed in noble Latin, its traditional language:[99] which – affirms the Constitution (Art. 36, Par. 1) – still remains, particular law remaining in force in the Latin rites.

A common line to be adhered to in the translation of liturgical texts is proposed (it is fitting) by the Instruction in n. 40.

Upon this there then follows the approval of the texts translated into the mother tongue by the competent territorial ecclesiastical authority (CL, Art. 36, 4; ICL, n. 30): hence the edition of books which contain the translation of the Latin liturgical texts into the mother tongue. From the document we are made to understand that the editions of such books (another problem directly connected with that of translation) are of two types: books from which the liturgical text is read to the people in the vernacular language (ICL, n. 40e); and bilingual liturgical books.

For the first type of books, the Instruction (n. 40e) recommends that consideration should be given to their dignity, so that the dignity of the book itself may move the faithful to a greater reverence for the word of God and for sacred things. Whereas for the bilingual liturgical books – that is, those which serve a liturgical use (cf. ICL, n. 57) duly approved by the Holy See (cf. ICL, n. 21) – the Instruction refers to them only at the end of n. 57 with regard to the missal, and in n. 89 with regard to the breviary.[100] As regards the ritual, there have been bilingual editions[101] since 1947 entitled *Collectio Rituum pro omnibus . . . dioecesibus. Ad instar Appendicis Ritualis Romani a S. Sed approbata.*[102]

Presumably reference has also been made to the theme of liturgical books and the translations of liturgical texts in n. 43 of the Instruction, which temporarily retains the force of particular liturgical books which were lawfully approved before the promulgation of the Constitution on the Sacred Liturgy (Dec. 4, 1963), and indults conceded up to that day.

If the use of the bilingual liturgy gives a positive and happy solution to an actually very distasteful situation and one which has been unfavorably protracted for too long a time in the Latin Church, it does not, however, totally resolve the problem: perhaps it will give rise to others, but of lesser import; one of these is already present in the document.

In n. 41 the Instruction takes note of a situation, today actually very widespread, to which the Church has directed its zealous and multiple cares: that is, the presence in different countries and regions of groups of immigrants, or of members of a personal parish, or similar instances. For such people active participation in liturgical celebrations finds a natural obstacle in the liturgy itself, which is now bilingual.

In order not to deprive these children of the true Christian spirit, the source of which is to be found in the liturgy (cf. CL, Art. 14), and of the full, conscious, and active participation in liturgical celebrations – their right and duty by reason of baptism (cf. CL, Art. 14) – the Instruction disposes that in liturgical services which are celebrated in some places with people of another language, it is lawful with the consent of the local ordinary to use the vernacular language known to these faithful (that is, that language proper to the groups mentioned above) in accordance with the extent of the use of the vernacular and its translation as legitimately approved by a competent territorial ecclesiastical authority of the respective language.

c *Celebration of the Word of God*

The liturgy, a rich source of instruction for the Christian people (CL, Art. 33), gives rise and form to another manner of effecting the marvelous dialog between God and his people, namely, that of the celebration of the Word of God, which constitutes the material out of which the liturgy itself is richly woven.[103] The celebration and proclamation of the Word of God exercised in the vernacular, the school of Christian life in which word, praise and prayer alternate, are fused together and aim at elevating the faithful to a meditated knowledge of the gospel message as the Word of life in which the very communal form of celebration is an invitation and an incentive to live the mystery of salvation solemnly announced among them and joyously accepted by them.

The different forms of instruction to the people (referred to in n. 7 of the Instruction) are expressed and attain an elevated form of religious service all its own, through the celebration of the Word of God, which is distinguished from the liturgy itself, even though it derives its form from it.

This type of assembly of prayer is not new nor is it peculiar to the Christian liturgy: it has been inherited from the sabbatical service in the synagogue and this still finds meaningful expression in the first part of the liturgical action of Good Friday. The liturgico-biblical movement, which has permeated the Church for the past twenty years, has contributed not a little to the perfection of the celebration of the Word of God in the living language.

When a precise distinction was made between liturgical action and pious exercises,[104] this sacred celebration of the Word of God became associated with the latter, but took on the name of bible vigil or liturgico-biblical vigil; this name was afterwards codified (n. 559) by the First Roman Synod in 1959.

As a pious exercise, the liturgico-biblical vigil had much success and assumed many forms.[105]

The development and full expression of this form of the celebration of the Word of God was slow and varied – passing through different experiences and methods, many of which were very positive.

It does not appear to be youthful enthusiasm to apply to this celebration also the expression which the Constitution of the Council (Art. 33) uses in reference to the sacred rites: "Thus not only when things are read 'which were written for our instruction' (Rom 15,4), but also when the Church prays or sings or acts, the faith of those taking part is nourished and their minds are raised to God, so that they may offer him their rational service and more abundantly receive his grace."

The Church is present in it in some way: in fact, with the Constitution of the Council (cf. Art. 35, 4) the Church confers upon the celebration of the Word of God[106] a special dignity and excellence, through which the celebration itself is distinguished from other pious exercises and acquires a place of permanence. Such dignity and excellence[107] of the sacred celebration of the Word stems from the same purpose and form which the Instruction – faithful and authoritative interpreter of the Constitution – has conferred upon the same celebration. This celebration is thus regulated by the document:

1) In the celebration of the Word of God, the vernacular is ordinarily used (cf. n. 37).

2) It is good to promote [foster] the celebration of the Word of God:

a) Every Sunday and on feast days of precept: in places which lack a priest . . . and there is no possibility of celebrating Mass (cf. n. 37). Judgment concerning the suitability or non-suitability of such a celebration pertains to the Ordinary of the place.

b) Elsewhere: on Sundays and feast days of precept, on vigils of the more solemn feasts, on some weekdays in Advent and Lent (cf. ICL, n. 38).

3) In places which lack a priest: a deacon or even a layman, authorized for this purpose, presides over the service (cf. ICL, n. 38).

4) Form or structure of this celebration.

a) When this supplies for the celebration of Mass – mentioned above in n. 2a – this celebration shall repeat, that is, be modeled upon, the pattern of the liturgy of the word in Mass (ICL, n. 37). And that is:

Introductory hymn	taken principally from the psalms[108]
First reading	the epistle of the Mass of the day
Meditation hymn	taken from the psalms
Second reading	the passage of the gospel of the Mass of the day
[Acclamations]	[joyous response to the Word of God][109]
Homily	given by the one presiding over the assembly[110]
Prayer of the faithful	in litany form[111]
Prayer of the Lord	the Lord's Prayer recited together by the entire assembly
[Final Hymn]	[possibly a psalm or hymn of praise][112]

b) In the other celebrations, mentioned above in n. 2, b, however, it is fitting that these should take into account the pattern of the liturgy of the word in Mass (ICL, n. 38).[113]

5) Number of readings.

a) In the celebration which repeats the pattern of the liturgy of the word in Mass and supplies for this – see above in n. 2, a); 4, a – there must be two readings (cf. ICL, n. 37).

b) In the other celebrations – see above n. 2, b; 4, b – there can be two or more, although there may be only a single reading. As regards the arrangement of several readings, see n. 38 of ICL.

6) Appropriate aids in order that these celebrations may be held with dignity and piety must be suggested or prepared by the diocesan liturgical commissions (ICL, n. 39).

The chapter on the celebration of the Word of God, in the field of the liturgy, has hardly begun. A serious,[114] varied and prolific study is awaited to bring to a fullness of expression this celebration, which the Constitution of the Council has chosen as a ripe fruit from the luxuriant tree of the piety of the Christian people, and has raised it to be, next to the sacred rites, a true school of the Christian people.

3 THE MASS, THE OTHER SACRAMENTS: THE SACRAMENTALS, AND THE OFFICE

The practical applications which the Instruction permits or establishes now, even before the renewal of the liturgical books (n. 3, 9), refer to the Roman rites alone (ICL, n. 9).

Generally they are simplifications, appropriate and expected retouches or even renovations in the sacred rites, effected according to the principles contained in n. 4-5 of the document. These are collected in chapters II, III and IV of the Instruction, under the same titles used by the Constitution and which, for practical purposes, are repeated in this second part of the commentary.

A The Eucharistic Mystery

While the revision of the entire Ordinary of the Mass is under study, so that from its structure the intrinsic nature and purpose of its several parts, as also the connection between them, may be more clearly manifested, and that devout and active participation by the faithful may be more easily achieved (CL, Art. 50), the Instruction up until now has introduced in the course of the Mass simplifications and innovations suited to outline more expressively the definitive ritual structure of the eucharistic celebration.

This consists of two parts, designated by the Commission as the *liturgy of the Word* and the *eucharistic liturgy*,[115] so closely connected with each other that they form but one single form of worship (CL, Art. 56). In turn, these two parts are accompanied by two other rites of lesser importance: by the *entrance rite* and by the *departure rite*.

The Instruction, in simplifying these two moments of the celebration, has given greater emphasis to the two principal components of the entire sacred action. By giving a worthy form to the liturgy of the Word, borrowed from its catechetic function,[116] and by harmoniously distinguishing in the eucharistic liturgy the Offertory, which concludes with the prayer over the offerings, recited in a loud voice; the Canon placed between the preface and the doxology *Per Ipsum* – this last prayer also said in a loud voice; and the Communion with the communal praying of the Lord's Prayer and with the embolism recited in a loud voice; the Instruction has given to the individual parts an appropriate distinction and importance. These appear more evident principally in the sung Mass and in the Mass with the participation of the people.

With this as an introduction, it is sufficient for the purpose of achieving a harmonious and exact application of the practical norms introduced by the Instruction in the eucharistic celebration to set them down in a clear presentation.

1 *Simplifications and Innovations in all Masses*[117]

1) *Omitted are:*
   - The kisses of the celebrant in putting on and removing his vestments, and the kisses of the server of the hand and of the objects which he offers or receives: cf. ICL, n. 36, d,
   - Psalm 42, *Judica me Deus,* in the prayers at the foot of the altar: ICL, n. 48, c[118]
   - The last Gospel: ICL, n. 48, j[119]
   - The Leonine prayers: ICL, n. 48, j[120]
2) *Recited in a loud voice or sung are:*
   - The Secret or prayer over the offerings: ICL, n. 48, e[121]
   - The prayer (embolism) *Libera nos,* which follows the Lord's Prayer: ICL, n. 48, h[122]
3) *Changed are:*
   - The rite completing the Canon: that is, by eliminating the five signs of the cross and by reciting in a loud voice or by singing the doxology *Per Ipsum*. Throughout the entire doxology the celebrant lifts up the chalice and the host for the Little Elevation. At the end he genuflects only after the response *Amen* is given by the people (ICL, n. 48, f)[123]
   - The formula and the procedure in the distribution of Communion to the faithful: ICL, n. 48, i[124]
4) *Moreover, it must be kept in mind that:*
   - The prayers at the foot of the altar (including the *Oramus te Domine*) are completely omitted whenever another liturgical service immediately precedes the Mass (ICL, n. 48, c). By another liturgical service is understood one[125] different in nature from the Mass. By immediately preceding the Mass is meant a service which introduces the Mass and is strictly connected with it: as, e.g., the canonical hour of Tierce, the *Asperges,* a procession,[126] funeral rites,[127] eucharistic blessing,[128] etc.; besides the cases already expressly indicated by number 424 of the Code of Rubrics.[129]
   - In low Masses the Lord's Prayer may be recited by the people together with the celebrant in the vernacular language;[130] in sung Masses it may be chanted by the people together with the celebrant in the Latin language.[131] It pertains to the competent territorial

ecclesiastical authority to decide whether the Lord's Prayer can be sung also in the vernacular language, to melodies approved by the same authority (ICL, n. 48, g; n. 42).

2 *Masses in the Vernacular with Participation by the People*

In this section it is above all necessary to bear in mind n. 57 of the Instruction concerning the texts which can be recited in the vernacular language.[132] *To determine what the vernacular languages are, and how and when they can be used depends upon the competent ecclesiastical authority.*

In the low Mass – commonly called the dialog or communal Mass[133] – in the sung and solemn Mass the celebrant:

- Does not read the parts of the Proper which are sung or recited by the schola or by the people (ICL, n. 48, a; cf. n. 32),[134] even if they are expressed in the vernacular (cf. ICL, n. 57, b).[135]
- May sing or recite the parts of the Ordinary together with the people or the schola (ICL, n. 48, b),[136] even if expressed in the vernacular, if the competent ecclesiastical authority has so disposed (ICL, n. 57, b).
- For the variations of the Ordinary: see Section A. In the sung and solemn Mass: the prayer over the offerings; the final doxology of the Canon, *Per Ipsum*, and the embolism, *Libera nos* are sung.[137]
- But the innovations of greater import which the Instruction has effected in the first part of the Mass – the liturgy of the Word – are represented by the rites whereby the proclamation of the Word of God takes place (cf. CL, Art. 51) and by the restoration of the Prayer of the Faithful or common prayer (cf. CL, Art. 53).

A PROCLAMATION OF THE WORD OF GOD

The rites whereby the proclamation of the Word of God is made – in the Readings, Epistles and Gospels[138] *– are ordained to give to the first part of the Mass (cf. CL, Art. 56) dignity, solemnity and an expressive form: as befits the celebration of the* magnalia Dei *of which the scriptures speak. Since this part can be read in the living or vernacular language (cf. ICL, n. 57, a); CL, Art. 36, 2; the opportunity presented itself of restoring to this first part of the Mass its original form of assembly,*[139] *of meeting, in which the celebrant reverts to wholly perform his role of presiding over the holy assembly.*[140] *The rites for the liturgy of the word are outlined by the Instruction moderately and without excessive ceremonial concern (unbecoming the nature of the document): however, they are suited to confirm to the place where the liturgical celebration takes place. In short:*[141]

a) *Readings*

- Are always read facing the people: ICL, n. 49 (cf. n. 40, e)
- Are read at the ambo or at the edge of the sanctuary area: ICL, n. 49, a-b

- Are read by:
  - The lector or by the deacon or priest in low and sung Masses: ICL, n. 50; 52, b, d[142]
  - The subdeacon and by the deacon in solemn Masses: ICL, n. 52, a
- In the vernacular in sung Masses: ICL, n. 51[143]
- The rites accompanying the readings:
  - In solemn Masses: ICL, n. 52, a[144]
  - In low and sung Masses: ICL, n. 50; 52, b, d[145]

b) *Chants between Readings*

- In sung and low Masses:
  - may be read by a qualified lector or server: ICL, n, 50; 52, b
  - by the choir or by the people: cf. ICL, n. 52, c
  - if this is necessary by the celebrant himself: ICL, n. 52, d
- In solemn Masses:
  - by the choir or by the people: cf. ICL, n. 52, a

c) *The Celebrant*

- In solemn Masses:
  - listens to the Lessons, the Epistle, Gospel and intervenient chants remaining at the bench: ICL, n. 52, a (with related ceremonies)
- In low and sung Masses:
  - Listens to all the readings: ICL, n. 52, a-b;
  - Reads the Gospel: he leaves the bench during the singing or reading of the intervenient chants: he goes to the lowest step of the altar and there bows deeply while saying *Munda cor meum;* then he goes to the ambo or to the edge of the sanctuary area to chant or recite the gospel: ICL, n. 52, c); 49, b)[146]
  - Reads the Epistle and Gospel: at the ambo or at the edge of the sanctuary area or at the altar, always facing the people; cf. ICL, n. 52, a); 49, b)[147]

B THE PRAYER OF THE FAITHFUL

The prayer of the faithful[148] *concludes the first part of the Mass. Here we limit ourselves to the structure of the prayer, outlined by the Instruction for Masses with participation on the part of the people. Concerning the introduction of this prayer, the formulas to be used, etc., n. 56 of the document must be read attentively.*

- The prayer of the faithful (ICL, n. 56)
  - Is read before the Offertory, after the word: *Oremus*
  - The celebrant directs it:
    - in solemn Masses from his seat: cf. ICL, n. 52, a);
    - in read and sung Masses, from his seat: cf. ICL, n. 52, b); 50; or from the same place where he has read the gospel and has given the homily: cf. n. 49, b; 52, c-d)
  - The concluding prayer is reserved to the celebrant[149]
  - The intentions or invocations may be chanted by a deacon[150] or a cantor or other qualified server: ICL, n. 56

• Other innovations or practical applications in the celebration of Mass:

1) *In a Solemn Mass:*

– The incensation of the celebrant after the chanting of the gospel is omitted: implicitly in ICL, n. 52, a)[151]

– The celebrant gives the homily to the people (cf. ICL, n. 53) from his seat[152]: this is deduced from ICL, n. 52, a)

– The Creed, if it is to be said, is intoned by the celebrant–and sung (cf. ICL, n. 48, b) with the ministers[153] together with the faithful – from his seat: ICL, n. 52, a)

– The subdeacon does not raise the paten, but leaves it on the altar: ICL, n. 48, d)[154]

2) *In low and sung Masses with the participation of the people:* the celebrant gives a homily to the people[155] from the place where he has listened to or read the gospel: implicitly contained in ICL, n. 52, b). Cf. also n. 49, b); 52, c-d)[156]

– The Creed, if it is to be said, is intoned by the celebrant – and sung or recited (cf. ICL, n. 48, b) together with the people – from the place where he has read the gospel and has given the homily: this is deduced from ICL, n. 52, b. Cf. also n. 49, b; 52, c-d

• Moreover:

– It is lawful to celebrate a sung Mass with a deacon only:[157] ICL, n. 48, k;

– It is lawful for bishops, if necessary, to celebrate a sung Mass according to the form used by priests: ICL, n. 48, l)[158]

With regard to the homily, an integrating part of the liturgical action (CL, Art. 52) 53-55 and 57 of the Instruction should be read attentively. The exposé of its nature and of its importance, also of serving a purpose toward a profitable liturgical formation of the faithful, deserves a fuller treatment, which we leave to others.

B *The Other Sacraments and the Sacramentals*

The higher principles expressed by the Constitution of the Council (III) concerning the other sacraments and sacramentals[159] practically converge on three questions:

1) On the revision of the rites of the sacraments and sacramentals so that they might more clearly express the nature and the purpose of the sacraments (cf. CL, Art. 62).[160]

2) On the great advantage which the use of the vernacular offers to the people principally in the administration of the sacraments and sacramentals (cf. CL, Art. 63).

3) On the preparation of particular rituals adapted to the needs of the different regions (also as regards the language employed) and having as their basis the new editions of the Roman Ritual (CL, Art. 63).

The first question is of vital importance to the present state of the liturgy: it is greatly felt by the pastors of souls and by priests in their immediate ministry. The motives are clear to all: also to the Commission which is concerned – as is known – with the reforming of the liturgical books. The study-group personally entrusted with the task of the revision of the Ritual and the Roman Pontifical, a delicate and not easy task, is (as other groups) already at work.[161]

In the meantime the Instruction, applying the principal note of simplification,[162] has already now made some corrections and opportune innovations of the sacraments and sacramentals called for by our times, so that the value of the sign included in them might also become more intelligible. The faithful in turn – through an appropriate catechesis – will be capable of easily understanding the sacramental signs and of frequenting with great eagerness those sacraments which were instituted to nourish the Christian life (CL, Art. 59).

The most important innovation, which call for our attention, concern the rites of confirmation, matrimony and the rites for the sick.

In what measure the vernacular can be introduced into the rites of the sacraments and sacramentals – the second question mentioned above – is clearly determined in n. 61 of the Instruction. The putting into practice, however, of such dispositions pertains only to the competent territorial authority only after the decrees have been approved or confirmed by the Apostolic See (ICL, n. 61). N. 61 of the Instruction[163] puts into effect Art. 63a of the Constitution of the Council in its fullest expression: in fact, with further possibilities, in conformity with Art. 40 of the same Constitution.

The simplifications and innovations of the Instruction introduced into the Roman Ritual – as it is at present – in connection with what has been established in n. 61, shall also become the simplifications and innovations to be introduced into the Collection of Rites (*Collectio Rituum . . . Ad instar Appendicis Rit. Rom.*)[164] presently in use in many dioceses (cf. ICL, n. 43) and approved at the time by the Holy See, awaiting a new redaction of such particular books, according to the criteria referred to above in the third question.

For a practical knowledge of the simplifications introduced now in certain rites of the sacraments and sacramentals, n. 62-63; 69; 76-77 of the Instruction should be read.[165] We here limit ourselves to pointing out the schema of the innovations of greater importance.

1 *Confirmation*

Of significant importance, to be grasped in all its fullness, is the attempt to relate or associate the rites of confirmation more visibly with the paschal mystery, proclaimed and celebrated in the Eucharist, in conjunction with the reference to baptism, through the renewal of the baptismal promises. A first step toward a renewed rite – as the Constitution of the Council indicates – in which the intimate connection which this sacrament has with the whole of Christian initiation is to be more clearly set forth (CL, Art. 71).[166]

The Instruction, following the path indicated by the Constitution in

Art. 71, and pointed to first by the MP (n. IV) of January of 1964, proposes (note the expression used) a pattern to be followed when confirmation is conferred within Mass.

Liturgy of the Word
Homily
Renewal of the baptismal promises
Sacrament of confirmation
[*Prayer of the faithful*]
Eucharistic liturgy

1) *The Mass within which confirmation is conferred may be celebrated as a votive Mass of class II, of the Holy Spirit:* ICL, n. 64.[167]

It is fitting that the Mass be celebrated by the bishop himself (ICL, n. 64): or by another (ICL, n. 66). In this case, it is fitting that the bishop assist wearing a white amice, stole and cope (Pont. Rom., Pars I, *De Confirmandis*) or of the color of the Mass (ICL, n. 66).

The homily is to be given by the bishop, even when he does not celebrate the Mass: ICL, n. 66.

2) *After the Gospel and homily, before the reception of Confirmation, it is praiseworthy that those to be confirmed should renew the promises of baptism, according to the rite legitimately in use in the individual regions. This renewal can take place even before Mass:* ICL, n. 65.

3) *The rite of confirmation is that of the Roman Pontifical, with the changes indicated in n. 67 of the Instruction.*[168] If the bishop himself celebrates the eucharistic sacrifice, he administers the sacrament vested in Mass vestments (ICL, n. 64);[169] if he assists only, then he wears a stole and cope (see 1. above). In this instance the celebrant remains at his seat throughout the entire rite: ICL, n. 66.

On the judgment of the bishop (cf. ICL, n. 56) the first part of the Mass can be concluded with a common prayer.[170] It pertains to the bishop himself to preside over or direct this prayer.

With regard to the second part of the Mass, may we point to two questions: in the eucharistic liturgy, celebrated by the bishop, would it not be praiseworthy, at the offertory, to introduce the offering of gifts by some of the newly-confirmed? Does the participation of the newly-confirmed in Mass require on their part a sacramental participation also?

It is clear that the rite of confirmation proposed by the Instruction is possible only when the number to be confirmed is not large or pastoral motives do not render the usual form, that of the Roman Pontifical, advisable. In this case would not a pattern similar to that given in n. 74 of the Instruction for the rite of matrimony outside of Mass be useful or possible?[171]

2 *The Rite of Matrimony*

The canonical solemnity of marriage actually consists in the solemn nuptial blessing, composed of three prayers: *Propitiare, Deus qui potestate* and *Deus Abraham* inserted in the *Missa pro Sponsis*.[172] This blessing, according to a constant tradition of the Church, is conferred during the celebration of the Mass and is therefore inseparable from it.[173]

The Constitution of the Council (Art. 78) now proposes also to gradually bring back into the eucharistic celebration the conjugal pact of the spouses entered into *coram Ecclesia,* which, as all know, is at the same time a sacrament for those who are baptized.[174]

The rite of matrimony[175] understood in its entirety, that is, as a conjugal pact and a nuptial blessing, wholly inserted in the eucharistic celebration, expresses the intimate union existing between the sacraments and the paschal mystery, from which they derive their efficacy (CL, Art. 61).

Before indicating the two outlines or patterns of the rite, adapted to the Instruction, it would be useful to arrange – after the manner of general norms – that which is common to both structures.

Matrimony is to be ordinarily celebrated[176] within the Mass: after the Gospel and the homily ICL, n. 70.

A just cause – the judge of which is the pastor – excuses from this ordinary form of the rite: ICL, n. 70

The homily, in both forms of the rite, must never be omitted: ICL, n. 70, 72, 74.

The nuptial blessing must never be omitted: not even in the prohibited season nor even if one or both of the spouses is entering a second marriage: ICL, n. 73, 74, d).[177]

If the marriage is celebrated during the prohibited season, the pastor shall advise the spouses to take into account the special character of this liturgical season: ICL, n. 75.[178]

Attention should be called to n. 35 of the Instruction.[179]

For the Rite of matrimony within Mass, the plan is the following:

Liturgy of the Word
Homily
Celebration of matrimony
[Prayer of the Faithful]
Eucharistic liturgy
Nuptial blessing

It is worth noting that:

1) *The votive Mass for Spouses (II Class) shall always be celebrated, even during the prohibited season; when it is prohibited by the rubrics, then a commemoration of the Mass,*[180] *conjoined with the prayer of the Mass of the day under one conclusion, is made:* ICL, n. 71. Code of Rubrics n. 378.[181]

As far as possible the Mass is to be celebrated by the pastor himself or by his delegate who assists at the marriage: ICL, n. 72.[182] The prescribed homily is given by the one assisting at the marriage: ICL, n. 72.

2) *The rite of matrimony is that of the Roman Ritual,* Tit. VIII, c. II. If it is performed by the celebrant (the pastor or his delegate), he assists wearing the vestments of the Mass (with the exception of the maniple): if, however, the priest who assists at the marriage does not cele-

brate the Mass, he wears the surplice, white stole and, according to local custom, also the cope: ICL, n. 72. In the form of the rite within Mass, pointed out by the Instruction, no reference is made to the common prayer of the faithful. This is highly recommended by the Instruction for the other form. From this is it lawful to conclude that the prayer of the faithful can also have a place in the Missa pro Sponsis? If an affirmative answer is given, a formula approved by the local ordinary, in which petitions for the spouses are also to be included, would be required (ICL, n. 74, c).

3) *The nuptial blessing after the Lord's Prayer and before the* Placeat *is always to be imparted by the priest who celebrates the Mass:* ICL, n. 72. Code of Rubrics, n. 381, b.

For the Rite of matrimony without Mass, the form (ICL, n. 74) adds to that given by MP, V:

Brief admonition
First reading: the epistle of the *Missa pro Sponsis*
(intervenient chant)
Second reading: the Gospel of the *Missa pro Sponsis*
Homily
Celebration of marriage
Prayer of the faithful
Nuptial blessing

It is to be remembered that:

1) *The brief admonition is not a homily, but a simple introduction to the celebration of matrimony* (ICL, n. 74a). This is provided for and advised for all the rites in Art. 35 3 of the Constitution. It has the purpose of creating a first separation from the profane and to posit the premises for starting the celebration of a sacred action.[184]

2) *The two readings are in the vernacular.*[185] If there does not exist a translation of these readings approved by the competent territorial authority, a text approved by the local ordinary can be used in the meantime (ICL, n. 74, b).

3) *The rite always ends with the nuptial blessing imparted according to the formula found in the Roman Ritual,* Tit. VII, c. III,[186] unless another blessing is given in particular rituals (ICL, n. 74, d).

The second form drawn from the Instruction truly achieves the form of a liturgical celebration, the constitutive elements of which are: the proclamation of the word of God, the celebration of marriage and the nuptial blessing. That special dignity and excellence conferred by the Conciliar Constitution on the proclamation of the word of God – to which reference was made previously[187] – attains here, in union with a sacramental rite, its fullest expression.[188]

3 *Continuous Rite of the Sacraments for the Sick*

The Instruction temporarily puts into practice for the first time Art. 74 of the Constitution, in which it is said that, in addition to the separate rites for anointing of the sick and for viaticum,[189] a continuous rite shall be prepared according to which the sick man is anointed after he has made his confession and before he receives viaticum.

This continuous rite does not substitute c. IV of Tit. V of the Roman Ritual, nor c. II of Tit. VI. The two rites still exist and are (or can be) used in the administration of the two sacraments for the sick,[190] conferred – in ordinary cases – separately, depending upon the period of the sickness; or when the conditions of the sick person are such as to permit the anointing only.

The continuous rite has received its first form – not its only one, however – from the different *Collectio Rituum*,[191] to which reference has been made, and it is very useful for pastoral purposes when the anointing of the sick and viaticum are administered at the same time (ICL, n. 68). The Instruction has outlined the form (n. 68), borrowing the elements from the cited chapters of the Roman Ritual.

The following is the form:

The sprinkling with holy water and related prayers: Roman Ritual (ed. Typ. 1952) Tit. VI, c. II, n. 3)

The priest, if it is necessary, hears the confession of the sick person

The Apostolic Blessing with the plenary indulgence at the hour of death: *Dominus noster Jesus Christus, Filius Dei vivi:* Rit. Rom. Tit. VI, c. VI, n. 6 only[192]

The anointing of the sick: Rit. Rom., Tit. VI, c. II, n. 7-12 Viaticum: Rit. Rom., Tit. V, c. IV, n. 18-22 and 27 only

The proposed form is for particular Rituals or for *Collectio Rituum* which at present do not have such a rite (ICL, n. 68); the vernacular can be used in it (cf. ICL, n. 63). For the dioceses or territories without a particular ritual – e.g., the dioceses of Italy – the disposition of the competent ecclesiastical authority must be followed (ICL, n. 22-23).

C *The Divine Office*

The Instruction recalls and more clearly defines certain norms of the Constitution, already given by the *Motu Proprio "Sacram Liturgiam,"* and repeats them with some necessary clarifications.[193]

1) These above all concern (cf. CL, Art. 95) the daily recitation of the divine office by those who have choral obligation (ICL, n. 78, a-b), with a particular concession, in mission lands, for members of chapters or religious who are lawfully absent from choir by reason of the pastoral ministry (ICL, n. 78, c).[194]

2) The faculty conceded to all ordinaries[195] of dispensing their subjects, in individual cases and for a just cause, from the obligation of the divine office in whole or in part or of commuting it, is also extended to major superiors of non-exempt clerical religious institutes and of societies of clerics who live the common life without vows (ICL, n. 79).[196]

3) Members of any institute dedicated to acquiring perfection who, according to their constitutions, are to recite any parts of the divine office or any short office, are to be considered performing the public prayer of the Church (MP, VIII).

What is meant by short office[197] composed on the pattern of the divine office (CL, Art. 89) is indicated in n. 81 of the Instruction; which, moreover, allows that for the interim, short offices may be used which have been lawfully approved up to the present time, reserving new short offices to the approval of the Holy See, in order to celebrate the public prayer of the Church (ICL, n. 81). The translation of the text of a short office into the vernacular language for use as the public prayer of the Church must be approved – as was precisely stated (cf. ICL, n. 30, 57 and 61) – by the competent territorial ecclesiastical authority (ICL, n. 82).

In this way the short offices, destined for the official prayer of the Church (ICL, n. 82), enter into the list of liturgical books, the primary source of the liturgy, the regulation of which, in those matters which affect the universal Church, pertains to the Holy See (cf. ICL, n. 21).

This, through the Instruction of the SRC (n. 84), now extends to members of institutes dedicated to acquiring perfection, obliged by reason of their constitutions to the common recitation of the divine office, or a short office, or parts of either, what the MP in n. VI has already conceded to those who are bound to the recitation of the divine office without choral obligation.[198]

Finally, the competent authority for its recitation is indicated in n. 83 of the Instruction.

4) The chapter then ends with certain norms on the language to be used in the recitation of the divine office: in the celebration of the divine office in choir, Latin is to be used (ICL, n. 85); in personal recitation, the faculty for the use of the vernacular is granted in individual cases to those clerics for whom the use of Latin constitutes a grave impediment to their praying the office properly (ICL, n. 86).

N. 86-87 of the Instruction indicate who is authorized to grant his last faculty and how the grave impediment is to be weighed: whereas n. 88 is concerned with the vernacular translation of the divine office according to a rite other than the Roman rite, and n. 89 makes reference to bilingual breviaries.[199]

4 THE ARRANGEMENT OF THE CHURCH

The last chapter of the document (c. V) contains suitable directions so that the temple – the place of fathering of the community of baptized persons – even in its architectural structure can render possible or facilitate the active participation of the faithful in solemn liturgical celebrations, the main purpose of the liturgical renewal.

It is a collection of practical observations to be kept in mind especially in the construction of new churches or in the repair and adaptation of already existing churches (ICL, n. 90).

From the entire chapter there appears an insistent concern that everyone in the temple truly form and express the community (ICL, n. 92, 96-98)[200] and that the participation required of them be aided also by the external senses of sight and hearing.

For this reason also, the traditional and characteristic position of Christian prayer toward the east is to be abandoned and the liturgical celebration is to be directed toward the people: during the celebration itself – as, for example, in the first part of the Mass (cf. ICL, n. 49-52, 56) – or, as the Instruction points out, by orientating the altar toward the congregation. Thus the altar becomes the center toward which the action of the sacred ministers and the congregation converges (ICL, n. 91- 95).

To understand the true pastoral significance of the directive expressed in n. 91 and 95 of the Instruction, it would be useful to read the study of Cyrille Vogel, *Versus ad Orientem: L'orientations dans les Ordines Romani du haut moyen âge.*[201]

The new orientation given to the main altar cannot be detrimental to the adoration, respect and worthy decorum due to the most holy Eucharist ordinarily reserved on the altar.[202]

The Instruction, in conformity with that which has been pointed out in n. 91, establishes that the most holy Eucharist shall be reserved:

1) In a solid and inviolable tabernacle placed in the middle of the main altar,

2) Or in a minor, but truly outstanding, altar,

3) Or, according to lawful customs and in particular cases to be approved by the local ordinary, also in some other noble and properly adorned part of the church (ICL, n. 95, cf. n. 94).

In this prescription is reflected the famous decree of SRC of June 1, 1957[203] *De forma et usu tabernaculi,*[204] still valid in its formulation.

It is to be hoped that in putting the norms mentioned above into practice, the advice and directives of the diocesan commission of liturgy and sacred art be given more consideration than personal skill or practical experience (cf. CL, Art. 46; ICL, n. 47). This commission will especially know how to show or suggest how successfully to put into practice the concession contained in n. 96 of the document: "It is lawful to celebrate Mass facing the people even if there is a tabernacle, small but suitable, on the altar."[205]

The words used in illustrating the Instruction have not always been able to capture and express the animating spirit of the document, which desires to be the faithful interpreter of the liturgical Constitution given to the Church by the Supreme Pontiff, Paul VI, happily reigning, together with the Fathers of the sacred ecumenical Council, Vatican II. For a proper acceptance of this document, for a better understanding of it and for putting it into practice in the spirit of docile obedience to the Church and to him who has in the Church the function of educating the faithful and of adoring the Father "in spirit and truth" (Jn. 4, 23), it is advisable to recall to mind the exhortation recently directed[206] by the Pope containing an open allusion to the present Document:

"During this time you will often hear a great deal on the sacred liturgy, spoken by many different voices and on different themes, but always based on the recent Constitution of the ecumenical Council and on the Instruction which followed it, which begins its gradual application. It is just that this be so: this new legislation concerning the public and official worship of the Church is very important, and deserves to be widely divulged and commented upon, also because one of its peculiar and principal ends is the participation of the faithful in the rites which the priest directs and personifies. And it is well to note that it is actually the authority of the Church that desires, promotes and sparks this new manner of prayer, for in this way it greatly favors its spiritual mission: it was and is the primary concern of the Church to protect the orthodoxy of prayer; and further care has been taken to render the expressions of cult stable and uniform; a great work, from which the spiritual life of the Church has derived immense benefits; now her care is widening, is modifying certain aspects of ritual discipline which today are inadequate, and aims courageously, but designedly, at penetrating the essential meaning, the communal need and the supernatural value of ecclesiastical worship by emphasizing, above all, the function exercised by the word of God, both that of sacred scripture and the didactic and commentarial word of the catechesis and of the homily; and by giving to the sacramental celebration its clear and at the same time mysterious centralness."

"To understand this religious progress and to enjoy its desired fruits all of us must modify the habitual mentality which has been formed concerning the sacred ceremonies and religious practices, especially when we believe that ceremonies are a simple execution of external rites and that practices exact nothing other than a passive and distracted assistance. It is necessary to realize that a new spiritual pedagogy has been born from the Council; it is a great newness; and we must not hesitate to become ourselves first of all disciples and then supporters of the school of prayer, which is about to begin. Perhaps the reform affects customs very dear to us, and perhaps also very respectable customs: it may be that the reform demands some effort which will not at first be pleasing; but we must be docile and must have confidence: the religious and spiritual plan, which has been opened before us by the new liturgical Constitution, is stupendous, for profundity and authenticity of doctrine, for rationality of Christian logic, for purity and richness of worship and art, for answering to the nature and needs of modern man. It is still the authority of the Church which so teaches us, and which so guarantees the goodness of the reform, in the pastoral effort to strengthen in souls faith and love for Christ and the religious sense of the world."

NOTES TO CHAPTER 10

ABBREVIATIONS

CL = Constitution on the sacred liturgy.
MP = *Motu Proprio "Sacram Liturgiam,"* January 21, 1964.
ICL = Instruction for the proper implementation of the Constitution on the sacred liturgy.
CIC = Code of Canon Law.

EL = *Ephemerides liturgicae.*
RL = *Rivista Liturgica* (nuova series, 1964).
MD = *La Maison-Dieu.*

1 Instituted with the *Motu Proprio,* January 21, 1964.

2 *L'Osservatore Romano,* March 5, 1964, 1. An account of the work thus far accomplished by the Commission has been given by the secretary, A. Bugnini: *"Sei mesi di attività del Consilium ad exsequendam Constitutionem de sacra Liturgia,"* in: *L'Osservatore Romano,* September 23, 1964, 5.

3 Cf. ICL, n. 2.

4 Cf. A. Bugnini, *art. cit.,* 5.

5 Cf. ICL, conclusion.

6 In the drawing up of the document the Commission had present certain directive criteria summarized by Fr. Bugnini, *art. cit.,* 5.

7 A. Bugnini, *art. cit.,* 5.

8 ICL, n. 1-3. Cf. MP, Intr.

9 Cf. CL, Art. 10.

10 Cf. CL, Art. 5-8.

11 Cf. ICL, n. 4, 8; CL, Art. 11 and 14.

12 Cf. RL, 356-360.

13 A careful reading should be made of the last part of the allocution addressed by the Holy Father to the members of the Commission on October 19, 1964, in: *L'Osservatore Romano,* October 13, 1964, 1.

14 Cf. C. Vagaggini, *"Lo spirito della Costituzione sulla Liturgia":* RL 511 (1964), 5-49. C. Vagaggini, *Il senso teologico della Liturgia* (Roma: 1958). A. G. Martimort, *La Chiesa in preghiera: Introduzione alla Liturgia* (Roma: 1963).

15 Cf. Rousseau, *Storia del movimento liturgico* (Roma: 1961). T. Federici, *"Date principali del movimento liturgico italiano,"* RL 51, 3 (1964), 379-397.

16 *L'Osservatore Romano,* April 15, 1964, 1.

17 Cf. MP, Intro.; EL 78 (1964), 406-408: a bibliographical list of the principal comments on the liturgical Constitution.

18 Cf. *Codex rubricarum Breviarii et Missalis Romani* (1960), 71-77. CL, Art. 102-104.

19 Pertaining to the Commission — as the Holy Father has recently declared — is the serious and difficult task of slowly putting into practice the renewal of the liturgy. *L'Osservatore Romano,* October 31, 1964, 1.

20 Cf. CL, Art. 22, par. 1, 3; MP, XI; ICL, n. 20.

21 Here the liturgical commissions — to which reference is made in n. 44-47 of the document — have the manner of performing the role assigned to them, by means of a positive and prompt action through an adequate knowledge and putting into effect of the Instruction.

22 Cf. ICL, n. 5.

23 Cf. CL, art. 2; MP, Intr.

24 Cf. Msgr. C. Rossi, *"Qual'e il vero concetto di Liturgia pastorale,"* RL 44 (1957), 11. L. Della Torre, *"Liturgia pastorale e pastorale liturgica nella Costituzione conciliare 'De sacra Liturgia,'"* RL 51, 1 (1964), 63-75.

25 Cf. *"Liturgia e pastorale: I principi; I mezzi della pastorale liturgica,"* in Vagaggini,

Senso teologico della Liturgia, 628-697. Ph. André, *"La Liturgie au coeur de la Catéchèse,"* MD 78 (1964), 61-81.

26 Cf. P. Visentin, *"Il mistero di Cristo nella Liturgia secondo la Costituzione liturgica,"* RL 51, par. 1, 3 (1964), 50-62; 293-307.

27 Cf. CL, Art. 3, 87.

28 Cf. CIC, can. 1; CL, Art. 3-4. The Latin rites — which have the ancient Roman liturgy as their basis — presently in force are: the Ambrosian, Dominican, Monastic, Premonstratensian, Cistercian, Carthusian, Carmelite of the old observance, and that of Braga Cf. F. Dell'Oro, *La semplificazione delle rubriche* (Napoli: 1960), 34.

29 Except what is proper and peculiar to the rites.

30 Cf. ICL, n. 9, 20-22, 88. CL, Art. 22, par. 1.

31 Cf. CL, Art. 22, par. 2. MP, ICL, n. 23. To these territorial episcopal bodies is expressly entrusted that which is contained in n. 34, 42, 44-45, 48g, 56-57, 61, 74b, 82 and 88 of the Instruction.

32 Cf. CIC, can. 198, par. 2; can. 1261, par. 1.

33 Cf. ICL, n. 37, 41, 78c:, 94-95. Moreover, the document appeals to the authority of the local ordinary in n. 11a, 34, 47, 74c.

34 Cf. ICL, n. 79 and 86.

35 ICL, n. 79, 83 and 86. Reference is also made to major superiors in n. 11a.

36 This is different from what is prescribed in CIC, can. 335, par. 2.

37 Cf. CL, Art. 22, par. 3. MP, XI.

38 All remember, e.g., the moderate lines of the pastoral and ritual preparation of the Instruction of the SRC, November 16, 1955 concerning the renewal of the rites of Holy Week.

39 Cf. *"Communicato della Commissione della Conferenza Episcopale Italiana,"* following the publication of the Instruction (*L'Italia,* November 1, 1964, 2).

40 *La Maison-Dieu* (organ of the CPL of France) has dedicated (1964) fascile n. 78, *La formation liturgique,* to the study of this complex but vital problem.

41 The discourse of the Supreme Pontiff at Monte Cassino on the occasion of the consecration of the reconstructed basilica of the historic Benedictine monastery, October 24, 1964 (*L'Osservatore Romano,* October 25, 1).

42 Cf. CL, Art. 14 and 19. See also Vagaggini, *Il senso teologico della Liturgia,* 648-659.

43 Cf. CL, Art. 15-18. MP, I.

44 Cf. F. Tollu, *"La formation liturgique des futurs prêtres,"* MD 78 (1964), 82-96. A. Hänggi, *De cleri institutione liturgica,* EL 78 (1964), 247-250.

45 Cf. Tollu, *art. cit.,* 82-84.

46 To establish therefore and to achieve an harmonious, fruitful equilibrium between personal prayer (also called private prayer) and liturgical prayer, the expression of the integral worship of the Mystical Body, cf. Biffi, *"I fondamenti della pietà liturgica e la pietà privata,"* RL 49 (1962), 52-58.

47 Tollu, *art. cit.,* 84.

48 Cf. also MP, I. Para. c of n. 11 is particularly directed to the formation of the young cleric, especially of those who are already working in the Lord's vineyard. Concerning the distribution of teaching matter, useful notes can be found in the cited article of Tollu (91-95). On the relation between theology and liturgy, see C. Vaggini, *Il senso teologico della Liturgia,* 416-419; 487-501.

49 Cf. also CL, Art. 17.

50 The term sacrament, as is obvious, is here understood as a sensible sign, which signifies and in a manner all its own realizes the sanctification of man (cf. CL, Art. 7). C. Vagaggini, *op. cit.*, 32, 89-108, 136-145; and for an over-all understanding of the theme, *Segno e Liturgia*, 38-108.

51 Cf. CL, Art. 19. To be recalled to mind are the three ways – principally the third which is effected in four stages – established by the Instruction of 1958 for an active participation of the faithful at Mass (n. 29-32) and the general principles of such a participation (n. 21-23): A. Bugnini, *Documenta pontificia ad instaurationem liturgicam spectantia II* (Roma: 1959), 79-79, 82-83.

52 Cf. CIC, can. 1367, para. 3.

53 Cf. SRC *Instructio,* September 3, 1958, n. 22: Bugnini, op. cit., II, 78-79.

54 Present in the house and whose participation is requested in a sung Mass, as has been said at the beginning of n. 15; therefore not only superiors and teachers.

55 See: A. G. Martimort, *"Le rituel de la concélébration eucharistique,"* in EL 77 (1963), 147-168. A. Nuij, *"Le rituel de la concélébration nouvelle,"* in *Les Questions lit. et par.* 45 (1964), 206-227.

56 Cf. note 50.

57 Cf. SRC *Instructio,* September 3, 1958, n. 40-42 (Bugnini, op. cit., II, 85); *Codex Rubr.*, n. 140.

58 Cf. CL, Art. 89a.

59 One should also bear in mind the last part of n. 16 of the Instruction: the chanting of Vespers in the cathedral church for the seminarians at least on major feast days.

60 Cf. CL, Art. 96.

61 Pius XII, *Mediator Dei,* November 20, 1947, P. IV, I, n. 170, 173: Bugnini, *Documenta pontificia,* I (Roma: 1953), 154.

62 *Mediator Dei,* P. IV, I, n. 173; Bugnini, *op. cit.,* I, 154.

63 *Mediator Dei,* P. IV, I, n. 171; Bugnini, *op. cit.,* I, 154.

64 See: *"Instituti Secolari,"* in *Enciclopedia Cattolica,* VII, 353-354.

65 Paul VI, to the faithful of the parish of the Great Mother of God, in Rome, March 8, 1964 (*L'Osservatore Romano,* March 15, 1).

66 *Ibid.,* 1.

67 Cf. MP, Intr.

68 Cf. SRC *Instructio,* September 3, 1958, n. 24-33: A. Bugnini, *op. cit.,* II, 79-83. *Liturgia viva* (Milano: 1962), 130-203.

69 ICL, n. 7.

70 Cf. Note 21.

71 In the liturgy, in fact, is expressed the most excellent part of the Church's activity (ICL, n. 1).

72 Cf. CIC, can. 1257, 1261, par. 1. *Mediator Dei,* p. I, V, n. 57: Bugnini, *op. cit.,* I, 117.

73 The faculties which the episcopal conferences had previously in liturgical matters are indicated by the Code of Rubrics, n. 117 and by the *"Additiones et variationes in Rituali Romano circa Ordinem Baptismi adultorum,"* c. 4, par. 2. *"Normae pro usu huius Ordinis,"* n. 3,6: EL 76 (1962), 425-426.

74 Cf. ICL, n. 3; CL, Art. 22, par. 2.

75 Cf. CIC, can. 1257. *Mediator Dei,* P. I. 5, n. 57: Bugnini, op. cit., I, 117.

76 Wherefore different from work with a pick and axe, as someone thought, it is the work of study, meditation and of prayer (Bugnini, *"Sei mesi di attività de Consilium,"* in *L'Osservatore Romano,* September 23, 1964, 52).

77 Bugnini, *art. cit.,* 5.

78 *L'Osservatore Romano,* October 31, 1964, 1.

79 Cf. CL, Art. 43; ICL, n. 4-7, 19.

80 Such a Commission, the Constitution says, should be assisted by experts in liturgical science, sacred music, art, and pastoral practice (Art. 44).

81 From 1947 the institution of such a commission was only recommended: *Nobis in votis est, ut in singulis dioecesibus . . . Consilium quoque constituatur ad liturgicum provehendum apostolatum . . .* (Pius XII, *Mediator Dei,* P. II, II, n. 108: Bugnini, *Documenta pontificia,* I, 134). It then became obligatory with the Instruction of the SRC (September 3, 1958); in each diocese commissions of sacred art and of sacred liturgy are likewise to be instituted (n. 118).

82 MP, II: ". . . for exploring and promoting the liturgical apostolate ever more diligently."

83 The expression "the following duties pertain to the diocesan liturgical commission, under the direction of the bishop . . . etc." of the Instruction does not seem to contradict the prescriptions of MP cited above.

84 Cf. RL 51, 3 (1964), 362-363.

85 Vagaggini, *Il senso teologico della Liturgia,* 35.

86 *L'Osservatore Romano,* October 31, 1964, 1.

87 Introduced in the liturgical action by the Instruction of 1958, (n. 96) (Bugnini, *Documenta pontificia,* II, 96-97), by the conciliar Constitution (Art. 29) and by the present Instruction (n. 13b), in which he is expressly named among the persons who exercise a genuine liturgical function at the altar (CL, Art. 29). See: A.-M. Roguet *"Le Commentateur,"* MD 60 (1959), 80-98. A. Duval, *"Le Concile de Trénte et les origines du 'Commentateur,'"* MD 61 (1960), 41-47.

88 Cf. CL, Art. 28, 32, 34.

89 It suffices to remember the simplification of the rubrics principally of missal and breviary (a. 1955-1960); the simplifying of the rites described in the second part of the Roman Pontifical (a. 1961) and the laborious path, through different experimental phases, of the renewal of the rites of Holy Week (1951-1955).

90 Cf. CL, Art. 34.

91 A rubrical norm appearing for the first time in the *Ordo hebdomadae sanctae instauratus* and amplified in 1960 with the *Codex rubricarum* (n. 473).

92 The term "clergy" used in para. b of n. 36 (notes Trimeloni in *Perfice Munus*) is understood in the strict sense: that is, there is question here of the clergy properly so-called, which comprises together the clerics who assist at a sacred function without giving direct service to the celebrant.

93 Only to be observed are: (a) the distinction which derives from the liturgical function and from sacred orders, and (b) the due honor to be given to civil authorities according to liturgical laws (CL, Art. 32).

94 This disposition will be put into practice by the abrogation of the distinction into what are called "classes" with respect to external solemnities especially of funerals, marriages, baptisms, etc.; by the abrogation of a place reserved in church to a certain faithful, and other such things. For all of this takes on the appearance of simony, and gives rise to a suspicion of profit-making on the part of the clergy. It

contradicts the communal nature of the liturgy, fosters vanity, and injures poverty (Famoso, in EL 78 (1964), 261).

95 By national language is meant the term "vernacular" – which is found in Varrone, *De lingua latina,* 5, 77 – used by the conciliar Constitution (Art. 36) and repeated by the Instruction. It indicates the language usually used in the homily and in the catechesis. In *Mediator Dei* and *Musicae sacrae disciplina* as also in the Instruction of 1958 the language spoken by the people was indicated by the term *"Lingua vulgaris,"* which, translated as "vulgar language," seems to give a deprecatory meaning to the common language. Others prefer instead to translate it as the "liturgical language," seeing that it is used in the sacred rites. Cf. P. Jounel, in MD 77 (1964), 69-70.

96 See: C. Braga, *"De lingua in Liturgia adhibenda,"*EL 78 (1964), 275 283.

97 Cf. CL, Art. 54.

98 Cf. CL, Art. 63.

99 Cf. note 41.

100 It seems that such books do not need further approval: the text in the vernacular, repeated in them, was already approved by the competent territorial ecclesiastical authority. With regard to certain texts of the Roman Pontifical translated into the vernacular (cf. ICL, n. 61b), it is not said whether they need or need not be incorporated in the edition of this book.

101 See a first list (1947-1955) in F. Dell'Oro, *La semplificazione delle rubriche,* p. 3, note 3. Other bilingual rituals: in 1958 for the dioceses of Brazil; in 1959 for Ireland and in 1961 (in the Latin-Zulu language) for the territory of the Union of South Africa.

102 On the introduction of the vernacular into the Ritual and successive developments, see: Card. P.M. Gerlier, *"I rituali bilingui e la pastorale dei sacramenti,"* in *La restaurazione liturgica nell'opera di Pio XII: Acts of the First International Congress on Pastoral Liturgy* (Assisi: September, 1956), 63-76.

103 See *Liturgia e Bibbia* in Vagaggini, *Il senso teologico della Liturgia,* 348-385.

104 SRC *Instructio,* September 3, 1958, n. 12-13: Bugnini, *Documenta pontificia,* II, 75-76.

105 Not equipped with a form-type, but youthfully anxious to grasp and contemplate the mystery of salvation, manifested fully in Christ, this communal form of religious service did not always maintain a harmonious balance among its constitutive elements: the Word of God, singing and prayer. At times the catechesis enjoyed predominance; at other times, however, there dominated the prayer-dialog, as the expression of the particular recurrences or feasts belonging to groups or societies or communities. Left to itself, that is, to the private inspiration of the redactor, the biblico-liturgical vigil became at times the mirror of a personal piety of different qualities.

106 Cf. E. Osenigo, *"La celebrazione della Parola di Dio," Ambrosius* 40, 4 (1964), 290-294.

107 Cf. Vagaggini, *Il senso teologico della Liturgia,* 101-108.

108 Since the two readings must be those of the Mass of the day, inspiration should be conveniently drawn from the psalm of the *Introit* of the Mass of the day. Useful aids: *Salterio corale* (Torino: Elle Di Ci); *Trenta salmi ed un cantico* (Torino: Elle Di Ci).

109 For example, a short but expressive phrase which draws its inspiration from the same passage read.

110 The one who presides shall give a homily, if he is a deacon; if not a deacon, he shall read a homily indicated by the bishop or the pastor (ICL, n. 37).

111 Cf. L. Della Torre, *"L'Oratio fidelium,"* RL 51, 2 (1964), 214-224; and also RL 52, 1 (1965). See also note 147.

112 For example, from Psalms 113-118 which form the great Hallel; or, from Psalms 119-135, expressive of the celebration itself.

113 Besides preferring the structure of the liturgy of the Word in the Mass, this reunion of communal prayer should reflect or express also the different liturgical seasons of the year. It is one thing to celebrate the Word of God in the feria of Advent and Lent, another to celebrate it on the vigil of Christmas or of Epiphany. It should also be possible to give to such a celebration that simple but expressive ceremonial form which truly helps to celebrate the Word of God, as the liturgy in the solemn Mass celebrates it.

114 A first study is that of Msgr. P. Borella, *"Bibbia e Liturgia nella Costituzione Liturgica del Concilio Ecum. Vat. II e nell'antico rito Ambrosiano," Ambrosius* 40, 4 (1964), 260-282.

115 The eucharistic liturgy consists of three moments: Offertory, Canon and Communion.

116 The restored *oratio fidelium* concludes this first part of the Mass.

117 The classification of the different types of Masses given by the Instruction of 1958 (Bugnini, *Documenta pontificia,* II, 74, n. 3), is implicitly changed by the recent document (cf. CL, Art. 48; 49; 56) as a result of this twofold distinction: Masses with participation of the people and Masses without participation of the people. The first can have a solemn form, that is, with sacred ministers and with a deacon only (cf. ICL, n. 48k) or read, with or without singing; the other (without participation of the people) is individual, and therefore always read. Then there is the pontifical Mass (cf. *Codex rubr.,* n. 271) and the concelebrated Mass (cf. CL, Art. 57-58). It is well to note that from ICL, n. 50 it is not clear that the Mass with a deacon is solemn.

118 With the promulgation of the new *Ritus servandus in celebratione Missae* (February 1965), drawn up in accordance with the norms fixed by the Instruction, we feel it superfluous to indicate the changes brought about in the preceding *Ritus serv.;* we limit ourselves to pointing out only those which refer to the *Codex rubricarum.* Cf. Dell'Oro, *op. cit.,* 331-333. Abrogated is n. 425 of the *Codex rubricarum.*

119 Cf. L. Agustoni-G. Wagner, *Partecipazione attiva alla liturgia: Atti del III Convegno internazionale di studi liturgici. Lugano, September 14-18, 1953,* (Como: 1953), 225, 241, 145. F. Dell'Oro, *La semplificazione delle rubriche,* 350-352. Totally abrogated are n. 509 and 510 of the *Codex rubr.;* consequently also the rubric which prescribes the reading of the Gospel with the account of the entrance of Jesus into Jerusalem in the Mass of the Second Sunday in Passiontide or Palm Sunday.

120 The Decree of SRC, March 9, 1960 is abrogated.

121 Cf. Agustoni-Wagner, *op. cit.,* p. 242. The prescription modifies n. 511 and 513 of the *Codex rubr.* In an intelligible voice the celebrant says, facing the server (or ministers), *Orate, fratres, ut meum* . . . etc. Without prefacing *Oremus* and with hands extended, he recites in a loud voice or sings the *oratio super oblato.* At the *Per Dominum nostrum,* he joins his hands before his chest up to the *per omnia* . . . etc., inclusive. After the *Amen* response of the assembly, the celebrant places his hands on the altar and says or sings *Dominus vobiscum,* raises his hands for the *Sursum corda,* and then continues the Preface in the usual way. The prayer over the offerings can be sung according to the ancient tone, the end of which (*per omnia saecula saeculorum*) is linked appropriately with the *Dominus vobiscum* of the Preface. It is appropriate then to sing also the Collect and the Postcommunion in the same tone.

122 Cf. Agustoni-Wagner, *op. cit.,* 243. The Instruction changes n. 511 and 513 of the *Codex rubricarum.* The celebrant recites or sings the entire *Pater Noster,* that is, up to the words *sed libera nos a malo* inclusive: both when he is accompanied by the faithful, and when he does so alone (see above, Par. b). The *Amen* is no longer said

as the conclusion (neither in a loud voice or secretly); this *Amen* will be then said at the end of the *Libera nos.* The embolism is for the time being recited or sung (the ancient tone of the prayer) while performing, according to the rubrics, the ceremony with the paten and the breaking of the host.

123 Cf. Agustoni-Wagner, *op. cit.,* 242, 243. Changed is n. 213 of the *Codex rubr.* The melody of *Per ipsum,* when it is sung, is that of the Preface.

124 Cf. Agustoni-Wagner, *op. cit.,* 244. Dell'Oro, *op. cit.,* 358, note 4. SRC Decree, April 25, 1964. The three *Domine non sum dignus* after the *Ecce Agnus Dei* are no longer recited by the celebrant, but only by those who are to receive Communion; this is deduced from ICL, n. 32.

125 To be recalled is the notion of liturgical actions given by the Instruction of 1958, n. 1 (Bugnini, *Documenta pontificia,* II, 73).

126 Cf. *Rituale Romanum,* Tit. X.

127 Cf. *Rituale Romanum,* Tit. VII, c. iii.

128 *"Benedictio Eucharistica est vere actio liturgica,"* SRC *Instructio* 1958, n. 47 (Bugnini, *op. cit.,* II, 86).

129 The distribution of Communion or the exposition of the most blessed Sacrament cannot be considered as another liturgical action; so also a Mass immediately following another. The decree of the SRC (December 7, 1964) has in mind the case of Christmas and November 2.

130 This faculty is directly given by the Instruction; it is the only one thus far pertaining to the vernacular.

131 ICL, n. 48g.

132 Cf. pp. 43-44.

133 In the dialog or communal form (a less appropriate term) it is accompanied by suitable hymns in the vernacular (cf. SRC *Instructio* 1958, n. 14b), 33: Bugnini *Documenta pontificia,* II, 76, 83).

134 These are: the antiphons of the Introit, Offertory, and Communion; the chants between Readings and the Sequence. When it is not possible to perform these antiphons in their own melody, they are to be sung in a psalm tone or *recto tono* (*Instructio,* September 3, 1958, n. 21c: Bugnini, *Documenta pontificia,* II, 78). In fact it would be desirable, so notes Trimeloni in *Perfice munus,* 1965, for the assembly to recite or sing, besides the antiphon and the versicle, the corresponding psalms, either entirely or in part.

135 Therefore when with the singing of the *Introit* — that is, the processional hymn (generally taken from the psalms with an appropriate refrain) — the Mass begins, the celebrant, after the usual prayers, ascends the altar, kisses it and remains in the middle for the recitation or singing of the *Kyrie* and of the *Gloria.* If it frequently happens that the proper parts are not said or sung by the choir or by the assembly, the celebrant reads them: a) in the vernacular and in a loud voice, provided the vernacular has been allowed for these parts, the assembly is not singing, and the commentator is not speaking; b) otherwise in Latin and secretly (Trimeloni, in *Perfice munus,* 1965). The recitation of these texts on the part of the celebrant is then obligatory when — according to the degree of participation — the assembly executes at the *Introit,* Offertory and Communion only religious hymns in harmony with the feast or liturgical season or with that part of the Mass (cf. *Instructio* 1958, n. 27b): Bugnini, *Documenta pontificia,* II, 81). It is to be remembered that after the Consecration no hymn is permitted (*Instructio,* n. 27e); and it is appropriate to conclude the celebration with a final hymn.

136 These are: *Kyrie, Gloria, Credo, Sanctus-Benedictus, Agnus Dei.* In read masses — always with the participation of the people — *Kyrie, Sanctus-Benedictus* and *Agnus Dei* can also be sung. In this case the celebrant begins the recitation of the Canon

(*Te igitur*) after the singing of the *Sanctus* has begun. However, he does not join in with the singing of the *Agnus Dei,* since this is an exclusive chant of the assembly; therefore, having completed the breaking of the host, he immediately begins the prayers for Communion. When the celebrant (and ministers) take part in the singing of the *Kyrie, Gloria* and *Credo,* they remain standing: at the altar or at their seats (or at the ambo). At the words *Et incarnatus est*... they bow their heads profoundly; a genuflection is made only — according to the rubrics — in the masses of Christmas and of the Annunciation (March 25).

137 The new melodies are published by the Ed. Vaticana.

138 The term "Readings" distinct from that of Epistle and Gospel refers to the passages of the Old and New Testament not taken from the group of New Testament readings: but it could also preannounce the restoration of the three readings in the Mass, as presently exists in the masses of the Ember Days and of Holy Wednesday and in the solemn liturgical action of Good Friday. On the readings of the Mass, besides the manuals of liturgy, see also: P. Kahle-Feld, *"L'Ordo lectionum Missae,"* in: Agustoni-Wagner, *op. cit.,* 209-219, found in *Liturgisches Jahrbuch,* 1953, 54-59; 301 309. French translation in MD 37 (1954), 134-143. H. Schurmann, *Eine dreijährige Perikopenordnung für Sonn und Festtage* (Regensburg: 1956; Düsseldorf; 1961). French translation in: *Paroisse et Liturgie,* 1957, 230-241). Jounel, *"Pour une réforme des lectures du Missel,* in MD 66 (1961), 36-69.

139 Cf. Agustoni-Wagner, *op. cit.,* 240.

140 It follows also that the seat of the celebrant must be properly placed with the celebration itself in view. That is, it must be easily seen, conveniently raised and decorous: not a common seat placed in a corner, nor an episcopal throne (cf. ICL, n. 72).

141 Cf. ICL, Art. 49-52.

142 The Lessons and the Epistle are proclaimed by the lector: a cleric (ICL, n. 13b) or one of the ministers or also a fit lay person (man or boy); never a woman, not even in an exclusive community of women. In performing such an office (cf. CL, Art. 29) the lector is to wear a cassock and a surplice or a tunic (possibly also the lay person). The Gospel is always proclaimed by the deacon or by a priest (who can be substituted for the celebrant himself): never by a lector and much less by a woman. The deacon or the priest wears the alb (or the surplice) and the deacon's stole. At the words which required a genuflection (for example, *Ut in nomine Iesu omne genuflectatur; Et Verbum caro factum est; Et procidentes adoraverunt eum,* etc.) only a simple bow of the head is made by all.

143 It depends upon the competent territorial ecclesiastical authority (ICL, n. 57).

144 The ceremonies preceding the reading which the subdeacon and deacon performed at the altar are now performed at the seat where the celebrant is, with these changes: the imposition of incense takes place during the chanting of the Gradual and *Alleluia;* the deacon carries the evangelary to the altar and there (kneeling) he recites the *Munda cor meum,* then he returns to the seat to receive (standing) the blessing of the celebrant. After the Gospel has been sung, the subdeacon brings the evangelary to the celebrant to be kissed. The celebrant, however, is not incensed.

145 In sung Masses, the Lessons, Epistle and Gospel, if they are proclaimed in the vernacular, may be recited without chant (ICL, n. 51). The deacon or priest who proclaims the Gospel performs the same ceremonies of the deacon in the solemn Mass (see the preceding note); when the reading has terminated, he brings the book to the celebrant to be kissed.

146 At the words which required a genuflection, for example, *Adiuva nos; Veni, sancte Spiritus,* etc., only a bow is made.

147 After the reading he kisses the book (*Per evangelica dicta*). In sung Masses

when incense is used (cf. *Codex rubricarum,* n. 426), the incense is administered immediately after the Epistle; the celebrant incenses the book (as the deacon does at a solemn Mass), and is not incensed after the reading.

148 See J. A. Jungmann, *Missarum sollemnia I* (Roma: 1953), 385-393. Righetti, *Storia liturgica III* (2a ed.; Milano: 1956). L. Della Torre, *"L'Oratio fidelium,"* RL 51, 2 (1964), 214-224. Agustoni-Wagner, *op. cit.p* 241.

149 The celebrant recites this prayer standing facing the altar. The conclusion is short: *Per Christum Dominum nostrum.*

150 Standing facing the people.

151 In a sung Mass, this ceremony was already eliminated in the revision of *Ritus serv. in celebr. Missae,* VI, 8.

152 Cf. note 140.

153 See note 136.

154 The *Ritus serv. in celebr. Missae,* VII, 9 is changed. The ceremonies to be followed, from the Offertory to the *Pater Noster,* could be – for the time being – those indicated by the manuals for the Mass of the Dead. Must the humeral veil still be used in the Mass? According to the *Ritus serv. in cel. Missae,* VII, 9, the subdeacon carries the chalice (with the paten and the host) covering it only with the sides of the humeral veil; after the ablution he carries it back to the credence table without the humeral veil (*Ritus,* XI, 3), since it is covered with the customary veil with the burse over it. The manuals of ceremonies teach that in the Mass for the Dead the humeral veil is not used, since the rubric says:"In Masses, however, of the dead, the paten is not held by the subdeacon" (*Ritus,* VII, 9). Therefore the answer to the question can only be negative. For ideas concerning this rite, which has finally been eliminated, see: Righetti, *Storia liturgica,* III, 289.

155 Cf. ICL, n. 53.

156 See note 140.

157 Cf. Homback, *"La 'Missa cum Diacono,'"* *Les Questions liturgiques et paroissiales* 38 (1957), 98-109.

158 Cf. also ICL, n. 36, 60.

159 On the Eucharist, sacrifice and sacrament (*mysterium fidei*), the Constitution has dedicated an entire chapter under the very significant title *"De sacrosancto Eucharistiae mysterio."*

160. The directive lines for such a renewal are indicated in Art. 64-82 of the Constitution.

161 Cf. Bugnini, *"Sei mesi di attività dei Consilium," L'Oss. Rom.,* September 23, 1964; 5. An attentive reading should be made of the first part of the discourse addressed by the Holy Father to the members of the Commission (October 29, 1964) in which he treats precisely of the *opus immensae molis,* which is the revision of the liturgical books (*L'Oss. Rom.,* October 31, 1964, 1).

162 Cf. pp. 15, 41-44.

163 The part that can be assigned to the vernacular.

164 See pp. 44-47.

165 Baptism, ordination to the priesthood, sacramentals.

166 See: R. Beraudy, *"L'iniziazione cristiana,"* in A.-G. Martimort, *La Chiesa in preghiera* (Italian ed.; Roma: 1963), 152 ff. Conclusions of the XII National Liturgical Week of CAL (Assisi: 3-7 July 1961) under the title: *"La Cresima: secondo momento della iniziazione cristiana,"* in RL 48 (1961), 282-285. See also the opening lecture

given by Card. Lercaro: *"L'iter storico della Cresima e i pensieri pastorali di un Vescovo,"* in RL 48 (1961), 244-523. P.M. Gy: *"Histoire liturgique du Sacrament de la Confirmation,"* in MD 58 (1959), 135-145.

167 With red-colored vestments. Cf. *Codex rubr.* 343-344. Cf. also the Mass celebrated in the vernacular with the participation of the people, 28ff. Desirable is an appropriate formulary, *In collatione Confirmationis* or *pro his qui confirmandi sunt,* to be recited with the prayer of the Mass under one conclusion.

168 Rite of confirmation.

169 When the rite begins, he removes the maniple, which is then resumed at the Offertory.

170 See p. 43. In this case, could not the final rubric of the Roman Pon., practically reduced to the common recitation of the Creed, Our Father and Hail Mary, already present (except the Hail Mary) in the Mass, be left out?

171 See pp. 46-47. Cf. I. Onatibia, *"De confirmatione,"* in *Commentario CL,* EL 78 (1964), 320.

172 Cf. L. Trimeloni, *Compendio di Liturgia pratica* (Torino: 1963), 184.

173 *Codex rubr.,* n. 381a). CIC, can. 1101, par. 1.

174 CIC, can. 1012.

175 Cf. Righetti, *Storia liturgica IV* 2a (2a ed.; Milano: 1959) 453-469. P. Jounel, *"Il Matrimonio,"* in A.-G. Martimort, *La Chiesa in preghiera,* 641 ff. J. Juard, *"La Liturgie nuptiale dans l'Eglise romaine": Les questions liturgiques et paroissiales* 38 (1957), 197-205. C. Braga, *"De Matrimonio,"* in *Commentario CL,* EL 78 (1964), 331-333.

176 Cf. MP, V.

177 Weakened are canons 1101, par. 1; 1108, par. 1, 2, 3; 1143 of the Code. *Rit. Rom.,* Tit. VIII, c. I, 16, 19. Changed are n. 380, 381 c) of the *Codex rubricarum.*

178 Cf. CIC, can. 1108, par. 3.

179 See 18-19.

180 When this is possible is pointed out in 343c); 379 of the *Codex rubr.* The second part of n. 379 is abrogated by ICL, n. 74d).

181 White-colored vestments. Cf. the Mass celebrated in the vernacular with the participation of the people.

182 If, however, he who celebrates the Mass does not assist at the marriage, then after the reading of the Gospel, he goes to the bench. He returns to the altar after the celebration of the marriage (or after the prayer of the faithful): ICL, n. 72.

183 Cf. ICL, n. 53 and p. 31.

184 Bugnini, *"Il Motu proprio 'Sacram Liturgiam,'" L'Osservatore Romano,* March 2-3, 1964, 1.

185 The reading in the vernacular of these two passages in the rite of Matrimony outside of Mass is not conditioned by any decree of the competent territorial authority: only the translation of the text depends upon this authority (cf. note 125).

186 Implicitly c. IV of Tit. VIII no longer has any value.

187 Cf. pp. 312-313.

188 The priest performs this celebration vested in surplice and white stole and, in accordance with local custom, also in cope.

189 The sacrament of Extreme Unction now assumes the name of the sacrament of the Anointing of the Sick. Cf. Dirks in EL 78 (1964), 333.

190 Cf. A.-G. Martimort, *"Pastorale liturgique des malades." Les questions liturgiques et paroissiales* 36 (1955), 231-243. A. Chavasse, *"Preghiere per gli ammalati e unzione sacramentale,"* in Martimort, *La Chiesa in preghiera,* 625 ff. Righetti, *Storia liturgica,* IV, 337-352.

191 For example, in the dioceses of Germany (1950), of the French language (2nd. ed. 1956), of Ireland (1959), of Belgium (1961) and of Holland (1962), etc. Cf. note 100. A. Dirks, *"De unctione informorum,"* in *Commentario CL,* EL 78 (1964), 325-326.

192 This blessing can be omitted or deferred to another time.

193 C. IV.

194 Cf. H. Schmidt, *"De obligatione Officii divini,"* in *Commentario CL,* EL 78 (1964), 352-354.

195 Cf. CIC, can. 198, par. 1.

196 CIC, can. 488, 8, 490. Cf. MP, VIII.

197 Cf. A. Bugnini, *"Parva breviaria fidelium,"* EL 68 (1954), 171-179. F. Vandenbroucke, *"Bréviaires des fidèles et livres d'houres" Les questions lit. et paroiss.* 33 (1952), 165-172. H. Schmidt, *Officium Parvum B. M. V. et Breviaria Parva: Introductio in Liturgiam Occidentalem* (Roma: 1960), 469-483. H. Chirat, *"De 'Officio divino parvo'"* EL 66 (1952), 83-89.

198 The faculty of being allowed to omit Prime and choose from among the other little hours one that best suits the time of day: MP, VI. (Cf. CL, Art. 89d-e.) Consequently this faculty—even though not expressly referred to by the Instruction—continues to be in effect for all those who, although not bound in choir, are bound to pray the divine office (cf. CL, Art. 96). Editor's note: On June 2, 1965, the Apostolic See granted to major religious superiors, according to their prudent judgment, the power to retain or declare non-obligatory the recitation of Prime by their subjects.

199 For the concluding chapter of the Instruction on the construction of churches and altars in order to facilitate the active participation of the faithful, we refer the reader to the comments of Fr. Marsili in this volume.

200 Cf. P. Massi, *"Il segno dell'Assemblea,"* RL 51, 2 (1964), 149-178. S. Rinaudo, *"L'Assemblea liturgica,"* RL 51, 2 (1964), 179-192. A.-G. Martimort, *"Precisions sur l'Assemblee,"* MD 60 (1959), 7-34.

201 In MD 70 (1962), 67-99 or also in *Studi medievali* (Spoleto), III serie, 1 (1960), 447-469. Cf. also J. Wagner, *Le lieu de la célébration eucharistique dans quelques églises anciennes d'Occident:* MD 70 (1962), 32-48. Roguet, *"L'autel,"* MD 63 (1963), 96-113.

202 Cf. Righetti, *Storia liturgica,* I, (3a ed.), 490-553.

203 Cf. Bugnini, *Documenta pontificia,* II, 66; with a brief comment in EL 61 (1957), 442-445. N. 4 of the decree is abrogated by n. 95 of the Instruction.

204 Cf. I. Musante, *"De tabernaculo eiusque ornatu,"* EL 60 (1956), 255-260.

205 To celebrate Mass on days of precept facing the people at a small altar erected in the middle of the sanctuary with the Blessed Sacrament at the celebrant's back and reserved in the tabernacle for an easier distribution of communion for the faithful, is a solution certainly contrary to the end and spirit of the Instruction.

206 The general audience on January 13, 1965: *L'Osservatore Romano,* January 14, 1.

Index

Roman numerals I and II refer to the volumes; arabic numbers to the pages. Although many cross references have been made, *see* and *see also,* if you cannot find a topic under a heading you think of first, try a related subject; e.g. for Sick Communion, look under Communion.

D

M

R

S

Z